Bloomsbury Keys

Spelling
Dictionary

BLOOMSBURY

Bloomsbury Keys

Spelling Dictionary

For David Griffiths

First published 1994 by
Bloomsbury Publishing Ltd,
2 Soho Square,
London W1V 5DE

Copyright © 1994 by Bloomsbury Publishing Ltd

A copy of the CIP entry for this book is
available from the British Library

ISBN 0 7475 1776 2

Typeset by Hewer Text, Edinburgh
Printed in Britain by
HarperCollins Manufacturing, Glasgow

Contents

INTRODUCTION

How to use the dictionary

Spelling can be difficult. To use a spelling dictionary effectively you need to be able to make a good guess at how a word might be spelt in order to find a likely place to look it up. This is not always easy. This book gives you three different types of help to make spellings easier to find.

Firstly, a list is given below of regular possible ways to spell sounds which may be spelled in different ways. If you do not find the word initially in the dictionary you should try these alternative spellings.

Secondly, where a group of words has an unusual or unexpected spelling, a note is given at the expected spelling to direct you to the unexpected one. For example at the letters fol . . ., near words like follow, a note directs you to look at fal . . . for words like false and falter.

Thirdly, for many words whose spelling is particularly difficult to guess, entries have been given for wrong spellings which direct you to the correct spelling. Wrong spellings may either be common misspellings like medecine (which should be medicine) or opthalmic (correctly ophthalmic) or they may reflect the sound of the word like fusha (fuchsia), or hurse (hearse). Wrong spellings are preceded by ✗.

Note that wrong spellings are only given for words in which the beginning part of the word is difficult to spell. Where the beginning of the word is reasonably straightforward, the word will be close to where you would look it up so no wrong spelling is given.

Note also that American spelling is not covered in this dictionary so a spelling such as gray is not given here even though it would be correct in American English

How to look up a word whose spelling you do not know

The main typical alternative spellings for consonant and vowel sounds are given below. If you cannot find the word you want in the first place you look for it, look at the examples below to find different possible spellings that you could try.

Consonants

Consonants are all the letters in the alphabet except a, e, i, o, u and sometimes y. Consonants can generally be doubled except for h, j, k, q, w and x. If you cannot find the word when looking for a single consonant, try looking for a doubled consonant. Similarly if you cannot find the word with a doubled consonant, try a single one.

ALTERNATIVE SPELLINGS FOR CONSONANTS

ch	tch	tu	
li**ch**en	ki**tch**en	punc**tu**re	
prea**ch**er	pa**tch**	crea**tu**re	

f	ph		
fair	**ph**one		
de**f**end	del**ph**inium		

j	g before e, i, or y		dg
jam	**g**em		ba**dg**e
ca**j**ole	ra**g**e		

k	c	ck	qu
kitten	**c**rowd	chi**ck**en	opa**qu**e

qu	kw		
li**qu**id	aw**kw**ard		

s	c before e, i, or y		sc
send	**c**entre		**sc**ent
ba**s**e	pa**c**e		a**sc**end

sh	ss	ti	
shop			
po**sh**	pa**ss**ion	pa**ti**ence	

w	u before vowel		
for**w**ard	pers**u**ade		

z	s before vowel		x
ra**z**e	plea**s**e		an**x**iety
mar**z**ipan	ea**s**y		**x**ylophone

There is also a sound somewhere between z and sh for which there is no consonant. It is usually spelt su as in pleasure or visual, but is also si in lesion.

VOWELS

The vowels in the alphabet are a, e, i, o, u and sometimes y. All the vowels have a 'long' vowel sound and a 'short' vowel sound. The 'long' sound is the sound of the letter as it would be pronounced when reciting the alphabet. The 'short' sounds are as in bad, bed, bid, body and bud. The letter y has the long and short sound of i as in cycle and bicycle.

The vowel on its own (between two consonants or at the beginning of a word) can have either the long or the short sound.

LONG VOWELS

In general a vowel followed by a single consonant and then an e (with the e not pronounced) is a long vowel, eg

> spade, these, bite, phone, prune, style

ALTERNATIVE SPELLINGS FOR LONG VOWELS FOR A, E, I, O, U

a	**ai**	**ay**	
make	complaint	day	
amiable	aim	say	

e	**ee**	**ea**	**ie**
lethal	sheep	peace	grief
even		eat	

ei			
ceiling			
either			

i	**igh**	**ie**	**y**
Friday	light	pie	cry
ice			

o	**oa**	**ow**	**oe**
ghost	roast	show	hoe
over	oats	own	

u	**ew**	**ue**	
huge	few	due	
union			

ALTERNATIVE SPELLINGS FOR SHORT VOWELS FOR A, E, I, O, U

e	**ea**
bed	bread
elephant	

i	y
him	gym
ink	

u	o
hundred	dozen

ALTERNATIVE SPELLINGS FOR OTHER VOWEL SOUNDS

oo	u		
foot	push		

ew	oo	o	ou
grew	goose	lose	group

ue	ui		
glue	fruit		

ow	ou		
cow	round		

aw	or	au	oo
straw	cord	fraud	door

ore	ough		
shore	ought		

Also:	all		
	fall		

air	ar		
pair	care		
	variable		

ur	**er**	**ir**	**ear**
c**ur**ve	m**er**ge	b**ir**th	p**ear**l

ar	**al**	**a**
h**ar**m	c**al**m	f**a**ther

ier	**eer**	**ea/ear**	**ere**
f**ier**ce	b**eer**	h**ear**	sev**ere**
		id**ea**	

Sounds like **wa**
oir
boud**oir**
mem**oir**

The very short vowel sound which is so short it is almost not pronounced at all, in barr**e**l, mis**e**rable, ref**e**ree, mon**a**rch, mon**a**cle, nob**o**dy, can be written as **e, a** or **o**.

WORD ENDINGS

Sounds like **i**

y	**ie**	**ey**
happ**y**	calor**ie**	mon**ey**

Sounds like **ij**

age	**idge**
man**age**	porr**idge**

Sounds like **er**

er	**or**	**re**	**our**
driv**er**	act**or**	lust**re**	arm**our**

A long **er** sound at the end of a word is often **ur**

oseur

Sounds like **shus**

| **ious** | **cious** | **scious** | **ceous** |
| autious | pernicious | conscious | curvaceous |

Sounds like **ius**

| **ous** | **eous** |
| elirious | hideous |

Sounds like **us**

| **us** | **ious** after **c** or **g** | **eous** after **c** or **g** |
| ecorous | delicious | courageous |

Sounds like **shun**

| **ion** | **sion** | **cion** |
| osition | mansion | coercion |

Sounds like **shul**

| **ial** | **cial** |
| ubstantial | commercial |

Sounds like **sul**

| **stle** | **sle** | **sel** |
| astle | tussle | mussel |

Sounds like **el** or **ul**

| **el** | **le** |
| arrelel | cattle |

Endings sounding like **ible** may also be spelt **able**

Endings sounding like **ent** may also be spelt **ant**

Endings sounding like **ence** may also be spelt **anc**

Main spelling rules

1. Adding s or es for plurals

The regular plural ending for nouns and the 3rd person singular ending for verbs is an added s. Words ending in ch, s, sh, x and z add es in the plural:

cat, cats
beech, beeches
batch, batches
boss, bosses
bush, bushes
fox, foxes
waltz, waltzes

Words ending in f or fe sometimes add s and sometimes change to ves:

scarf, scarves

Exceptions: the plural of bus is buses and the plural of gas is gases but the 3rd person singular of 'to bus' is busses and of 'to gas' is gasses.

2. Changing y to ie

Words that end in y keep the y before ing but change to ies and ied for the noun plural, the 3rd person singular and the past tense:

worry, worries, worried, worrying
try, tries, tried, trying
cherry, cherries

Names of people and places that end in y keep the y
and just add s in the plural, eg Mr and Mrs Perry, the
Perrys.

3. Verbs ending in ie

Verbs like lie, tie and die replace ie with y in the
present participle

lie, lies, lied, lying
die, dies, died, dying

Note the difference between die above and dye,
dyes, dyed, dyeing.

4. Dropping e before ing

Words which end in a consonant and then e
generally lose the e before ing (also ish, ism, ise,
ize, ist) and ed (also er, en)

like, liked, liking

Exceptions are the present participles of singe
(=burn), which is singeing (to avoid confusion
with 'singing'), and age which can be spelt ageing
or aging. Note also swingeing (=large), spelt with an
e to avoid confusion with 'swinging'.

5. Words ending in c

Words ending in c add k before ed and ing

panic, panics, panicked, panicking

An exception is arc for which the participles are arced and arcing.

6. Doubling the consonant before ed, ing, er

Single syllable words which end in a single vowel and a consonant usually double the consonant before ed, ing and er, eg

    hit, hitting, hitter
    flap, flapped, flapping

Words where the stress is on the last syllable which end in a single vowel and a consonant also usually double the consonant before ed, ing and er

    regret, regretted, regretting
    omit, omitted, omitting

7. ie, ei

The well known rule 'i before e except after c' applies when the vowel rhymes with 'sheep'

    shriek, niece, 'i before e'
    ceiling, deceit, 'except after c'

There are several exceptions such as seize, weird and the names Sheila and Keith.

8. Verbs ending in ise or ize

For words like characterise, the traditional spelling in British English is usually ise but the American ize spelling is becoming more common. However, the following verbs are only ever spelt ise:

advertise   excise
advise   exercise
apprise   improvise
arise   merchandise
chastise   prise (open)
circumcise   revise
comprise   rise
compromise   supervise
despise   surmise
devise   surprise
enfranchise   televise

Capsize, prize and size are only ever spelt ize.

Alternative spellings

This list gives some of the main possible alternative spellings:

acs try acc:	accelerate
air try aer:	aerial
anti try ante:	antelope
ay try eye:	eyelash
ca try cha:	character
ce try ca:	camellia, canary
ce try che:	chemist
clor try chlor:	chlorine
co try cho:	cholera
cr try chr:	Christmas
disim try disem:	disembark
disin try disen:	disenchant
ecs try ex:	exact
ef try af:	affection, afraid

egs try exh:	exhaust
fer try fur:	furry
fol try fal:	false
for try four:	fourteen
gi try gui:	guilt
hart try heart:	hearty
hi try high:	higher
ho try who:	whole
idiol try ideol:	ideology
infen try infan:	infant
inse try insu:	insubstantial
meca try mecha:	mechanic
na try kna:	knack, knave
ne try kne:	knee, knell
ni try kni:	knife, knit
no try kno:	knob, know
nur try neur:	neurosis
nut try neut:	neutral
o try au:	Australia, austere
ocs try ox:	oxtail
pel try pol:	polite
per try pur:	purple
pre try pro:	provide
quo try qua:	qualification, quarrel
ra try wra:	wrap
re try wre:	wreck
ri try wri:	wriggle, write
se try sce:	scene, scent
si try sci:	science, scissors
sic try psych:	psychology
sosh try soci:	social

spesh try speci:	special, species
squo try squa:	squabble, squash
uf try euph:	euphoria
uph try euph:	euphoria
ur try eur:	Europe
vial try viol:	violin
wa try wha:	whale, whack
wawl try wal:	walnut
we try whe:	when, wheel
wi try whi:	which, while
wo try wa:	wander, wash
wod try wad:	waddle
wor try wa:	water
wun try one:	one-sided
wur try wor:	work

A

aardvark
aback
abacus
abacuses
baft
balone
bandon
abandons
abandoned
abandoning
abandoned
abandonment
abase
abases
abased
abasing
abasement
abashed
abate
abates
abated
abating
abattoir
abayance = abeyance
abbé
abbés
abbess
abbesses
abbey
abbeys
abbot
abbreviate

abbreviates
abbreviated
abbreviating
abbreviation
abdicate
abdicates
abdicated
abdicating
abdomen
abdominal
abdominally
abduct
abducts
abducted
abducting
abduction
abductor
abecedarian
abed
Aberavon
Aberdeen
Abergavenny
aberrant
aberration
Abertillery
Aberystwyth
abet
abets
abetted
abetting
abeyance
abeyant
abhor
abhors
abhorred
abhorring
abhorrence
abhorrent
abide
abides

abode or
abided
abiding
ability
abilities
abject
abjection
abjectly
abjure
abjures
abjured
abjuring
ablative
ablaut
ablaze
able
able-bodied
ablution
ably
abnegate
abnegates
abnegated
abnegating
abnormal
abnormality
abnormalities
abnormally
aboard
abode
abolish
abolishes
abolished
abolishing
abolishable
abolisher
abolishment
abolition
A-bomb
abominable
abominably

abominate

abominate
abominates
abominated
abominating
abomination
✘ abor = abhor
✘ abord = aboard
aboriginal
aborigine
abort
aborts
aborted
aborting
abortion
abortionist
abortive
abound
abounds
abounded
abounding
about
above
abracadabra
abrade
abrades
abraded
abrading
abrasion
abrasive
abrasively
abreast
abridgable
abridge
abridges
abridged
abridging
abridgement
abridgment
abroad
abrogate

abrogates
abrogated
abrogating
abrupt
abruptly
abruptness
✘ absail = abseil
abscess
abscesses
abscond
absconds
absconded
absconding
absconder
abseil
abseils
abseiled
abseiling
absence
absences
absent
absents
absented
absenting
absentee
absenteeism
absently
absent-minded
✘ absess = abscess
absinth (plant)
absinthe (drink)
absolute
absolutely
absolution
absolutism
absolvable
absolve
absolves
absolved
absolving

absolver
absorb
absorbs
absorbed
absorbing
absorbability
absorbable
absorbency
absorbent
absorbent
absorbing
absorption
absorptive
abstain
abstains
abstained
abstaining
abstemious
abstemiously
abstemiousness
abstention
abstinence
abstract
abstracts
abstracted
abstracting
abstracted
abstractedly
abstraction
abstruse
abstrusely
abstruseness
absurd
absurdity
absurdities
absurdly
absurdness
abundance
abundant
abundantly

buse
abuses
abused
abusing
buser
busive
busively
busiveness
but
abuts
abutted
abutting
buzz
bysmal
bysmally
byss
abysses
cacia
cademe
cademia
cademic
cademically
cademician
cademy
academies
canthus
acanthuses *or*
acanthi
ACAS
a cappella
ccede
accedes
acceded
acceding
cceder
ccelerate
accelerates
accelerated
accelerating
cceleration

accelerative
accelerator
accent
accents
accented
accenting
accentuate
accentuates
accentuated
accentuating
accentuation
accept
accepts
accepted
accepting
acceptability
acceptable
acceptableness
acceptably
acceptance
accepted
accepter
access
accesses
accessed
accessing
accessibility
accessible
accessibly
accession
accessional
accessory
accessories
accidence
accident
accidental
accidentally
acclaim
acclaims
acclaimed

acclaiming
acclaimer
acclamation
acclamatory
acclimatisation
acclimatise
acclimatises
acclimatised
acclimatising
acclimatization
acclimatize
acclimatizes
acclimatized
acclimatizing
acclivity
acclivities
accolade
accommodate
accommodates
accommodated
accommodating
accommodating
accommodatingly
accommodation
accompaniment
accompanist
accompany
accompanies
accompanied
accompanying
accomplice
accomplish
accomplishes
accomplished
accomplishing
accomplishable
accomplishment
accord
accords
accorded

according
accordance
according
accordingly
accordion
accordionist
accost
accosts
accosted
accosting
account
accounts
accounted
accounting
accountability
accountable
accountably
accountancy
accountant
accounting
accoutrement
Accra
accredit
accredits
accredited
accrediting
accreditation
accrue
accrues
accrued
accruing
accumulable
accumulate
accumulates
accumulated
accumulating
accumulation
accumulative
accumulatively
accumulativeness

accumulator
accuracy
accuracies
accurate
accursed
accursedly
accursedness
accusal
accusation
accusative
accusatively
accuse
accuses
accused
accusing
accuser
accusing
accusingly
accustom
accustoms
accustomed
accustoming
accustomed
AC/DC
ace
acephalous
acerbate
acerbates
acerbated
acerbating
acerbic
acerbically
acerbity
acetate
acetic
acetone
ache
aches
ached
aching

achier
achiest
achievable
achieve
achieves
achieved
achieving
achievement
achiever
aching
achy
acid
acidhead
acidic
acidification
acidifier
acidify
acidifies
acidified
acidifying
acidity
acidities
acidly
acidometer
acknowledge
acknowledges
acknowledged
acknowledging
acknowledgement
acknowledgment
acme
acne
acolyte
aconite
acorn
acoustic
acoustically
acoustician
acoustics
acquaint

acquaints
acquainted
acquainting
acquaintance
acquaintanceship
acquainted
acquiesce
  acquiesces
  acquiesced
  acquiescing
acquirable
acquire
  acquires
  acquired
  acquiring
acquirer
acquisition
acquisitive
acquisitively
acquisitiveness
acquit
  acquits
  acquitted
  acquitting
acquittal
acquittance
acre
acreage
acrid
acridity
acridness
acrimonious
  acrimoniously
  acrimoniousness
acrimony
  acrimonies
acrobat
acrobatic
acrobatically
acrobatics

acronym
acronymous
acrophobia
across
across-the-board
acrostically
acrylic
acs try acc
✗ acseed = accede
act
  acts
  acted
  acting
action
actionable
activate
  activates
  activated
  activating
active
  actively
activism
activist
activity
  activities
actor
actress
  actresses
actual
actualise
  actualises
  actualised
  actualising
actuality
  actualities
actualize
  actualizes
  actualized
  actualizing
actually

actuarial
actuary
  actuaries
actuate
  actuates
  actuated
  actuating
acuity
acumen
acupressure
acupuncture
acupuncturist
acute
acutely
acuteness
acyclic
AD
adage
adagio
  adagios
adamant
adapt
  adapts
  adapted
  adapting
adaptability
adaptable
adaptableness
adaptation
adapter
adaptive
adaptor
add
  adds
  added
  adding
addendum
addenda
adder
addict

addiction
addictive
adding
addition
additional
additionally
additive
addle
addles
addled
addling
add-on
address
addresses
addressed
addressing
addressee
adduce
adduces
adduced
adducing
adduceable
adducible
Adelaide
adenoid
adenoidal
adenoidectomy
adenoidectomies
adept
adeptly
adeptness
adequacy
adequacies
adequate
adequately
adhere
adheres
adhered
adhering
adherence

adherent
adhesion
adhesive
adhesively
adhesiveness
ad hoc
adieu
adieus or
adieux
ad infinitum
adios
adipose
adjacency
adjacent
adjacently
adjectival
adjective
adjoin
adjoins
adjoined
adjoining
adjourn
adjourns
adjourned
adjourning
adjournment
adjudge
adjudges
adjudged
adjudging
adjudicate
adjudicates
adjudicated
adjudicating
adjudication
adjudicative
adjudicator
adjunct
adjure
adjures

adjured
adjuring
adjust
adjusts
adjusted
adjusting
adjustable
adjuster
adjustment
adjutant
✗ adlevise =
edelweiss
ad-lib
ad-libs
ad-libbed
ad-libbing
ad-libber
admeasure
admeasures
admeasured
admeasuring
admin
administer
administers
administered
administering
administrate
administrates
administrated
administrating
administration
administrative
administratively
administrator
admirable
admirably
admiral
admiralty
admiralties
admiration

admire
  admires
  admired
  admiring
admirer
admiringly
admissibility
admissible
admission
admit
  admits
  admitted
  admitting
admittance
admittedly
admixture
admonish
  admonishes
  admonished
  admonishing
admonition
ad nauseam
ado
adobe
adolescence
adolescent
Adonis
adopt
  adopts
  adopted
  adopting
adopted
adoption
adoptive
adorable
adorably
adoration
adore
  adores
  adored

adoring
adorer
adoring
adoringly
adorn
  adorns
  adorned
  adorning
adornment
adrenal
adrenaline
Adriatic
adrift
adroit
adroitly
adroitness
adulation
adulatory
adult
adulterate
  adulterates
  adulterated
  adulterating
adulteration
adulterer
adulteress
  adulteresses
adulterous
adulterously
adultery
  adulteries
adulthood
advance
  advances
  advanced
  advancing
advanced
advancement
advances
advancingly

advantage
  advantages
advantageous
advantageously
advent
Advent
adventitious
adventure
  adventures
adventurer
adventurism
adventurous
adventurously
adverb
adverbial
adverbially
adversarial
adversary
  adversaries
adverse
adversely
adversity
  adversities
advert
advertise
  advertises
  advertised
  advertising
advertisement
advertiser
advertising
advice
advisability
advisable
advisableness
advisably
advise
  advises
  advised
  advising

advised
advisedly
adviser
advisor
advisory
advocaat
advocacy
  advocacies
advocate
  advocates
  advocated
  advocating
adze
  adzes
Aegean
Aegean Sea
aegis
aeon
  aeons
aerate
  aerates
  aerated
  aerating
aeration
aerial
aerobatics
aerobic
aerobics
aerodrome
  aerodromes
aerodynamic
aerodynamics
aerofoil
aerogram
  aerograms
aerogramme
  aerogrammes
aeronautical
aeronautics
aeroplane

aerosol
aerospace
aesthete
aesthetic
aesthetically
aesthetician
aestheticism
aesthetics
aether
aethereal
afar
affability
affable
affair
affect
  affects
  affected
  affecting
affectation
affected
  affectedly
  affectedness
affection
affectionate
affectionately
affidavit
  affidavits
affiliate
  affiliates
  affiliated
  affiliating
affinity
  affinities
affirm
  affirms
  affirmed
  affirming
affirmation
affirmative
affirmatives

affirmatively
affix
  affixes
  affixed
  affixing
afflict
  afflicts
  afflicted
  afflicting
affliction
affluence
affluent
afford
  affords
  afforded
  affording
affordability
affordable
afforest
  afforests
  afforested
  afforesting
afforestation
affray
affront
  affronts
  affronted
  affronting
affusion
afghan
Afghan
Afghanistan
aficionado
  aficionados
afield
afloat
aflutter
afoot
aforementioned
aforesaid

afraid
afresh
African
African-American
Afrikaans
Afrikaner
Afro
  Afros
aft
after
afterbirth
aftercare
afterdeck
aftereffect
afterglow
afterlife
  afterlives
aftermath
afternoon
afterpains
afters
aftershave
  aftershaves
aftershock
aftertaste
afterthought
afterwards
afterword
Aga
  Agas
again
against
agape (= wide
  open)
Agape (= Christian
  love)
✗ agarst = aghast
agate
  agates
age

ages
aged
ageing *or*
aging
aged
ageing
ageism
ageless
agency
  agencies
agenda
  agendas
agent
agentive
agent provocateur
  agents provoca-
    teurs
✗ ageraphobia =
  agoraphobia
ages
agglomerate
agglomerates
agglomerated
agglomerating
agglomeration
aggrandisement
aggrandizement
aggravate
aggravates
aggravated
aggravating
aggravation
aggregate
aggregates
aggregated
aggregating
aggregation
aggregative
aggression
aggressive

aggressively
aggressiveness
aggressor
aggrieve
aggrieves
aggrieved
aggrieving
aggrieved
aggrievedly
aggro
aghast
agile
agility
agin
aging
agism
agist
agitate
agitates
agitated
agitating
agitated
agitatedly
agitation
agitato
agitator
AGM
agnostic
agnosticism
ago
agog
agonise
agonises
agonised
agonising
agonize
agonizes
agonized
agonizing
agonizingly

agony
  agonies
agoraphobia
agoraphobic
agrarian
agrarianism
agree
  agrees
  agreed
  agreeing
agreeable
agreeableness
agreeably
agreed
agreeing
agreement
agrees
agribusiness
  agribusinesses
agricultural
agriculturalist
agriculture
agrochemical
agronomist
agronomy
aground
ague
  agues
ah
aha
ahead
ahem
ahoy
AI
aid (= help → aide)
  aids
  aided
  aiding
aide (= military
  officer → aid)

aide-de-camp
  aides-de-camp
aide-mémoire
  aides-mémoire
AIDS
aikido
ail (= cause trouble
  for → ale)
  ails
  ailed
  ailing
ailerons
ailing
ailment
aim
  aims
  aimed
  aiming
aimless
aimlessly
aimlessness
ain't
aïoli
air try aer
air (= gas → heir)
  airs
  aired
  airing
airborne
airbrick
Airbus
aircraft
  aircraft
aircraftman
  aircraftmen
aircraftsman
  aircraftsmen
aircrew
airdrop
Airedale

✗ airess = heiress
airfield
airier
airiest
airily
airiness
airing
airless
airlift
  airlifts
  airlifted
  airlifting
airline
  airlines
airliner
airlock
✗ airloom = heirloom
airmail
airman
  airmen
airplane
airport
airs
airship
airshow
airsick
airspace
airspeed
airstrip
airtight
airtime
airwaves
airway
airworthy
airy (= open to the
  air → eyrie)
  airier
  airiest
aisle (= passage or
  corridor → isle)

aisles
aitch
  aitches
aitchbone
  aitchbones
ajar
akimbo
akin
alabaster
à la carte
alack
alacritous
alacrity
à la mode
alarm
  alarms
  alarmed
  alarming
alarmed
alarming
  alarmingly
alarmism
alarmist
alas
Alastair
Albania
Albanian
albatross
  albatrosses
albeit
albinism
albino
  albinos
album
albumen
albumin
alchemist
alchemy
  alchemies
alcohol

alcoholic
alcoholise
  alcoholises
  alcoholised
  alcoholising
alcoholism
alcoholize
  alcoholizes
  alcoholized
  alcoholizing
alcove
  alcoves
Aldeburgh
aldehyde
  aldehydes
alder
alderman
  aldermen
ale (= beer → ail)
  ales
alehouse
alert
  alerts
  alerted
  alerting
alertly
alertness
alewife
  alewives
Alexander
Alexandra
Alexandrian
Alexandrine
alfalfa
  alfalfas
alfresco
algae
algal
algebra
  algebras

algebraic
Algeria
Algerian
algicide
algorithm
alias
  aliases
alibi
  alibis
alien
alienable
alienate
  alienates
  alienated
  alienating
alienation
alight
  alights
  alighted or
  alit
  alighting
align
  aligns
  aligned
  aligning
alignment
  alignments
alike
aliment
alimentary
alimentation
alimony
  alimonies
✗ aline = align
alit
alive
alkali
  alkalis or
  alkalies
alkaline

alkalinity
alkaloid
all (= every one of
→ awl)
Allah
allargando
allay
allays
allayed
allaying
allegation
allege
alleges
alleged
alleging
alleged
allegedly
allegiance
allegiances
allegorical
allegorise
allegorises
allegorised
allegorising
allegorize
allegorizes
allegorized
allegorizing
allegory
allegories
allegretto
allegrettos
allegro
allegros
alleluia
allergen
allergic
allergist
allergy
allergies

alleviate
alleviates
alleviated
alleviating
alleviation
alleviative
alley
alleyway
Allhallows
alliance
allied
allies
✗alligation =
allegation
alligator
✗alligery = allegory
✗alliluya = alleluia
alliterate
alliterates
alliterated
alliterating
alliteration
alliterative
allocate
allocates
allocated
allocating
allocation
allocution
allopath
allopathic
allopathy
allot
allots
allotted
allotting
allotment
allow
allows
allowed

allowing
allowable
allowably
allowance
allowances
alloy
allspice
allude
alludes
alluded
alluding
allure
allures
allured
alluring
alluringly
allusion
alluvial
alluvion
alluvium
ally
allies
allied
allying
alma mater
alma maters
almanac
almightily
almightiness
almighty
Almighty
almond
almost
alms (= gifts for the
poor → arms)
almshouse
almshouses
Alnwick
aloe

aloes	altercate	amalgamated
loft	altercates	amalgamating
lone	altercated	amalgamation
long	altercating	amanuensis
longside	altercation	amanuensises
loof	alternate	amaryllis
loud	alternates	amass
lpaca	alternated	amasses
alpacas	alternating	amassed
lpha	alternately	amassing
alphas	alternation	amateur
lphabet	alternative	amateurish
lphabetical	alternatives	amatory
lphabetically	alternatively	amaze
lphabetise	alternativeness	amazes
alphabetises	alternator	amazed
alphabetised	although	amazing
alphabetising	altimeter	amazement
lphabetize	altissimo	amazing
alphabetizes	altitude	amazingly
alphabetized	alto	Amazon
alphabetizing	altos	ambassador
lpha-fetoprotein	altogether	ambassadorial
lpine	Altrincham	ambassadorship
lpinist	altruism	amber
lready	altruistic	ambergris
lright	altruistically	ambidextrous
Alsatian	alum	ambience
lso	aluminium	ambient
lstroemeria	alumna	ambiguity
alstroemerias	alumnae	ambiguities
altar (= structure in	alumnus	ambiguous
church → alter)	alumni	ambiguously
altarpiece	always	ambiguousness
alter (= change →	am	ambit
altar)	AM	ambition
alters	a.m.	ambitious
altered	amalgam	ambitiously
altering	amalgamate	ambitiousness
alteration	amalgamates	ambivalence

ambivalent
amble
  ambles
  ambled
  ambling
ambrosia
ambrosian
ambulance
ambulant
ambulatory
ambuscade
ambush
  ambushes
  ambushed
  ambushing
✗ ameba = amoeba
ameliorable
ameliorate
  ameliorates
  ameliorated
  ameliorating
amelioration
amen
Amen
amenability
amenable
amend (= to put
  right → emend)
  amends
  amended
  amending
amendable
amendment
amends
amenity
  amenities
amenorrhoea
American
Americana
Americanise

Americanises
Americanised
Americanising
Americanism
Americanize
Americanizes
Americanized
Americanizing
Amerindian
amethyst
amiability
amiable
amiably
amicable
amicably
amid
amidships
amidst
amigo
amino acid
Amish
amiss
amity
  amities
ammeter
ammo
ammonia
  ammonias
ammonite
ammonium
ammunition
amnesia
amnesiac
amnesty
  amnesties
amniocentesis
  amniocenteses
amniotic
amoeba
  amoebae or

amoebas
amoebic
amok
among
amongst
amontillado
  amontillados
amoral
amorality
amorous
amorphous
amorphously
amorphousness
amortise
  amortises
  amortised
  amortising
amount
amour
amp
amperage
ampere
ampersand
amphetamine
amphibian
amphibious
amphitheatre
ampicillin
ample
amplification
amplifier
amplify
  amplifies
  amplified
  amplifying
amplitude
amply
ampoule
amputate
  amputates

amputated
amputating
amputee
amuck
amulet
amuse
amuses
amused
amusing
amusement
amusing
amusingly
an
Anabaptist
anabolic
anachronic
anachronism
anachronistic
anachronistically
anaconda
anaemia
anaemic
anaerobic
anaesthesia
anaesthetic
anaesthetics
anaesthetise
   anaesthetises
   anaesthetised
   anaesthetising
anaesthetist
anaesthetization
anaesthetize
   anaesthetizes
   anaesthetized
   anaesthetizing
Anaglypta
anagram
anal
analgesia

analgesic
analog
analogous
analogously
analogue
   analogues
analogy
   analogies
analyse
   analyses
   analysed
   analysing
analysis
   analyses
analyst
analytic
   analytical
anaphoric
anarchic
anarchical
anarchically
anarchism
anarchist
anarchy
   anarchies
anastigmatic
anathema
anathematise
   anathematises
   anathematised
   anathematising
anathematize
   anathematizes
   anathematized
   anathematizing
Anatolian
anatomical
anatomist
anatomy
   anatomies

ANC
✗ ancer = anchor
ancestor
ancestral
ancestry
   ancestries
anchor
   anchors
   anchored
   anchoring
anchorage
anchorite
anchorman
   anchormen
anchovy
   anchovies
ancient
ancillary
   ancillaries
and
andante
   andantes
andantino
andiron
androgynous
androgyny
android
✗ anemia = anaemia
anemometer
anemone
anencephalic
anencephaly
aneroid
✗ anesthesia =
   anaesthesia
anesthetic
anew
angel
angelfish
angelic

angelica
angelically
Angelus
✗angenu = ingenue
anger
angers
angered
angering
angina
angle
angles
angled
angling
angler
Anglesey
Anglian
Anglican
Anglicanism
anglicise
anglicises
anglicised
anglicising
Anglicism
anglicize
anglicizes
anglicized
anglicizing
angling
Anglo
Anglophile
Anglophobe
Anglophone
Angola
angora
angry
angrier
angriest
✗angshus = anxious
angst
anguish

anguished
angular
angularity
anima
animal
animate
animates
animated
animating
animatedly
animation
animato
animator
animosity
animosities
✗anirobic = anaerobic
aniseed
ankle
anklebone
anklet
ankylosaur
ankylosis
annals
annelid
annex (= take
control of → an-
nexe)
annexes
annexed
annexing
annexation
annexe (= building
→ annex)
annihilate
annihilates
annihilated
annihilating
annihilation
annihilator

anniversary
anniversaries
anno Domini
annotate
annotates
annotated
annotating
annotation
announce
announces
announced
announcing
announcement
announcer
annoy
annoys
annoyed
annoying
annoyance
annoyer
annoyingly
annual
annuity
annuities
annul
annuls
annulled
annulling
annulment
Annunciation
anode
anodise
anodises
anodised
anodising
anodize
anodizes
anodized
anodizing
anodyne

anoint
  anoints
  anointed
  annointing
  anointer
anointment
anomalous
anomalously
anomalousness
anomaly
  anomalies
anon
anonymity
anonymous
anonymously
anonymousness
anorak
anorexia
anorexic
another
Anschluss
answer
  answers
  answered
  answering
answerable
ant
antacid
antagonise
  antagonises
  antagonised
  antagonising
antagonism
antagonist
antagonistic
antagonistically
antagonize
  antagonizes
  antagonized
  antagonizing

Antarctic
ante- (= before
  → anti-)
anteater
antecedent
antechamber
antedate
  antedates
  antedated
  antedating
antediluvian
antelope
antemeridian
antenatal
antenna
  antennae (= part
    of insect) *or*
  antennas (=
    aerial)
antepenultimate
anterior
anteriority
anteroom
anthem
anther
anthological
anthology
  anthologies
Anthony
anthracite
anthrax
anthropic
anthropocentric
anthropogenesis
anthropoid
anthropological
anthropology
anthropomorphic
anthropomorphism
anti try ante

anti- (= against
  → ante-)
antibiotic
antibody
  antibodies
antic
Antichrist
anticipate
  anticipates
  anticipated
  anticipating
anticipation
anticlimactic
anticlimax
  anticlimaxes
anticlockwise
anticoagulant
anticonvulsant
antics
anticyclone
  anticyclones
anticyclonic
antidepressant
antidote
antifreeze
antigen
antiglobulin
antihero
  antiheroes
antihistamine
anti-inflammatory
antilogarithm
antimacassar
antimagnetic
antimalarial
antimatter
antinuclear
antioxidant
antipasto
  antipastos

antipathetic
antipathy
  antipathies
antiperistalsis
antipersonnel
antiperspirant
antipodean
antipodes
antiquarian
antiquary
  antiquaries
antiquated
antique
antiquity
  antiquities
antirrhinum
  antirrhinums
anti-Semite
antiseptic
antiserum
antisocial
antithesis
  antitheses
antitoxin
antitrust
antler
Antony
antonym
antonymous
anus
  anuses
anvil
anxiety
  anxieties
anxious
anxiously
any
anybody
anyhow
✗ anyilate = annihilate

anymore
anyone
anyplace
anyroad
anything
anyway
anywhere
Anzac
AOB
A-OK
A-okay
A-one
aorta
  aortas or
  aortae
aortal
aortic
apace
Apache
apart
apartheid
apartment
apathetic
apathy
ape
apeman
  apemen
apéritif
  apéritifs
aperture
apery
  aperies
apex
  apexes or
  apices
APEX
aphid
  aphids
aphis
aphrodisiac

apiarist
apiary
  apiaries
apices
apiece
apish
aplenty
aplomb
apocalypse
  apocalypses
apocalyptic
apocalyptically
apocryphal
apolitical
apologetic
apologetically
apologia
apologise
  apologises
  apologised
  apologising
apologist
apologize
  apologizes
  apologized
  apologizing
apology
  apologies
apoplectic
apoplexy
apostasy
  apostasies
apostate
apostatical
a posteriori
apostle
apostolic
apostrophe
apostrophise
  apostrophises

apostrophised
apostrophising
apostrophize
apostrophizes
apostrophized
apostrophizing
apothecary
apothecaries
apotheosis
apotheoses
appal
appals
appalled
appalling
Appalachian
appall = appal
appallingly
Appaloosa
apparatus
apparatus or
apparatuses
apparel
apparent
apparently
apparition
appassionato
appeal
appeals
appealed
appealing
appealing
appealingly
appear
appears
appeared
appearing
appearance
appeasable
appease
appeases

appeased
appeasing
appeasement
appellant
appellate
appellation
append
appends
appended
appending
appendage
appendicectomy
appendicectomies
appendicitis
appendix
appendixes or
appendices
appertain
appertains
appertained
appertaining
appetiser
appetising
appetite
appetizer
appetizing
applaud
applauds
applauded
applauding
applaudingly
applause
apple
Appleby
applecart
applejack
appliance
applicable
applicant

application
applicator
applied
appliqué
appoint
appoints
appointed
appointing
appointee
appointees
appointment
apportion
apportions
apportioned
apportioning
apportionment
apposite
apposition
appraisal
appraise
appraises
appraised
appraising
appraiser
appreciable
appreciably
appreciate
appreciates
appreciated
appreciating
appreciation
appreciative
appreciatively
apprehend
apprehends
apprehended
apprehending
apprehension
apprehensive
apprentice

apprenticeship
apprise
  apprises
  apprised
  apprising
apprize
  apprizes
  apprized
  apprizing
approach
  approaches
  approached
  approaching
approachability
approachable
approachableness
approbation
appropriacy
appropriate
  appropriates
  appropriated
  appropriating
appropriately
appropriateness
appropriation
approval
approve
  approves
  approved
  approving
approved
approx.
approximate
  approximates
  approximated
  approximating
approximately
approximation
approximative
appurtenance

APR
après-ski
apricot
April
a priori
apron
apropos
apse
apt
aptitude
aquaerobics
aqualung
aquamarine
aquaphobia
aquaplane
  aquaplanes
  aquaplaned
  aquaplaning
aquarist
aquarium
Aquarius
aquatic
aquatics
aquatint
aqueduct
aqueous
aquifer
aquilegia
aquiline
arabesque
Arabian
Arabic
arable
arachnid
arachnophobia
Araldite℠
Aran
arbiter
arbitrage
arbitrageur

arbitrarily
arbitrariness
arbitrary
arbitrate
  arbitrates
  arbitrated
  arbitrating
arbitration
arboreal
arboretum
arboriculture
arbour
arc
arcade
Arcadian
arcane
arcanely
arcaneness
arch
  arches
  arched
  arching
archaeological
archaeology
archaic
archaically
archaism
archangel
archbishop
archbishopric
archdeacon
archdeaconry
  archdeaconries
archdiocese
  archdioceses
archducal
archduchess
  archduchesses
archduchy
  archduchies

archduke
  archdukes
arched
archeological
archeology
archer
archery
archetype
archetypical
archfiend
archimandrite
Archimedes
arching
archipelago
architect
architectural
architecturally
architecture
architrave
archival
archive
archivist
archly
archway
‹arcipelago =
  archipelago
‹arcitect = architect
‹arcitype = archetype
‹arcive = archive
arcs
Arctic
ardent
ardently
ardour
arduous
are
area
arena
aren't
areola

areolar
areolate
areole
arête
argent
Argentina
argie-bargie
argon
Argonaut
argot
arguable
arguably
argue
  argues
  argued
  arguing
argument
argumentation
argumentative
Argus
argy-bargy
  argy-bargies
Argyll
aria
arid
aridity
Aries
aright
arise
  arises
  arose
  arisen
  arising
aristocracy
  aristocracies
aristocrat
aristocratic
arithmetic
arithmetical
arithmetically

arithmetician
ark
Ark
arm
  arms
  armed
  arming
armada
armadillo
  armadillos
Armageddon
Armagh
Armagnac
Armalite™
armament
armature
armband
armchair
armed
Armenia
Armenian
armful
armhole
arming
armistice
  armistices
armoire
armour
armoured
armoury
  armouries
armpit
armrest
arms (= weapons
  → alms)
army
  armies
arnica
✗arnt = aunt
aroma

aromas
aromatherapist
aromatherapy
aromatic
aromaticity
arose
around
arousal
arouse
arouses
aroused
arousing
arpeggio
arpeggios
arraign
arraigns
arraigned
arraigning
arraignment
✗arrain = arraign
arrange
arranges
arranged
arranging
arrangement
arranger
arrant
array
arrays
arrayed
arraying
arrears
arrest
arrestingly
arrhythmia
arrival
arrive
arrives
arrived
arriving

arrivederci
arrivisme
arriviste
arrogance
arrogant
arrogantly
arrogate
arrogates
arrogated
arrogating
arrow
arrowroot
arrows
arse
arsehole
arsenal
arsenic
arson
art
artefact
arterial
arterially
arteriosclerosis
    arterioscleroses
artery
arteries
Artex⊤ᴹ
artful
artfully
artfulness
arthritic
arthritis
arthropod
Arthurian
artic
artichoke
article
articulacy
articulate
articulates

articulated
articulating
articulately
articulation
articulatory
artier
artiest
artifact
artifice
artifices
artificial
artificialise
artificiality
artificially
artillery
artilleryman
artillerymen
artisan
artisanal
artist (= painter etc
    → artiste)
artiste (= performer
    → artist)
artistic
artistically
artistry
artless
artlessly
arts
artwork
arty
    artier
    artiest
arty-crafty
Arundel
Aryan
as
asafetida
asafoetida
a.s.a.p.

asbestos
asbestosis
ascend
  ascends
  ascended
  ascending
ascendancy
ascendant
ascendency
ascendent
ascending
ascension
Ascension
ascent
ascertain
  ascertains
  ascertained
  ascertaining
ascetic
ascetically
asceticism
ASCII
ascot
ascribable
ascribe
  ascribes
  ascribed
  ascribing
ASEAN
✗ asend = ascend
✗ asent = ascent
aseptic
✗ asertain = ascertain
✗ asetic = ascetic
asexual
asexually
ash
  ashes
ashamed
ashamedly

ashen
ashes
ashore
ashram
ashtray
✗ ashure = assure
ashy
Asia
Asian
Asiatic
aside
✗ asine = assign
asinine
asininity
ask
  asks
  asked
  asking
askance
askew
asleep
ASLEF
✗ asolt = assault
asp
asparagus
aspect
aspen
asperity
asperities
aspersion
asphalt
  asphalts
  asphalted
  asphalting
asphyxia
asphyxiate
  asphyxiates
  asphyxiated
  asphyxiating
asphyxiation

aspic
aspidistra
  aspidistras
aspirate
  aspirates
  aspirated
  aspirating
aspiration
aspire
  aspires
  aspired
  aspiring
aspirin
✗ asprin = aspirin
asquint
ass
  asses
assail
  assails
  assailed
  assailing
assailable
assailant
assam
assassin
assassinate
  assassinates
  assassinated
  assassinating
assassination
assault
  assaults
  assaulted
  assaulting
assay
  assays
  assayed
  assaying
assemblage
assemble

assembles
assembled
assembling
assembly
assemblies
assent
assents
assented
assenting
assert
asserts
asserted
asserting
assertion
assertive
assertively
assertiveness
assess
assesses
assessed
assessing
assessment
assessor
asset
assiduity
assiduous
assiduously
assign
assigns
assigned
assigning
assignable
assignation
assignment
assimilable
assimilate
assimilates
assimilated
assimilitating
assimilation

assimilative
assimilatory
assist
assists
assisted
assisting
assistance
assistant
assister
assizes
associate
associates
associated
associating
associateship
association
associative
assonance
assort
assorts
assorted
assorting
assorted
assortment
assuage
assuages
assuaged
assuaging
assumable
assume
assumes
assumed
assuming
assumed
assumption
Assumption
assurance
assure
assures
assured

assuring
assuredly
assuredness
Assyrian
aster
asterisk
asterisks
asterisked
asterisking
astern
asteroid
asthma
asthmatic
asthmatically
astigmatic
astigmatism
astir
astonish
astonishes
astonished
astonishing
astonishingly
astonishment
astound
astounds
astounded
astounding
astoundingly
astrakhan
astral
astray
astride
astringence
astringency
astringent
astrologer
astrological
astrologist
astrology
astronaut

astronomer
astronomical
astronomically
astronomy
astrophysics
astute
astutely
astuteness
asunder
asylum
asymmetric
  asymmetrical
  asymmetrically
asymmetry
asymptomatic
asymptomatically
at
atavism
atavistic
ate (= consumed
  food → eight)
ateen = eighteen
atheism
atheist
atherosclerosis
athlete
athletic
athletically
athleticism
athletics
athwart
atieth = eightieth
atilt
Atlantic
atlas
  atlases
atmosphere
atmospheric
atmospherically
atmospherics

atoll
atom
atomic
atomise
atomises
atomised
atomising
atomiser
atomize
atomizes
atomized
atomizing
atomizer
atonal
atonality
atonally
atone
atones
atoned
atoning
atonement
atop
atopic
atrium
atrocious
atrociously
atrocity
  atrocities
atrophy
  atrophies
  atrophied
  atrophying
attaboy
attach
  attaches
  attached
  attaching
attaché
  attached
  attachment

attack
  attacks
  attacked
  attacking
attackable
attacker
attain
  attains
  attained
  attaining
attainability
attainable
attainment
attempt
  attempts
  attempted
  attempting
attemptable
attend
  attends
  attended
  attending
attendance
attendant
attention
attentive
attentively
attentiveness
attenuate
  attenuates
  attenuated
  attenuating
attenuation
attest
  attests
  attested
  attesting
attestable
attestation
attested

attic
attire
attitude
Attlee, Clement
attorney
    attorneys
attorneyship
attract
    attracts
    attracted
    attracting
attractant
attraction
attractive
attractively
attractiveness
attractor
attributable
attribute
    attributes
    attributed
    attributing
attribution
attributive
attributively
attrition
attune
✗ aty = eighty
atypical
atypically
auberge
aubergine
aubretia
aubrietia
auburn
Auchterarder
Auchtermuchty
Auckland
auction
    auctions

auctioned
auctioning
auctioneer
audacious
audaciously
audacity
audibility
audible
audibly
audience
audio
audiogram
audiotypist
audiovisual
audit
    audits
    audited
    auditing
audition
auditor
auditorium
    auditoriums or
    auditoria
auditory
au fait
Augean
auger (= tool
    → augur)
aught
augment
    augments
    augmented
    augmenting
augmentation
augmentative
augur (= be a sign
    of → auger)
    augurs
    augured
    auguring

augury
august
August
auk
auld
aunt
auntie
aunty
    aunties
aura
    auras or
    aurae
aural
aureole
au revoir
auricle
auricular
aurora
    auroras or
    aurorae
aurora borealis
auroral
auspices
auspicious
Aussie
Austen, Jane
austere
austerely
austerity
Australasia
Australasian
Australia
Australian
Austria
Austrian
autarchic
autarchy
    autarchies
authentic
authentically

authenticate
  authenticates
  authenticated
  authenticating
authentication
authenticator
authenticity
author
  authors
  authored
  authoring
authoress
  authoresses
authorial
authorisation
authorise
  authorises
  authorised
  authorising
authoritarian
authoritarianism
authoritative
authoritatively
authority
  authorities
authorize
  authorizes
  authorized
  authorizing
authorship
autism
autistic
auto
  autos
autobahn
autobiographical
autobiography
  autobiographies
autocracy
  autocracies

autocrat
  autocratic
autocross
auto-da-fé
  autos-da-fé
autograph
  autographs
  autographed
  autographing
autoimmune
automate
  automates
  automated
  automating
automatic
automation
automaton
automobile
automotive
autonomous
autonomously
autonomy
  autonomies
autopilot
autopsy
  autopsies
autoroute
  autoroutes
autos-da-fé
autumn
autumnal
auxiliary
  auxilliaries
avail
  avails
  availed
  availing
availability
available
availably

avalanche
  avalanches
avant-garde
avarice
avaricious
avariciously
avatar
avenge
  avenges
  avenged
  avenging
avenger
avenue
aver
  avers
  averred
  averring
average
  averages
  averaged
  averaging
averagely
averment
averred
averring
averse
aversely
aversion
avert
  averts
  averted
  averting
avgolemono
avian
aviary
  aviaries
aviation
aviator
avid
avidity

avidly
avocado
avocados
avocation
avocet
avoid
avoids
avoided
avoiding
avoidable
avoidably
avoidance
avoider
avoirdupois
avow
avows
avowed
avowing
avowal
avowed
avuncular
await
awaits
awaited
awaiting
awake
awakes
awoke *or*
awaked
awoken *or*
awaked
awaking
awaken
awakens
awakened
awakening
awakes
awaking
award
awards

awarded
awarding
awardable
aware
awareness
awash
away
awe (= feeling of wonder → or, oar)
awes
awed
awing
awesome
awful
awfully
awfulness
✗ awile = awhile
awkward
awl (= tool → all)
awkward
awkwardness
✗ awlder = alder
awning
awoke
awoken
AWOL
awry
axe
axes
axed
axing
axeman
axemen
axes
axiom
axiomatic
axis
axes
axle
ay try eye

ay
ayah
ayatollah
aye (= yes → eye)
Aylesbury
Ayr
azalea
Azerbaidjan
Aztec
azure

B

backward

BA
baa
  baas
  baaed
  baaing
baba
babble
  babbles
  babbled
  babbling
babbler
babe
Babel
baboon
babushka
  babushkas
baby
baby-boomer
Baby-bouncer™
babyhood
babyish
Babylonian
baby-sit
  baby-sits
  baby-sat
  baby-sitting
baby-sitter
baccalaureate
baccarat
bacchanal
bacchanalia
bacchanalian

Bacchic
baccy
Bach, Johann Se-
  bastian
bachelor
bacillary
bacillus
  bacilli
back
  backs
  backed
  backing
backache
backbeat
backbench
backbencher
backbiter
backbiting
backboard
backbone
backbreaking
backchat
backcloth
  backcloths
backcomb
  backcombs
  backcombed
  backcombing
backdate
  backdates
  backdated
  backdating
backdown
backdrop
backed
backer
backfill
  backfills
  backfilled
  backfilling

backfire
  backfires
  backfired
  backfiring
backgammon
background
backhand
backhanded
backhander
backing
backlash
backlog
backpack
  backpacks
  backpacked
  backpacking
back-pedal
  back-pedals
  back-pedalled
  back-pedalling
backscratcher
backside
back-slapping
backslide
  backslides
  backslid
  backsliding
backspace
backspin
backstage
backstairs
backstitch
backstreet
backstroke
backtrack
  backtracks
  backtracked
  backtracking
backup
backward

backwardation
backwards
backwash
backwater
backwoods
backwoodsman
  backwoodsmen
baclava
bacon
bacteria
bacterial
bactericide
bacteriological
bacteriologically
bacteriologist
bacteriology
bacterium
  bacteria
Bacup
bad
  worse
  worst
baddie
  baddies
baddy
  baddies
bade
badge
badger
  badgers
  badgered
  badgering
badinage
badlands
badly
badminton
bad-mouth
  bad-mouths
  bad-mouthed
  bad-mouthing

baffle
baffles
baffled
baffling
bafflement
bag
bags
bagged
bagging
bagatelle
bagel
baggage
  baggages
bagged
bagging
baggy
  baggier
  baggiest
bagpipes
bags
baguet
baguette
bah
Bahamiam
Bahraini
Bahreini
✗baige = beige
bail (= money;
empty out water
→ bale)
bails
bailed
bailing
bailey
  baileys
bailiff
bain-marie
  bains-marie
bairn
bait (= food to

catch on animal
→ baked)
baits
bated
bating
baize
bake
bakes
baked
baking
Bakelite™
baker
bakery
  bakeries
baking
baklava
baksheesh
balalaika
  balalaikas
balance
  balances
  balanced
  balancing
balanced
balcony
  balconies
bald
balder
baldest
balderdash
baldheaded
balding
baldy
baldness
bale (= bundle;
jump out of aircraft
→ bail)
bales
baled
baling

Balearic
baleen
baleful
balefully
baler
balk
  balks
  balked
  balking
Balkan
ball (= round object
  → bawl)
ballad
balladeer
ballast
ballerina
  ballerinas
ballet
balletic
ballistic
ballistics
balloon
  balloons
  ballooned
  ballooning
ballooning
balloonist
ballot
  ballots
  balloted
  balloting
ballpark
ballpoint
ballroom
balls
bally
ballyhoo
balm
balmier
balmiest

balmy (= warm
  → barmy)
  balmier
  balmiest
baloney
balsa
balsam
balsamic
Baltic
balustrade
bambino
  bambinos or
  bambini
bamboo
bamboozles
  bamboozles
  bamboozled
  bamboozling
bamboozler
ban (= forbid
  → banns)
  bans
  banned
  banning
banal
banality
  banalities
banally
banana
  bananas
band
  bands
  banded
  banding
bandage
  bandages
  bandaged
  bandaging
bandana
bandanna

bandicoot
bandier
bandies
bandiest
bandit
bandmaster
bandoleer
bandolier
bandsman
  bandsmen
bandstand
bandwagon
bandy
  bandies
  bandied
  bandying
bandy-legged
bane
baneful
banefully
bang
  bangs
  banged
  banging
banger
Bangkok
Bangladesh
Bangladeshi
bangle
banish
  banishes
  banished
  banishing
banishment
banisters
banjo
bank
  banks
  banked
  banking

bankable
banker
banking
banknote
bankroll
  bankrolls
  bankrolled
  bankrolling
bankrupt
  bankrupts
  bankrupted
  bankrupting
bankruptcy
  bankruptcies
banksman
  banksmen
banlieue
  banlieues
banned
banner
banning
bannisters
bannock
banns(= for a
  wedding → ban)
banquet
  banquets
  banqueted
  banqueting
banshee
bantam
bantamweight
banter
  banters
  bantered
  bantering
Bantu
banyan
baobab
bap

baptise
  baptises
  baptised
  baptising
baptism
baptismal
Baptist
baptize
  baptizes
  baptized
  baptizing
bar
  bars
  barred
  barring
Bar
barb
Barbadian
barbarian
barbarianism
barbaric
barbarically
barbarise
  barbarises
  barbarised
  barbarising
barbarism
barbarity
  barbarities
barbarous
barbarously
barbecue
  barbecues
  barbecued
  barbecuing
barbed
barbell
barber
barbershop

barbican
barbie
  barbies
barbiturate
barbwire
bard
bare (= without a
  covering → bear)
  bares
  bared
  baring
  barer
  barest
bareback
barefaced
barefacedly
barefoot
barely
bareness
bargain
  bargains
  bargained
  bargaining
barge
  barges
  barged
  barging
bargee
  bargees
bargepole
baric
baritone
barium
bark (= make noise
  like a dog
  → barque)
  barks
  barked
  barking
barley

barleys
arleycorn
arm = balm
armaid
arman
barmen
army (= mad
→ balmy)
barmier
barmiest
arn
arnacle
arney
barneys
arnsley
arnstaple
arnstorm
barnstorms
barnstormed
barnstorming
arnyard
arometer
arometric
arometry
aron (= nobleman
→ barren)
aronage
aroness
baronesses
aronet
aronetcy
baronetcies
aronial
arony
baronies
aroque
aroscope
aroscopic
arperson
barpersons

barque (= sailing
ship → bark)
barrack
barracks
barracked
barracking
barracks
barracuda
barracuda or
barracudas
barrage
barred
barrel
barrel-chested
barrelful
barren (= unfruitful
→ baron)
barrette
barricade
barricades
barricaded
barricading
barrier
barring
barrio
barrister
barrow
barrowful
bars
bartender
barter
barters
bartered
bartering
bartsia
basal
basalt
basaltic
base
bases

based
basing
baseball
baseboard
Basel
baseless
baseline
basely
baseman
basemen
basement
baseness
bases
bash
bashes
bashed
bashing
bashful
bashfully
bashfulness
bashibazouk
basic
basically
basics
basil
basilica
basilisk
basin
basinful
basis
bases
bask
basks
basked
basking
basket
basketball
basketful
basketry
basketwork

Basque
bas-relief
  bas-reliefs
bass
  basses
basset
bassinet
bassist
bassoon
bassoonist
bast
bastard
bastardisation
bastardise
  bastardises
  bastardised
  bastardising
bastardization
bastardize
  bastardizes
  bastardized
  bastardizing
bastardy
baste
  bastes
  basted
  basting
bastinado
basting
bastion
bat
  bats
  batted
  batting
batch
  batches
  batched
  batching
bated (= bated
  breath → bait)

bath
baths
bathed
bathing
bathe
bathes
bathed
bathing
bather
bathers
bathing
bathos
bathrobe
baths
bathtub
bathyscaph
bathysphere
batik
batiste
batman
  batmen
baton
bats
batsman
  batsmen
battalion
batted
batten
  battens
  battened
  battening
batten
Battenburg
batter
  batters
  battered
  battering
batterer
battering

battery
  batteries
battik
batting
battle
  battles
  battled
  battling
battledress
battlefield
battlement
battleship
batty
  battier
  battiest
batwing
batwoman
  batwomen
bauble
baud (= measure of
  speed → bawd,
  bored)
baulk
bauxite
bavarois
bawbee
bawd (= prostitute
  → baud, bored)
bawdier
bawdiest
bawdy
  bawdier
  bawdiest
bawl (= shout
  → ball)
  bawls
  bawled
  bawling
bay
  bays

bayed
baying
bayonet
bayonets
bayoneted *or*
bayonetted
bayoneting *or*
bayonetting
bayou
bazaar
bazar
bazooka
bazookas
be
am
are
is
was
were
been
being
each (= sea shore
→ beech)
beaches
beached
beaching
beachcomber
beachhead
beacon
bead
beaded
beadier
beadiest
beading
beadle
beadwork
beady
beadier
beadiest
beagle

beak
beaked
beaker
beam
beams
beamed
beaming
bean
beanbag
beanfeast
beano
beanos
beanpole
beanstalk
bear (= animal;
carry; put up with
→ bare)
bears
bore
borne *or*
born
bearing
bearable
bearably
beard
beards
bearded
bearding
beardless
bearer
bearing
bearish
bearishly
Béarnaise
bears
bearskin
beast
beastie
beastly
beastlier

beastliest
beat (= defeat
→ beet)
beats
beat
beaten
beating
beaten
beater
beatific
beatifically
beatification
beatify
beatifies
beatified
beatifying
beatitude
Beatitudes
beatnik
Beatrice
beats
beau
beaus *or*
beaux
Beaujolais
Beaulieu
beaus
beaut
beauteous
beautician
beautification
beautiful
beautifully
beautify
beautifies
beautified
beautifying
beauty
beauties

beaux
beaux-arts
beaver
  beavers
  beavered
  beavering
bebop
becalmed
became
because
beck
Becket, Thomas à
Beckett, Samuel
beckon
  beckons
  beckoned
  beckoning
become
  becomes
  became
  become
  becoming
becoming
becomingly
becomingness
becquerel
bed
  beds
  bedded
  bedding
bedaub
  bedaubs
  bedaubed
  bedaubing
bedazzle
  bedazzles
  bedazzled
  bedazzling
bedazzlement
bedbug

bedchamber
bedclothes
beddable
bedded
bedder
bedding
bedeck
  bedecks
  bedecked
  bedecking
bedevil
  bedevils
  bedevilled
  bedevilling
bedevilment
bedewed
bedfellow
bedlam
bedlamite
Bedouin
bedpan
bedpost
bedraggled
bedridden
bedrock
bedroll
bedroom
beds
bedside
bedsitter
bedsore
bedspread
bedstead
bedtime
bed-wetting
bee
bees
Beeb
beech (= tree
  → beach)

beeches
beechnut
✗ beeday = bidet
beef
  beefs
  beefed
  beefing
beefburger
beefcake
beefeater
beefier
beefiest
beefs
beefsteak
beefy
beehive
beekeeper
beeline
Beelzebub
been
beep
  beeps
  beeped
  beeping
beer (= drink
  → bier)
beerier
beeriest
beery
beeswax
beet (= vegetable
  → beat)
Beethoven, Ludwig
van
beetle
  beetles
  beetled
  beetling
beetle-browed
beetroot

beezer
befall
befit
  befalls
  befell
  befallen
  befalling
befitting
befittingly
befog
  befogs
  befogged
  befogging
before
beforehand
beforetime
befoul
  befouls
  befouled
  befouling
befriend
  befriends
  befriended
  brefriending
befuddle
  befuddles
  befuddled
  befuddling
befuddlement
beg
  begs
  begged
  begging
begad
began
begat
  begets
  begot *or*
  begat
  begotten *or*

begot
begetting
begetter
beggar
  beggars
  beggard
  beggaring
beggarly
beggary
begged
begging
✗begile = beguile
begin
  begins
  began
  begun
  beginning
beginner
beginning
begone
begonia
  begonias
begorra
begot
begotten
begrudge
  begrudges
  begrudged
  begrudging
  begrudgingly
  begs
beguile
  beguiles
  beguiled
  beguiling
beguilement
beguiler
  beguiling
  beguilingly
  begun

behalf
behave
  behaves
  behaved
  behaving
behaviour
behavioural
behaviourism
behaviourist
behead
  beheads
  beheaded
  beheading
beheld
behemoth
behest
behind
behindhand
behold
  beholds
  beheld
  beholding
  beholden
  beholder
behove
  behoves
  behoved
  behoving
beige
beigel
Beijing
being
Beirut
bejabers
bejewelled
belabour
  belabours
  belaboured
  belabouring
Belarus

belated
belatedly
belatedness
belch
  belches
  belched
  belching
beleaguer
  beleaguers
  beleaguered
  beleaguering
belfry
  belfries
Belgian
Belgium
belie
  belies
  blied
  belying
belief
believability
believable
believably
believe
  believes
  believed
  believing
believer
believing
belittle
  belittles
  belittled
  belittling
belittlement
bell
belladonna
bellboy
belle
  belles
belles-lettres

bellflower
bellicose
bellicosity
belligerence
belligerency
belligerent
bellow (= shout
  → below)
bellows
bellowed
bellowing
bellows
belly
  bellies
bellyache
  bellyaches
  bellyached
  bellyaching
bellybutton
bellyful
belong
  belongs
  belonged
  belonging
  belongings
Belorussian
beloved
below (= under-
  neath → bellow)
belt
  belts
  belted
  belting
beltway
beluga
belvedere
bemoan
  bemoans
  bemoaned

bemoaning
bemused
bemusedly
ben
Ben Nevis
bench
  benches
bend
  bends
  bent
  bending
bender
bendier
bendiest
bends
bendy
beneath
Benedictine
benediction
benefaction
benefactor
benefactoress
  benefactoresses
beneficence
beneficent
beneficently
beneficial
beneficiary
  beneficiaries
benefit
  benefits
  benefited
  benefiting
benevolence
benevolent
benevolently
Bengali
benighted
benightedly
benign

benignity
benignly
bent
bentonite
benumb
  benumbs
  benumbed
  benumbing
bequeath
  bequeaths
  bequeathed
  bequeathing
bequeather
bequest
berate
  berates
  berated
  berating
Berber
berberis
bereave
  bereaves
  bereaved
  bereaving
bereavement
bereft
beret
berg
bergamot
beriberi
berk
Berkhampstead
berm
berme
Bern
berry (= small fruit
  → bury)
  berries
berserk
berth (= ship's

mooring place
  → birth)
berths
berthed
berthing
Berwick
beseech
  beseeches
  besought *or*
  beseeched
  beseeching
beseecher
beseeching
beseechingly
beset
  besets
  beset
  besetting
beside
besides
besiege
  besieges
  besieged
  besieging
besmear
  besmears
  besmeared
  besmearing
besmirch
  besmirches
  besmirched
  besmirching
besom
besotted
besought
bespangled
bespattered
bespeak
  bespeaks
  bespoke

bespoken
bespeaking
bespectacled
bespoke
besprinkled
best
bestial
bestiality
  bestialities
bestially
bestiary
  bestiaries
bestir
  bestirs
  bestirred
  bestirring
bestow
  bestows
  bestowed
  bestowing
bestowal
bestrew
  bestrews
  bestrewed
  bestrewn *or*
  bestrewed
  bestrewing
bestride
  bestrides
  bestrode
  bestridden
  bestriding
bet
  bets
  bet *or*
  betted
  betting
beta
beta-blocker
betacarotene

betake
  betakes
  betook
  betaken
  betaking
betel
bête noire
  bêtes noires
bethink
  bethinks
  bethought
  bethinking
bethought
betide
betimes
bêtise
  bêtises
betoken
  betokens
  betokened
  betokening
betook
betray
  betrays
  betrayed
  betraying
betrayal
betrayer
betrothal
betrothed
bets
betted
better
betterment
betting
between
betwixt
bevel
  bevels
  bevelled

bevelling
beverage
bevies
bevy
bewail
  bewails
  bewailed
  bewailing
beware
bewhiskered
bewilder
  bewilders
  bewildered
  bewildering
  bewilderingly
  bewilderment
bewitch
  bewitches
  bewitched
  bewitching
  bewitchingly
beyond
bezique
bhajee
  bhajees
bhaji
  bhajis
bhang
biannual
biannually
bias
  biases or
  biasses
  biased or
  biassed
  biasing or
  biassing
biathlon

biaxial
bib
Bible
biblical
Biblicist
bibliographic
bibliography
  bibliographies
bibliomania
bibliophile
bibulous
bicameral
bicarb
bicarbonate
bicentenary
  bicentenaries
biceps
Bicester
bichloride
bicker
  bickers
  bickered
  bickering
bickie
  bickies
bicolour
bicoloured
bicycle
bid
  bids
  bade or
  bid
  bidden or
  bid
  bidding
biddable
bidden
bidder
bidding
biddy

biddies
bide
 bides
 bided *or*
 bode
 bided
 biding
bidet
biding
bidirectional
biennial
biennially
bier (= table for
 dead body → beer)
bierkeller
biff
 biffs
 biffed
 biffing
bifocal
bifocals
bifurcate
 bifurcates
 bifurcated
 bifurcating
 bifurcation
big
 bigger
 biggest
bigamist
bigamous
bigamy
bigger
biggest
bighead
big-hearted
bight
bigot
bigotry
bigwig

bijou
bike
 bikes
 biked
 biking
 biker
bikini
 bikinis
bilabial
bilateral
bilaterally
bilberry
 bilberries
bile
bilge
bilharzia
bilinear
bilingual
bilingualism
bilingually
bilious
 biliousness
bilirubin
bilk
 bilks
 bilked
 bilking
bill
 bills
 billed
 billing
billabong
billboard
Billericay
billet
 billets
 billeted
 billeting
billet-doux
billets-doux

billfold
billhook
billiard
 billiards
billing
billion
billionaire
billow
 billows
 billowed
 billowing
 billowy
billposter
billy
 billies
billycock
billyo
bilobate
biltong
bimbo
 bimbos
bimonthly
bin
 bins
 binned
 binning
binary
bind
 binds
 bound
 binding
binder
binding
bindweed
binge
 binges
 binged
 bingeing *or*
 binging
bingo

binman
  binmen
binning
binocular
  binoculars
binomial
binomially
bins
bio-
biochemical
biochemistry
biodegradable
biodegradation
biodiversity
biodynamics
biofeedback
biographer
biographical
biographically
biography
  biographies
biological
biologically
biologist
biology
biomass
bionic
biophysicist
biophysics
biopic
biopsy
  biopsies
biorhythm
biosphere
biotechnological
biotechnology
bipartisan
bipartite
biped
biplane

birch
  birches
  birched
  birching
bird
birdbath
bird-brained
birdcage
birdhouse
birdie
  birdies
birdlime
birdman
  birdmen
birdseed
birdshot
birdsong
biretta
biriani
Birmingham
Biro ⓣⓜ
birth (= being born
  → berth)
birthday
  birthdays
birthmark
birthplace
birthright
birthstone
biryani
biscuit
bisect
  bisects
  bisected
  bisecting
bisection
bisexual
bisexuality
bisexually
bishop

bishopric
Bismarck, Otto von
bismuth
bison
  bisons or
  bison
bisque
bistro
  bistros
bisulphate
bisulphide
bisulphite
bit
bitch
  bitches
  bitched
  bitching
bitchier
bitchiest
bitchy
  bitchier
  bitchiest
bite (= cut with
  mouth → byte)
  bites
  bit
  bitten
  biting
biting
bitten
bitter
bitterly
bitterness
bitters
bittersweet
bitty
  bittier
  bittiest
bitumen
bituminous

bivalve
bivalvular
bivouac
  bivouacs
  bivouacked
  bivouacking
biweekly
biyearly
bizarre
bizarrely
bizarreness
blab
  blabs
  blabbed
  blabbing
blabbed
blabber
  blabbers
  blabbered
  blabbering
blabbermouth
blabbing
blabs
black
  blacks
  blacked
  blacking
blackamoor
blackball
  blackballs
  blackballed
  blackballing
blackberry
  blackberries
blackbird
blackboard
blackcap
blackcurrant
blacken
  blackens

blackened
blackening
blackface
blackfly
  blackflies
blackguard
blackhead
blacking
blackjack
blackleg
blacklist
  blacklists
  blacklisted
  blacklisting
blackmail
  blackmails
  blackmailed
  blackmailing
blackout
blacksmith
blackthorn
blacktop
bladder
bladderwort
blade
blaeberry
  blaeberries
✗ blagard =
  blackguard
blah
blame
  blames
  blamed
  blaming
blamed
blameless
blamelessly
blamelessness
blameworthy
✗ blamonge =

blancmange
blanch
  blanches
  blanched
  blanching
blancmange
bland
  blander
  blandest
blandishments
blank
blanket
  blankets
  blanketed
  blanketing
blankly
blankness
blare
  blares
  blared
  blaring
blarney
blasé
blaspheme
  blasphemes
  blasphemed
  blaspheming
blasphemer
blasphemous
blasphemously
blasphemy
  blasphemies
blasted
  blast
  blasts
  blasted
  blasting
blastoff
blatant
blatantly

blather
blathers
blathered
blathering
blaze
blazes
blazed
blazing
blazer
blazes
blazon
blazons
blazoned
blazoning
bleach
bleaches
bleached
bleaching
bleachers
bleak
blearier
bleariest
bleary
blearier
bleariest
bleary-eyed
bleat
bleats
bleated
bleating
bled
bleed
bleeds
bled
bleeding
bleeder
bleeding
bleep
bleeps
bleeped

bleeping
bleeper
blemish
blemishes
blemished
blemishing
blench
blenches
blenched
blenching
blend
blends
blended
blending
blende
blender
blenny
blennies
blepharitis
bless
blesses
blessed or
blest
blessed
blesses
blessing
blest
blether
blethers
blethered
blethering
blew
blight
blights
blighted
blighting
blighter
blimey

blimp
blind
blinds
blinded
blinding
blinders
blindfold
blindfolds
blindfolded
blindolding
blinding
blindworm
blini
blinis
blink
blinks
blinked
blinking
blinkered
blinkers
blinking
blintz
blintzes
blintze
blintzes
blip
bliss
blissful
blisfully
blister
blisters
blistered
blistering
blistering
blisteringly
blithe
blithely
blithering
blithesome
blitz

blitzes
blitzed
blitzing
litz
Blitzes
itzkrieg
izzard
oated
oater
ob
oc
lock
blocks
blocked
blocking
ockade
blockades
blockaded
blockading
lockader
lockage
lockboard
lockbuster
lockbusting
locked
locker
lockhead
lockhouse
locking
lockish
loke
londe
lood
loodbath
loodcurdling
looded
loodhound
loodied
loodier
loodies

bloodiest
bloodless
bloodlessly
bloodlessness
bloodline
bloodroot
bloodshed
bloodshot
bloodstained
bloodstock
bloodstone
bloodstream
bloodsucker
bloodthirsty
bloodthirstier
bloodthirstiest
bloodworm
bloody
bloodier
bloodiest
bloodies
bloodied
bloodying
bloody-minded
bloom
blooms
bloomed
blooming
bloomer
bloomers
blooming
blooper
blossom
blossoms
blossomed
blossoming
blot
blots
blotted
blotting

blotch
blotches
blotted
blotter
blotting
blotto
blouse
blouson
blow
blows
blew
blown
blowing
blowed
blower
blowfly
blowflies
blowhard
blowhole
blowier
blowiest
blowing
blowlamp
blown
blowout
blowpipe
blowsier
blowsiest
blowsy
blowsier
blowsiest
blowtorch
blowy
blowier
blowiest
blowzier
blowziest
blowzy
blowzier
blowziest

blub
blubs
blubbed
blubbing
blubber
bludgeon
bludgeons
bludgeoned
bludgeoning
blue
bluer
bluest
bluebell
blueberry
blueberries
bluebird
bluebook
bluebottle
bluefish
bluefish
bluegrass
blueish
blueprint
bluer
blues
bluest
bluestocking
bluestone
bluethroat
bluetit
bluetongue
blueweed
bluff
bluffs
bluffed
bluffing
bluish
blunder
blunders
blundered

blundering
blunderbuss
blunt
blur
blurs
blurred
blurring
blurb
blurred
blurring
blurt
blurts
blurted
blurting
blush
blushes
blushed
blushing
blusher
bluster
blusters
blustered
blustering
✗bo = beau
boa
boar (= animal →
bore)
board
boards
boarded
boarding
boarder (= one who
boards → border)
boarding
boardroom
boardsailing
boardwalk
boarfish
boast
boasts

boasted
boasting
boastful
boastfully
boastfulness
boat
boater
boathook
boathouse
boating
boatman
boatmen
boatswain
bob
bobs
bobbed
bobbing
bob
bobbed
bobbejaan
bobbin
bobbing
bobble
bobby
bobbies
bobby-dazzler
bobbysoxer
bobcat
bobfloat
boblet
bobotie
bobsled
bobsleigh
bobstay
bobtail
bocage
bod
bode
bodes
boded

boding
bodega
bodge
bodges
bodged
bodging
bodger
bodice
bodiless
bodily
bodkin
body
bodies
bodyguard
bodysuit
bodywork
Boer
boffin
bog
bogs
bogged
bogging
bogey
bogeys
bogeyman
bogeymen
boggart
bogged
bogging
boggle
boggles
boggled
boggling
bogie
bogies
Bogota
bogus
bogwood
bogy
bogies

boil
boils
boiled
boiling
boiler
boilermaker
boilerplate
boiling
boilover
boisterous
boisterously
boisterousness
bold
bolder
boldest
boldface
boldfaced
boldly
boldness
bole
bolero
boleros
boletus
boletuses *or*
boleti
Bolivia
boll
bollard
bollocking
bollocks
bollworm
bolometer
bolometric
boloney
Bolshevik
bolshie
bolshier
bolshiest
bolshy
bolshier

bolshiest
bolster
bolsters
bolstered
bolstering
bolt
bolts
bolted
boting
bolus
bomb
bombs
bombed
bombing
bombard
bombards
bombarded
bombarding
bombardier
bombardment
bombastic
bombastically
bombed
bomber
bombshell
bombsight
bonanza
Bonaparte, Napoleon
bonbon
bonce
bond
bonds
bonded
bonding
bondage
bonded
bondholder
bonding
bondmaid
bondservant

bondsman
  bondsmen
bone
  bones
  boned
  boning
bone-dry
bonehead
boneshaker
boneyard
bonfire
bong
bongo
  bongos *or*
  bongoes
bonhomie
bonier
boniest
bonk
  bonks
  bonked
  bonking
bonkers
bonne
bonnet
bonny
  bonnier
  bonniest
bonsai
bony
bonzer
boo
  boos
  booed
  booing
boob
  boobs
  boobed
  boobing
boo-boo

booby
  boobies
booed
boogie
  boogies
  boogied
  boogieing
boogie-woogie
boohoo
booing
book
  books
  booked
  booking
bookbinder
bookbinding
bookcase
bookie
  bookies
  booking
bookish
bookishness
booklet
bookmaker
bookmark
bookplate
books
bookstall
booksy
bookworm
bool
✗ boolabase =
  bouillabaisse
✗ boolimia = bulimia
boom
  booms
  boomed
  booming
boomer
boomerang

boon
boondocks
boor
boorish
boorishly
boorishness
boos
boost
  boosts
  boosted
  boosting
booster
boot
  boots
  booted
  booting
bootblack
booted
bootee (= shoe for
  a baby → booty)
  bootees
booth
booting
bootlace
bootleg
  bootlegs
  bootlegged
  bootlegging
bootlegger
bootless
bootstraps
booty (= stolen
  goods → bootee)
booze
  boozes
  boozed
  boozing
boozer
boozier
booziest

oozy	✗ borld = bald	bosun
boozier	✗ borderdash =	botanical
booziest	balderdash	botanically
op	born (= came to life	botanise
bops	→ borne, bourn)	botanises
bopped	borne (= carried;	botanised
bopping	put up with	botanising
oracite	→ born, bourn)	botanist
orage	bornite	botanize
orax	boron	botanizes
orazon	boronia	botanized
orbon = bourbon	borough	botanizing
ordeaux	borrow	botany
ordel	borrows	botch
ordello	borrowed	botches
bordellos	borrowing	botched
order (= frontier	borsch	botching
→ boarder)	borscht	botcher
borders	borshcht	botchier
bordered	borstal	botchiest
bordering	borzoi	botchy
orderer	boscage	botchier
orderland	Bosch, Hieronymus	botchiest
orderline	bosh	botfly
ore (= not interest	bo's'n	botflies
→ boar)	Bosnia	both
bores	bosom	bother
bored	bosomy	bothers
boring	boss	bothered
oreal	bosses	bothering
ored (= uninter-	bossed	botheration
esting → bawd,	bossing	bothersome
baud)	bossa nova	bothies
oredom	bossed	bothy
orehole	bosses	bothies
orer	boss-eyed	Botswana
oric	bossier	Botticelli
oride	bossiest	bottle
oring	bossing	bottles
orjoir = bourgeois	bossy	bottled

bottling
bottlebrush
bottled
bottleful
bottleneck
bottler
bottling
bottom
  bottoms
  bottomed
  bottoming
bottomless
bottommost
botulin
botulinus
botulism
bouclé
boudoir
bouffant
bougainvillaea
  bougainvillaeas
bougainvillea
  bougainvilleas
bough (= branch of
  a tree → bow)
bought
bouillabaisse
bouillon
boulder (= large
  stone → bold)
boules
boulevard
bounce
  bounces
  bounced
  bouncing
bouncer
bouncier
bounciest
bouncing

bouncy
bouncier
bounciest
bound
bounds
bounded
bounding
boundary
  boundaries
bounded
bounden
bounder
boundless
boundlessly
boundlessness
bounds
bounteous
bounteously
bounteousness
bountiful
bounty
  bounties
Bounty
bouquet
bourbon
bourgeois
bourgeoise
bourgeoisie
bourn (= stream
  → born, borne)
bout
boutique
boutonniere
bovine
bovver
bow (= bend body
  in respect
  → bough)
bows
bowed

bowing
bowdlerise
  bowdlerises
  bowdlerised
  bowdlerising
bowdlerize
  bowdlerizes
  bowdlerized
  bowdlerizing
bowed
bowel
  bowels
bower
bowfin
bowing
bowknot
bowl
  bowls
bowled
bowling
bow-legged
bowler
bowlful
bowline
bowling
bowman
bowmen
bowsaw
bowshot
bowsprit
bow-wow
box
  boxes
  boxed
  boxing
boxcar
boxer
boxers
boxful
boxing

boxroom
boxwood
boy (= male child
  → buoy)
boycott
  boycotts
  boycotted
  boycotting
boyfriend
boyhood
boyish
boyishly
boyishness
boysenberry
  boysenberries
bra
brace
  braces
  braced
  bracing
bracelet
braces
brachah
brachial
brachiosaurus
brachium
bracing
bracken
bracket
  brackets
  bracketed
  bracketing
bracketing
brackish
brackishly
brackishness
bradawl
bradycardia
brae (= hillside
  → bray)

brag
brags
bragged
bragging
braggadocio
braggart
bragged
bragging
Brahman
Brahmans
Brahmin
Brahmin or
Brahmins
Brahms, Johannes
braid
braids
braided
braiding
Braille
brain
brains
brained
braining
brainbox
brainchild
braindead
brainier
brainiest
brainless
brainpower
brainstem
brainstorm
brainstorming
brain-teaser
brainwash
brainwashes
brainwashed
brainwashing
brainy
braise

braises
braised
braising
brake (= for stop-
  ping → break)
brakes
braked
braking
✗ brakedown =
  breakdown
✗ brakewater =
  breakwater
bramble
brambling
Bramley
bran
branch
branches
branched
branching
brand
brands
branded
branding
brandish
brandishes
brandished
brandishing
brandy
brandies
brash
brashly
brashness
Brasilia
brass
brasses
brasserie
brasseries
brassica
brassicas

brassier
brassiere
brassy
  brassier
  brassiest
brat
bratpack
bratwurst
bravado
brave
  braver
  bravest
bravely
bravery
bravissimo
bravo
  bravos
bravura
brawl
  brawls
  brawled
  brawling
brawn
brawnier
brawniest
brawny
  brawnier
  brawniest
bray (= make sound
like a donkey
→ brae)
  brays
  brayed
  braying
brazen
  brazens
  brazened
  brazening
Brazil
brazier

Brazilian
breach (= break
  → breech)
  breaches
  breached
  breaching
bread (= food
  → bred)
breadbasket
breadboard
breadcrumb
breadfruit
breadline
breadth
breadthways
breadwinner
breadwise
break (= become
broken → brake)
  breaks
  broke
  broken
  breaking
breakable
breakage
breakaway
break-dance
breakdown
breaker
breakeven
breakfast
  breakfasts
  breakfasted
  breakfasting
breaking
breakneck
breakthrough
breakwater
bream
  breams or

bream
breast
  breasts
  breasted
  breasting
breastbone
breastpin
breastplate
breaststroke
breastwork
breath
breathalyse
  breathalyses
  breathalysed
  breathalysing
breathalyser
breathalyze
  breathalyzes
  breathalyzed
  breathalyzing
breathalyzer
breathe
  breathes
  breathed
  breathing
breather
breathier
breathiest
breathing
breathless
breathtaking
breathy
  breathier
  breathiest
Brechin
Brecht, Bertolt
Brecon
bred (= produced
young → bread)
breech (= as in

brink

breech birth
→ breath)
breeches
breed
  breeds
  bred
  breeding
breeder
breeding
breeks
breeze
  breezes
  breezed
  breezing
breezier
breeziest
breezy
  breezier
  breeziest
brethren
Breton
Breughel, Pieter
breve
breviary
  breviaries
brevity
brew
  brews
  brewed
  brewing
brewer
brewery
briar
bribe
  bribes
  bribed
  bribing
bribery
bric-a-brac
brick

bricks
bricked
bricking
brickbat
brickearth
✗ brickette = briquette
brickie
brickies
bricklayer
bricklaying
brickwork
brickyard
bridal
bride
bridegroom
bridesmaid
bridewell
bridge
  bridges
  bridged
  bridging
bridgehead
bridges
bridgework
bridging
bridie
bridle
  bridles
  bridled
  bridling
Brie
brief
  briefs
  briefed
  briefing
  briefer
  briefest
briefcase
briefing
brier

brig
brigade
brigadier
brigand
brigantine
bright
  brighter
  brightest
brightens
brightens
brightened
brightening
bright-eyed
brightly
brightness
Brighton
brill
brilliance
brilliant
brilliantine
brilliantly
brills
brim
  brims
  brimmed
  brimming
brimful
brimfull
brimmed
brimming
brimstone
brindled
brine
bring
  brings
  brought
  bringing
brinier
briniest
brink

brinkmanship
brioche
  brioches
briony
  brionies
briquette
Brisbane
brisk
  brisker
  briskest
brisket
briskly
briskness
bristle
  bristles
  bristled
  bristling
bristletail
bristols
Brit
Britain (= country
  → Briton)
Britannia
Britannic
britches
Briticism
British
Britisher
Briton (= person
  → Britain)
brittle
brittleness
broach (= introduce
  a subject
  → brooch)
  broaches
  broached
  broaching
broad

broader
broadest
broadband
broadbrim
broadbrush
broadcast
  broadcasts
  broadcasted
  broadcasting
broadcloth
broaden
  broadens
  broadened
  broadening
broadleaf
broad-leaved
broadloom
broad-minded
broadsheet
broadside
broadsword
brocade
  brocades
  brocaded
  brocading
broccoli
brochette
brochure
brock
brogue
broil
  broils
  broiled
  broiling
broiler
broke
broken
brokenhearted
broker
brokerage

brolly
  brollies
bromeliad
bromide
bromine
Bromley
bronchia
bronchial
bronchiole
bronchitic
bronchitis
broncho-
bronchopneumonia
bronco
  broncos
Brontë (sisters)
brontosaurus
  brontosauri
bronze
  bronzes
  bronzed
  bronzing
brooch (= piece of
  jewellery
  → broach)
  brooches
brood
  broods
  brooded
  brooding
brooder
broodier
broodiest
broody
  broodier
  broodiest
brook
  brooks
  brooked
  brooking

brooklet
brookweed
broom (= brush
　→ brume)
broomstick
✗brosher = brochure
broth
brothel
brother
brotherhood
brotherly
brougham
brought
brouhaha
brow
browband
browbeat
　browbeats
　browbeat
　browbeaten
　browbeating
brown
　browns
　browned
　browning
brownie
　brownies
Brownie
　Brownies
browning
brownout
browse
　browses
　browsed
　browsing
brucellosis
bruin
bruise
　bruises
　bruised

bruising
bruiser
bruit
bruits
bruited
bruiting
Brûlé
brume (= mist
　→ broom)
Brummie
　Brummies
brunch
brunches
brunette
brunt
brush
brushes
brushed
brushing
brushmark
brushoff
brushwood
brushwork
brusque
brusquely
brusqueness
Brussels
brutal
brutalise
　brutalises
　brutalised
　brutalising
brutality
brutalities
brutalize
　brutalizes
　brutalized
　brutalizing
brutally
brute

brutish
brutishly
✗bruwem = brougham
bryony
bryonies
BSc
bub
bubble
bubbles
bubbled
bubbling
bubbly
bubblier
bubbliest
bubonic
buccaneer
buck
bucks
bucked
bucking
buckaroo
buckaroos
buckboard
bucket
buckets
bucketed
bucketing
buckeye
buckhorn
buckle
buckles
buckled
buckling
buckler
buckram
buckshee
buckshot
buckskin
buckthorn
bucktooth

buckteeth
buckwheat
bucolic
bucolically
bud
  buds
  budded
  budding
Buddha
Buddhism
budding
buddleia
  buddleias
buddy
  buddies
budge
  budges
  budged
  budging
budgerigar
budget
  budgets
  budgeted
  budgeting
budgie
  budgies
buff
  buffs
  buffed
  buffing
buffalo
  buffalos
  buffaloes
buffer
  buffers
  buffered
  buffering
buffet
  buffets
  buffeted

buffeting
buffoon
buffoonery
bug
  bugs
  bugged
  bugging
bugaboo
  bugaboos
bugbear
bugged
bugger
  buggers
  buggered
  buggering
buggery
bugging
buggy
  buggies
bughouse
bugle
bugler
bugloss
build
  builds
  built
  building
builder
  building
built
✗ buion = bouillon
bulb
bulbiferous
bulbous
Bulgaria
Bulgarian
bulge
  bulges
  bulged
  bulging

bulgur
bulimia
bulimic
bulk
bulkhead
bulkier
bulkiest
bulkily
bulkiness
bulky
  bulkier
  bulkiest
bull
bullace
bulldog
bulldoze
  bulldozes
  bulldozed
  bulldozing
bulldozer
bullet
bulletin
bulletproof
bullfight
bullfighter
bullfighting
bullfinch
  bullfinches
bullfrog
bull-headed
bull-headedly
bullhorn
bullion
bullish
bullishly
bullishness
bullock
bullring
bullshit
  bullshits

bullshitted
bullshitting
bully
  bullies
  bullied
  bullying
bullyboy
bulrush
  bulrushes
bulwark
bum
  bums
  bummed
  bumming
bumbailiff
bumble
  bumbles
  bumbled
  bumbling
bumblebee
bumf
bumfreezer
bummed
bummer
bumming
bump
  bumps
  bumped
  bumping
bumper
bumph
bumpier
bumpiest
bumpkin
bumptious
bumptiously
bumptiousness
bumpy
  bumpier
  bumpiest

bun
bunch
  bunches
  bunched
  bunching
bund
bundle
  bundles
  bundled
  bundling
bung
  bungs
  bunged
  bunging
bungalow
bunghole
bungle
  bungles
  bungled
  bungling
bunion
bunk
  bunks
  bunked
  bunking
bunker
bunkhouse
bunkum
bunny
  bunnies
bunt
  bunts
  bunted
  bunting
bunting
buoy (= floating
  object → boy)
  buoys
buoyancy
buoyant

buoyantly
bur
Burberry℠
  Burberries
burble
  burbles
  burbled
  burbling
burbot
burden
  burdens
  burdened
  burdening
burdensome
burdock
bureau
  bureaux
bureaucracy
  bureaucracies
bureaucrat
bureaucratically
bureaucratisation
bureaucratization
burette
burgeon
  burgeons
  burgeoned
  burgeoning
burger (= round
  piece of meat
  → burgher)
burgess
  burgesses
burgh
burgher (= person
who lives in a town
→ burger)
burglar
burglarize
  burglarizes

burglarized
burglarizing
burglary
  burglaries
burgle
  burgles
  burgled
  burgling
burgomaster
burial
buried
buries
burk
burlap
burlesque
burliness
burly
Burma
Burmese
burn
  burns
  burnt *or*
  burned
  burning
burner
burnet
burning
burnish
  burnishes
  burnished
  burnishing
burnoose
burnous
burnouse
burnout
burnsides
burnt
✗ buro = bureau
✗ burocracy =
  bureaucracy

✗ burocrat =
  bureaucrat
burp
  burps
  burped
  burping
burr
burrito
  burritos
burro
  burros
burrow
  burrows
  burrowed
  burrowing
bursar
bursarial
bursary
  bursaries
burst
  bursts
  burst
  bursting
burthen
  burthens
  burthened
  burthening
burton
burweed
bury (= put into the
  ground → berry)
  buries
  buried
  burying
bus
  busses *or*
  buses
  bussed *or*
  bused
  bussing *or*

busing
busby
  busbies
bused
buses
bush
bushbaby
  bushbabies
bushed
bushel
bushfire
bushfly
  bushflies
bushier
bushiest
Bushman
  Bushmen
bushwhack
  bushwhacks
  bushwhacked
  bushwhacking
bushwhacker
bushy
  bushier
  bushiest
busied
busier
busies
busiest
busily
business
  businesses
businesslike
businessman
  businessmen
businesswoman
  businesswomen
busing
busk
  busks

busked
busking
busman
busmen
bussed
busses
bussing
bust
  busts
  busted *or*
  bust
  busting
bustard
busted
buster
bustier
bustiest
busting
bustle
  bustles
  bustled
  bustling
busty
  bustier
  bustiest
busy
  busies
  busied
  busying
  busier
  busiest
busybody
  busybodies
busying
but
butane
butanol
butch
butcher
  butchers

butchered
butchering
butchery
✗ butiful = beautiful
✗ butishun =
  beautician
butler
butlery
butt
  butts
  butted
  butting
butte
butter
  butters
  buttered
  buttering
butterbur
buttercup
butterfingers
butterfly
  butterflies
buttermilk
butternut
butterscotch
butterwort
buttery
buttock
button
  buttons
  buttoned
  buttoning
buttonhole
buttress
  buttresses
  buttressed
  buttressing
butty
  butties
✗ buty = beauty

butyl
buxom
buy (= purchase
  → by, bye)
  buys
  bought
  buying
buyer
  buying
buyout
buzz
  buzzes
  buzzed
  buzzing
buzzard
buzzer
by (= near → buy,
  bye)
by-
✗ bycycle = bicycle
bye (= goodbye;
  sports match
  → buy, by)
  byes
bye-bye
bye-election
bye-law
by-election
Byelorussian
bygone
bylaw
bypass
  bypasses
  bypassed
  bypassing
by-product
byre
bystander
byte (= in a
  computer → bite)

byway
byword
Byzantine

C

ca try cha
cab
cabal
cabala
cabalistic
cabaret
cabbage
cabbogy
cabbala
cabbalah
cabbie
   cabbies
cabby
   cabbies
caber
Cabernet Sauvignon
cabin
cabinet
cable
   cables
   cabled
   cabling
cabochon
caboodle
caboose
cabriole
cabriolet
cacao
cacciatore
cache (= hidden
   store → cash)
cachepot

cachet
cachou (= scented
   sweet → cashew)
   cachous
cack-handed
cackle
   cackles
   cackled
   cackling
cacophonous
cacophony
   cacophonies
cactus
   cactuses *or*
   cacti
cad
cadaver
cadaverous
CADCAM
caddie (= in golf)
   caddies
   caddied
   caddying
caddish
caddy (= tea caddy)
   caddies
cadence
cadenza
cadet
cadge
   cadges
   cadged
   cadging
cadmium
cadre
Caernarfon
Caernarvon
Caerphilly
Caesarean
Caesarian

caesium
caesura
café
cafe
cafeteria
cafetiere
caffeine
caftan
cage
  cages
  caged
  caging
cagey
  cagier
  cagiest
cagoule
cahoots
caïque
cairn
Cairo
caisson
Calcutta
California
cajole
  cajoles
  cajoled
  cajoling
cajolery
Cajun
cake
  cakes
  caked
  caking
calabash
calaboose
calabrese
calamine
calamitous
calamitously
calamity

calamities
calcareous
calceolaria
calciferol
calcification
calcify
  calcifies
  calcified
  calcifying
calcine
  calcines
  calcined
  calcining
calcium
calculable
calculate
  calculates
  calculated
  calculating
calculation
calculator
calculus
caldera
Caledonian
calendar (= to show
  days, weeks, etc
  → colander)
calender (= ma-
  chine → colander)
calendula
calf
  calves
calfskin
calibrate
  calibrates
  calibrated
  calibrating
calibre
calices
calico

caliper
calipers
caliph
caliphate
calix
  calices
call
  calls
  called
  calling
Callanetics
calligrapher
calligraphist
calligraphy
calling
callipers
callisthenics
callosity
callous
callow
callus
calm
  calms
  calmed
  calming
calmative
calomel
calorie
calorific
calumniate
  calumniates
  calumniated
  calumniating
calumny
  calumnies
calvary
  calvaries
calve (= give birth
  to a calf → carve)
  calves

calved
calving
Calvinism
Calvinist
calvinistic
calyces
calypso
  calypsos *or*
  calypsoes
calyx
  calyces *or*
  calyxes
cam
camaraderie
Camarthen
camber
Cambodia
cambric
camcorder
came
✗ cameelion =
  chameleon
camel
camellia
  camellias
Camembert
cameo
  cameos
camera
cameraman
  cameramen
Cameroon
camiknickers
camise
camisole
camomile
camouflage
  camouflages
  camouflaged
  camouflaging

camp
camps
camped
camping
campaign
campaigns
campaigned
campaigning
campaigner
campanile
campanologist
campanology
campanula
  campanulas
Campari™
camper
camphor
campion
campus
  campuses
camshaft
Camus, Albert
can
Canaan
Canaanite
Canadian
canaille
Canada
canal
canalise
  canalises
  canalised
  canalising
canalize
  canalizes
  canalized
  canalizing
canapé
canard
canary

canaries
canasta
cancan
cancel
cancels
cancelled
cancelling
cancellation
cancer
cancerophobia
candelabrum
  candelabrums *or*
  candelabra
candid
candida
candidacy
  candidacies
candidate
candidature
candied
candle
candlelight
Candlemas
candlestick
candlewick
candour
candy
candyfloss
candytuft
cane
  canes
  caned
  caning
canine
caning
canister
canker
cankerous
cannabis
canned

cannelloni
canneloni
canner
cannery
  canneries
cannibal
cannibalise
  cannibalises
  cannibalised
  cannibalising
cannibalism
cannibalize
  cannibalizes
  cannibalized
  cannibalizing
cannily
canning
cannon (= large gun
  → canon)
  cannons *or*
  cannon
  cannons
  cannoned
  cannoning
cannonade
cannonball
cannonry
cannot
canny
  cannier
  canniest
canoe
  canoes
  canoed
  canoeing
canoeist
canon (= law of
  Christian church
  → cannon)
canonical

canonisation
canonise
  canonises
  canonised
  canonising
canonize
  canonizes
  canonized
  canonizing
canoodle
  canoodles
  canoodled
  canoodling
canopy
  canopies
canst
cant
  cants
  canted
  canting
can't
Cantab.
cantaloup
cantankerous
cantankerously
cantankerousness
cantata
  cantatas
canteen
canter (= gallop
  → cantor)
Canterbury
  canters
  cantered
  cantering
canticle
cantilever
canto
  cantos
canton

Cantonese
cantor (= leader of
  singers → canter)
canvas (= thick
  cloth → canvass)
  canvases
canvass (= find out
  opinions → can-
  vas)
  canvasses
  canvassed
  canvassing
canyon
canzonetta
  canzonettas
✗ caos = chaos
cap
  caps
  capped
  capping
capability
capable
capacious
capaciously
capaciousness
capacitor
capacity
  capacities
caparison
cape
caper
  capers
  capered
  capering
capercaillie
  capercaillies
capillary
  capillaries
capita
capital

capitalisation

capitalisation
capitalise
capitalises
capitalised
capitalising
capitalism
capitalist
capitalization
capitalize
capitalizes
capitalized
capitalizing
capitation
capitulate
capitulates
capitulated
capitulating
capitulation
capitulatory
capon
capped
capping
cappuccino
cappuccinos
capriccioso
caprice
capricious
capriciously
capriciousness
Capricorn
capsicum
capsicums
capsize
capsizes
capsized
capsizing
capstan
capsule
captain
captains

captained
captaining
caption
captious
captiously
captivate
captivates
captivated
captivating
captive
captivity
captor
capture
captures
captured
capturing
Capuchin
capybara
capybaras
car
Caracas
carafe
caramel
caramelise
caramelises
caramelised
caramelising
caramelize
caramelizes
caramelized
caramelizing
carapace
carat (= measure of
 purity of gold
 → caret, carrot)
Caravaggio
caravan
caravanning
caravanserai
caraway

carbine
carbohydrate
carbolic
carbon
carbonaceous
carbonade
carbonated
carboniferous
carbonise
carbonises
carbonised
carbonising
carbonize
carbonizes
carbonized
carbonizing
carboy
carbuncle
carburation
carburetter
carcase
carcass
carcasses
carcinogen
carcinogenic
carcinoma
carcinomas
card
cardamom
cardamum
cardboard
cardi-
cardiac
cardie
Cardiff
cardigan
cardinal
cardiogram
cardiograph
cardiological

carte blanche

ardiology
ardiopulmonary
ardiovascular
ardoon
ards
ardsharp
are
  cares
  cared
  caring
areen
  careens
  careened
  careening
areer
areerism
areerist
arefree
areful
arefully
arefulness
areless
arelessly
arelessness
arer
aress
  caresses
  caressed
  caressing
aressingly
aret (= symbol
  used in printing
  → carat, carrot)
aretaker
areworn
arfare
argo
  cargoes *or*
  cargos
Caribbean

caribou
  caribous *or*
  caribou
caricature
  caricatures
  caricatured
  caricaturing
caries
carillon
  caring
Carlisle
Carmelite
carmine
carnage
carnal
carnally
carnation
carnelian
carnival
carnivore
carnivorous
carnivorously
carob
carol
  carols
  carolled
  carolling
Carolingian
carotene
carousal (= merry-
  making → carou-
  sel, carrousel)
carouse
  carouses
  caroused
  carousing
carousel (= merry-
  go-round → carou-
  sal)
carouser

carp
  carps
  carped
  carping
carpel
carpenter
carpentry
carpet
  carpets
  carpeted
  carpeting
carpetbagger
  carpeting
carping
carport
carrel
carriage
carriageway
carrier
✗ carrige = carriage
carrion
carrot (= vegetable
  → carat, caret)
carroty
carrousel (= merry-
  go-round → carou-
  sal)
carry
  carries
  carried
  carrying
carrycot
carrying-on
  carryings-on
carsick
cart
  carts
  carted
  carting
carte blanche

cartel
cartful
carthorse
cartilage
cartilaginous
cartload
cartographer
cartographic
cartography
carton
cartoon
cartoonist
cartouch
cartouche
cartridge
cartwheel
cartwright
carve (= cut meat
→ calve)
  carves
carved
carving
carver
carvery
  carveries
carving
caryatid
casbah
cascade
  cascades
  cascaded
  cascading
case
  cases
  cased
  casing
casebook
casework
cash (= money →
  cache)

cashes
cashed
cashing
cashew (= nut
  → cachou)
cashier
cashless
cashmere
cash-point
casing
casino
  casinos
cask
casket
casque
cassava
  cassavas
casserole
  casseroles
  casseroled
  casseroling
cassette
cassock
cassoulet
cassowary
  cassowaries
cast
  casts
  cast
  casting
castanets
castaway
caste
castellated
caster
castigate
  castigates
  castigated
  castigating
casting

castle
castor
castrate
  castrates
  castrated
  castrating
castration
castrato
castrator
casual
casually
casualness
casualty
  casualties
casuist
casuistic
casuistical
casuistry
cat
catabolic
cataclysm
cataclysmic
catacomb
Catalan
catalepsy
cataleptic
catalogue
  catalogues
  catalogued
  cataloguing
catalpa
catalysis
catalyst
catalytic
catamaran
catapult
  catapults
  catapulted
  catapulting
cataract

catarrh
catarrhal
catastrophe
catastrophic
catastrophically
catatonic
catcall
catch
  catches
  caught
  catching
catch-22
catcher
catches
catchier
catchiest
catching
catchment
catchword
catchy
  catchier
  catchiest
catechise
  catechises
  catechised
  catechising
catechism
catechist
catechize
  catechizes
  catechized
  catechizing
categorial
categorical
categorically
categorise
  categorises
  categorised
  categorising
categorize

categorizes
categorized
categorizing
category
  categories
cater
  caters
  catered
  catering
caterer
catering
caterpillar
caterwaul
  caterwauls
  caterwauled
  caterwauling
catfish
  catfish or
  catfishes
catgut
catharsis
  catharses
cathartic
cathedra
cathedral
catheter
catheterise
  catheterises
  catheterised
  catheterising
catheterize
  catheterizes
  catheterized
  catheterizing
cathodal
cathode
catholic
catholicisation
catholicise
  catholicises

catholicised
catholicising
Catholicism
catholicization
catholicize
catholicizes
catholicized
catholicizing
catkin
catmint
catnap
  catnaps
  catnapped
  catnapping
catnip
cat-o'-nine-tails
Catseye℠
catsuit
cattery
  catteries
cattleman
  cattlemen
catty
  cattier
  cattiest
catwalk
Caucasian
caucus
  caucuses
caudal
caught
cauldron
cauliflower
caulk (= block up
  cracks in → cork)
  caulks
  caulked
  caulking
causal
causality

causally
causation
causative
causatively
cause
  causes
  caused
  causing
causeway
caustic
cauterise
  cauterises
  cauterised
  cauterising
cauterize
  cauterizes
  cauterized
  cauterizing
caution
  cautions
  cautioned
  cautioning
cautionary
cautious
  cautiously
  cautiousness
cavalcade
cavalier
cavalry
cavalryman
  cavalrymen
cave
  caves
  caved
  caving
caveat
caveman
  cavemen
cavern
cavernous

cavernously
caviar
cavil
  cavils
  cavilled
  cavilling
caving
cavity
  cavities
cavort
  cavorts
  cavorted
  cavorting
caw
  caws
  cawed
  cawing
✗ cayli = ceilidh
CB
CD
CD-ROM
ce try ca
ce try che
ceanothus
  ceanothuses
cease
  ceases
  ceased
  ceasing
ceaseless
  ceaselessly
cedar
cede (= give up
  → seed)
  cedes
  ceded
  ceding
cedilla
  cedillas

Ceefax
✗ ceesh = quiche
ceilidh
ceiling
celandine
✗ celebacy = celibacy
celebrant
celebrate
  celebrates
  celebrated
  celebrating
celebration
celebrity
  celebrities
celeriac
celerity
celery
celestial
celibacy
celibate
cell (= room in a
  prison; unit of
  living matter
  → sell)
cellar
cellarage
cellist
cello
  cellos
cellphone
cellular
cellulite
celluloid
cellulose
Celsius
Celt
Celtic
cembalo
  cembali or
  cembalos

cement
  cements
  cemented
  cementing
cemetery
  cemeteries
cenotaph
censor (= take
  parts out of a film
  etc → censure)
  censors
  censored
  censoring
censorious
censoriously
censoriousness
censorship
censure (= express
  disapproval of
  → censor)
  censures
  censured
  censuring
census
  censuses
cent
centaur
centavo
  centavos
centenarian
centenary
  centenaries
centesimal
centigrade
centigram
centigramme
centilitre
centime
centimetre
centipede

central
centralisation
centralise
  centralises
  centralised
  centralising
centralism
centrality
centralization
centralize
  centralizes
  centralized
  centralizing
centrally
centre
  centres
  centred
  centring
centrefold
centrepiece
centrifugal
centrifugally
centrifuge
centripetal
centrist
centurion
century
  centuries
cephalic
cephalopod
ceramic
ceramics
cereal (= grain crop
  → serial)
cerebellum
cerebral
cerebrally
cerebration
cerebrum
  cerebrums or

cerebra
ceremonial
ceremonially
ceremonious
ceremoniously
ceremony
  ceremonies
cerise
cert
certain
certainly
certainty
  certainties
certifiable
certificate
  certificated
certification
certificatory
certified
certify
  certifies
  certified
  certifying
certitude
cerulean
cervical
cervix
  cervices or
  cervixes
Cesarean
cesium
cessation
cession
cesspool
cetacean
cetologist
cetology
cf
CFC
Chablis

cha-cha-cha
chafe
    chafes
    chafed
    chafing
chaff
    chaffs
    chaffed
    chaffing
chaffinch
    chaffinches
chagrin
chain
    chains
    chained
    chaining
chair
    chairs
    chaired
    chairing
chairman
    chairmen
chairmanship
chairperson
    chairpersons
chairwoman
    chairwomen
chaise
chalet
chalice
chalk
    chalks
    chalked
    chalking
chalkiness
chalky
challenge
    challenges
    challenged
    challenging

chamber
chamberlain
chambermaid
chambers
chambray
chameleon
chammy
chamois
chamomile
champ
    champs
    champed
    champing
champagne
✗ champane =
    champagne
champion
championship
chance
    chances
    chanced
    chancing
chancel
chancellery
chancellor
chancery
chancy
    chancier
    chanciest
chandelier
chandler
chandlery
change
    changes
    changed
    changing
changeability
changeable
changeless
changeling

changeover
channel
    channels
    channelled
    channelling
chant
    chants
    chanted
    chanting
chantry
    chantries
chanty
chaos
chaotic
chaotically
chap
    chaps
    chapped
    chapping
chaparral
chapel
chaperon
    chaperons
    chaperoned
    chaperoning
chaperone
    chaperones
    chaperoned
    chaperoning
chaplain
chaplaincy
chaplet
chapped
chappie
chapping
chaps
chapter
char
    chars
    charred

charring
charabanc
character
characterisation
characterise
  characterises
  characterised
  characterising
characteristic
characteristically
characterization
characterize
  characterizes
  characterized
  characterizing
charade
charades
charcoal
chard
Chardonnay
charge
  charges
  charged
  charging
chargeable
chargé d'affaires
  chargés d'affaires
charger
charier
chariest
charily
chariness
chariot
charioteer
charisma
charismatic
charitable
charitably
charity
  charities

charlady
  charladies
charlatan
charleston
charlie
charm
  charms
  charmed
  charming
charmer
charming
charmingly
charnel
Charolais
Charollais
charred
charring
chart
  charts
  charted
  charting
charter
Chartism
chartist
chartreuse℠
charwoman
  charwomen
chary
  charier
  chariest
chase
  chases
  chased
  chasing
chaser
chasm
chassis
  chassis
chaste
chastely

chasten
chastens
chastened
chastening
chastise
chastises
chastised
chastising
chastisement
chastity
chasuble
chat
  chats
  chatted
  chatting
château
  châteaus *or*
  châteaux
chatelaine
chatline
chatted
chattel
chatter
  chatters
  chattered
  chattering
chatterbox
  chatterboxes
chatterer
chatting
chatty
  chattier
  chattiest
chauffeur
  chauffeurs
  chauffeured
  chauffeuring
chauffeuse
chauvinism
chauvinist

chauvinistic
chauvinistically
cheap (= not ex-
 pensive → cheep)
cheapen
 cheapens
 cheapened
 cheapening
cheaply
cheapness
cheapo
cheapskate
cheat
 cheats
 cheated
 cheating
check (= look for
 mistakes → che-
 que)
 checks
 checked
 checking
checker
checklist
checkmate
checkout
checkpoint
checkup
cheddar
cheek
 cheeks
 cheeked
 cheeking
cheekbone
cheeky
 cheekier
 cheekiest
cheep (= noise
 made by a bird →
 cheap)

cheeps
cheeped
cheeping
cheer
 cheers
 cheered
 cheering
cheerful
cheerfully
cheerfulness
cheerier
cheeriest
cheerio
cheerleader
cheerless
cheerlessly
cheers
cheery
 cheerier
 cheeriest
cheese
cheeseboard
cheeseburger
cheesecake
cheesecloth
cheesemonger
cheeseparing
cheesewood
cheesy
 cheesier
 cheesiest
cheetah
chef
chef d'oeuvre
 chefs d'oeuvre
Chekhov, Anton
✗ chellist = cellist
✗ chello = cello
chemical
chemically

chemise
chemist
chemistry
chemotherapeutic
chemotherapy
chenille
cheque (= used as
 means of payment
 → check)
chequebook
chequered
chequers
cherish
 cherishes
 cherished
 cherishing
Cherokee
cheroot
cherry
 cherries
cherub
 cherubs or
 cherubim
cherubic
cherubically
cherubim
chervil
chess
chessboard
chessman
 chessmen
chest
chesterfield
chestier
chestiest
chestnut
chesty
 chestier
 chestiest
chevalier

chevron
chew
  chews
  chewed
  chewing
chewy
  chewier
  chewiest
Cheyenne
chianti
chiaroscuro
chic (= elegant
  → sheikh, sheik)
Chicago
chicanery
chichi
chick
chickadee
chicken
  chickens
  chickened
  chickening
chickenpox
chickpea
chickweed
chicle
chicly
chicory
chide
  chides
  chided or
  chid
  chid or
  chidden
  chiding
chief
chiefly
chieftain
chiffon
chiffonier

chiffonnier
chigger
chignon
chihuahua
chilblain
child
  children
  childbirth
  childcare
  childhood
  childish
  childishly
  childishness
  childlike
  children
Chile
chill
  chills
  chilled
  chilling
  chiller
  chilli
  chillies
  chilliness
  chilly
  chillier
  chilliest
chimaera
chime
  chimes
  chimed
  chiming
chimera
chimerical
chimney
  chimneys
chimneypiece
chimneypot
chimp
chimpanzee

chin
China
china
chinchilla
chine
Chinese
chink
  chinks
  chinked
  chinking
chinless
chino
chinos
chintz
chintzy
  chintzier
  chintziest
chinwag
chip
  chips
  chipped
  chipping
chipboard
chipmunk
chipolata
  chipped
  chipper
Chippewa
  chipping
chippy
  chippies
chiromancy
chiropodist
chiropody
chiropractic
chiropractor
chirp
  chirps
  chirped
  chirping

chirpy
  chirpier
  chirpiest
chisel
  chisels
  chiselled
  chiselling
chiseller
chit
chitchat
chitin
chitterlings
chitty
  chitties
chivalrous
chivalrously
chivalry
chives
chivvy
  chivvies
  chivvied
  chivvying
chivy
  chivies
  chivied
  chivying
chlorate
chloride
chlorinate
  chlorinates
  chlorinated
  chlorinating
chlorine
chlorite
chlorofluorocarbon
chloroform
chlorophyll
chloroplast
chlorosis
choc

chocaholic
chock
  chocks
  chocked
  chocking
chocoholic
chocolate
Choctaw
choice
choir (= group of
  singers → coir,
  quire)
choirboy
choirmaster
choke
  chokes
  choked
  choking
choker
chokey
choky
choler
cholera
choleric
cholerically
cholesterol
chomp
  chomps
  chomped
  chomping
choose
  chooses
  chose
  chosen
  choosing
choosy
  choosier
  choosiest
chop
  chops

chopped
chopping
chophouse
chopped
chopper
choppers
chopping
choppy
  choppier
  choppiest
chops
chopsticks
chop suey
choral (sung by a
  choir → coral,
  corral)
chorale
chord (= musical
  notes → cord)
chording
chore
choreograph
  choreographs
  choreographed
  choreographing
choreographer
choreographic
choreography
chorister
chorizo
  chorizos
✗ chork = chalk
chortle
  chortles
  chortled
  chortling
chorus
  choruses
  chorused
  chorusing

chose
chosen
choux
chow
chowder
chow mein
Christ
christen
  christens
  christened
  christening
Christendom
christening
Christian
Christianise
  Christianises
  Christianised
  Christianising
Christianity
Christianize
  Christianizes
  Christianized
  Christianizing
Christlike
Christmas
Christmassy
Christmastide
chromate
chromatic
chrome
chromite
chromium
chromosome
chronic
chronically
chronicle
  chronicles
  chronicled
  chronicling
chronicler

chronograph
chronological
chronologically
chronologist
chronology
chrysalis
chrysalises
chrysanthemum
chrysanthemums
chubby
chubbier
chubbiest
chuck
chucks
chucked
chucking
chuckle
chuckles
chuckled
chuckling
chuffed
chug
chugs
chugged
chugging
chukka
chukker
chum
chums
chummed
chumming
chummy
chummier
chummiest
chump
chunk
chunky
chunkier
chunkiest
Chunnel

church
churches
churchier
churchiest
Churchill, Winston
churchman
churchmen
churchwarden
churchwoman
churchwomen
churchy
churchier
churchiest
churchyard
churl
churlish
churlishly
churlishness
churn
churns
churned
churning
chute (= slide →
  shoot)
chutney
chutneys
CIA
✗ cianti = chianti
ciao
cicada
cicadas
cicatrice
cicatrices
cicatrix
cicatrices
cicerone
CID
cider
cig

cigar
cigarette
cigarillo
  cigarillos
ciggy
  ciggies
✗ cimera = chimera
cinch
cincture
cinder
cinema
cinematographer
cinematographic
cinematography
cinnabar
cinnamon
Cinzano ⓉⓂ
cipher
  ciphers
  ciphered
  ciphering
circa
circadian
✗ circit = circuit
✗ circitry = circuitry
circle
  circles
  circled
  circling
circlet
circuit
circuitous
circuitously
circular
circularise
  circularises
  circularised
  circularising
circularity
circularize

circularizes
circularized
circularizing
circulate
circulates
circulated
circulating
circulation
circumcise
circumcises
circumcised
circumcising
circumcision
circumference
circumferential
circumflex
circumlocution
circumlocutory
circumnavigate
circumnavigates
circumnavigated
circumnavigating
circumnavigation
circumscribe
circumscribes
circumscribed
circumscribing
circumscription
circumspect
circumspection
circumspectly
circumstance
circumstantial
circumstantially
circumvent
circumvents
circumvented
circumventing
circus
circuses

✗ cirosis = cirrhosis
cirque
cirrhosis
cirrus
CIS
cissy
  cissies
Cistercian
cistern
citadel
citation
cite (= give as an
  example → site,
  sight)
  cites
  cited
  citing
citizen
citizenry
citizenship
citric
citron
citronella
citrus
  citruses
city
  cities
civet
civic
civics
civies
civil
civilian
civilisation
civilise
  civilises
  civilised
  civilising
civilised
civility

vilization
vilize
civilizes
civilized
civilizing
vilized
villy
vvies
vvy
lack
clacks
clacked
clacking
lad
ladding
laggy
claggier
claggiest
laim
claims
claimed
claiming
laimant
lairvoyance
lairvoyant
lairvoyantly
lam
clams
clammed
clamming
lamber
clambers
clambered
clambering
lammed
lamming
lammy
clammier
clammiest
lamour

clamours
clamoured
clamouring
clamp
clamps
clamped
clamping
clampdown
clan
clandestine
clandestinely
clandestineness
clang
clangs
clanged
clanging
clanger
clank
clanks
clanked
clanking
clannish
clannishly
clannishness
clansman
clansmen
clap
claps
clapped
clapping
clapper
clapperboard
clappers
clapping
claptrap
claque
claret
clarification
clarify
clarifies

clarified
clarifying
clarinet
clarinetist
clarinettist
clarion
clarity
✗ clark = clerk
clarkia
clash
clashes
clashed
clashing
clasp
clasps
clasped
clasping
class
classes
classed
classing
classic
classical
classicism
classicist
classics
classier
classiest
classification
classified
classify
classifies
classified
classifying
classism
classless
classmate
classroom
classy
classier

classiest
clatter
  clatters
  clattered
  clattering
clause (= part of a
  sentence → claws)
claustrophobia
claustrophobic
clavichord
clavicle
claw (= animal's
  sharp nail
  → clause)
  claws
  clawed
  clawing
clay
claymore
clean
  cleans
  cleaned
  cleaning
clean-cut
cleaner
cleanliness
cleanly
cleanse
  cleanses
  cleansed
  cleansing
cleanser
cleanup
clear
  clears
  cleared
  clearing
clearance
clear-cut
clearing

clearly
clear-sighted
clearstory
  clearstories
clearway
cleat
cleavage
cleave
  cleaves
  cleaved or
  clove
  cleaved or
  cleft or
  cloven
  cleaving
cleaver
Cleethorpes
clef
cleft
cleg
clematis
clemency
clement
clementine
clemently
clench
  clenches
  clenched
  clenching
✗ clens = cleanse
✗ clenser = cleanser
clerestory
  clerestories
clergy
clergyman
  clergymen
cleric
clerical
clericalism
clerically

clerihew
clerk
Cleveland
clever
cleverdick
cleverly
cleverness
clew
clianthus
✗ clic = clique
cliché
clichéd
click
  clicks
  clicked
  clicking
client
clientele
cliff
cliffhanger
climacteric
climacterical
climactic
climactically
climate
climatic
climatically
climatological
climatologically
climatology
climax
  climaxes
climb (= got to the
  top of → clime)
  climbs
  climbed
  climbing
climber
clime (= climate
  → climb)

✗climer = climber
✗clinch
  clinches
  clinched
  clinching
clincher
cline
cling
  clings
  clung
  clinging
clingfilm
clinic
clinical
clinically
clinician
clink
  clinks
  clinked
  clinking
clinker
clip
  clips
  clipped
  clipping
clipboard
clipped
clipper
clippers
clipping
clique
cliquish
cliquishness
✗clishay = cliché
clitoral
clitoris
  clitorises
cloak
  cloaks
  cloaked

cloaking
cloakroom
clobber
  clobbers
  clobbered
  clobbering
cloche
clock
  clocks
  clocked
  clocking
clockmaker
clockwise
clockwork
clod
cloddish
clodhopper
clog
  clogs
  clogged
  clogging
cloisonné
cloister
  cloisters
  cloistered
  cloistering
clone
  clones
  cloned
  cloning
clop
  clops
  clopped
  clopping
clor try chlor
close
  closes
  closed
  closing
  closer

closest
close-fisted
close-grained
close-hauled
close-knit
closely
closeness
closet
  closets
  closeted
  closeting
✗closh = cloche
closing
closure
clot
  clots
  clotted
  clotting
cloth
clothe
  clothes
  clothed
  clothing
clothes
clotheshorse
clothesline
clothier
clothing
clotted
cloture
cloud
  clouds
  clouded
  clouding
cloudberry
  cloudberries
cloudburst
cloudier
cloudiest
cloudless

cloudy
  cloudier
  cloudiest
clout
  clouts
  clouted
  clouting
clove
cloven
clover
cloverleaf
clown
  clowns
  clowned
  clowning
cloy
  cloys
  cloyed
  cloying
cloze test
club
  clubs
  clubbed
  clubbing
clubby
clubhouse
cluck
  clucks
  clucked
  clucking
clue
  clues
  clued
  cluing
clued-up
clueless
clump
  clumps
  clumped
  clumping

clumsy
  clumsier
  clumsiest
clung
clunk
  clunks
  clunked
  clunking
cluster
  clusters
  clustered
  clustering
clutch
  clutches
  clutched
  clutching
clutter
  clutters
  cluttered
  cluttering
✗ clwasonay =
  cloisonné
Clwyd
Clyde
cm
CND
co try cho
Co.
c/o
coach
  coaches
  coached
  coaching
coach-builder
coachman
coachmen
coachwork
coaction
coactive
coactively

coadjutor
coagulable
coagulant
coagulate
  coagulates
  coagulated
  coagulating
coagulation
coagulative
coal
coalesce
  coalesces
  coalesced
  coalescing
coalescence
coalface
coalfield
coalition
coalman
coalmen
✗ coam = comb
coarse (= rough
  → course)
coarsen
  coarsens
  coarsened
  coarsening
coast
  coasts
  coasted
  coasting
coaster
coastguard
coastline
coat
  coats
  coated
  coating
coating
coauthor

coax
  coaxes
  coaxed
  coaxing
cob
cobalt
cobber
cobble
  cobbles
  cobbled
  cobbling
cobbled
cobbler
cobblers
cobblestone
cobnut
cobra
  cobras
cobweb
coca
cocaine
coccyx
  coccyxes *or*
  coccyges
✗ cocetry = coquetry
cocette = coquette
cochineal
cochlea
  cochlea *or*
  cochleae
cock
  cocks
  cocked
  cocking
cockade
cock-a-doodle-doo
cock-a-hoop
cock-a-leekie
cockalorum
cockatiel

cockatoo
  cockatoos *or*
  cockatoo
cockatrice
cockchafer
cockcrow
cockerel
cockeyed
cockfight
cockhorse
cockier
cockiest
cockiness
cockle
cockleshell
cockney
  cockneys
cockpit
cockroach
cockscomb
cocksure
cocktail
cockup
cocky
  cockier
  cockiest
cocoa
coconut
cocoon
  cocoons
  cocooned
  cocooning
cocotte
✗ cocsyx = coccyx
cod
COD
coda
  codas
coddle
  coddles

coddled
coddling
code
  codes
  coded
  coding
codeine
codename
codeword
codex
  codices
codger
codices
codicil
codification
codify
  codifies
  codified
  codifying
codling
codpiece
codswallop
co-ed
coeducation
coefficient
coelacanth
coeliac
coequal
coequally
coerce
  coerces
  coerced
  coercing
coercion
coercive
coercively
coerciveness
coeval
coexist
  coexists

coexisted
coexisting
coexistence
coextensive
✗ coff = cough
coffee
coffeepot
coffer
cofferdam
coffin
cog
cogency
cogent
  cogently
cognac
cognate
cognisance
cognisant
cognition
cognitive
cognitively
cognizance
cognizant
cognomen
cognominal
cognoscenti
cogwheel
cohabit
  cohabits
  cohabited
  cohabiting
cohabitant
cohabitation
cohabiter
cohere
  coheres
  cohered
  cohering
coherence
coherent

coherently
cohesion
cohesive
cohesively
cohesiveness
cohort
coif
coiffed
coiffeur
coiffure
coiffured
coil
  coils
  coiled
  coiling
coin
  coins
  coined
  coining
coinage
coincide
  coincides
  coincided
  coinciding
coincidence
coincident
coincidental
coincidentally
Cointreau
coir (= material
  used for mats,
  ropes etc → choir)
✗ coit = quoit
coital
coition
coitus
coitus interruptus
coke
col
cola

colander
cold
  colder
  coldest
cold-blooded
cold-hearted
coldly
coldness
Coleraine
coleslaw
coley
  coleys
colic
colicky
coliseum
colitis
collaborate
  collaborates
  collaborated
  collaborating
collaboration
collaborationism
collaborationist
collaborative
collaborator
collage (= picture
  → college)
collagen
collapse
  collapses
  collapsed
  collapsing
collapsibility
collapsible
collar
  collars
  collared
  collaring
collarbone
collard

collate
  collates
  collated
  collating
collateral
collation
collator
colleague
collect
  collects
  collected
  collecting
collectable
collected
collectedly
collection
collective
collectively
collectivisation
collectivization
collector
colleen
college (= school → college)
collegial
collegiate
collegium
collide
  collides
  collided
  colliding
collie
  collies
collier
colliery
  collieries
collision
collocate
  collocates
  collocated

collocating
collocation
colloid
colloquial
colloquialism
colloquially
colloquialness
colloquy
collude
  colludes
  colluded
  colluding
collusion
collusive
collywobbles
Colne
cologne
✗ colone = cologne
Colombia (country)
colon
colonel (= military officer → kernel)
colonial
colonialism
colonialist
colonially
colonise
  colonises
  colonised
  colonising
colonist
colonize
  colonizes
  colonized
  colonizing
colonnade
  colonnaded
colonoscope
colony
  colonies

coloration
coloratura
colossal
colossally
colosseum
colossus
  colossuses *or*
  colossi
colostrum
colour
  colours
  coloured
  colouring
coloured
colourfast
colourful
colourfully
colourise
  colourises
  colourised
  colourising
colourize
  colourizes
  colourized
  colourizing
colourless
colourlessly
colt
coltish
coltishly
coltishness
coltsfoot
columbine
column
columnar
columnist
coma
  comas
Comanche
comatose

comb
  combs
  combed
  combing
combat
  combats
  combatted
  combatting
combatable
combatant
combative
combatively
comber
combinable
combination
combinative
combine
  combines
  combined
  combining
combo
  combos
combustibility
combustible
combustion
come
  comes
  came
  come
  coming
comeback
comedian
comedienne
comedown
comedy
  comedies
comeliness
comely
comer
comestible

comet
comeuppance
comfier
comfiest
comfit
comfort
  comforts
  comforted
  comforting
comfortable
comfortably
comforter
comforting
comfortingly
comfortless
comfy
  comfier
  comfiest
comic
comical
comically
coming
comity
  comities
✗ comly = comely
comma
  commas
command
  commands
  commanded
  commanding
commandant
commandeer
commander
commandership
commanding
commandingly
commandment
commando
  commandos or

commandoes
comeuppance
commedia dell'arte
comme il faut
commemorate
  commemorates
  commemorated
  commemorating
commemoration
commemorative
commemoratively
commence
  commences
  commenced
  commencing
commencement
commend
  commends
  commended
  commending
commendable
commendably
commendation
commendatory
commensurate
comment
  comments
  commented
  commenting
commentary
  commentaries
commentate
  commentates
  commentated
  commentating
commentator
commerce
commercial
commercialisation
commercialise
  commercialises

commercialised
commercialising
commercialism
commercialization
commercialize
commercializes
commercialized
commercializing
commercially
commie
commies
commiserate
commiserates
commiserated
commiserating
commiseration
commissar
commissariat
commissary
commissaries
commission
commissions
commissioned
commissioning
commissionaire
commissioner
commissionership
commit
commits
committed
committing
commitment
committal
committed
committee
committeeman
committeemen
committeewoman
committeewomen
commode

commodious
commodiously
commodiousness
commodity
commodities
commodore
common
commonality
commoner
commonly
commonness
commonplace
commons
common sense
commonsensical
commonweal
commonwealth
Commonwealth
commotion
communal
communally
commune
communes
communed
communing
communicable
communicably
communicant
communicate
communicates
communicated
communicating
communication
communicative
communicatively
communicator
communion
communiqué
communism
communist

community
communities
commutability
commutable
commutableness
commutation
commutative
commutator
commute
commutes
commuted
commuting
commuter
compact
compacts
compacted
compacting
compaction
compactly
compactness
compadre
companion
companionability
companionable
companionableness
companionably
companionless
companionship
companionway
company
companies
comparable
comparability
comparably
comparative
comparatively
compare
compares
compared
comparing

comparison
compartment
compartmental
compartmentalisa-
tion
compartmentalise
compartmentali-
ses
compartmenta-
lised
compartmentalis-
ing
compartmentaliza-
tion
compartmentalize
compartmentali-
zes
compartmenta-
lized
compartmentaliz-
ing
compass
compassion
compassionate
compassionately
compatibility
compatible
compatibly
compatriot
compeer
compel
compels
compelled
compelling
compelling
compellingly
compendious
compendiously
compendiousness
compendium

compendiums *or*
compendia
compensate
compensates
compensated
compensating
compensation
compensatory
compere
comperes
compered
compering
compete
competes
competed
competing
competence
competency
competent
competently
competition
competitive
competitively
competitiveness
competitor
compilation
compile
compiles
compiled
compiling
compiler
complacency
complacent
complacently
complain
complains
complained
complaining
complainant
complainer

complaining
complainingly
complaint
complaisance
complaisant
complaisantly
complement (=
make something
complete → com-
pliment)
complements
complemented
complementing
complementary
complementation
complete
completes
completed
completing
completely
completeness
completion
completive
complex
complexes
complexion
complexioned
complexity
complexities
compliance
compliant
compliantly
complicate
complicates
complicated
complicating
complicated
complication
complicity
complied

complies
compliment (= flattering remark → complement)
compliments
complimented
complimenting
complimentary
compline
comply
complies
complied
complying
component
componential
comport
comports
comported
comporting
comportment
compose
composes
composed
composing
composed
composedly
composer
composite
composition
compositor
compos mentis
compost
composts
composted
composting
composure
compote
compound
compounds
compounded

compounding
comprehend
comprehends
comprehended
comprehending
comprehensible
comprehension
comprehensive
comprehensively
compress
compresses
compressed
compressing
compressibility
compressible
compression
compressor
comprisal
comprise
comprises
comprised
comprising
compromise
compromises
compromised
compromising
comptroller
compulsion
compulsive
compulsively
compulsiveness
compulsorily
compulsoriness
compulsory
compunction
computation
compute
computes
computed
computing

computer
computerisation
computerise
computerises
computerised
computerising
computerization
computerize
computerizes
computerized
computerizing
comrade
comradely
comradeship
coms
✗ comuppance =
comeuppance
con
cons
conned
conning
concatenate
concatenates
concatenated
concatenating
concatenation
concave
concavity
concavities
concavo-concave
concavo-convex
conceal
conceals
concealed
concealing
concealable
concealer
concealment
concede
concedes

conceded
conceding
conceit
conceited
conceitedly
conceitedness
conceivability
conceivable
conceivably
conceive
  conceives
  conceived
  conceiving
concentrate
  concentrates
  concentrated
  concentrating
concentration
concentrative
concentric
concentrically
concept
conception
conceptual
conceptualisation
conceptualise
  conceptualises
  conceptualised
  conceptualising
conceptualization
conceptualize
  conceptualizes
  conceptualized
  conceptualizing
conceptually
concern
  concerns
  concerned
  concerning
concerned

concernedly
concerning
concernment
✗ conceror =
  conqueror
concert
concerted
concertedly
concertgoer
concertina
  concertinas
concertmaster
concerto
  concertos
concession
concessionaire
concessionary
concessive
conch
  conches
✗ concherto = concerto
conchie
  conchies
conchologist
conchology
concierge
conciliate
  conciliates
  conciliated
  conciliating
conciliation
conciliator
conciliatory
concise
concisely
conciseness
concision
conclave
conclude
  concludes

concluded
concluding
conclusion
conclusive
conclusively
concoct
  concocts
  concocted
  concocting
concoction
concomitant
concomitantly
concord
concordance
concordant
concordantly
concordat
Concorde
concourse
concrete
  concretes
  concreted
  concreting
concretise
  concretises
  concretised
  concretising
concretize
  concretizes
  concretized
  concretizing
concubinage
concubine
concupiscence
concupiscent
concur
  concurs
  concurred
  concurring
concurrence

confident

concurrent
concurrently
concuss
  concusses
  concussed
  concussing
concussion
condemn
  condemns
  condemned
  condemning
condemnable
condemnably
condemnation
condemnatory
condemning
condemningly
condensation
condense
  condenses
  condensed
  condensing
condenser
condescend
  condescends
  condescended
  condescending
condescending
condescension
condign
condignly
condiment
condition
  conditions
  conditioned
  conditioning
conditional
conditionally
conditioned
conditioner

conditioning
condolatory
condole
  condoles
  condoled
  condoling
condolence
condom
condominium
condonable
condone
  condones
  condoned
  condoning
condor
conduce
  conduces
  conduced
  conducing
conducive
conduciveness
conduct
  conducts
  conducted
  conducting
conduction
conductive
conductivity
conductor
conductress
  conductresses
conduit
cone
  cones
  coned
  coning
coney
  coneys
confabulate
confabulates

confabulated
confabulating
confabulation
confection
confectioner
confectionery
confederacy
confederate
  confederates
  confederated
  confederating
confederation
confederative
confer
  confers
  conferred
  conferring
conference
conferment
confess
  confesses
  confessed
  confessing
confessed
confessedly
confession
confessional
confessor
confetti
confidant (= person
  with whom one
  shares secrets →
  confident)
confidante
confide
  confides
  confided
  confiding
confidence
confident (= certain

that one will suc-
ceed → confidant)
confidential
confidently
confiding
confidingly
confidingness
configuration
confinable
confine
confines
confined
confining
confineable
confinement
confiner
confirm
confirms
confirmed
confirming
confirmation
confirmatory
confirmed
confiscate
confiscates
confiscated
confiscating
confiscation
confiscatory
conflagration
conflate
conflates
conflated
conflating
conflation
conflict
conflicts
conflicted
conflicting

conflictingly
confluence
conform
conforms
conformed
conforming
conformance
conformation
conformist
conformity
confound
confounds
confounded
confounding
confounded
confoundedly
confraternity
confraternities
confrère
confront
confronts
confronted
confronting
confrontation
confrontational
Confucian
Confucianism
confusability
confusable
confuse
confuses
confused
confusing
confused
confusedly
confusedness
confusing
confusingly
confusion
confutable

confutation
confute
confutes
confuted
confuting
congé
congeal
congeals
congealed
congealing
congenial
congeniality
congenially
congenital
congenitally
conger
congested
congestion
Congleton
conglomerate
conglomeration
congrats
congratulate
congratulates
congratulated
congratulating
congratulation
congratulations
congratulative
congratulatory
congregate
congregates
congregated
congregating
congregation
congregational
Congregationalism
congress
congresses
Congress

congressional
Congressman
  Congressmen
Congresswoman
  Congresswomen
congruence
congruent
congruity
congruous
conic
conical
conifer
coniferous
conjectural
conjecturally
conjecture
  conjectures
  conjectured
  conjecturing
conjoin
  conjoins
  conjoined
  conjoining
conjoint
conjointly
conjugal
conjugate
  conjugates
  conjugated
  conjugating
conjugation
conjunction
conjunctive
conjunctivitis
conjuncture
conjure
  conjures
  conjured
  conjuring
conjurer

conjuror
conk
  conks
  conked
  conking
conker (= horse
  chestnut → con-
  quer)
  conkers
conman
  conmen
connect
  connects
  connected
  connecting
  connecter
  Connecticut
  connection
  connective
  connector
  conned
Connemara
  connexion
  conning
conniption
connivance
connive
  connives
  connived
  conniving
  connivingly
connoisseur
connotation
connotative
connote
  connotes
  connoted
  connoting
connotive
connubial

conquer (= defeat
  → conker)
  conquers
  conquered
  conquering
conquest
conquistador
consanguine
consanguinity
✗ conschence =
  conscience
✗ conschientious =
  conscientious
conscience
conscientious
conscientiously
conscientiousness
conscious
consciously
consciousness
conscript
  conscripts
  conscripted
  conscripting
conscription
consecrate
  consecrates
  consecrated
  consecrating
Consecration
consecutive
consecutively
consensual
consensus
consent
  consents
  consented
  consenting
consequence
consequences

consequent
consequential
consequently
conservancy
conservation
conservationist
conservatism
conservative
conservativeness
conservatoire
conservatory
   conservatories
conserve
   conserves
   conserved
   conserving
consider
   considers
   considered
   considering
considerable
considerably
considerate
considerately
considerateness
consideration
considered
considering
consign
   consigns
   consigned
   consigning
consignee
consigner
consignment
consignor
consist
   consists
   consisted
   consisting

consistency
   consistencies
consistent
consistently
consolable
consolation
consolatory
console
   consoles
   consoled
   consoling
consolidate
   consolidates
   consolidated
   consolidating
consolidation
   consolingly
consols
consommé
consonance
consonant
consort
   consorts
   consorted
   consorting
consortium
   consortiums *or*
   consortia
conspectus
   conspectuses
conspicuous
conspicuously
conspicuousness
conspiracy
   conspiracies
conspirator
conspiratorial
conspiratorially
conspire
   conspires

conspired
conspiring
constable
constabulary
   constabularies
constancy
constant
Constantinople
constellation
consternation
constipate
   constipates
   constipated
   constipating
constipation
constituency
   constituencies
constituent
constitute
   constitutes
   constituted
   constituting
constitution
constitutional
constitutionalism
constitutionality
constitutionally
constrain
   constrains
   constrained
   constraining
constrained
constrainedly
constraint
constrict
   constricts
   constricted
   constricting
constriction
constrictive

constrictor
construct
  constructs
  constructed
  constructing
constructer
construction
constructional
constructive
constructively
constructiveness
constructor
construe
  construes
  construed
  construing
consubstantiation
consul
consular
consulate
consulship
consult
  consults
  consulted
  consulting
consultancy
  consultancies
consultant
consultation
consultative
consulting
consumable
consume
  consumes
  consumed
  consuming
consumer
consumerism
consuming
consumingly

consummate
  consummates
  consummated
  consummating
consummately
consummation
consumption
consumptive
consumptively
contact
  contacts
  contacted
  contacting
contactable
contagion
contagious
contagiously
contagiousness
contain
  contains
  contained
  containing
container
containerisation
containerise
  containerises
  containerised
  containerising
containerization
containerize
  containerizes
  containerized
  containerizing
containment
contaminant
contaminate
  contaminates
  contaminated
  contaminating
contamination

contango
  contagos
contd
contemplate
  contemplates
  contemplated
  contemplating
contemplation
contemplative
contemporaneity
contemporaneous
contemporaneously
contemporarily
contemporary
contempt
contemptibility
contemptible
contemptibly
contemptuous
contemptuously
contend
  contends
  contended
  contending
contender
content
  contents
  contented
  contenting
contented
contentedly
contention
contentious
contentiously
contentiousness
contently
contentment
contest
  contests
  contested

contesting
contestable
contestant
contester
context
contextual
contextualisation
contextualise
contextualises
contextualised
contextualising
contextualization
contextualize
contextualizes
contextualized
contextualizing
contextually
contiboard℠
contiguity
contiguous
contiguously
continent
continental
contingency
contingencies
contingent
contingently
continual
continually
continuance
continuation
continue
continues
continued
continuing
continuingly
continuity
continuo
continuos
continuous

continuously
continuousness
continuum
continuums or
continua
contort
contorts
contorted
contorting
contortion
contortionist
contour
contra-
contraband
contrabass
contrabasses
contrabassist
contraception
contraceptive
contract
contracts
contracted
contracting
contractible
contractile
contraction
contractionary
contractor
contractual
contractually
contradict
contradicts
contradicted
contradicting
contradiction
contradictory
contradistinction
contraflow
contrail
contraindication

contralto
contraltos
contraption
contrapuntal
contrarily
contrariness
contrariwise
contrary
contrast
contrasts
contrasted
contrasting
contrastive
contravene
contravenes
contravened
contravening
contravention
contretemps
contribute
contributes
contributed
contributing
contribution
contributive
contributor
contributory
contrite
contritely
contrition
contrivance
contrive
contrives
contrived
contriving
control
controls
controlled
controlling
controllability

controllable
controllably
controller
controversial
controversially
controversy
  controversies
contumacious
contumacy
contumelious
contumely
contusion
conundrum
  conundrums
conurbation
convalesce
  convalesces
  convalesced
  convalescing
convalescence
convalescent
convection
convector
convene
  convenes
  convened
  convening
convener
convenience
convenient
conveniently
convenor
convent
conventicle
convention
conventional
conventionalism
conventionality
  convertionalities
conventionally

converge
converges
converged
converging
convergence
convergent
conversant
conversation
conversational
conversationalist
conversationally
conversazione
  conversaziones *or*
  conversazioni
converse
converses
conversed
conversing
conversely
conversion
convert
converts
converted
converting
converter
convertibility
convertible
convertor
convex
convexly
convey
conveys
conveyed
conveying
conveyance
conveyancer
conveyancing
conveyer
conveyor
convict

convicts
convicted
convicting
conviction
convince
convinces
convinced
convincing
convivial
conviviality
convivially
convocation
convoke
convokes
convoked
convoking
convoluted
convolution
convolvulus
  convolvuluses
convoy
convulse
convulses
convulsed
convulsing
convulsion
convulsive
convulsively
cony
  conies
✗ conyac = cognac
✗ conyoshenti =
  cognoscenti
coo
  coos
  cooed
  cooing
✗ cood = could
✗ coodnt = couldn't
cooee

cooey
cook
  cooks
  cooked
  cooking
cooker
cookery
cookhouse
cookie
  cookies
cool
  cools
  cooled
  cooling
  cooler
  coolest
coolant
cooler
coolie
  coolies
coolish
coolly
coolness
coomb
coon
coop
  coops
  cooped
  cooping
co-op
cooper
cooperate
  cooperates
  cooperated
  cooperating
co-operate
  co-operates
  co-operated
  co-operating
cooperation

co-operation
cooperative
co-operative
cooperatively
co-operatively
cooperativeness
co-operativeness
co-opt
  co-opts
  co-opted
  co-opting
coordinate
  coordinates
  coordinated
  coordinating
coordinately
coordinates
coordination
coordinator
✗ coorier = courier
✗ cooshette =
  couchette
coot
✗ cooture = couture
cop
  cops
  copped
  copping
cope
  copes
  coped
  coping
  copied
copier
  copies
copilot
coping
copious
copiously
copped

copper
copperhead
copperplate
coppice
  coppices
  coppiced
  coppicing
copping
copra
copse
Coptic
copula
copulate
  copulates
  copulated
  copulating
copulation
copy
  copies
  copied
  copying
copybook
copycat
  copying
copyist
copyright
  copyrights
  copyrighted
  copyrighting
copywriter
coq au vin
coquetry
  coquetries
coquette
coquettish
coquettishly
coquettishness
coracle
coral (= stonelike
  substance → cor-

ral, choral)
or anglais
  cors anglais
orbel
ord (= string or
  rope → chord)
ordage
orded
ordial
ordiality
ordially
ordite
ordless
ordon
ordon bleu
ordon sanitaire
ords
orduroy
  corduroys
ore (= centre
  → corps)
  cores
  cored
  coring
oreligionist
orrespondent (=
  person cited in a
  divorce case →
  correspondent)
orgi
  corgis
oriander
Corinthian
ork (= stopper for
  wine bottle
  → caulk)
  corks
  corked
  corking
orkage

corked
corker
corkscrew
corm
cormorant
corn
cornball
corncob
corncockle
corncrake
cornea
  corneas
corned
cornelian
corner
  corners
  cornered
  cornering
cornerstone
cornet
cornetist
cornfield
cornflakes
cornflour
cornflower
cornice
corniche
cornier
corniest
cornily
corniness
Cornish
cornucopia
corny
cornier
corniest
corollary
  corollaries
corona
  coronas or

coronae
coronary
  coronaries
coronation
coroner
coronet
✗ cor onglaze =
  cor anglaise
corpora
corporal
corporate
corporately
corporation
corporeal
corporeally
corps (= group of
  soldiers → core)
corpse
corpulence
corpulent
corpus
  corpora or
  corpuses
corpuscle
corral (= area for
  animals → coral,
  choral)
correct
  corrects
  corrected
  correcting
correction
correctional
correctitude
corrective
correctively
correctly
correctness
correlate
  correlates

correlated
correlating
correlation
correlative
correspond
correspondence
correspondent (=
person one writes
to → corespon-
dent)
corridor
corrigendum
corrigenda
corroborate
corroborates
corroborated
corroborating
corroboration
corroborative
corroborator
corrode
corrodes
corroded
corroding
corrosion
corrosive
corrosively
corrosiveness
corrugated
corrugation
corrupt
corrupts
corrupted
corrupting
corruptibility
corruptible
corruption
corruptly
corruptness
corsage

corsair
✗ corse = course or
coarse
corselet
corset
corsetry
✗ cort = court or
caught
cortege
cortège
cortex
cortices
corticosteroid
cortisone
corundum
coruscate
coruscates
coruscated
coruscating
coruscation
corvette
cos
cosh
coshes
coshed
coshing
cosier
cosiest
cosignatory
cosignatories
cosily
cosine
cosiness
cosmetic
cosmetically
cosmetician
cosmic
cosmically
cosmogony
cosmology

cosmonaut
cosmopolitan
cosmos
Cossack
cosset
cossets
cossetted
cossetting
cost
costs
cost
costing
costa
Costa Rica
co-star
co-stars
co-starred
co-starring
costermonger
costing
costive
costly
costume
costumier
cosy
cosier
cosiest
cot
cotangent
cotangential
Cote D'Ivoire
coterie
coteries
coterminous
coterminously
✗ cotiledon =
cotyledon
cotillion
Cotswolds
cottage

cottager
cottaging
cotton
  cottons
  cottoned
  cottoning
cottonwood
couch
  couches
  couched
  couching
couchette
cougar
cough
  coughs
  coughed
  coughing
cought = caught or
court
couldn't
couldst
council (= elected
  body → counsel)
councillor
councilman
  councilmen
councilwoman
  councilwomen
counsel (= give
  advice → council)
  counsels
  counselled
  counselling
counsellor
count
  counts
  counted
  counting
countable
countdown

countenance
counter
counteract
  counteracts
  counteracted
  counteracting
counterattack
  counterattacks
  counterattacked
  counterattacking
counterattraction
counterbalance
  counterbalances
  counterbalanced
  counterbalancing
counterblast
counterclaim
counterclockwise
counterespionage
counterfeit
  counterfeits
  counterfeited
  counterfeiting
counterfeiter
counterfoil
countermand
  countermands
  countermanded
  countermanding
countermeasure
counteroffensive
counterpane
counterpart
counterpoint
counterpoise
counterproductive
countersign
  countersigns
  countersigned
  countersigning

countersignature
countervailing
countess
  countesses
✗ countinance =
  countenance
countless
countrified
country
  countries
countryman
  countrymen
countryside
countrywoman
  countrywomen
county
  counties
coup
coup de grâce
coup d'état
  coups d'état
coupé
couple
  couples
  coupled
  coupling
coupledom
coupler
couplet
coupling
coupon
courage
courageous
courageously
courageousness
courgette
courier
  couriers
  couriered
  couriering

course (= path → covet
  coarse)
court
  courts
  courted
  courting
court-bouillon
courteous
courteously
courteousness
courtesan
courtesy
courthouse
courtier
courtly
court-martial
  courts-martial or
  court-martials
  court-martials
  court-martialled
  court-martialling
courtroom
courtship
courtyard
couscous
cousin
couture
couturier
cove
coven
covenant
Coventry
cover
  covers
  covered
  covering
coverage
covering
coverlet
covert

covet
covets
coveted
coveting
covetous
covetously
cow
coward
cowardice
cowardly
cowbell
cowboy
cowcatcher
cower
cowers
cowered
cowering
cowgirl
cowherd
cowhide
cowl
cowlick
cowling
cowman
cowmen
cowpat
cowpox
cowpuncher
cowrie
cowry
cowslip
cox
coxes
coxcomb
coxswain
coy
coyly
coyness
coyote
coypu

coypus or
coypu
cozen
cozens
cozened
cozening
cr try chr
crab
crabs
crabbed
crabbing
crabbed
crabby
crabbier
crabbiest
crabs
crabstick
crabwise
crack
cracks
cracked
cracking
crackbrained
crackdown
cracker
crackers
cracking
crackle
crackles
crackled
crackling
crackling
crackpot
crackup
cradle
cradles
cradled
cradling
cradlesnatching
craft

crafts
crafted
crafting
craftier
craftiest
craftily
craftiness
craftsman
craftsmen
craftswoman
craftswomen
crafty
craftier
craftiest
crag
craggy
cram
crams
crammed
cramming
crammer
cramp
cramps
cramped
cramping
crampon
cranberry
cranberries
crane
cranes
craned
craning
cranesbill
cranial
craniology
cranium
craniums *or*
crania
crank
cranks

cranked
cranking
crankier
crankiest
crankiness
crankshaft
cranky
crankier
crankiest
cranny
crannies
crap
craps
crapped
crapping
crape
craps
crash
crashes
crashed
crashing
crass
crassly
crassness
crate
crates
crated
crating
crater
cravat
crave
craves
craved
craving
craven
craving
crawfish
crawfishes *or*
crawfish
crawl

crawls
crawled
crawling
crawler
Crawley
crayfish
crayfishes *or*
crayfish
crayon
crayons
crayoned
crayoning
craze
crazed
crazily
craziness
crazy
crazier
craziest
creak
creaks
creaked
creaking
cream
creams
creamed
creaming
creamer
creamery
creameries
creamy
creamier
creamiest
crease
creases
creased
creasing
create
creates
created

creating
creation
creationism
creationist
creative
creatively
creativeness
creator
creature
crèche
credence
credentials
credibility
credible
credibly
credit
  credits
  credited
  crediting
creditable
creditably
creditor
credits
creditworthy
credo
  credos
credulity
credulous
credulously
credulousness
Cree
creed
creek
creel
creep
  creeps
  crept
  creeping
creeper
creeps

creepy
creepier
creepiest
creepy-crawly
cremate
cremates
cremated
cremating
cremation
crematorium
crematoriums *or*
  crematoria
crème
crenellated
creole
creosote
  creosotes
  creosoted
  creosoting
crepe
crêpes suzettes
crept
crepuscular
crescendo
  crescendos
crescent
✘ cresh = crèche
cress
crest
crested
crestfallen
cretin
cretinism
cretinous
cretonne
crevasse
crevice
crew (= team of
  people → cruise)
  crews

crewed
crewing
Crewe (town)
crib
  cribs
  cribbed
  cribbing
cribbage
Criccieth
crick
  cricks
  cricked
  cricking
cricket
cricketer
cricketing
cried
crier
cries
crikey
crime
criminal
criminalise
  criminalises
  criminalised
  criminalising
criminality
criminalize
  criminalizes
  criminalized
  criminalizing
criminally
criminologist
criminology
crimp
  crimps
  crimped
  crimping
Crimplene℠
crimson

cringe
  cringes
  cringed
  cringing
crinkle
  crinkles
  crinkled
  crinkling
crinkly
crinoline
cripes
cripple
  cripples
  crippled
  crippling
crisis
  crises
crisp
  crisps
  crisped
  crisping
crispy
crisscross
  crisscrosses
  crisscrossed
  crisscrossing
criterion
  criteria *or*
  criterions
critic
critical
critically
criticise
  criticises
  criticised
  criticising
criticism
criticize
  criticizes
  criticized

criticizing
critique
croak
  croaks
  croaked
  croaking
Croatia
Croatian
crochet
  crochets
  crocheted
  crocheting
crock
crockery
crocodile
crocodilian
crocus
  crocuses
croft
crofter
crofting
croissant
Cromer
cromlech
crone
crony
  cronies
crook
  crooks
  crooked
  crooking
crooked
crookedly
crookedness
croon
  croons
  crooned
  crooning
crop
  crops

cropped
cropping
cropper
croquet
croquette
✗ croshay = crochet
crosier
cross
  crosses
  crossed
  crossing
cross-
  crossbar
cross-bench
cross-bencher
crossbill
crossbones
crossbow
crossbred
crossbreed
crosscheck
  crosschecks
  crosschecked
  crosschecking
crossed
cross-eyed
crossfire
crossing
cross-legged
crossover
crosspatch
  crosspatches
crosspiece
crossroads
crosswind
crosswise
crotch
  crotches
crotchet
crotchety

crouch
  crouches
  crouched
  crouching
croup
croupier
crouton
crow
  crows
  crowed
  crowing
crowbar
crowd
  crowds
  crowded
  crowding
crowed
crowing
crown
  crowns
  crowned
  crowning
crozier
crucial
crucially
crucible
crucifix
  crucifixes
crucifixion
cruciform
crucify
  crucifies
  crucified
  crucifying
crud
crude
crudely
crudity
  crudities
cruel

cruelly
cruelty
cruet
cruise (= sea voyage → crews)
  cruises
  cruised
  cruising
cruiser
cruller
crumb
crumble
  crumbles
  crumbled
  crumbling
crumbly
crummy
  crummier
  crummiest
crumpet
crumple
  crumples
  crumpled
  crumpling
crunch
  crunches
  crunched
  crunching
crusade
  crusades
  crusaded
  crusading
crusader
cruse
crush
  crushes
  crushed
  crushing
✘ crushel = crucial
crust

crustacean
crustaceous
crusty
  crustier
  crustiest
crutch
  crutches
crux
✘ crwason = croissant
cry
  cries
  cried
  crying
cryogenics
cryonics
crypt
cryptic
cryptically
cryptographer
cryptographic
cryptography
✘ crysalis = chrysalis
✘ crysanthemum = chrysanthemum
crystal
crystalise
  crystalises
  crystalised
  crystalising
crystalize
  crystalizes
  crystalized
  crystalizing
crystalline
crystallise
  crystallises
  crystallised
  crystallising
crystallize
  crystallizes

crystallized
crystallizing
cub
Cuba
Cuban
cubbing
cubbyhole
cube
  cubes
  cubed
  cubing
cubic
cubicle
cubiform
cubism
cubist
cubit
cuckold
  cockolds
  cockolded
  cockolding
cuckoo
  cuckoos
cucumber
cucurbit
cud
cuddle
  cuddles
  cuddled
  cuddling
cuddly
cudgel
  cudgels
  cudgelled
  cudgelling
cue (= signal to
  speak; billiard stick
  → queue)
  cues
  cued

cueing
cuff
cuffs
cuffed
cuffing
cuirass
cuisine
cul-de-sac
  cul-de-sacs *or*
  culs-de-sac
culinary
cull
  culls
  culled
  culling
cullender
culminate
  culminates
  culminated
  culminating
culmination
culottes
culpa
culpability
culpable
culpably
culprit
culs-de-sac
cult
cultivable
cultivar
cultivate
  cultivates
  cultivated
  cultivating
cultivation
cultivator
cultural
culture
cultured

culvert
cum
cumbersome
cumin
cum laude
cummerbund
cumquat
cumulative
cumulatively
cumulus
cuneiform
cunnilingus
cunning
cunningly
cunt
✗ countryside =
  countryside
✗ cuntry = country
cup
  cups
  cupped
  cupping
Cupar
cupbearer
cupboard
cupcake
cupful
Cupid
cupidity
✗ cuple = couple
cupola
cuppa
cupped
cupping
cupric
cur
curable
curably
curacy
  curacies

✗ curage = courage
✗ curagus =
  courageous
curate
curative
curator
curatorship
curb (= control
  → kerb)
  curbs
  curbed
  curbing
curd
curdle
  curdles
  curdled
  curdling
cure
  cures
  cured
  curing
curé
curettage
curfew
curia
  curiae
curio
  curios
curiosity
  curiosities
curious
curiously
✗ curit = curate
curl
  curls
  curled
  curling
curler
curlew
curlicue

curling
curly
  curlier
  curliest
curmudgeon
curmudgeonly
currant (= dried
  grape → current)
currency
  currencies
current (= flow of
  electricity; happen-
  ing now → currant)
curricular
curriculum
  curricula or
  curriculums
curry
  curries
  curried
  currying
curse
  curses
  cursed
  cursing
cursed
cursedly
cursive
cursor
cursorily
cursory
curt
curtail
  curtails
  curtailed
  curtailing
curtailment
curtain
  curtains
  curtained

curtaining
curtly
curtsey
  curtseys
  curtseyed
  curtseying
curtsy
  curtsies
  curtsied
  curtsying
curvaceous
curvaceously
curvature
curve
  curves
  curved
  curving
cushion
  cushions
  cushioned
  cushioning
cushy
  cushier
  cushiest
✗ cusin = cousin
cusp
cuss
  cusses
  cussed
  cussedly
  cussedness
custard
custodial
custodian
custodianship
custody
custom
customarily
customary
customer

customise
  customises
  customised
  customising
customize
  customizes
  customized
  customizing
customs
cut
  cuts
  cut
  cutting
cutaway
cutback
cute
  cuter
  cutest
cutely
cuteness
cuticle
cutie
  cuties
cutlass
  cutlasses
cutler
cutlery
cutlet
cutoff
cutout
cutpurse
cutter
cutthroat
cutting
cuttingly
cuttlefish
  cuttlefish
✗ cuzin = cousin
CV
cwt

✗ cwisine = cuisine
cyan
cyanide
cybernetic
cybernetically
cybernetics
cyclamate
cyclamen
  cyclamen
cycle
  cycles
  cycled
  cycling
cyclic
cyclical
cyclically
cyclist
cyclone
cyclops
cyclotron
cyder
cygnet
cylinder
cylindrical
cylindrically
cymbal
cymbalist
cymbalo
  cymbalos
cynic
cynical
cynically
cynicism
cynosure
cypher
cypress
  cypresses
Cypriot
Cyprus
Cyrillic

cyst
cystic
cystic fibrosis
cystitis
cytologist
cytology
czar
Czech
Czechoslovakia
Czechoslovakian

D

dab
  dabs
  dabbed
  dabbing
dabble
  dabbles
  dabbled
  dabbling
dabchick
dachshund
Dacron℠
✘ dacsund = dachshund
dactyl
dad
daddy
  daddies
daddy-longlegs
dado
  dadoes
daemon
daemonic
daemonically
daffodil
daft
  dafter
  daftest
  daftly
dagger
dago
  dagos *or*
  dagoes
dahlia

dahlias
✘ daify = deify
daily
  dailies
daintily
dainty
  daintier
  daintiest
daiquiri
  daiquiris
dairy
  dairies
dairymaid
dairyman
dairymen
dais
  daises
daisy
  daisies
daisywheel
✘ daity = deity
✘ dajavu = déjà vu
dale
Dales
✘ dalia = dahlia
dalliance
dally
  dallies
  dallied
  dallying
Dalmatian
dam
  dams
  dammed
  damming
damage
  damages
  damaged
  damaging
damascene

Damascus
damask
dame
dammit
damn
  damns
  damned
  damning
damnable
damnably
damnation
damned
  damnedest
  damning
damoiselle
damp
  damps
  damped
  damping
dampcourse
dampen
  dampens
  dampened
  dampening
damper
damsel
damselfly
  damselflies
damson
dan
dance
  dances
  danced
  dancing
D and C
dandelion
dander
dandified
✘ dandilion =
  dandelion

dandle
  dandles
  dandled
  dandling
dandruff
dandy
  dandies
Dane
danger
dangerous
dangerously
dangle
  dangles
  dangled
  dangling
Danish
dank
dankness
danse macabre
Danube
daphnia
  daphnias
dapper
dappled
dare
  dares
  dared
  daring
daredevil
daren't
daresay
daring
daringly
dark
  darker
  darkest
darken
  darkens
  darkened
  darkening

darkey
  darkeys
darkie
  darkies
darkly
darkness
darkroom
darky
  darkies
darling
darn
  darns
  darned
  darning
dart
  darts
  darted
  darting
dartboard
  darts
Darwinian
Darwinism
dash
  dashes
  dashed
  dashing
dashboard
  dashing
  dashingly
dastardly
data
database
date
  dates
  dated
  dating
dateless
dateline
dating
dative

daub
  daubs
  daubed
  daubing
daughter
daughterly
daunt
  daunts
  daunted
  daunting
dauntless
dauntlessly
dauphin
✗ dauter = daughter
davenport
davit
dawdle
  dawdles
  dawdled
  dawdling
dawn
  dawns
  dawned
  dawning
day
dayboy
daybreak
daycare
daycentre
daydream
  daydreams
  daydreamed *or*
  daydreamt
  daydreaming
daydreamer
daygirl
Day-Glo℠
daylight
daylights
daytime

daze
  dazes
  dazed
  dazing
  dazedly
dazzle
  dazzles
  dazzled
  dazzling
D-day
DDT
deacon
deaconess
  deaconesses
deaconry
  deaconries
deactivate
  deactivates
  deactived
  deactivating
deactivation
dead
deadbeat
deaden
  deadens
  deadened
  deadening
deadhead
  deadheads
  deadheaded
  deadheading
deadlier
deadliest
deadline
deadlock
deadlocked
deadly
  deadlier
  deadliest
deadpan

deaf
deafen
  deafens
  deafened
  deafening
deafness
deal
  deals
  dealt
  dealing
dealer
  dealings
dealt
dean
deanery
  deaneries
dear (= well-loved;
  expensive → deer)
  dearer
  dearest
dearie
  dearies
dearness
dearth
deary
  dearies
death
deathblow
deathless
deathlessly
deathly
deathtrap
deathwatch
debacle
debar
  debars
  debarred
  debarring
debase
  debases

debased
debasing
debasement
debatable
debate
  debates
  debated
  debating
debater
debauch
  debauches
  debauched
  debauching
debauchedly
debauchee
debauchery
debenture
debilitate
  debilitates
  debilitated
  debilitating
debilitation
debilitative
debility
  debilities
debit
  debits
  debited
  debiting
debonair
debouch
  debouches
  debouched
  debouching
debrief
  debriefs
  debriefed
  debriefing
debris
debt

debtor
✗debue = debut
debug
  debugs
  debugged
  debugging
debunk
  debunks
  debunked
  debunking
debunker
debut
debutante
decade
decadence
decadent
decadently
decaffeinated
decalitre
decamp
  decamps
  decamped
  decamping
decant
  decants
  decanted
  decanting
decanter
decapitate
  decapitates
  decapitated
  decapitating
decapitation
decathlete
decathlon
decay
  decays
  decayed
  decaying
decease

deceased
deceit
deceitful
deceitfully
deceitfulness
deceivable
deceive
  deceives
  deceived
  deceiving
deceiver
deceivingly
decelerate
  decelerates
  decelerated
  decelerating
deceleration
December
decencies
decency
decennial
decent (= accepta-
  ble → descent)
decently
decentralisation
decentralise
  decentralises
  decentralised
  decentralising
decentralization
decentralize
  decentralizes
  decentralized
  decentralizing
deception
deceptive
deceptively
deceptiveness
decibel
decide

decides
decided
deciding
decided
decidedly
deciduous
decilitre
decimal
decimalise
  decimalises
  decimalised
  decimalising
decimalize
  decimalizes
  decimalized
  decimalizing
decimate
  decimates
  decimated
  decimating
decimation
decimetre
decipher
  deciphers
  deciphered
  deciphering
decipherable
decision
decisive
decisively
decisiveness
deck
  decks
  decked
  decking
declaim
  declaims
  declaimed
  declaiming
declaimer

declamation
declamatory
declarable
declaration
declarative
declare
  declares
  declared
  declaring
declassification
declassify
  declassifies
  declassified
  declassifying
declension
declination
decline
  declines
  declined
  declining
declivity
  declivities
declutch
  declutches
  declutched
  declutching
decoction
decode
  decodes
  decoded
  decoding
décolletage
décolleté
decolonisation
decolonise
  decolonises
  decolonised
  decolonising
decolonization
decolonize

decolonizes
decolonized
decolonizing
decompose
  decomposes
  decomposed
  decomposing
decomposition
decompression
decongestant
deconsecrate
  deconsecrates
  deconsecrated
  deconsecrating
deconsecration
decontaminate
  decontaminates
  decontaminated
  decontaminating
decontamination
decontrol
  decontrols
  decontrolled
  decontrolling
decor
décor
decorate
  decorates
  decorated
  decorating
decoration
decorative
decoratively
decorator
decorous
decorously
decorum
decoupage
decoy
  decoys

decoyed
decoying
decrease
  decreases
  decreased
  decreasing
decreasingly
decree
  decrees
  decreed
  decreeing
decree absolute
  decrees absolute
decree nisi
  decrees nisi
decrepit
decrepitude
decrescendo
decriminalise
  decriminalises
  decriminalised
  decriminalising
decriminalize
  decriminalizes
  decriminalized
  decriminalizing
decry
  decries
  decried
  decrying
dedicate
  dedicates
  dedicated
  dedicating
dedicated
dedicatedly
dedication
deduce
  deduces
  deduced

deducing
deducible
deduct
  deducts
  deducted
  deducting
deductible
deductive
deductively
deed
deejay
  deejays
deem
  deems
  deemed
  deeming
deep
  deeper
  deepest
deepen
  deepens
  deepened
  deepening
deeply
deep-rooted
deep-seated
deer (= animal
  → dear)
  deer
deerskin
deface
  defaces
  defaced
  defacing
defacement
de facto
defamation
defamatory
defame
  defames

defamed
defaming
default
  defaults
  defaulted
  defaulting
defeat
  defeats
  defated
  defeating
defeatism
defeatist
defecate
  defecates
  defecated
  defecating
defect
  defects
  defected
  defecting
defection
defective
defectively
defectiveness
defector
defence
defenceless
defencelessly
defencelessness
defend
  defends
  defended
  defending
defendable
defendant
defender
defensible
defensibly
defensive
defensively

defensiveness
defer
  defers
  deferred
  deferring
deferable
deference
deferential
deferentially
deferment
deferrable
deferred
deferring
defiance
defiant
defiantly
defibrillation
defibrillator
deficiency
  deficiencies
deficient
deficiently
deficit
defile
  defiles
  defiled
  defiling
defilement
defiler
definable
define
  defines
  defined
  defining
definite
definitely
definition
definitive
definitively
deflate

deflates
deflated
deflating
deflation
deflationary
deflect
deflects
deflected
deflecting
deflection
deflector
deflower
deflowers
deflowered
deflowering
defoliant
defoliate
defoliates
defoliated
defoliating
defoliation
deforest
deforests
deforested
deforesting
deforestation
deform
deforms
deformed
deforming
deformation
deformity
deformities
defraud
defrauds
defrauded
defrauding
defraudment
defray
defrays

defrayed
defraying
defrock
defrocks
defrocked
defrocking
defrost
defrosts
defrosted
defrosting
defroster
deft
deftly
deftness
defunct
defuse
defuses
defused
defusing
defy
defies
defied
defying
Degas, Edgar
degeneracy
degenerate
degenerates
degenerated
degenerating
degeneration
degenerative
degradability
degradable
degradation
degrade
degrades
degraded
degrading
degradingly

degree
degrees
dehumanisation
dehumanise
dehumanises
dehumanised
dehumanising
dehumanization
dehumanize
dehumanizes
dehumanized
dehumanizing
dehumidifier
dehydrate
dehydrates
dehydrated
dehydrating
dehydration
de-ice
de-ices
de-iced
de-icing
de-icer
deification
deify
deifies
deified
deifying
deign
deigns
deigned
deigning
Deirdre
deism
deity
deities
déjà vu
dejected
dejectedly
dejection

de jure
dekko
delay
  delays
  delayed
  delaying
delectability
delectable
delectably
delectation
delegate
  delagates
  delegated
  delegating
delegation
delete
  deletes
  deleted
  deleting
deleterious
deletion
Delhi
deliberate
  deliberates
  deliberated
  deliberating
deliberately
deliberateness
deliberation
deliberative
delicacy
  delicacies
delicate
delicately
delicatessen
delicious
deliciously
deliciousness
delight
  delights

delighted
delighting
delightedly
delightful
delightfully
delightfulness
delimit
  delimits
  delimited
  delimiting
delimitation
delinquency
delinquent
deliquescence
deliquescent
delirious
deliriously
delirium
  deliriums
delirium tremens
deliver
  delivers
  delivered
  delivering
deliverance
deliverer
delivery
  deliveries
deliveryman
  deliverymen
dell
Delphic
delphinium
delta
  deltas
delude
  deludes
  deluded
  deluding
deluge

deluges
deluged
deluging
delusion
delusional
delusive
delusively
delusory
deluxe
delve
  delves
  delved
  delving
demagogic
demagogue
demagoguery
demand
  demands
  demanded
  demanding
  demandingly
demarcate
  demarcates
  demarcated
  demarcating
demarcation
demean
  demeans
  demeaned
  demeaning
demeanour
demented
dementedly
dementia
demerara
demerit
demigod
demijohn
demilitarisation

demilitarise
 demilitarises
 demilitarised
 demilitarising
demilitarization
demilitarize
 demilitarizes
 demilitarized
 demilitarizing
demimonde
demise
demist
 demists
 demisted
 demisting
demister
demo
 demos
demob
 demobs
 demobbed
 demobbing
demobilisation
demobilise
 demobilises
 demobilised
 demobilising
demobilization
demobilize
 demobilizes
 demobilized
 demobilizing
democracy
 democracies
democrat
democratic
 democratically
democratisation
democratise
 democratises

democratised
democratising
democratization
democratize
 democratizes
 democratized
 democratizing
démodé
demographer
demographic
demography
demolish
 demolishes
 demolished
 demolishing
demolition
demon
demoniac
 demoniacal
demonic
demonically
 demonstrability
demonstrable
demonstrably
demonstrate
 demonstrates
 demonstrated
 demonstrating
demonstration
demonstrative
 demonstratively
 demonstrativeness
demonstrator
demoralisation
demoralise
 demoralises
 demoralised
 demoralising
demoralization
demoralize

demoralizes
demoralized
demoralizing
demos
demote
 demotes
 demoted
 demoting
demotic
demur
 demurs
 demurred
 demurring
demure
 demurely
 demureness
demystification
demystify
 demystifies
 demystified
 demystifying
den
denationalisation
denationalise
 denationalises
 denationalised
 denationalising
denationalization
denationalize
 denationalizes
 denationalized
 denationalizing
deniable
deniably
denial
denier
denigrate
 denigrates
 denigrated
 denigrating

depoliticizes

denigration
denim
denims
Denis
denizen
denomination
Denmark
denominational
denominator
denotation
denotative
denotatively
denote
  denotes
  denoted
  denoting
denouement
denounce
  denounces
  denounced
  denouncing
denouncer
dense
densely
denseness
density
  densities
dent
  dents
  dented
  denting
dental
dentifrice
dentine
dentist
dentistry
dentition
denture
denude
  denudes

denuded
denuding
denunciation
denunciatory
deny
  denies
  denied
  denying
deodar
deodorant
deodorise
  deodorises
  deodorised
  deodorising
deodorizer
  deodorizes
  deodorized
  deodorizing
deoxygenate
  deoxygenates
  deoxygenated
  deoxygenating
deoxygenation
deoxyribonucleic
depart
  departs
  departed
  departing
department
departmental
departmentalise
  departmentalises
  departmentalised
  departmentalising
departmentalize
  departmentalizes
  departmentalized
  departmentalizing
departure
depend

depends
depended
depending
dependability
dependable
dependably
dependant
dependence
dependency
  dependencies
dependent
depict
  depicts
  depicted
  depicting
depiction
depilatory
deplete
  depletes
  depleted
  depleting
depletion
deplorable
deplorably
deplore
  deplores
  deplored
  deploring
deploy
  deploys
  deployed
  deploying
deployment
✗ depo = depot
depoliticise
  depoliticises
  depoliticised
  depoliticising
depoliticize
  depoliticizes

depoliticized
depoliticizing
depopulate
depopulates
depopulated
depopulating
depopulation
deport
deports
deported
deporting
deportation
deportee
deportment
depose
deposes
deposed
deposing
deposit
deposits
deposited
depositing
deposition
depositor
depository
depositories
depot
depravation
deprave
depraves
depraved
depraving
depravity
deprecate
deprecates
deprecated
deprecating
deprecatory
depreciate
depreciates

depreciated
depreciating
depreciation
depredation
✗ depreshiate =
depreciate
✗ depreshiation =
depreciation
depress
depresses
depressed
depressing
depressant
depressing
depressingly
depression
depressive
depressurisation
depressurise
depressurises
depressurised
depressurising
depressurization
depressurize
depressurizes
depressurized
depressurizing
deprivation
deprive
deprives
deprived
depriving
depth
deputation
depute
deputes
deputed
deputing
deputise
deputises

deputised
deputising
deputize
deputizes
deputized
deputizing
deputy
deputies
derail
derails
derailed
derailing
derailment
deranged
derangement
derby
derbies
deregulate
deregulates
deregulated
deregulating
deregulation
deregulatory
derelict
dereliction
deride
derides
derided
deriding
de rigueur
derision
derisive
derisively
derisory
derivable
derivation
derivative
derivatively
derive
derives

desk

derived
deriving
dermatitis
dermatological
dermatologist
dermatology
derogate
derogates
derogated
derogating
derogatory
derrick
derring-do
✘ derth = dearth
derv
dervish
dervishes
desalinate
desalinates
desalinated
desalinating
desalination
descale
descales
descaled
descaling
descant
descend
descends
descended
descending
descendant
descent (= going
down → descent)
describe
describes
described
describing
description
descriptive

descriptively
descriptiveness
descry
descries
descried
descrying
desecrate
desecrates
desecrated
desecrating
desecration
desegregate
desegregates
desegregated
desegregating
desegregation
deselect
deselects
deselected
deselecting
✘ desend = descend
desensitisation
desensitise
desensitises
desensitised
desensitising
desensitization
desensitize
desensitizes
desensitized
desenitizing
desert (= leave;
area of arid land
→ dessert)
deserts
deserted
deserting
deserter
desertification
desertion

deserve
deserves
deserved
deserving
deservedly
deserving
deservingly
deshabille
desiccant
desiccate
dessicates
dessicated
dessicating
desideratum
desiderata
design
designs
designed
designing
designate
designates
designated
designating
designedly
designer
designing
desirability
desirable
desirably
desire
desires
desired
desiring
desirous
desirously
desist
desists
desisted
desisting
desk

deskill
  deskills
  deskilled
  deskilling
desktop
desolate
  desolated
desolation
despair
  despairs
  despaired
  despairing
despairingly
despatch
  despatches
  despatched
  despatching
desperado
  desperadoes *or*
  desperados
desperate
desperately
desperation
despicable
despicably
despise
  despises
  despised
  despising
despite
despoil
  despoils
  despoiled
  despoiling
despondency
despondent
despondently
despot
despotic
despotically

despotism
dessert (= sweet
  food → desert)
dessertspoon
destabilisation
destabilise
  destabilises
  destabilised
  destabilising
destabilization
destabilize
  destabilizes
  destabilized
  destabilizing
destination
destined
destiny
  destinies
destitute
destitution
destroy
  destroys
  destroyed
  destroying
destroyer
destructibility
destructible
destruction
destructive
destructively
destructiveness
desultorily
desultory
✗ det = debt
detach
  detaches
  detached
  detaching
detachable
detached

detachment
detail
  details
  detailed
  detailing
detain
  detains
  detained
  detaining
detainee
detect
  detects
  detected
  detecting
detectable
detection
detective
detector
détente
detention
deter
  deters
  deterred
  deterring
detergent
deteriorate
  deteriorates
  deteriorated
  deteriorating
deterioration
determinant
determination
determine
  determines
  determined
  determining
determined
determinedly
determiner
determinism

determinist
deterministic
deterrence
deterrent
detest
  detests
  detested
  detesting
detestable
detestably
detestation
detonate
  detonates
  detonated
  detonating
detonation
detonator
✗ detont = detente
detour
detract
  detracts
  detracted
  detracting
detraction
detractor
detriment
detrimental
detritus
de trop
✗ dettor = debtor
✗ detur = detour
deuce
deuced
deus ex machina
devaluation
devalue
  devalues
  devalued
  devaluing
devastate

devastates
devastated
devastating
devastation
develop
  develops
  developed
  developing
developer
development
developmental
deviance
deviant
deviate
  deviates
  deviated
  deviating
deviation
deviationist
device
devil
devilish
devilishly
devilled
devilment
devilry
devious
deviously
deviousness
devise
  devises
  devised
  devising
Devises
devoid
devolution
devolve
  devolves
  devolved
  devolving

Devonian
devote
  devotes
  devoted
  devoting
devotedly
devotedness
devotee
devotion
devotional
devour
  devours
  devoured
  devouring
devout
devoutly
devoutness
dew (= moisture on
  ground → due)
dewdrop
dewy
  dewier
  dewiest
dewy-eyed
dexter
dexterity
dexterous
dexterously
dextrose
dextrous
dextrously
Dhaka
diabetes
diabetic
diabolical
diabolically
diacritic
diadem
diaeresis
  diaereses

diagnose
  diagnoses
  diagnosed
  diagnosing
diagnosis
  diagnoses
diagnostic
diagnostician
diagnostics
diagonal
diagonally
diagram
diagrammatic
diagrammatically
dial
  dials
  dialled
  dialling
dialect
dialectic
dialectical
dialectics
dialogue
dialyse
  dialyses
  dialysed
  dialysing
dialyser
dialysis
diameter
diametric
diametrically
diamond
✗diamontay =
  diamonté
diaphanous
diaphragm
✗diaphram =
  diaphragm
diarist

diarrhea
diarrhoea
diary
  diaries
Diaspora
diatonic
diatribe
dibber
dibble
  dibbles
  dibbled
  dibbling
dibs
dice
  dices
  diced
  dicing
dicey
  dicier
  diciest
dichotomy
  dichotomies
dicier
diciest
dick
dickens
Dickens, Charles
Dickensian
dickhead
dicky
  dickies
✗dicotomy =
  dichotomy
dicta
Dictaphone
dictate
  dictates
  dictated
  dictating
dictation

dictator
dictatorial
dictatorially
dictatorship
diction
dictionary
  dictionaries
dictum
dicta
did
didactic
didactically
didacticism
diddle
  diddles
  diddled
  diddling
didgeridoo
didn't
die (= become dead
  → dye)
dies
died
dying
dieback
die-casting
die-hard
dieresis
diereses
diesel
diet
  diets
  dieted
  dieting
dietary
dieter
dietetic
dietetics
dietician

dietitian
differ
  differs
  differed
  differing
difference
different
differential
differentiate
  differentiates
  differentiated
  differentiating
differentiation
differently
difficult
difficulty
  difficulties
diffidence
diffident
diffidently
diffract
  diffracts
  diffracted
  diffracting
diffraction
diffuse
  diffuses
  diffused
  diffusing
diffusely
diffuseness
diffuser
diffusion
diffusor
dig
  digs
  dug
  digging
digest
  digests

digested
digesting
digestibility
digestible
digestif
digestion
digestive
digger
digit
digital
digitalis
digitalise
  digitalises
  digitalised
  digitalising
digitalize
  digitalizes
  digitalized
  digitalizing
digitise
  digitises
  digitised
  digitising
digitize
  digitizes
  digitized
  digitizing
dignified
dignify
  dignifies
  dignified
  dignifying
dignitary
dignity
digraph
digress
  digresses
  digressed
  digressing
digression

digs
dike (= wall to keep
  back water →
  dyke)
diktat
dilapidated
dilapidation
dilate
  dilates
  dilated
  dilating
dilation
dilatory
dildo
  dildos
dilemma
  dilemmas
dilettante
diligence
diligent
diligently
dill
dilute
  dilutes
  diluted
  diluting
dilution
dim
  dims
  dimmed
  dimming
  dimmer
  dimmest
dime
dimension
dimensional
dimensionality
diminish
  diminishes
  diminished

diminishing
diminuendo
diminuendos
diminution
diminutive
diminutively
dimity
dimmed
dimmer
dimmest
dimming
dimple
dim sum
dimwit
dim-witted
din
dins
dinned
dinning
dine
dines
dined
dining
diner
ding-dong
dinghy
dinghies
dingle
dingo
dingoes
dingy
dingier
dingiest
dingily
dinginess
dinky
dinned
dinner
dinning
dinosaur

dint
diocesan
diocese
Dionysian
Dionysus
dioxide
dioxin
dip
dips
dipped
dipping
diphtheria
diphthong
diplodocus
diplodocuses
diploid
diploma
diplomacy
diplomat
diplomatic
diplomatically
diplomatist
dipped
dipper
dipping
dippy
dipsomania
dipsomaniac
dipstick
✗ diptheria =
diphtheria
✗ dipthong =
diphthong
diptych
diptychs
dire
direct
directs
directed
directing

direction
directional
directionality
directive
directly
directness
director
directorate
directorship
directory
directories
direful
dirge
dirigible
dirk
dirndl
dirt
dirties
dirtied
dirtying
dirtier
dirtiest
disability
disabilities
disable
disables
disabled
disabling
disabled
disablement
disabuse
disabuses
disabused
disabusing
disadvantage
disadvantaged
disadvantageous
disadvantageously
disaffected
disaffiliate

disaffiliates
disaffiliated
disaffiliating
disafforest
disafforests
disafforested
disafforesting
disafforestation
disagree
disagrees
disagreed
disagreeing
disagreeable
disagreeably
disagreement
disallow
disallows
disallowed
disallowing
disambiguate
disambiguates
disambiguated
disambiguating
disappear
disappears
disappeared
disappearing
disappoint
disappoints
disappointed
disappointing
disappointedly
disappointingly
disappointment
disapproval
disapprove
disapproves
disapproved
disapproving
disapprovingly

disarm
disarms
disarmed
disarming
disarmament
disarming
disarmingly
disarray
disassociate
disassociates
disassociated
disassociating
disaster
disastrous
disastrously
disavow
disavows
disavowed
disavowing
disband
disbands
disbanded
disbanding
disbandment
disbar
disbars
disbarred
disbarring
disbarment
disbelief
disbelieve
disbelieves
disbelieved
disbelieving
disburse
disburses
disbursed
disbursing
disbursement
disc

discard
discards
discarded
discarding
discern
discerns
discerned
discerning
discernible
discernibly
discerning
discerningly
discernment
discharge
discharges
discharged
discharging
disciple
discipleship
disciplinarian
disciplinary
discipline
disciplines
disciplined
disciplining
disclaim
disclaims
disclaimed
disclaiming
disclaimer
disclose
discloses
disclosed
disclosing
disclosure
disco
discos
discoloration
discolour
discolours

discoloured
discolouring
discomfit (= annoy
slightly → discom-
fort)
  discomfits
  discomfited
  discomfiting
discomfiture
discomfort (= lack
of comfort →
discomfit)
discompose
  discomposes
  discomposed
  discomposing
disconcert
  disconcerts
  disconcerted
  disconcerting
disconcertingly
disconnect
  disconnects
  disconnected
  disconnecting
disconnectedly
disconsolate
disconsolately
discontent
discontented
discontinue
  discontinues
  discontinued
  discontinuing
discontinuity
  discontinuities

discord
discordant
discordantly
✗ discorse = discourse
discotheque
discount
  discounts
  discounted
  discounting
discountenance
discourage
  discourages
  discouraged
  discouraging
discouragement
discouragingly
discourse
  discourses
  discoursed
  discoursing
discourteous
discourteously
discourteousness
discourtesy
  discourtesies
discover
  discovers
  discovered
  discovering
discoverer
discovery
  discoveries
discredit
  discredits
  discredited
  discrediting
discreditable
discreditably
discreet (= careful
and sensitive →

discrete)
discreetly
discreetness
discrepancy
  discrepancies
discrete (= distinct
→ discreet)
discretely
discreteness
discretion
discretionary
discriminate
  discriminates
  discriminated
  discriminating
discriminatingly
discrimination
discriminatory
✗ discurage =
discourage
discursive
discursively
discursiveness
✗ discurtious =
discourteous
✗ discurtisy =
discourtesy
discus (= object for
throwing → dis-
cuss)
  discuses or
  disc
discuss (= talk
about → discus)
  discusses
  discussed
  discussing
discussion
✗ discuver = discover
✗ discuvery =

disin

discovery
disdain
  disdains
  disdained
  disdaining
disdainful
disdainfully
disease
diseased
disembark
  disembarks
  disembarked
  disembarking
  disembarkation
disembodied
disembowel
  disembowels
  disembowelled
  disembowelling
disenchanted
disenfranchise
  disenfranchises
  disenfranchised
  disenfranchising
  disenfranchisement
disengage
  disengages
  disengaged
  disengaging
disentangle
  disentangles
  disentangled
  disentangling
disequilibrium
disestablish
  disestablishes
  disestablished
  disestablishing
  disestablishment
disfavour

disfigure
disfigues
disfigured
disfiguring
disfigurement
disforest
  disforests
  disforested
  disforesting
  disforestation
disfranchise
  disfranchises
  disfranchised
  disfranchising
  disfranchisement
✗ disgise = disguise
✗ disgize = disguise
disgorge
  disgorges
  disgorged
  disgorging
disgrace
  disgraces
  disgraced
  disgracing
disgraceful
disgracefully
disgruntled
disguise
  disguises
  disguised
  disguising
disgust
  disgusts
  disgusted
  disgustedly
  disgusting
  disgustingly
dish

dishes
dished
dishing
dishabille
disharmonious
disharmony
dishcloth
dishearten
  disheartens
  disheartened
  disheartening
  dishearteningly
dished
dishevelled
dishier
dishiest
dishing
dishonest
dishonestly
dishonesty
dishonour
  dishonours
  dishonoured
  dishonouring
dishonourable
dishonourableness
dishonourably
dishpan
dishwasher
dishwater
dishy
  dishier
  dishiest
disillusion
  disillusions
  disillusioned
  disillusioning
  disillusionment
disim try disem
disin try disen

disincentive
disinclination
disinclined
disinfect
  disinfects
  disinfected
  disinfecting
disinfectant
disinformation
disingenuous
disingenuously
disintegrate
  disintegrates
  disintigrated
  disintigrating
disintegration
disinter
  disinters
  disinterred
  disinterring
disinterested
disinterestedly
disjointed
disjointedly
disk
diskette
dislikable
dislike
  dislikes
  disliked
  disliking
dislikeable
dislocate
  dislocates
  dislocated
  dislocating
dislocation
dislodge
  dislodges
  dislodged

dislodging
disloyal
disloyally
disloyalty
dismal
dismally
dismantle
  dismantles
  dismantled
  dismantling
dismay
dismember
  dismembers
  dismembered
  dismembering
dismiss
  dismisses
  dismissed
  dismissing
dismissal
dismissive
dismount
  dismounts
  dismounted
  dismounting
disobedience
disobedient
disobediently
disobey
  disobeys
  disobeyed
  disobeying
disobliging
disobligingly
✗disoner = dishonour
✗disonest = dishonest
disorder
  disorders
  disordered
  disordering

disorderliness
disorderly
disorganisation
disorganise
disorganises
disorganised
disorganising
disorganization
disorganize
disorganizes
disorganized
disorganizing
disorient
disorients
disoriented
disorienting
disorientate
disorientates
disorientated
disorientating
disorientation
disown
disowns
disowned
disowning
disparagement
disparaging
disparagingly
disparate
disparately
disparity
disparities
dispassionate
dispassionately
dispatch
dispatches
dispatched
dispatching
dispel
dispels

dispelled
dispelling
dispensable
dispensary
dispensaries
dispensation
dispense
dispenses
dispensed
dispensing
dispenser
dispersal
dispersant
disperse
disperses
dispersed
dispersing
dispersion
dispirited
dispiritedly
dispiriting
displace
displaces
displaced
displacing
displacement
display
displays
displayed
displaying
displease
displeases
displeased
displeasing
displeasure
disposable
disposal
dispose
disposes
disposed

disposing
disposition
dispossess
dispossesses
dispossessed
dispossessing
dispossession
disproof
disproportion
disproportionate
disproportionately
disprove
disproves
disproved
disproving
disputable
disputably
disputation
disputatious
dispute
disputes
disputed
disputing
disqualification
disqualify
disqualifies
disqualified
disqualifying
disquiet
disquiets
disquieted
disquieting
disquietingly
disquietude
disregard
disregards
disregarded
disregarding
disrepair

disreputable
disreputably
disrepute
disrespect
disrobe
disrobes
disrobed
disrobing
disrupt
disrupts
disrupted
disrupting
disruption
disruptive
disruptively
dissatisfy
dissatisfies
dissatisfied
dissatisfying
dissect
dissects
dissected
dissecting
dissection
dissemble
dissembles
dissembled
dissembling
disseminate
disseminates
disseminated
disseminating
dissemination
dissension
dissent
dissents
dissented
dissenting
dissenter
dissertation

disservice
dissidence
dissident
dissimilar
dissimilarity
dissimilarly
dissimulate
  dissimulates
  dissimulated
  dissimulating
dissimulation
dissipate
  dissipates
  dissipated
  dissipating
dissipation
dissociate
  dissociates
  dissociated
  dissociating
dissociation
dissolute
dissolutely
dissolution
dissolve
  dissolves
  dissolved
  dissolving
dissonance
dissonant
dissuade
  dissuades
  dissuaded
  dissuading
dissuasion
distaff
distance
  distances
  distanced
  distancing

distant
distantly
distaste
distasteful
distastefully
distastefulness
distemper
distend
  distends
  distended
  distending
distension
distil
  distils
  distilled
  distilling
distillation
distiller
distillery
  distilleries
distinct
distinction
distinctive
distinctively
distinctly
distinctness
distinguish
  distinguishes
  distinguished
  distinguishing
distinguishable
distinguished
distort
  distorts
  distorted
  distorting
distortion
distract
  distracts
  distracted

distracting
distractedly
distraction
distraught
✗ distraut = distraught
distress
  distresses
  distressed
  distressing
distressingly
distribute
  distributes
  distributed
  distributing
distribution
distributive
distributively
distributor
district
distrust
  distrusts
  distrusted
  distrusting
distrustful
distrustfully
disturb
  disturbs
  disturbed
  disturbing
disturbance
disturbed
disturbing
disturbingly
disunite
  disunites
  disunited
  disuniting
disunity
disuse

disused
disyllabic
ditch
  ditches
  ditched
  ditching
dither
  dithers
  dithered
  dithering
ditto
  dittos
ditty
  ditties
diuretic
diurnal
divan
dive
  dives
  dived
  diving
diver
diverge
  diverges
  diverged
  diverging
divergence
divergent
divergently
divers
diverse
diversely
diversification
diversify
  diversifies
  diversified
  diversifying
diversion
diversionary
diversity

divert
diverts
diverted
diverting
divest
divests
divested
divesting
divestiture
divestment
divide
divides
divided
dividing
dividend
divider
divination
divine
divines
divined
divining
divinely
diviner
diving
divinity
divisible
division
divisive
divisively
divisor
divorce
divorces
divorced
divorcing
divorcé
divorcée
divulge
divulges
divulged
divulging

divulgence
Diwali
dizzy
dizzier
dizziest
djinn
DNA
do
does
did
done
doing
doc
docile
docility
dock
docks
docked
docking
docker
docket
dockets
docketed
docketing
dockland
dockyard
doctor
doctors
doctored
doctoring
doctoral
doctorate
doctrinaire
doctrinal
doctrine
docudrama
document
documents
documented
documenting

documentary
documentaries
documentation
dodder
dodders
doddered
doddering
doddery
dodge
dodges
dodged
dodging
dodgem
dodger
dodgy
dodgier
dodgiest
dodo
dodos *or*
dodoes
doe (= female deer
→ dough)
doer (= someone
who does things
→ dour)
does
doesn't
✗doey = doughy
doff
doffs
doffed
doffing
dog
dogs
dogged
dogging
doge
dogfight
dogfish
dogfish *or*

dogfishes
dogged
doggedly
doggedness
doggerel
doggie
dogging
doggo
doggy
doggies
dogleg
dogma
dogmatic
dogmatically
dogmatism
dogmatist
do-gooder
dogsbody
dogsbodies
dogtrot
dogwood
doh
doily
doilies
doing
doings
Dolby⒯ⓜ
doldrums
dole
doles
doled
doling
doleful
dolefully
dolefulness
doll
dolls
dolled
dolling
dollar

dollop
dolly
dollies
dolmen
doloroso
dolorous
dolorously
dolphin
dolphinarium
dolphinariums
dolt
domain
dome
domed
domesday
domestic
domestically
domesticate
domesticates
domesticated
domesticating
domestication
domesticity
domicile
domiciled
domiciliary
dominance
dominant
dominate
dominates
dominated
dominating
domination
domineering
Dominican
Dominican Republic
dominion
domino
dominoes
don

dons
donned
donning
Don
Doña
donate
donates
donated
donating
donation
done
Donegal
Don Juan
donkey
donkeys
donned
donning
donnish
donor
don't
✗ donut = doughnut
doodah
doodle
doodles
doddled
doodling
doodlebug
doom
doomed
door
doorframe
doorjamb
doorman
doormen
doormat
doorpost
doorstep
doorstop
doorway
dope

dopes
doped
doping
dopey
dopier
dopiest
dopy
dopier
dopiest
Doric
dormant
dormer
dormitory
dormitories
Dormobile℠
dormouse
dormice
dorsal
dosage
dose
doses
dosed
dosing
dosh
do-si-do
doss
dosses
dossed
dossing
dosser
dosshouse
dossier
dost
dot
dots
dotted
dotting
dotage
dotard
dote

dotes
doted
doting
doth
✗ doti = dhoti
dotted
dotting
dotty
dottier
dottiest
double
doubles
doubled
doubling
double-barrelled
double-breasted
double-decker
double-dutch
double-edged
double-jointed
doublet
doubloon
doubly
doubt
doubts
doubted
doubting
doubtful
doubtfully
doubtless
douche
dough (= uncooked
bread; money
→ doe)
doughnut
doughty
doughy
Douglas
dour (= gloomy
→ doer)

dourly
douse
  douses
  doused
  dousing
✗ douty = doughty
dove
dovecote
Dover
dovetail
  dovetails
  dovetailed
  dovetailing
dowager
dowdily
dowdy
dowel
  doweling
  dowelling
down
  downs
  downed
  downing
downbeat
downer
downfall
downgrade
  downgrades
  downgraded
  downgrading
downhearted
downhill
download
  downloads
  downloaded
  downloading
downpour
downright
downs
downside

downstage
downstairs
downstream
downtime
downtown
downtrodden
downturn
downward
downwards
downwind
downy
dowry
  dowries
dowse
  dowses
  dowsed
  dowsing
doyen
doyenne
doyly
  doylies
doz.
dozed
dozen
dozily
doziness
dozing
dozy
  dozier
  doziest
DPhil
DPP
Dr
drab
drabs
drachma
  drachmas or
  drachmae
✗ dracma = drachma
draconian

draft (= write →
  draught)
  drafts
  drafted
  drafting
draftsman
draftsmen
draftswoman
draftswomen
✗ drafty = draughty
drafty
  draftier
  draftiest
drag
  drags
  dragged
  dragging
draggy
dragnet
dragoman
  dragomans
dragon
dragonfly
  dragonflies
dragoon
  dragoons
  dragooned
  dragooning
dragster
drain
  drains
  drained
  draining
drainage
drainer
drainpipe
drake
dram
drama
dramatic

dramatically
dramatics
dramatisation
dramatise
  dramatises
  dramatised
  dramatising
dramatis personae
dramatist
dramatization
dramatize
  dramatizes
  dramatized
  dramatizing
drank
drape
  drapes
  draped
  draping
draper
drapery
  draperies
drastic
drastically
drat
dratted
draught (= current
  of air → draft)
draughts
draughtsman
  draughtsmen
draughtswoman
  draughtswomen
draughty
  draughtier
  draughtiest
draw
  draws
  drew
  drawn

drawing
drawback
drawbridge
drawer
drawl
  drawls
  drawled
  drawling
drawn
drawstring
dray
dread
  dreads
  dreaded
  dreading
dreadful
dreadfully
dreadfulness
dreadlocks
dreadnought
dream
  dreams
  dreamed *or*
  dreamt
  dreaming
dreamboat
dreamer
dreamier
dreamiest
dreamland
dreamt
dreamy
  dreamier
  dreamiest
drear
dreary
  drearier
  dreariest
dredge
  dredges

dredged
dredging
dredger
dregs
drench
  drenches
  drenched
  drenching
dress
  dresses
  dressed
  dressing
dressage
dresser
dressmaker
dressy
  dressier
  dressiest
drew
dribble
  dribbles
  dribbled
  dribbling
dried
drier
dries
driest
drift
  drifts
  drifted
  drifting
drifter
driftwood
drill
  drills
  drilled
  drilling
drily
drink
  drinks

drank
drunk
drinking
drinker
drip
drips
dripped
dripping
drip-dry
dripped
dripping
drippy
drive
drives
drove
driven
driving
drivel
drivels
drivelled
drivelling
driven
driver
driveway
driving
drizzle
drizzles
drizzled
drizzling
Drogheda
droll
drollery
drolly
dromedary
dromedaries
drone
drones
droned
droning
drool

drools
drooled
drooling
droop
droops
drooped
drooping
drop
drops
dropped
dropping
drop-kick
droplet
dropout
dropper
dropping
droppings
dropsy
dross
drought
✗ drout = drought
drove
drover
droves
drown
drowns
drowned
drowning
drowse
drowses
drowsed
drowsing
drowsy
drowsier
drowsiest
drubbing
drudge
drudges
drudged
drudging

drudgery
drug
drugs
drugged
drugging
druggie
druggies
drugstore
druid
druidic
druidical
drum
drums
drummed
drumming
drumbeat
drummer
drumstick
drunk
drunkard
drunken
dry
dries
dried
drying
drier
driest
dryad
dry-clean
dryer
dryly
dual (= consisting
of two parts
→ duel)
dualism
dualistic
duality
dub
dubs
dubbed

dubbing
dubbin
dubious
dubiously
dubiousness
Dublin
ducal
ducat
◄ duce = deuce
duchess
　duchesses
duchy
　duchies
duck
　ducks
　ducked
　ducking
duckling
duckweed
ducky
duct
ductile
ductility
dud
dude
due (= owed or
　owing → dew)
duel (= fight
　→ dual)
　duels
　duelled
　duelling
duenna
dues
duet
duff
duffel
duffer
dug
dugout

duke
dukedom
dulcet
dulcimer
dull
　dulls
　dulled
　dulling
dullard
duly
dumb
dumbbell
dumbfound
　dumbfounds
　dumbfounded
　dumbfounding
dumbly
dumbwaiter
Dumfries
dummy
　dummies
dump
　dumps
　dumped
　dumping
dumper
dumpier
dumpiest
dumpling
dumps
dumpy
　dumpier
　dumpiest
dun
dunce
Dundalk
dunderhead
dune
dung
dungarees

dungeon
dunk
　dunks
　dunked
　dunking
dunno
duo
　duos
duodecimal
duodenal
duodenum
　duodena or
　duodenums
duos
dupe
　dupes
　duped
　duping
duplex
duplicate
　duplicates
　duplicated
　duplicating
duplication
duplicator
duplicitous
duplicity
durability
durable
duration
duress
Durex℠
Durham
during
durst
dusk
duskiness
dusky
dust
　dusts

dusted
dusting
dustbin
duster
dustier
dustiest
dustman
 dustmen
dustpan
dustsheet
dusty
 dustier
 dustiest
Dutch
Dutchman
 Dutchmen
dutiable
dutiful
dutifully
duty
 duties
duvet
✗duzen = dozen
dwarf
 dwarfs *or*
 dwarves
 dwarfs
 dwarfed
 dwarfing
dwell
 dwells
 dwelt *or*
 dwelled
 dwelling
dwelling
dwelt
dwindle
 dwindles
 dwindled
 dwindling

✗dyceeri = daiquiri
dye (= colour →
 die)
dyes
dyed
dyeing
Dyfed
dying
dyke (= lesbian →
 dike)
dynamic
dynamically
dynamics
dynamism
dynamite
 dynamites
 dynamited
 dynamiting
dynamo
 dynamos
dynastic
dynasty
 dynasties
dysentery
dyslexia
dyslexic
dysmenorrhoea
dyspepsia
dyspeptic
dystrophy

E

each
eager
 eagerly
 eagerness
eagle
eaglet
Ealing
✗ean = eon
ear
earache
eardrops
eardrum
eared
earful
earl
earldom
earliness
early
 earlier
 earliest
earmark
 earmarks
 earmarked
 earmarking
earmuff
earn (= deserve
 → urn)
 earns
 earned
 earning
earnest
earnings

earphone
earpiece
earplug
earring
earshot
earth
earthed
earthbound
earthen
earthenware
earthier
earthiest
earthliness
earthling
earthly
  earthlier
  earthliest
earthquake
earthshaking
earthward
earthwards
earthwork
earthworm
earthy
  earthier
  earthiest
earwax
earwig
earwigging
ease
  eases
  eased
  easing
easel
easement
easier
easiest
easily
easiness
east

eastbound
Easter
easterly
  easterlies
eastern
easternmost
easting
eastward
eastwards
easy
  easier
  easiest
eat
  eats
  ate (= took food
    → eight)
  eaten
  eating
eatable
eatables
eaten
eater
eatery
  eateries
eats
eaves
eavesdrop
  eavesdrops
  eavesdropped
  eavesdropping
  eavesdropper
✗ eazy = easy
ebb
  ebbs
  ebbed
  ebbing
Ebbw Vale
E-boat
ebony

ebonies
ebullience
ebulliency
ebullient
ebulliently
eccentric
eccentrically
eccentricity
  eccentricities
Eccles
ecclesiastic
ecclesiastical
ecclesiasticism
ECG
echelon
echidna
  echidnas or
  echidnae
echo
  echoes
  echoed
  echoing
echt
eclair
eclampsia
eclat
eclectic
eclectically
eclecticism
eclipse
  eclipses
  eclipsed
  eclipsing
✗ eco = echo
ecological
ecologically
ecologist
ecology
econometric
econometrics

economic	eddies	editorializing
economical	eddied	✗ edlevise =
economically	eddying	edelweiss
economics	edelweiss	educable
economise	✗ edema = oedema	educate
economises	edge	educates
economised	edges	educated
economising	edged	educating
economiser	edgily	education
economist	edginess	educational
economize	edging	educationalist
economizes	edgeways	educationally
economized	edgy	educative
economizing	edgier	educator
economizer	edgiest	Edwardian
economy	edible	EEC
economies	edibles	eel
ecospecies	edict	e'en
ecospecific	edification	e'er (= ever → air;
ecosphere	edifice	ere; heir)
ecosystem	edify	eerie (= spooky
ecru	edifies	→ eyrie)
ecs try ex	edified	eerier
✗ ecsema = eczema	edifying	eeriest
✗ ecsentric = eccentric	Edinburgh	eeriness
ecstasy	edit	ef try af
ecstasies	edits	eff
ecstatic	edited	efface
ecstatically	editing	effaces
ectomorph	edition	effaced
ectopia	editor	effacing
ectopic	editorial	effaceable
ectoplasm	editorially	effacement
Ecuador	editorialise	effacer
ecumenical	editorialises	effect (= result, or
ecumenicism	editorialised	bring about
eczema	editorialising	→ affect)
eczematous	editorialize	effects
Edam (= cheese)	editorializes	effected
eddy	editorialized	effecting

effecter
effective
effectively
effector
effects
effectual
effectuality
effeminacy
effeminate
effendi
  effendis
effervesce
  effervesces
  effervesced
  effervescing
effervescent
effervescently
effete
efficacious
efficacy
efficiency
  efficiencies
efficient
efficiently
effigy
  effigies
effishunsy =
  efficiency
effluence
effluent
effluvial
effluvium
  effluviums or
  effluvia
effort
effortless
effortlessly
effrontery
  effronteries
effusion

effusive
effusively
egad
egalitarian
egalitarianism
egest
egests
egested
egesting
egestion
egg
  eggs
egged
egging
egghead
eggnog
eggplant
eggshell
eglantine
ego
  egos
egocentric
egocentrically
egocentricity
egocentrism
egoism
egoist
egomania
egomaniacal
egos
egotism
egotist
egregious
egress
egression
egret
egs try exh
Egypt
Egyptian
Egyptology

Egyptologist
eh
eider
eiderdown
eigenfrequency
eigenfunction
eigentone
eigenvalue
eight (= number
  → ate)
eighteen
eighteenth
eightfold
eighth
eightieth
eighty
  eighties
Einstein
einsteinium
Eire
eisteddfod
  eisteddfods or
  eisteddfodau
either
Eleanor
Eliot, George
Eliot, T.S.
Elizabeth
ejaculate
  ejaculates
ejaculated
ejaculating
ejaculation
eject
ejects
ejected
ejecting
ejection
ejective
ejector

eke
  ekes
  eked
  eking
elaborate
  elaborates
  elaborated
  elaborating
elaboration
eland
elapse
  elapses
  elapsed
  elapsing
elastic
elastically
elasticate
  elasticates
  elasticated
  elasticating
elastication
elasticises
  elasticises
  elasticised
  elasticising
elasticity
elasticize
  elasticizes
  elasticized
  elasticizing
elastomer
elate
  elates
  elated
  elating
elation
elbow
  elbows
  elbowed
  elbowing

elbowroom
elder
elderberry
  elderberries
elderliness
elderly
eldest
elect
  elects
  elected
  electing
electable
election
electioneering
elective
electivity
elector
electoral
electorally
electorate
electric
electrical
electrically
electrician
electricity
electrifiable
electrification
electrifier
electrify
  electrifies
  electrified
  electrifying
electrocardiogram
electrocardiograph
electrocardiography
electrocute
  electrocutes
  electrocuted
  electrocuting
electrocution

electrode
electroencephalo-
  gram
electroencephalo-
  graph
electrolysis
electrolyte
electromagnet
electromagnetic
electromagnetically
electromagnetics
electromagnetism
electron
electronic
electronically
electronics
electroplate
  electroplates
  electroplated
  electroplating
electroplater
electrostatic
elegance
elegant
elegantly
elegiac
elegiacally
elegise
  elegises
  elegised
  elegising
elegize
  elegizes
  elegized
  elegizing
elegy
  elegies
element
elemental
elementally

elementary
elephant
elephantiasis
elephantine
elevate
  elevates
  elevated
  elevating
elevation
elevator
eleven
elevenses
eleventh
elf
  elves
elfin
elfish
elflock
elicit
  elicits
  elicited
  eliciting
eligible
eliminate
  eliminates
  eliminated
  eliminating
elimination
eliminator
eliminatory
elision
elite
elitism
elitist
elixir
Elizabethan
elk
  elk or
  elks
ell

ellipse
ellipsis
ellipsoid
ellipsoidal
elliptic
elliptical
elliptically
elm
elocution
elongate
  elongates
  elongated
  elongating
elongation
elope
  elopes
  eloped
  eloping
  elopement
  eloper
eloquence
eloquent
El Salvador
else
elsewhere
elucidate
  elucidates
  elucidated
  elucidating
elucidation
elude
  eludes
  eluded
  eluding
elusion
elusive
elusively
elver
elves
elvish

emaciated
emaciation
emanate
  emanates
  emanated
  emanating
  emanation
emancipate
  emancipates
  emancipated
  emancipating
emancipation
emancipative
emancipator
emancipatory
emasculate
  emasculates
  emasculated
  emasculating
emasculation
embalm
  embalms
  embalmed
  embalming
  embalmer
embalmment
embankment
✗ embarass = embarrass
embargo
  embargoes
  embargoed
  embargoing
embark
  embarks
  embarked
  embarking
✗ embarm = embalm
embarrass
  embarrasses

embarrassed
embarrassing
embarrassingly
embarrassment
embassy
  embassies
embattled
embed
  embeds
  embedded
  embedding
embellish
  embellishes
  embellished
  embellishing
embellisher
embellishment
ember
embezzle
  embezzles
  embezzled
  embezzling
embezzlement
embezzler
embittered
embitterment
emblazon
  emblazons
  emblazoned
  emblazoning
emblem
embodiment
embody
  embodies
  embodied
  embodying
embolism
embonpoint
emboss
  embosses

embossed
embossing
embosser
embouchure
embrace
  embraces
  embraced
  embracing
embracer
embrasure
  embrasured
embrocation
embroider
  embroiders
  embroidered
  embroidering
embroiderer
embroidery
  embroideries
embroil
  embroils
  embroiled
  embroiling
embryo
  embryos
embryology
embryonic
emcee
emend (= correct a
  text → amend)
  emends
  emended
  emending
emendation
emerald
emerge
  emerges
  emerged
  emerging
emergence

emergency
  emergencies
emergent
emeritus
emersion
emery
emesis
emetic
emetically
emigrant
emigrate
  emigrates
  emigrated
  emigrating
emigré
emigration
Emily
eminence
eminency
  eminencies
eminent
emir
emirate
emissary
  emissaries
emission
emissive
emissivity
emit
  emits
  emitted
  emitting
emitter
Emma
Emmenthal
✗ emnity = enmity
emollience
emollient
emolument
emotion

emotional
emotionally
emotionless
emotionlessly
emotive
emotively
empathic
empathically
empathise
  empathises
  empathised
  empathising
empathize
  empathizes
  empathized
  empathizing
empathy
emperor
emphasis
  emphases
emphasise
  emphasises
  emphasised
  emphasising
emphasize
  emphasizes
  emphasized
  emphasizing
emphatic
emphatically
emphysema
empire
empiric
empirical
empirically
empiricism
empiricist
employ
  employs
  employed

employing
employability
employable
employee
employer
employment
emporium
  emporiums or
  emporia
empoverish
  empoverishes
  empoverished
  empoverishing
empoverishment
empower
  empowers
  empowered
  empowering
empowerment
empress
emptiable
emptily
emptiness
empty
  empties
  emptied
  emptying
empty
  emptier
  emptiest
emu
  emus or
  emu
emulate
  emulates
  emulated
  emulating
emulation
emulsifiable
emulsification

emulsifier
emulsify
  emulsifies
  emulsified
  emulsifying
emulsion
enable
  enables
  enabled
  enabling
enablement
enabler
enact
  enacts
  enacted
  enacting
enactment
enactor
enamel
  enamels
  enamelled
  enamelling
enameller
enamellist
enamelwork
enamoured
encampment
encapsulate
  encapsulates
  encapsulated
  encapsulating
encapsulation
encase
  encases
  encased
  encasing
enceinte
encephalic
encephalin
encephalitic

encephalitis
encephalogram
encephalograph
encephalographic
encephalographically
encephalography
encephaloma
   encephalomas or
   encephalomata
encephalomyelitic
encephalomyelitis
encephalon
   encephala
encephalopathy
encephalous
enchant
   enchants
   enchanted
   enchanting
enchanter
enchantingly
enchantment
enchantress
enchilada
✗ enciclopedia =
   encyclopaedia or
   encyclopedia
encipher
   enciphers
   enciphered
   enciphering
encipherer
encipherment
encircle
   encircles
   encircled
   encircling
encirclement
encircling
enclave

enclitic
enclosable
enclose
   encloses
   enclosed
   enclosing
encloser
enclosure
encode
   encodes
   encoded
   encoding
encodement
encoder
encomium
   encomiums or
   encomia
encompass
   encompasses
   encompassed
   encompassing
encompassment
encore
encounter
   encounters
   encountered
   encountering
encounterer
encourage
   encourages
   encouraged
   encouraging
encouragement
   encouragingly
encroach
   encroaches
   encroached
   encroaching
encroacher

encroachment
encrust
   encrusts
   encrusted
   encrusting
encumbrance
encyclical
encyclopaedia
encyclopaedic
encyclopaedically
encyclopedia
encyclopedic
encyclopedically
end
   ends
   ended
   ending
endanger
   endangers
   endangered
   endangering
endangerment
endbrain
endear
   endears
   endeared
   endearing
endearingly
endearment
endeavour
   endeavours
   endeavoured
   endeavouring
endeavourer
endemic
endemical
endemically
endgame
ending
endive

endless
endlessly
endmost
endocardium
  endocardia
endocarp
endocranium
  endocrania
endocrine
endocrinologic
endocrinology
endocrinous
endometriosis
endometrium
  endometria
endomorph
endoplasm
endorphin
endorsable
endorse
  endorses
  endorsed
  endorsing
endorsee
endorsement
endorser
endorsor
endoscope
endoscopic
endoscopist
endoscopy
endoskeleton
endosperm
endospore
endosporous
endothelium
  endothelia
endothermic
endow
  endows

endowed
endowing
endower
endowment
endpaper
endplate
endplay
endurability
endurable
endurably
endurance
endure
  endures
  endured
  enduring
endways
enema
  enemas
enemy
  enemies
energetic
energid
energise
  energises
  energised
  energising
energize
  energizes
  energized
  energizing
energy
  energies
enervate
  enervates
  enervated
  enervating
enfeeble
  enfeebles
  enfeebled
  enfeebling

enfeeblement
enfeebler
✗ enflame = inflame
✗ enflict = inflict
enfold
  enfolds
  enfolded
  enfolding
enforce
  enforces
  enforced
  enforcing
enforceability
enforceable
enforceably
enforcement
enforcer
enfranchise
  enfranchises
  enfranchised
  enfranchising
enfranchisement
enfranchiser
engage
  engages
  engaged
  engaging
engagement
engager
engender
  engenders
  engendered
  engendering
engine
engineer
engineering
English
engorge
  engorges
  engorged

engorging
engorgement
engrave
engraves
engraved
engraving
engraver
engraving
engross
engrosses
engrossed
engrossing
engrossment
engulf
engulfs
engulfed
engulfing
enhance
enhances
enhanced
enhancing
enhancement
enhancer
enharmonic
enigma
enigmatic
enjoin
enjoins
enjoined
enjoining
enjoy
enjoys
enjoyed
enjoying
enjoyable
enjoyably
enjoyer
enjoyment
enlarge
enlarges

enlarged
enlarging
enlargeable
enlargement
enlarger
enlighten
enlightens
enlightened
enlightening
enlightenment
enlist
enlists
enlisted
enlisting
enlister
enlistment
enliven
enlivens
enlivened
enlivening
enlivener
enlivenment
enmesh
enmeshes
enmeshed
enmeshing
enmeshment
Enniskillen
enmity
enmities
ennoble
ennobles
ennobled
ennobling
ennoblement
ennobler
ennobling
ennui
enormity
enormities

enormous
enormously
enough
enquire
enquires
enquired
enquiring
enquirer
enquiry
enquiries
enrage
enrages
enraged
enraging
enragement
enrapture
enraptures
enraptured
enrapturing
enrich
enriches
enriched
enriching
enricher
enrichment
enrobe
enrobes
enrobed
enrobing
enrober
enrol
enrols
enrolled
enrolling
enrolment
ensconce
ensconces
ensconced
ensconcing
ensemble

✗ enshure = ensure

✗ ensiclopedia =
   encyclopaedia or
   encyclopedia

ensign

enslave
   enslaves
   enslaved
   enslaving

enslavement

enslaver

ensnare
   ensnares
   ensnared
   ensnaring

ensnarement

ensnarer

ensue
   ensues
   ensued
   ensuing

ensure
   ensures
   ensured
   ensuring

✗ ensyclopedia =
   encyclopaedia or
   encyclopedia

entail
   entails
   entailed
   entailing

entailment

entangle
   entangles
   entangled
   entangling

entanglement

entangler

entente

enter
   enters
   entered
   entering

enteric

enteritis

enterprise

enterprising

entertain
   entertains
   entertained
   entertaining

entertainer

entertaining

entertainingly

entertainment

enthral
   enthrals
   enthralled
   enthralling

enthuse
   enthuses
   enthused
   enthusing

enthusiasm

enthusiast

enthusiastic

enthusiastically

entice
   entices
   enticed
   enticing

enticement

enticer

enticing

enticingly

entire

entirely

entirety

entireties

entitle
   entitles
   entitled
   entitling

entitlement

entity
   entities

entoderm

entomb
   entombs
   entombed
   entombing

entombment

entomological

entomology

entourage

entozoic

entozoon

entrails

entrance
   entrances
   entranced
   entrancing

entrancing

entrancingly

entrancement

entrant

entrap
   entraps
   entrapped
   entrapping

entrapment

entrapper

entreat
   entreats
   entreated
   entreating

entreatment

entreaty

entreaties
entrechat
entrecôte
entrée
entrench
  entrenches
  entrenched
  entrenching
entrencher
entrenchment
entrepôt
entrepreneur
entropy
  entropies
entrust
  entrusts
  entrusted
  entrusting
entry
  entries
entwine
  entwines
  entwined
  entwining
✗ enuf = enough
enumerable
enumerate
  enumerates
  enumerated
  enumerating
enumeration
enumerative
enumerator
enunciable
enunciate
  enunciates
  enunciated
  enunciating
enunciation
enunciator

enuresis
enuretic
envelop (= to wrap)
  envelops
  enveloped
  enveloping
envelope (= sta-
  tionery)
envelopment
enviable
enviably
envious
environment
environmental
environmentalism
environmentalist
environmentally
environs
envisage
  envisages
  envisaged
  envisaging
envisagement
envision
  envisions
  envisioned
  envisioning
envoy
envy
  envies
  envied
  envying
enzyme
eolith
Eolithic
Eozoic
EP
epaulet
epaulette
ephedrine

ephemera
ephemeras or
  ephemerae
ephemeral
ephemerally
ephemerality
epic
epically
epicanthus
  epicanthi
epicardium
  epicardia
epicarp
epicene
epicentre
epicure
epicurean
epidemic
epidemiological
epidemiology
epidermis
epididymis
  epididymides
epidural
epiglottis
epigram
epigraph
epilepsy
epileptic
epilogue
epiphany
  epiphanies
episcopacy
episcopal
episcopalian
episiotomy
  episiotomies
episode
episodic
episodically

epistemological
epistemologically
epistemologist
epistemology
epistle
epitaph
epithelium
  epitheliums or
  epithelia
epithet
epitome
epitomise
  epitomises
  epitomised
  epitomising
epitomize
  epitomizes
  epitomized
  epitomizing
epizoic
epizoite
epizoon
epizootic
epoch
epochal
eponym
eponymous
eponymy
epoxy
  epoxies
epsilon
equable
equal
  equals
  equalled
  equalling
equalise
  equalises
  equalised
  equalising

equaliser
equality
  equalities
equalize
  equalizes
  equalized
  equalizing
equalizer
equalled
equally
equals
equanimity
equanimous
equatability
equatable
equate
  equates
  equated
  equating
equation
equator
equatorial
equerry
  equerries
equestrian
equestrianism
equiangular
equidistant
equilateral
equilibrium
  equilibriums or
  equilibria
equine
equinoctial
equinox
equip
  equips
  equipped
  equipping
equipage

equipment
equipoise
equipper
equitable
equity
  equities
equivalence
equivalency
equivalent
equivocal
equivocally
equivocate
  equivocates
  equivocated
  equivocating
equivocation
equivocator
equivocatory
era
eradicable
eradicably
eradicate
  eradicates
  eradicated
  eradicating
eradication
eradicator
erasable
erase
  erases
  erased
  erasing
eraser
erasure
erbium
ere (= before
  → air; e'er; heir)
erect
  erects
  erected

erecting
erectable
erecter
erectile
erectility
erection
erector
erelong
erewhile
erg
ergo
ergonomic
ergonomics
ergonomist
Eritrea
erlking
✗ erk = irk
✗ erksome = irksome
✗ erl = earl
✗ erly = early
ermine
✗ ern = earn *or* urn
✗ ernest = earnest
✗ ernings = earnings
erode
  erodes
  eroded
  eroding
erogenous
erosion
erosive
erotic
erotica
erotically
eroticism
err (= do wrong
  → er)
  errs
  erred
  erring

errand
errant
errata
erratic
erratically
erratum
errata
erroneous
error
ersatz
Erse
erstwhile
✗ erth = earth
✗ erthenware =
  earthenware
✗ erther = earther
erudite
eruditely
erudition
erupt
erupts
erupted
erupting
eruptible
eruption
eruptive
eruptivity
erysipelas
erythrocyte
erythrocytic
erythromycin
escalate
escalates
escalated
escalating
escalator
escalope
escapable
escapade
escape

escapes
escaped
escaping
escapee
escaper
escapism
escapist
escapologist
escargot
escarpment
✗ escetology =
  eschatology
eschatological
eschatology
escort
escorts
escorted
escorting
escudo
escudos
✗ eshelon = echelon
✗ esholzia =
  eschscholtzia
Eskimo
  Eskimos or
  Eskimo
✗ esophagus =
  oesophagous
esoteric
ESP
espadrille
espalier
España
especial
especially
Esperanto
espionage
esplanade
espousal
espouse

espouses
espoused
espousing
espresso
  espressos
esprit
espy
  espies
  espied
  espying
esquire
essay
essayist
essence
essential
essentially
establish
  establishes
  established
  establishing
establisher
establishment
estate
esteem
esteemed
ester
✗esthete = aesthete
✗esthetic = aesthetic
estimable
estimate
  estimates
  estimated
  estimating
estimation
estimator
✗estrogen =
  oestrogen
Estonia
estuary
  estuaries

eta
etc.
etcetera
etch
  etches
  etched
  etching
eternal
eternally
eternity
  eternities
ethane
ethanol
ether
ethereal
ethereally
etheric
ethic
ethical
ethics
Ethiopia
Ethiopian
ethnic
ethnicity
ethnocentrism
ethnographic
ethnography
ethnologist
ethnology
ethnomethodology
ethos
ethyl
ethylene
✗eticet = etiquette
etiquette
Etruscan
etymological
etymology
  etymologies
eucalyptus

eucalyptuses or
  eucalypti
Eucharist
eugenic
eugenically
eugenicist
eugenics
eugenist
eulogise
  eulogises
  eulogised
  eulogising
eulogize
  eulogizes
  eulogized
  eulogizing
eulogy
  eulogies
eunuch
euphemism
euphonic
euphonically
euphonium
euphony
  euphonies
euphoria
euphoric
Eurasian
eureka
eurhythmic
eurocrat
eurocurrency
eurodeposit
eurodollar
euromarket
Europe
European
europium
euthanasia
evacuate

evacuates
evacuated
evacuating
evacuation
evacuee
evadable
evade
evades
evaded
evading
evader
evaluate
evaluates
evaluated
evaluating
evaluation
evaluative
evaluator
evanescent
evangelical
evangelically
evangelisation
evangelise
evangelises
evangelised
evangelising
evangeliser
evangelism
evangelist
evangelistic
evangelistically
evangelization
evangelize
evangelizes
evangelized
evangelizing
evangelizer
evaporability
evaporable
evaporate

evaporates
evaporated
evaporating
evaporation
evaporative
evaporator
evapotranspiration
evasion
evasive
evasively
eve
even
evening
evenings
evenly
evens
evensong
event
eventer
eventful
eventfully
eventide
eventing
eventual
eventuality
eventualities
eventually
ever
Everest
evergreen
everlasting
evermore
every
everybody
everyday
everyone
everything
everywhere
Evesham
evict

evicts
evicted
evicting
eviction
evictor
evidence
evident
evidential
evidently
evil
evildoer
evilly
evince
evinces
evinced
evincing
evincible
eviscerate
eviscerates
eviscerated
eviscerating
evisceration
eviscerator
evocative
evocatively
evoke
evokes
evoked
evoking
evoker
evolution
evolutionary
evolutionist
evolve
evolves
evolved
evolving
evolvement
ewe (= sheep →
yew; you)

ewer
ex
exacerbate
  exacerbates
  exacerbated
  exacerbating
exacerbation
exact
  exacts
  exacted
  exacting
exactable
exacter
exacting
exactingly
exactitude
exactly
exactor
exaggerate
  exaggerates
  exaggerated
  exaggerating
exaggeration
exaggerator
exalt (= raise →
 exult)
  exalts
  exalted
  exalting
exaltation
exalted
exam
examinable
examination
examine
  examines
  examined
  examining
examinee
examiner

example
exasperate
  exasperates
  exasperated
  exasperating
exasperatingly
exasperation
excavate
  excavates
  excavating
excavator
exceed
  exceeds
  exceeded
  exceeding
exceedable
exceeder
exceeding
exceedingly
excel
  excels
  excelled
  excelling
excellence
Excellency
  Excellencies
except (= apart
 from, or to leave
 out → accept)
  excepts
  excepted
  excepting
exception
exceptionable
exceptionably
exceptional
exceptionally
✘ excercise = exercise
excerpt

excess
excessive
exchange
  exchanges
  exchanged
  exchanging
exchangeability
exchangeable
exchangeably
exchequer
excipient
excisable
excise
  excises
  excised
  excising
excision
excitability
excitable
excitably
excitation
excite
  excites
  excited
excitedly
exciting
excitement
exclaim
  exclaims
  exclaimed
  exclaiming
exclaimer
exclamation
exclamatory
excludable
exclude
  excludes
  excluded
  excluding
excluder

exclusion
exclusionary
exclusionism
exclusionist
exclusive
exclusivity
excommunicate
  excommunicates
  excommunicated
  excommunicating
excrement
excrescence
excrescent
excreta
excretal
excrete
  excretes
  excreted
  excreting
excreter
excretion
excretive
excretory
excruciating
exculpable
exculpatory
excursion
excursive
excusable
excusably
excuse
  excuses
  excused
  excusing
exeat
execrable
execute
  executes
  executed
  executing

execution
executioner
executive
executor
executory
executrix
executrixes or
  executrices
✗ exeed = exceed
exegesis
  exegeses
✗ exel = excel
✗ exellent =
  excellent
exemplar
exemplarily
exemplariness
exemplary
exemplifiable
exemplification
exemplifier
exemplify
  exemplifies
  exemplified
  exemplifying
exempt
  exempts
  exempted
  exempting
exemption
✗ exept = except
✗ exeptional =
  exceptional
exercise (= activity
  → exorcise)
  exercises
  exercised
  exercising
exerciser
exert

exerts
exerted
exerting
exertion
✗ exess = excess
exeunt
exfoliation
exhalable
exhalant
exhale
  exhales
  exhaled
  exhaling
exhaust
  exhausts
  exhausted
  exhausting
exhaustibility
exhaustible
exhaustibly
exhausting
exhaustingly
exhaustion
exhaustive
exhaustively
exhibit
  exhibits
  exhibited
  exhibiting
exhibition
exhibitioner
exhibitionism
exhibitionist
exhibitor
exhilarate
  exhilarates
  exhilarated
  exhilarating
exhilaration
exhort

exhorts
exhorted
exhorting
exhortation
exhortative
exhortatory
exhumation
exhume
exhumes
exhumed
exhuming
exhumer
✗ exibit = exhibit
✗ exibition =
exhibition
✗ exicrable =
execrable
exigency
exigent
exiguous
✗ exilarate =
exhilarate
✗ exilaration =
exhilaration
exile
✗ exilerate =
exhilarate
✗ exileration =
exhilaration
✗ exise = excise
exist
exists
existed
existing
existence
existent
existential
existentialism
existing
exit

exits
exited
exiting
✗ exitable = excitable
✗ exite = excite
✗ exiting = exciting
✗ exitment =
excitement
exocarp
exocrine
exoderm
exodus
exogenous
exonerate
exonerates
exonerated
exonerating
exoneration
exonerative
exonerator
exorbitance
exorbitant
exorcise (= get rid
of spirits → ex-
ercise)
exorcises
exorcised
exorcising
exorcize (= get rid
of spirits → ex-
ercise)
exorcizes
exorcized
exorcizing
✗ exorst = exhaust
✗ exorstion =
exhaustion
✗ exort = exhort
✗ exortation =
exhortation

exoskeleton
exosmic
exosmosis
exosmotic
exosphere
exospore
exoteric
exotic
exotica
exotically
exoticism
expand
expands
expanded
expanding
expandable
expander
expanse
expansibility
expansible
expansile
expansion
expansionary
expansionism
expansionist
expansionistic
expansive
expansivity
expat
expatriate
expatriation
expect
expects
expected
expecting
expectancy
expectant
expectantly
expectation
expectative

expecting
expectorant
expediency
expedient
expedite
  expedites
  expedited
  expediting
expediter
expedition
expeditionary
expeditious
expeditor
expel
  expels
  expelled
  expelling
expellant
expellent
expend
  expends
  expended
  expending
expendable
expender
expenditure
expense
expensive
expensively
experience
  experiences
  experienced
  experiencing
experiential
experientially
experiment
  experiments
  experimented
  experimenting
experimental

experimentalist
experimentally
experimentation
experimenter
expert
expertise
expiate
  expiates
  expiated
  expiating
expiation
expiatory
expiration
expiratory
expire
  expires
  expired
  expiring
expirer
expiry
  expiries
explain
  explains
  explained
  explaining
explainable
explainer
explanation
explanatorily
explanatory
expletive
explicable
explicably
explicate
  explicates
  explicated
  explicating
explication
explicative
explicatory

explicit
explicitly
explode
explodes
exploded
exploding
exploder
exploit
exploits
exploited
exploiting
exploitable
exploitative
exploitive
exploration
explorative
exploratory
explore
explores
explored
exploring
explorer
explosion
explosive
expo
expos
exponent
exponential
exponentially
export
exports
exported
exporting
exportable
exportation
exporter
exposable
exposal
expose
exposes

exposed
exposing
exposé
exposer
exposition
expositor
expostulate
   expostulates
   expostulated
   expostulating
expostulation
exposure
expound
   expounds
   expounded
   expounding
expounder
express
   expresses
   expressed
   expressing
expresser
expressible
expression
expressionism
expressionist
expressionistic
expressionless
expressive
expressively
expressly
expropriate
   expropriates
   expropriated
   expropriating
expropriation
expropriator
expulsion
expulsive
expunction

expunge
expunges
expunged
expunging
expurgate
   expurgates
   expurgated
   expurgating
expurgatorial
expurgatory
exquisite
extant
extemporaneous
extempore
extemporisation
extemporise
   extemporises
   extemporised
   extemporising
extemporiser
extemporization
extemporize
   extemporizes
   extemporized
   extemporizing
extemporizer
extend
   extends
   extended
   extending
extendability
extendable
extended
extender
extendibility
extendible
extensibility
extensible
extensibleness
extension

extensive
extensively
extensor
extent
extenuating
extenuation
exterior
exterminable
exterminate
   exterminates
   exterminated
   exterminating
extermination
exterminator
external
externalisation
externalise
   externalised
   externalising
externalization
externalize
   externalizes
   externalized
   externalizing
externally
exteroceptor
exterritorial
extinct
extinction
extinguish
   extinguishes
   extinguished
   extinguishing
extinguishable
extinguisher
extinguishment
extol
   extols
   extolled
   extolling

extort
  extorts
  extorted
  extorting
extortion
extortionate
extortionately
extortioner
extortionist
extra
extracellular
extract
  extracts
  extracted
  extracting
extractability
extractable
extraction
extractions
extractive
extractor
extracurricular
extraditable
extradite
  extradites
  extradited
  extraditing
extradition
extramarital
extramural
extraneous
extranuclear
extraordinarily
extraordinariness
extraordinary
extraordinarily
extrapolate
  extrapolates
  extrapolated
  extrapolating

extrapolation
extrasensory
extraterrestrial
extraterritorial
extravagance
extravagant
extravagantly
extravaganza
extravehicular
extraversion
extremal
extreme
extremely
extremism
extremist
extremity
  extremities
extricate
  extricates
  extricated
  extricating
extrinsic
extrinsically
✘ extrordinary =
  extraordinary
extroversion
extrovert
extroverted
extrude
  extrudes
  extruded
  extruding
extrusible
extrusion
extrusive
exuberance
exuberant
exude
  exudes
  exuded

exuding
exult (= be happy
  → exalt)
  exults
  exulted
  exulting
exultant
exultation
exultingly
✘ exumation =
  exhumation
✘ exume = exhume
eye
  eyes
  eyed
  eyeing or
  eying
eyeball
eyebrow
eyed (= looked at
  → I'd)
eyeful
eyelash
eyelet
eyelevel
eyelid
eyeliner
eyes
eyesight
eyesore
eyestrain
eyetooth
eyewitness
eying
eyrie (= eagle's
  nest → eerie)
  eyries

F

fab
Fabian
fable
fabled
fabric
fabricate
  fabricates
  fabricated
  fabricating
fabulous
facade
face
  faces
  faced
  facing
faceless
facet
  faceted
facetious
facetiously
facetiousness
facia
facial
facile
facilitate
facilitation
facilitative
facilitator
facility
facsimile
fact
faction

factious
factitious
factitiously
factitiousness
factive
factoid
factor
factorage
factorial
factoring
factorise
  factorises
  factorised
  factorising
factorize
  factorizes
  factorized
  factorizing
factory
  factories
factotum
factual
faculty
fad
fade
  fades
  faded
  fading
fadeless
faecal
faeces
faerie
Faeroese
faery
fag
  fags
  fagged
  fagging
faggot
fah

Fahrenheit
fail
  fails
  failed
  failing
failure
fain (= would like
  → feign)
faint (= lose con-
  sciousness
  → feint)
  faints
  fainted
  fainting
fair (= funfair
  → fare)
  fairer
  fairest
fairground
fairies
fairing
fairish
fairly
fairway
fairy
  fairies
fairyland
fairy-tale
faith
faithful
faithfully
faithfulness
faithless
fake
  fakes
  faked
  faking
fakir
falafel
falcon

falconer
falconry
falderal
fall
  falls
  fell
  fallen
  falling
fallacious
fallaciously
fallaciousness
fallacy
  fallacies
fallible
falling
fallow
Falmouth
false
falsehood
falsetto
falsies
falsification
falsify
  falsifies
  falsified
  falsifying
falsity
Falstaffian
falter
  falters
  faltered
  faltering
fame
familial
familiar
familiarisation
familiarise
  familiarises
  familiarised
  familiarising

familiariser
familiarity
familiarization
familiarize
  familiarizes
  familiarized
  familiarizing
familiarly
familiarness
family
  families
famine
famous
fan
  fans
  fanned
  fanning
fanatic
fanatical
fanatically
fanaticism
fancied
fancier
fanciful
fancy
  fancies
  fancied
  fancying
fandango
  fandangos
✗fane = feign
fanfare
fang
fanlight
fanned
fanning
fanny
fantail
fantasia
fantasise

fantasises
fantasised
fantasising
fantasize
fantasizes
fantasized
fantasizing
fantastic
fantastically
fantasy
fanzine
faqir
far
farad
faraday
faradic
faradise
  faradises
  faradised
  faradising
faradism
faradize
  faradizes
  faradized
  faradizing
faraway
farce
farcemeat
farcical
fare (= get on
  → fair)
  fares
  fared
  faring
✗farenhite =
  Fahrenheit
farewell
farina
farinaceous
farinose

farm
  farms
  farmed
  farming
farmer
farmhouse
farmland
farmstead
farmyard
Faroese
farraginous
farrago
farrier
farriery
farrow
  farrows
  farrowed
  farrowing
Farsi
farther
farthermost
farthest
farthing
farthingale
fascia
fascicle
fascinate
  fascinates
  fascinated
  fascinating
fascinator
fascism
Fascism
fascist
Fascist
✗ fasen = fasten
✗ fashel = facial
✗ fasher = fascia
fashion
  fashions

fashioned
fashioning
fashionable
✗ fashism = fascism
✗ fashist = fascist
✗ fasinate = fascinate
fast
  fasts
  fasted
  fasting
fastback
fasten
  fastens
  fastened
  fastening
fast-food
fast-forward
fastidious
fastidiously
fastidiousness
fastness
fat
  fatter
  fattest
fatal
fatalism
fatality
  fatalities
fatally
fate
fated
fateful
father
  fathers
  fathered
  fathering
fatherhood
father-in-law
fatherland
fatherless

fatherly
fathers-in-law
fathom
  fathoms
  fathomed
  fathoming
fathomless
fatigue
  fatigues
  fatigued
  fatiguing
fatted
fatten
  fattens
  fattened
  fattening
fatter
fattest
fatty
  fattier
  fattiest
fatuity
fatuous
fatwa
fatwah
faucal
fauces
faucet
faugh
Faulkner, William
fault
faultless
faulty
  faultier
  faultiest
faun (= an imaginary
  creature → fawn)
fauna
favour
  favours

favoured
favouring
favourable
favourite
favouritism
fawn
fawns
fawned
fawning
fawn (= baby deer;
brown colour
→ faun)
fax
faxes
faxed
faxing
faze
fazes
fazed
fazing
fealty
fear
fears
feared
fearing
fearful
fearfully
fearfulness
fearsome
feasible
feast
feat (= a deed
→ feet)
feather
feathers
feathered
feathering
featherbed
featherbeds
featherbedded

featherbedding
featherbrain
featherweight
feature
featureless
febrifacient
febrific
febrifugal
febrifuge
febrile
febrility
February
✗ Febuary = February
✗ feces = faeces
feckless
fecula
feculent
fecund
fecundity
fed
federal
federalise
federalises
federalised
federalising
federalism
Federalist
federalize
federalizes
federalized
federalizing
federate
federation
fedora
fee
feeble
feed
feeds
fed
feeding

feedback
feeder
feel
feels
felt
feeling
feeler
feeling
✗ feesh = fiche
feet (= plural of
foot → feat)
feign (= pretend
→ fain)
feigns
feigned
feigning
✗ feilty = fealty
feint (= to make a
mock attack or
movement → faint)
feints
feinted
feinting
felafel
feldspar
feldspathic
feldspathoid
felicitate
felicitates
felicitated
felicitating
felicitation
felicitous
felicitously
felicitousness
felicity
feline
felinity
fell
fellatio

feller
felloe
fellow
fellowship
felon
felonious
feloniously
feloniousness
felony
✗felorn = forlorn
felspar
felspathic
felt
felting
felucca
felwort
female
✗fem fatal =
femme fatale
feminine
femininity
feminise
  feminises
  feminised
  feminising
feminism
feminize
  feminizes
  feminized
  feminizing
femoral
femur
fen
fence
  fences
  fenced
  fencing
fencer
fend
  fends

fended
fending
fender
fenestration
Fenian
fennec
fennel
✗fennig = pfennig
fenny
fenugreek
feoff
fer try fur
feral
Fermanagh
ferment
  ferments
  fermented
  fermenting
fermentation
fermenter
fermion
fern
fernery
ferocious
ferociously
ferociousness
ferocity
ferrate
ferreous
ferret
  ferrets
  ferreted
  ferreting
ferri-
ferric
ferriferous
ferrite
ferroelectric
ferroelectricity
ferrotype

ferrous
ferruginous
ferrule
ferry
  ferries
  ferried
  ferrying
fertile
fertilisation
fertilise
  fertilises
  fertilised
  fertilising
fertiliser
fertility
fertilization
fertilize
  fertilizes
  fertilized
  fertilizing
fertilizer
ferula
ferulaceous
ferule
fervency
fervent
✗ferver = fervour
fervour
fescue
fess
fesse
fester
  festers
  festered
  festering
festination
festival
festive
festivity
festoon

festoons
festooned
festooning
festschrift
feta
✗ fetal = foetal
fetation
fetch
fetches
fetched
fetching
fete
fetes
feted
feting
fête
fêtes
fêted
fêting
fetid
fetish
fetishism
fetlock
fetor
fetter
fetters
fettered
fettering
fettle
fettucini
fettucine
✗ fetus = foetus
feu
feud
feudal
feudalism
feudality
feudatory
feudist
feuilleton

fever
feverfew
feverish
few
fey
fez
fezzes
fiancé (= man)
fiancée (= woman)
fiasco
fiascoes
fiascos
fiat
fib
fibs
fibbed
fibbing
fibre
fibreboard
fibreglass
fibriform
fibril
fibrillation
fibrilliform
fibrillose
fibrin
fibrinogen
fibrinogenic
fibrinogenous
fibrinolysis
fibrinolytic
fibrinous
fibroid
fibroma
fibromatous
fibrosis
fibrositis
fibrotic
fibrous
fibula

fiche
fichu
fickle
fictile
fiction
fictionalise
fictionalises
fictionalised
fictionalising
fictionalize
fictionalizes
fictionalized
fictionalizing
fictitious
fictitiously
fictitiousness
fictive
ficus
fiddle
fiddles
fiddled
fiddling
fiddle-de-dee
fiddlededee
fiddledeedee
fiddler
fiddlesticks
fiddly
fiddlier
fiddliest
fidelity
fidget
fidgets
fidgeted
fidgeting
fiducial
fiducially
fiduciarily
fiduciary
fie

fief
fiefdom
field
 fields
 fielded
 fielding
fielder
fieldfare
fieldmouse
fieldwork
fiend
fiendish
fierce
fiery
 fierier
 fieriest
fiesta
 fiestas
fife
fifteen
fifteenth
fifth
fifthly
fiftieth
fifty
fifty-fifty
fig
fight
 fights
 fought
 fighting
fighter
figment
figuline
figural
figurate
figuration
figurative
figure
 figures

figured
figuring
figurehead
figurine
figwort
Fiji
Fijian
filagree
filament
filamentary
filbert
filch
 filches
 filched
 filching
file
 files
 filed
 filing
filial
filibeg
filibuster
 filibusters
 filibustered
 filibustering
filibusterer
filicide
filiform
filigree
filings
Filipino
 Filipinos
fill
 fills
 filled
 filling
fillagree
filler
fillet
 fillets

filleted
filleting
filling
fillip
filly
 fillies
film
 films
 filmed
 filming
filmy
 filmier
 filmiest
filo
Filofax™
 Filofaxes™
filose
filter
 filters
 filtered
 filtering
filterable
filth
filthy
 filthier
 filthiest
filtrate
 filtrates
 filtrated
 filtrating
filtration
filum
fimbriate
fin
finable
finagle
 finagles
 finagled
 finaling
finagler

final
finale
finalise
  finalises
  finalised
  finalising
finalism
finalist
finality
finalize
  finalizes
  finalized
  finalizing
finally
finals
finance
  finances
  financed
  financing
financial
financially
finch
  finches
find
  finds
  found
  finding
finder
fine
  fines
  fined
  fining
fineable
fine-drawn
finely
fineness
finery
finesse
finger
  fingers

fingered
fingering
fingernail
fingerprint
fingertip
finical
finicky
fining
finis
finish
  finishes
  finished
  finishing
finisher
finite
Finland
Finn
finned
finner
Finnish
finny
fino
finos
✗ fionsay = fiancé or fiancée
fiord
fioritura
fir
fire
  fires
  fired
  firing
firearm
firebird
firebomb
firebreak
firebrick
firecracker
firedamp
firedog

firefighter
firefly
  fireflies
fireguard
firelock
fireman
  firemen
fireplace
fireproof
fireside
firestone
fireweed
firework
  fireworks
firing
firkin
firm
  firms
  firmed
  firming
firmament
firmamental
firmware
firn
firry
firrier
firriest
first
firstly
first-rate
firth
✗ firy = fiery
fiscal
fish
  fishes or
  fish
  fished
  fishing
✗ fishen = fission
fisher

fisherman
  fishermen
fishery
  fisheries
fishmonger
fishnet
fishtail
fishwife
  fishwives
fishy
  fishier
  fishiest
fissile
fissility
fission
fissionable
fissiparous
fissure
fist
fistful
  fistfuls
fisticuffs
fistula
  fistulas *or*
  fistulae
fistulous
fit
  fits
  fitted
  fitting
fitch
fitter
fittest
fitful
fitfully
fitly
fitment
fitness
fitter
five

fivefold
fiver
fives
fix
  fixes
  fixed
  fixing
fixate
  fixates
  fixated
  fixating
fixation
fixative
fixedly
fixer
fixings
fixity
fixture
fizz
  fizzes
  fizzed
  fizzing
fizzle
  fizzles
  fizzled
  fizzling
fjord
flab
flabbergast
  flabbergasts
  flabbergasted
  flabbergasting
flabby
  flabbier
  flabbiest
flabellate
flaccid
flaccidity
flack
flacon

flag
  flags
  flagged
  flagging
flagellant
flagellate
  flagellates
  flagellated
  flagellating
flagellum
  flagella *or*
  flagellums
flageolet
flagging
flagitious
flagitiously
flagitiousness
flagon
flagpole
flagrant
flagship
flagstone
flail
  flails
  flailed
  flailing
flair (= style
  → flare)
flak
flake
  flakes
  flaked
  flaking
flaky
  flakier
  flakiest
flambé
flambeau
flambée
flamboyance

flamboyancy
flamboyant
flamboyantly
flame
flames
flamed
flaming
flamenco
flamencos
flameproof
flamingo
flamingos *or*
flamingoes
flammable
flan
flange
flanges
flanged
flanging
flank
flanks
flanked
flanking
flanker
flannel
flannelette
flap
flaps
flapped
flapping
flapjack
flapper
flare (= flame
→ flair)
flares
flared
flaring
flash
flashes
flashed

flashing
flashback
flasher
flashlight
flashy
flashier
flashiest
flask
✗ flassid = flaccid
flat
flatter
flattest
flatboat
flatfish
flatiron
flatlet
flatmate
flatted
flatten
flattens
flattened
flattening
flatter
flatters
flattered
flattering
flattest
flattish
flatulence
flatulent
flatus
flatworm
flaunt
flaunts
flaunted
flaunting
flautist
flavescent
flavin

flavine
flavone
flavonoid
flavour
flavours
flavoured
flavouring
flaw
flaws
flawed
flawing
flax
flaxen
flay
flays
flayed
flaying
flea (= insect
→ flee)
fleabite
fleam
fleapit
flèche
fleck
flecks
flecked
flecking
flection
fled
fledged
fledgeling
fledgling
flee (= run away
from → flea)
flees
fled
fleeing
fleece
fleeces
fleeced

fleecing
fleecy
  fleecier
  fleeciest
fleet
fleeting
Fleming
Flemish
flesh
flesher
fleshly
  fleshlier
  fleshliest
fleshpots
fleshy
  fleshier
  fleshiest
fleur-de-lis
  fleurs-de-lis
fleur-de-lys
  fleurs-de-lys
flew (to fly → flu,
  flue)
flex
  flexes
  flexed
  flexing
flexible
flexile
flexion
flexitime
flexor
flexuous
flexure
flibbertigibbet
flick
  flicks
  flicked
  flicking
flicker

flickers
flickered
flickering
flier
flies
flight
flightless
flighty
  flightier
  flightiest
flimflam
flimsy
  flimsier
  flimsiest
flinch
  flinches
  flinched
  flinching
fling
  flings
  flung
  flinging
flint
flintlock
flinty
  flintier
  flintiest
flip
  flips
  flipped
  flipping
flip-flop
flippant
flipper
flipping
flirt
  flirts
  flirted
  flirting
flirtation

flirtatious
flirtatiously
flirtatiousness
flit
  flits
  flitted
  flitting
flitch
  flitches
float
  floats
  floated
  floating
floatage
floatation
floater
floaty
  floatier
  floatiest
flocci
floccose
flocculate
floccule
flocculent
flocculus
  flocculi
floccus
  flocci
flock
  flocks
  flocking
  flocked
floe
floes
flog
  flogs
  flogged
  flogging
✗flombay = flambé
flood

floods
  flooded
  flooding
floodgate
floodlight
floor
  floors
  floored
  flooring
floorage
floosie
floozie
floozy
flop
  flops
  flopped
  flopping
floppy
  floppier
  floppiest
floral
floreated
Florentine
florescence
✗ floresense =
  fluorescence
floret
floriated
floribunda
floriculture
florid
✗ floride = fluoride
floridity
floriferous
florigen
florin
✗ florine = fluorine
florist
floristic
floristics

floss
flossy
  flossier
  flossiest
flotage
flotation
flotilla
  flotillas
flotsam
flounce
  flounces
  flounced
  flouncing
flounder
  flounders
  floundered
  floundering
flour (= powder
  made from grain
  → flower)
flourish
  flourishes
  flourished
  flourishing
flout
  flouts
  flouted
  flouting
flow
  flows
  flowed
  flowing
flower (= to bloom
  → flour)
  flowers
  flowered
  flowering
flowerage
floweret
flowerless

flowery
  flowerier
  floweriest
flowmeter
flown
flu (= illness
  → flue, flew)
fluctuant
fluctuate
  fluctuates
  fluctuated
  fluctuating
fluctuation
✗ flud = flood
✗ fludlight =
  floodlight
flue (= chimney
  → flu)
fluency
fluent
fluff
  fluffs
  fluffed
  fluffing
fluffy
  fluffier
  fluffiest
flugelhorn
fluid
fluidic
fluidics
fluidise
  fluidises
  fluidised
  fluidising
fluidity
fluidize
  fluidizes
  fluidised
  fluidizing

fluke
flukey
flukier
flukiest
fluky
flukier
flukiest
flume
flummox
flummoxes
flummoxed
flummoxing
flung
flunk
flunks
flunked
flunking
flunkey
flunkeys
flunky
flunkies
fluor-
fluoresce
fluorescence
fluorescent
fluoric
fluoridate
fluoridates
fluoridated
fluoridating
fluoridation
fluoride
fluorinate
fluorinates
fluorinated
fluorinating
flfluorine
fluoro-
fluorocarbon
fluorometer

✗flurish = flourish
flurry
flurries
flurried
flurrying
flush
flushes
flushed
flushing
fluster
flusters
flustered
flustering
flute
flutes
fluted
fluting
flutist
flutter
flutters
fluttered
fluttering
fluvial
flux
fluxmeter
fly
flies
flew
flown
flying
flyblown
flyer
flying
flyleaf
flyleaves
flyover
flyweight
flywheel
✗fo pas = faux pas
foal

foals
foaled
foaling
foam
foams
foamed
foaming
foamy
foamier
foamiest
fob
fobs
fobbed
fobbing
focal
fo´c´sle
fo´c´s´le
focus
focusses or
foci
focus
focuses or
focusses
focused or
focussed
focusing or
focussing
fodder
foe
foetal
foetid
foetor
foetus
foetuses
fog
fogs
fogged
fogging
fogey
fogeys or

fogies
foggy
  foggier
  foggiest
fogy
  fogies
föhn
foible
foil
  foils
  foiled
  foiling
foist
  foists
  foisted
  foisting
✗ foke = folk
✗ fokelore = folklore
✗ fokesy = folksy
fol try fal
folacin
fold
  folds
  folded
  folding
foldaway
folder
folderol
folia
foliaceous
foliage
foliar
foliate
  foliates
  foliated
  foliating
foliation
folio
  folios
foliolate

foliose
folium
  folia
folk
Folkestone
folklore
folksy
  folksier
  folksiest
follicle
follicular
folliculated
follow
  follows
  followed
  following
follower
folly
  follies
✗ folt = fault
✗ foltless = faultless
✗ folty = faulty
foment
  foments
  fomented
  fomenting
fomentation
fomenter
fond
fondant
fondle
  fondles
  fondled
  fondling
fondue
font
fontanelle
food
foodie
foodstuff

fool
  fools
  fooled
  fooling
foolery
foolhardy
  foolhardier
  foolhardiest
foolish
foolproof
foolscap
foot
  feet
foot
  foots
  footed
  footing
footage
football
foothill
foothold
footie
footing
footle
  footles
  footled
  footling
footlights
footling
footloose
footman
  footmen
footnote
footpath
footprint
footsie
footsore
footstep
footstool
footwear

foreshadow

footwork
footy
fop
foppery
fopperies
for try four
for
forage
forages
foreaged
foraging
foramen
foramina or
foramens
foray
forays
forayed
foraying
forbade
forbear
forbears
forbore or
forbearing
forbearance
forbid
forbids
forbade
forbidding
forbidden
forbidder
forbidding
forbore
forborne
force
forces
forced
forcing
forcedly
forceful
forcefully

forcefulness
forcemeat
forceps
forcible
forcibly
ford
fords
forded
fording
fore (= front
→ four)
✗forein = foreign
✗forenolidge =
foreknowledge
✗forfit = forfeit
✗forin = foreign
forearm
forearms
forearmed
forearming
forebear
foreboding
forebodingly
forebrain
forecast
forecasts
forecast
forecasting
forecastle
foreclose
forecloses
foreclosed
foreclosing
foreclosure
forefather
forefend
forefinger
forefront
foregather
foregathers

foregathered
foregathering
forego
foregoes
forewent
foregone
foregoing
foregoer
foreground
forehead
foreign
foreigner
foerignness
foreknowledge
foreleg
forelock
foreman
foremen
foremast
foremost
forenamed
forenoon
forensic
forensically
forensics
foreordain
foreordination
forepaw
foreplay
forequarters
forerunner
foresaid
foresail
foresee
foresees
foresaw
foreseeing
foreseeable
foreseer
foreshadow

foreshadows
foreshadowed
foreshadowing
foreshore
foreshorten
foreshortens
foreshortened
foreshortening
foresight
foreskin
forest
forestall
forestalls
forestalled
forestalling
forestaller
forestalment
forester
forestry
foretaste
foretastes
foretasted
foretasting
foretell
foretells
foretold
foretelling
foreteller
forethought
forever
forevermore
forewarn
forewarns
forewarned
forewarning
forewarner
forewent
forewing
forewoman
forewomen

foreword
forfeit
forfeits
forteited
forfeiting
forfeiture
forfend
forfex
forfices
forficate
forgather
forgathers
forgathered
forgathering
forgave
forge
forges
forged
forging
forgery
forgeries
forget
forgets
forgot
forgotten
forgetting
forgetful
forgetfully
forgetfulness
forgettable
forgetter
forging
forgivable
forgivably
forgive
forgives
forgave
forgiven
forgiving
forgiveness

forgiver
forgiving
forgivingly
forgivingness
forgo
forgoes
forwent
forgone
forgoing
forgoer
forgot
forgotten
fork
forks
forked
forking
forlorn
forlornly
forlornness
form
forms
formed
forming
formal
formaldehyde
formalin
formalise
formalises
formalised
formalising
formalism
formality
formalize
formalizes
formalized
formalizing
format
formate
formation
formational

formative
forme
former
formerly
formic
Formica℠
formicary
formication
formidable
formless
formula
  formulas *or*
  formulae
formulaic
formularise
  formularises
  formularised
  formularising
formularize
  formularizes
  formularized
  formularizing
formulary
formulate
  formulates
  formulated
  formulating
formulism
formyl
fornicate
  fornicates
  fornicated
  fornicating
fornication
forsake
  forsakes
  forsook
  forsaken
  forsaking
forsaker

forsooth
forswear
  forswears
  forswore
  forsworn
  forswearing
forswearer
forsythia
fort
forte (= talent
  → forty)
forth (= forward
  → fourth)
forthcoming
forthright
forthwith
fortieth
fortification
fortify
  fortifies
  fortified
  fortifying
fortissimo
fortitude
fortnight
Fortran℠
fortress
  fortresses
fortuitism
fortuitist
fortuitous
fortuitously
fortuitousness
fortuity
fortunate
fortune
forty (= number
  → forte)
forum
  forums *or*

fora
forward
forwards
forwarded
forwarding
forwards
forwent
fossa
fosse
fossil
fossiliferous
fossilise
  fossilises
  fossilised
  fossilising
fossilize
  fossilizes
  fossilized
  fossilizing
foster
  fosters
  fostered
  fostering
fosterage
foudroyant
fought
foul (= horrible
  → fowl)
fouler
foulest
foully
foulness
found
  founds
  founded
  founding
foundation
founder (starter)
founder (= sink)
  founders

foundered
foundering
foundling
foundry
  foundries
fount
fountain
fountainhead
four (= number
  → fore)
fourfold
four-poster
fourscore
foursome
fourteen
fourteenth
fourth (= number
  → forth)
fourthly
fovea
foveae
foveolar
foveolate
fowl (= hen → foul)
fowling
fox
  foxes
fox
  foxes
  foxed
  foxing
foxglove
foxhound
fox-hunting
foxtrot
  foxtrots
  foxtrotted
  foxtrotting
foxy
  foxier

foxiest
foyer
fracas
fractal
fraction
fractional
fractionary
fractionate
  fractionates
  fractionated
  fractionating
fractionise
  fractionises
  fractionised
  fractionising
fractionize
  fractionizes
  fractionized
  fractionizing
fractious
fracture
  fractures
  fractured
  fracturing
fraenum
  fraena
fragile
fragility
fragment
fragmentary
fragmentation
fragrance
fragrant
frail
frailty
frame
  frames
  framed
  framing
franc (= money →

frank)
France
Frances (female)
franchise
Francis (male)
Franciscan
francium
Francophile
Francophobe
Francophone
frangible
frangipane
frangipani
Franglais
frank (= honest
  → franc)
frankfurter
frankincense
frankly
frantic
frantically
frappé
✗ frate = freight
✗ frater = freighter
fraternal
fraternalism
fraternally
fraternise
  fraternises
  fraternised
  fraternising
fraternity
  fraternities
fraternize
  fraternizes
  fraternized
  fraternizing
fratricide
fraud
fraudulence

fraudulent
fraught
fraxinella
fray
frays
frayed
fraying
frazzle
frazzles
frazzled
frazzling
freak
freaks
freaked
freaking
freakish
freaky
freakier
freakiest
freckle
freckles
freckled
freckling
free
freer
freest
free
frees
freed
freeing
freebie
freebooter
freed
freedom
Freephone℠
freehold
freeholder
freeing
freelance
freelances

freelanced
freelancing
freeloader
freeman
freemen
freemartin
freemason
freemasonry
Freepost℠
free-range
freesheet
freesia
freesias
freeway
freewheel
freewheels
freewheeled
freewheeling
freeze (= become
ice → frieze)
freezes
froze
frozen
freezing
freezer
freight
freightage
freighter
fremitus
fremitus
French
✘ frend = friend
frenetic
frenetically
freneticness
frenzied
frenzy
Freon℠
frequence
frequency

frequencies
frequent
frequentation
frequentative
frequenter
fresco
frescoes or
frescos
fresh
freshen
freshens
freshened
freshening
fresher
freshet
fresnel
fret
frets
fretting
fretted
fretful
fretwork
Freudian
Freud, Sigmund
friable
friar
friary
fricassee
fricassees
fricasseeing
fricasseed
fricative
friction
Friday
fridge
fried
friend
friendliness
friendly
frier

fries
Friesian
frieze (= ornament
→ freeze)
frig
  frigs
  frigged
  frigging
frigate
fright
frighten
  frightens
  frightened
  frightening
frightful
frightfully
frigid
frigidity
✗frigit = frigate
frigorific
frill
  frills
  frilled
  frilling
fringe
  fringes
  fringed
  fringing
frippery
  fripperies
Frisbee (TM)
Frisian
frisk
  frisks
  frisked
  frisking
frisky
  friskier
  friskiest
frit

frits
fritted
fritting
fritillary
  fritillaries
fritt
  fritts
  fritted
  fritting
fritter
  fritters
  frittered
  frittering
frivolity
frivolous
frizz
  frizzes
  frizzed
  frizzing
frizzle
  frizzles
  frizzled
  frizzling
frizzy
  frizzier
  frizziest
fro
frock
  frocks
  frocked
  frocking
froe
frog
  frogs
  frogged
  frogging
frogman
  frogmen
frogmarch
  frogmarches

frogmarched
frogmarching
✗froidian = Freudian
frolic
  frolics
  frolicked
  frolicking
frolicsome
from
frond
frondescence
frondescent
front
frontage
frontal
frontier
frontispiece
frontlet
frontrunner
frontwards
frost
  frosts
  frosted
  frosting
frostbite
frostbitten
frosty
  frostier
  frostiest
froth
  froths
  frothed
  frothing
frottage
froufrou
frouzy
  frousier
  frousiest
frown
  frowns

frowned
frowning
frowsty
  frowstier
  frowstiest
frowzy
  frowzier
  frowziest
froze
frozen
fructan
fructiferous
fructification
fructify
  fructifies
  fructified
  fructifying
fructose
fructuous
frugal
frugality
frugivorous
fruit
  fruits
  fruited
  fruiting
fruitage
fruitarian
fruitarianism
fruiter
fruiterer
fruitful
fruition
fruitless
fruity
  fruitier
  fruitiest
frumentaceous
frump
frumpy

frumpier
frumpiest
frustrate
  frustrates
  frustrated
  frustrating
frustration
frustule
frustum
frutescence
frutescent
fry
  fries
  fried
  frying
  fryer
fucivorous
fuck
  fucks
  fucked
  fucking
  fucker
fucoid
fucous
fucus
  fucuses
✗ fudal = feudal
✗ fudalism =
   feudalism
fuddle
  fuddles
  fuddled
  fuddling
fuddy-duddy
✗ fude = feud
fudge
  fudges
  fudged
  fudging
fuel

fuels
fuelled
fuelling
fug
fugacious
fugaciously
fugaciousness
fugacity
fugal
✗ fuge = fugue
fugitive
fugue
fulcrum
fulfil
  fulfils
  fulfilled
  fulfilling
fulfiller
fulfilment
fulgent
fuliginous
full
  fulls
  fulled
  fulling
fullback
fuller
full-time
fully
fulmar
fulminant
fulminate
  fulminates
  fulminated
  fulminating
fulsome
fulvous
fumarole
fumarolic
fumble

fumbles
fumbled
fumbling
fume
  fumes
  fumed
  fuming
fumet
fumigant
fumigate
  fumigates
  fumigated
  fumigating
fun
funambulism
funambulist
function
functional
functionalism
functionary
  functionaries
fund
  funds
  funded
  funding
fundament
fundamental
fundamentalism
fundus
  fundi
funebrial
funeral
funerary
funereal
funereally
funfair
fungal
fungi
fungible
fungic

fungicide
fungiform
fungoid
fungus
  fungi *or*
  funguses
funicle
funicular
funiculate
funiculus
funk
funky
  funkier
  funkiest
funnel
funny
  funnier
  funniest
fur
  furs
  furred
  furring
furbelow
furbish
  furbishes
  furbished
  furbishing
furcation
Furies (= fates)
furious
  furiously
furl
  furls
  furled
  furling
furlong
furnace
furnish
  furnishes
  furnished

furnishing
furnishings
furniture
furore
furrier
furriery
furrow
  furrows
  furrowed
  furrowing
furry
  furrier
  furriest
further
furtherance
furthermore
furthermost
furthest
furtive
fury
  furies
furze
fuse
  fuses
  fused
  fusing
fuselage
✗ fusha = fuchsia
✗ fusher = fuchsia
fusible
fusiform
fusile
fusilier
fusillade
fusion
fuss
  fusses
  fussed
  fussing
fussy

G

fussier
fussiest
fustian
fusty
  fustier
  fustiest
✗ fut = phut
futile
futility
futon
futtock
future
futurism
futuristic
futurity
futurology
fuzee
fuzz
  fuzzes
  fuzzed
  fuzzing
fuzzy
  fuzzier
  fuzziest
f-word

gab
  gabs
  gabbed
  gabbing
gabardine
gabble
  gabbles
  gabbled
  gabbling
gabby
  gabbier
  gabbiest
gaberdine
gable
  gabled
Gabon
gad
  gads
  gadded
  gadding
gadfly
  gadflies
gadget
gadgetry
gadroon
gadzooks
Gael
Gaelic
gaff (= blow the
  gaff → gaffe)
gaffe (= blunder
  → gaff)

gaffer
gaffsail
gag
  gags
  gagged
  gagging
gaga
✗ gage = guage
gage
gagger
gaggle
gaiety
gaily
gain
  gains
  gained
  gaining
gainer
gainful
gainly
  gainlier
  gainliest
gains
gainsay
  gainsays
  gainsaid
  gainsaying
gait (= walk
  → gate)
gaiter
gal
gala
  galas
galactic
galactose
galah
Galahad
galantine
galatea
Galashiels

Galatians
galavant
 galavants
 galavanted
 galavanting
galaxy
 galaxies
galbanum
gale
✗ galic = Gaelic
galivant
 galivants
 galivanted
 galivanting
gall
 galls
 galled
 galling
gallant
gallantry
 gallantries
galleon
gallery
 galleries
galley
 galleys
gallfly
 gallflies
galliard
gallic
Gallic
Gallicism
gallimaufry
galling
gallium
gallivant
 gallivants
 gallivanted
 gallivanting
gallon

gallonage
gallop
 gallops
 galloped
 galloping
Galloway
gallows
galoot
galore
galoshes
galtonia
galumph
 galumphs
 galumphed
 galumphing
galvanic
galvanise
 galvanises
 galvanised
 galvanising
galvanism
galvanize
 galvanizes
 galvanized
 galvanizing
galvanometer
galvanotropic
galvanotropism
Galway
✗ galy = gaily
gam
gambado
 gambados or
 gambadoes
Gambia
gambit
gamble (= play
 games of chance
 → gambol)
gambles

gambled
gambling
gamboge
gambogian
gambol (= frolic
 → gamble)
gambols
gambolled
gambolling
game
games
gamed
gaming
gamekeeper
gamelan
gamely
gameness
gamesmanship
gamesome
gamester
gamete
gametic
gametogenesis
gametophyte
gamey
gamier
gamiest
gamic
gamin
gamine
gaming
gamma
gammon
gammy
gamp
gamut
gamy
gamier
gamiest
gander

Gandhi
Gandhian
gang
  gangs
  ganged
  ganging
ganger
gangling
ganglion
gangrene
gangrenous
gangster
gangue
gangway
ganister
ganja
gannet
gannister
gantlet
gantline
gantry
  gantries
gaol
  gaols
  gaoled
  gaoling
gap
gape
  gapes
  gaped
  gaping
gaper
garage
  garages
  garaged
  garaging
✗ garantee =
  guarantee
✗ garantor =
  guarantor

garb
garbs
garbed
garbing
garbage
garble
garbles
garbled
garbling
garboard
garçon
✗ gard = guard
gardaí
✗ garded = guarded
garden
gardens
gardened
gardening
gardener
gardenia
✗ gardian = guardian
✗ gardsman =
  guardsman
garfish
gargantuan
garget
gargle
gargles
gargled
gargling
gargoyle
garibaldi
garish
garland
garlic
garlicky
garlickier
garlickiest
garment
garner

garners
garnered
garnering
garnet
garnierite
garnish
garnishes
garnished
garnishing
garnishee
garnishment
garniture
garotte
garottes
garotted
garotting
garotter
garpike
garret
garrison
garrisons
garissoned
garissoning
✗ garrit = garret
garron
garrotte
garrottes
garrotted
garrotting
garrotter
garrulity
garrulous
garter
garth
gas
gasses
gassed
gassing
gas
gases *or*

gasses
gasconade
gaselier
gaseous
gash
gashes
gashed
gashing
✗ gasius = gaseous
gasiform
gasify
gasifies
gasified
gasifying
gasket
gaskin
gasolene
gasoline
gasometer
gasp
gasps
gasped
gasping
gasper
gassed
gasser
gasses
gassing
gassy
gassier
gassiest
gasteropod
✗ gastly = ghastly
gastrectomy
gastric
gastritic
gastritis
gastroenterology
gastroenterostomy
gastronome

gastronomic
gastronomy
gastropod
gastropodan
gastropodous
gastroscope
gastroscopy
gat
gate (= barrier
→ gait)
gates
gated
gating
gateau
gateaux or
gateaus
gatepost
gateway
gather
gathers
gathered
gathering
✗ gato = gateau
gauche
gaucho
gauchos
gaudy
gaudier
gaudiest
gauffer
gauffers
gauffered
gauffering
gauge
gauges
gauged
gauging
gauger
Gauguin, Paul
Gauleiter

Gaullism
gault
gaunt
gauntlet
gauntry
gauntries
gaup
gaups
gauped
gauping
gauss
gaussmeter
gauze
gauzy
gauzier
gauziest
gave
gavel
gavotte
gavottes
gavotted
gavotting
gawk
gawks
gawked
gawking
gawky
gawkier
gawkiest
gawp
gawps
gawped
gawping
gay
gayer
gayest
✗ gayety = gaiety
✗ gayly = gaily
gaze
gazes

gazed
gazing
gazebo
  gazebos *or*
  gazeboes
gazelle
gazette
  gazettes
  gazetted
  gazetting
gazetteer
gazpacho
gazump
  gazumps
  gazumped
  gazumping
  gazumper
GCHQ
GCSE
geanticlinal
geanticline
gear
  gears
  geared
  gearing
gearing
gearshift
gecko
  geckos *or*
  geckoes
gee
  gees
  geed
  geeing
✗ gee = ghee
gee-gee
geek
geese
geisha
  geishas *or*

geisha
gel
  gels
  gelled
  gelling
gelatin
gelatine
gelatinisation
gelatinise
  gelatinises
  gelatinised
  gelatinising
gelatinization
gelatinize
  gelatinizes
  gelatinized
  gelatinizing
gelatinoid
gelatinous
gelation
geld
  gelds
  gelded
  gelding
gelding
gelid
gelidity
gelignite
  gelled
  gelling
✗ gelore = galore
✗ geloshes = galoshes
  or goloshes
gelsemium
✗ gelumf = galumph
gem
  gems
  gemmed
  gemming
gemfish

gemfish *or*
gemfishes
geminate
  geminates
  geminated
  geminating
gemination
Gemini
gemma
gemmate
gemmation
gemmiferous
gemmiparous
gemmological
gemmologist
gemmology
gemological
gemologist
gemology
gemsbok
gen
  gens
  genned
  genning
gendarme
gendarmerie
gender
gene
genealogical
genealogy
genera
generable
general
generalisation
generalise
  generalises
  generalised
  generalising
generalist
generality

generalization
generalize
  generalizes
  generalized
  generalizing
generally
generate
  generates
  generated
  generating
generation
generative
generator
generic
generically
generosity
generous
genesis
genet
genetic
genetically
geneticist
genetics
genial
geniality
✗ genialogical =
  genealogical
✗ genialogy =
  genealogy
genic
genicular
geniculate
geniculation
genie
  genies
genii
genital
genitalia
genitals
genitival

genitive
genitor
genius
  geniuses
genom
genome
genotype
genre
gent
genteel
genteelly
genteelness
gentian
gentile
gentilesse
gentility
gentle
gentleman
  gentlemen
gentleness
gentlewoman
  gentlewomen
gentrification
gentrify
  gentrifies
  gentrified
  gentrifying
gentry
  gentries
gents
genuflect
genuine
genus
  genera *or*
  genuses
geocentric
geochronology
geode
geodesic
geodesy

geodetic
geodic
geodynamics
Geoffrey
geognostic
geognosy
geographer
geographical
geographically
geography
geoid
geological
geologically
geologist
geology
geomagnetic
geomagnetism
geometric
geometrical
geomtrically
geometry
geophagist
geophagous
geophagy
geophysics
geophyte
geophytic
geopolitical
geopolitics
geoponic
geoponics
Geordie
George
georgette
Georgia
Georgian
geoscience
geosphere
geostatic
geostatics

gibes

geostrophic
geotaxis
geotectonic
geothermal
geotropic
geotropism
geranium
   geraniums
gerbil
gerfalcon
geriatric
geriatrician
geriatrics
✗ gerilla = gorilla *or*
   guerrilla
✗ gerkin = gherkin
germ
German
germane
germanely
germaneness
Germanic
germanium
Germanophile
Germanophobe
Germany
germicide
germinal
germinant
germinate
   germinates
   germinated
   germinating
gerontic
gerontocracy
gerontocratic
gerontological
gerontology
gerrymander
   gerrymanders

gerrymandered
gerrymandering
gerund
gerundial
gerundival
gerundive
✗ gess = guess
gesso
✗ gest = guest
Gestalt
Gestapo
gestate
   gestates
   gestated
   gestating
gestation
gestative
gesticulate
   gesticulates
   gesticulated
   gesticulating
gesticulation
gesticulator
gesticulatory
gesture
   gestures
   gestured
   gesturing
get
   gets
   got
   getting
get-at-able
getter
✗ getto = ghetto
geum
gewgaw
geyser
G-force
Ghana

ghastly
ghastlier
ghastliest
ghee
gherkin
ghetto
   ghettos *or*
   ghettoes
ghillie
ghost
   ghosts
   ghosted
   ghosting
ghostly
   ghostlier
   ghostliest
ghostwrite
ghoul
GHQ
gi *try* gui
GI
giant
giantess
giantism
giardiasis
gib
   gibs
   gibbed
   gibbing
gibber
   gibbers
   gibbered
   gibbering
gibberish
gibbet
gibbon
gibbosity
gibbous
gibe
   gibes

gibed
gibing
giblets
giddy
giddier
giddiest
✗gie = guy
gift
gifts
gifted
gifting
giftwrap
gig
gigs
gigged
gigging
gigahertz
gigantic
gigantically
giganticness
giggle
giggles
giggled
giggling
GIGO
gigolo
gigolos
gigot
gigue
gilbert
Gilbertian
gild
gilds
gilded or gilt
gilding
gilet
gill
gilled
✗gilleteen =
guillotine

gillie
gilliflower
✗gillimot = guillemot
gillion
gillyflower
gilt (= gold paint
→ guilt)
gimbals
gimcrack
gimlet
gimlet-eyed
gimmick
gin
gins
ginned
ginning
ginger
gingerbread
gingerly
gingery
ginerier
gingeriest
gingham
gingiva
gingival
gingivitis
ginkgo
ginned
ginning
ginormous
ginseng
Gioconda
gip
gips
gipped
gipping
gipsy
giraffe
girandole
girasol

gird
girds
girded or
girt
girding
girder
girdle
girdles
girdled
girdling
girl
girlfriend
girlhood
girlish
giro
giros
giron
girosol
girt
girth
gismo
gismos
gist
git
give
gives
gave
given
giving
giveaway
gizmo
gizzard
glabella
glabellar
glabrescent
glabrous
glacé
glacial
glaciate
glaciates

glaciated
glaciating
glacier
glad
gladder
gladdest
gladden
gladdens
gladdened
gladdening
glade
gladiator
gladiatorial
gladiolus
gladioli *or*
gladioluses
gladsome
Glamorgan
glamorise
glamorises
glamorising
glamorised
glamorous
glamorize
glamorizes
glamorized
glamorizing
glamour
glance
glances
glanced
glancing
gland
glanders
glandular
glandule
glans
glandes
glare
glares

glared
glaring
Glasgow
✗glashel = glacial
glass
glasses
✗glassay = glacée
glassful
glassfuls
✗glassier = glacier
glassware
glassy
glassier
glassiest
Glaswegian
glaucoma
glaucomatous
glaucous
glaze
glazes
glazed
glazing
glazier
gleam
gleams
gleamed
gleaming
glean
gleans
gleaned
gleaning
glebe
glee
gleeful
gleet
glen
Glenrothes
gley
glib
glibly

glide
glides
glided
gliding
glider
glimmer
glimmers
glimmered
glimmering
glimpse
glint
glints
glinted
glinting
glissade
glissades
glissaded
glissading
glissando
glisten
glistens
glistened
glistering
glister
glitch
✗glitsy = glitzy
glitter
glitters
glittered
glittering
glitterati
glitz
glitzy
glitzier
glitziest
gloaming
gloat
gloats
gloated
gloating

glob
global
globalisation
globalization
globate
globe
globetrotter
globin
globoid
globose
globosity
globular
globularity
globule
globulin
globus
glockenspiel
gloom
gloomy
  gloomier
  gloomiest
glorification
glorify
  glorifies
  glorified
  glorifying
gloriole
glorious
glory
  glories
  gloried
  glorying
gloss
  glosses
  glossed
  glossing
glossarial
glossary
  glossaries
glossitis

glossolalia
glossy
  glossier
  glossiest
glottal
glottic
glottis
Gloucester
✗ gloucoma =
  glaucoma
glove
  gloves
  gloved
  gloving
glover
glow
  glows
  glowed
  glowing
glower
  glowers
  glowered
  glowering
gloxinia
glucose
glucosic
glucoside
glue
  glues
  glued
  gluing
glum
  glummer
  glummest
glut
  gluts
  glutted
  glutting
glutaeal
glutamate

glutamine
gluten
gluteus
  glutei
glutinosity
glutinous
glutton
gluttony
glyceric
glyceride
glycerin
glycerine
glycerol
glyceryl
glycine
glycogen
glycol
glycolic
glycose
glycoside
glycosidic
glyph
glyptal
glyptic
glyptics
G-man
GMT
gnarled
gnash
  gnashes
  gnashed
  gnashing
gnat
gnathic
gnathite
gnaw
  gnaws
  gnawed
  gnawed *or*
  gnawn

gnawing
gneiss
gnocchi
gnome
gnomic
gnomon
gnomonic
gnosis
gnostic
Gnosticism
gnotobiotics
gnu
   gnus
go
   goes
   went
   gone
   going
goa
goad
   goads
   goaded
   goading
goal
goalie
goalkeeper
✗ goash = gauche
goat
goatee
goatherd
goatish
goatskin
gob
   gobs
   gobbed
   gobbing
gobbet
gobble
   gobbles
   gobbled

gobbling
gobbledegook
gobbledygook
gobbler
goblet
goblin
gobo
   gobos or
   goboes
gobsmacked
gobstopper
goby
   gobies
go-by
god
God
Godalming
godchild
goddamn
goddaughter
✗ goddauter =
   goddaughter
goddess
   goddesses
godet
godetia
godfather
God-fearing
godforsaken
godless
godlike
godly
godmother
godparent
godsend
godson
goer
goes
gofer
goffer

go-getter
goggle
   goggles
   goggled
   goggling
go-go
✗ gographer =
   geographer
✗ gography =
   geography
going
going-over
   goings-over
goitre
go-kart
gold
goldcrest
gold-digger
golden
goldenrod
goldfinch
   goldfinches
goldfish
goldfish or
   goldfishes
goldilocks
goldsmith
golf
   golfs
   golfed
   golfing
golfer
Golgotha
Goliath
golliwog
golly
goloshes
✗ gometry = geometry
gonad
gonadic

gonadotrophin
✗ gondarm =
gendarme
gondola
gondolas
gondolier
Gondwanaland
gone
goner
gong
goniometer
gonococcus
gonococci
gonocyte
gonopod
gonorrhoea
gonosome
✗ gonre = genre
goo
goober
good
better
best
goodbye
goodbyes
good-humoured
goodies
good-looking
goodly
good-natured
goodness
goods
good-sized
good-tempered
goodwill
goody
goody-goody
gooey
gooier
gooiest

goof
goofy
goofier
goofiest
googly
googlies
googol
✗ gool = ghoul
gook
gooly
goolies
goon
✗ goord = gourd
✗ goormay = gourmet
✗ goormond =
gourmand
goosander
goose
geese
goose
gooses
goosed
goosing
gooseberry
gooseberries
goosefoot
goosegrass
goose-step
✗ gooy = gooey
gopher
Gorbachev, Mikhail
✗ gord = gourd
gore
gores
gored
goring
gorge
gorgeous
gorgeously
Gorgio

Gorgios
gorgon
Gorgonzola (cheese)
gorilla (= animal →
guerrilla)
gormand
gormandise
gormandises
gormandised
gormandising
gormandize
gormandizes
gormandized
gormandizing
gormless
gorse
gory
gorier
goriest
gosh
goshawk
✗ goshe = gauche
gosling
gospel
gospeller
gossamer
gossip
gossips
gossiped
gossiping
gossipmonger
✗ gost = ghost
got
Gothic
Götterdämmerung
gouache
✗ gouash = gouache
gouge
gouges
gouged

gouging
gouger
goujon
goulash
gourd
gourmand
gourmandise
  gourmandises
  gourmandised
  gourmandising
gourmandize
  gourmandizes
  gourmandized
  gourmandizing
gourmet
gout
✗ goverment =
  government
govern
  governs
  governed
  governing
governance
governess
government
governmental
governor
gown
  gowns
  gowned
  gowning
goy
  goyim or
  goys
grab
  grabs
  grabbed
  grabbing
graben
grace

graces
graced
gracing
graceful
graceless
gracious
gradable
gradation
grade
grades
graded
grading
grader
gradient
gradual
gradualism
graduand
graduate
  graduates
  graduated
  graduating
graduation
graffitist
graffito
graffiti
graft
  grafts
  grafted
  grafting
Graham
grail
grain
graining
grainy
  grainier
  grainiest
gram
grama
✗ gramaphone =
  gramophone

graminaceous
gramineous
graminicolous
graminivorous
grammar
grammarian
grammatical
grammatically
grammaticalness
gramme
gramophone
gramophonic
grampus
  grampuses
gran
granadilla
granary
  granaries
grand
  grander
  grandest
grandam
✗ grandauter =
  granddaughter
grandaunt
grandchild
granddad
granddaughter
grandee
grandeur
grandfather
grandfatherly
grandiloquence
grandiloquent
grandiloquently
grandiose
grandiosity
grandma
grandmaster
grandmother

grandmotherly
grandnephew
grandniece
grandpa
grandparent
grandsire
grandson
grandstand
granduncle
grange
granite
granitic
granitite
granivore
granivorous
grannie
granny
  grannies
grant
  grants
  granted
  granting
grantee
grantor
granular
granularity
granulate
  granulates
  granulated
  granulating
granulation
granule
granulite
granulitic
granulomatous
grape
grapefruit
  grapefruits
grapeshot
grapevine

graph
graphic
  graphically *or*
  graphicly
graphics
graphite
graphitic
graphologist
graphology
grapnel
grappa
grapple
  grapples
  grappled
  grappling
grasp
  grasps
  grasped
  grasping
grass
  grasses
  grassed
  grassing
grasshopper
grassland
grassy
  grassier
  grassiest
grate (= rub into
  small pieces; fire-
  place → great)
  grates
  grated
  grating
grateful
  gratefully
grater
gratification
gratify
gratifies

gratified
gratifying
gratin
gratis
gratitude
gratuitous
gratuitously
gratuitousness
gratuity
  gratuities
gratulate
  gratulates
  gratulated
  gratulation
gravadlax
grave
gravel
gravelly
graven
gravestone
graveyard
gravid
gravidity
gravitate
  gravitates
  gravitated
  gravitating
gravitation
gravitational
gravity
gravlax
gravure
gravy
  gravies
✗gray = grey
✗grayhound =
  greyhound
graylag
✗grayness = greyness
graze

grazes
grazed
grazing
grazier
grease
greases
greased
greasing
greasepaint
greaser
greasewood
greasy
greasier
greasiest
great (= very large/
good → grate)
greater
greatest
great-aunt
greatcoat
great-hearted
great-nephew
great-niece
great-uncle
grebe
Grecian
Greco-Roman
✗ gredation =
gradation
Greece
greed
greedy
greedier
greediest
greegree
Greek
green
greenback
Greene, Graham
greenery

greenfield
greenfinch
greenfinches
greenfly
greenflies
greengage
greengrocer
greenhorn
greenhouse
greening
greenroom
greenshank
Greenwich
greenwood
✗ greshen = Grecian
greet
greets
greeted
greeting
greetings-card
gregarious
gregariously
gregariousness
Gregorian
greisen
gremlin
grenade
grenadier
grew
grey
greyer
greyest
greyhound
greylag
greywacke
gricer
griddle
gridiron
gridlock
grief

Grieg, Edvard
✗ griere = Gruyère
grievance
grieve
grieves
grieved
grieving
grievous
griffin
grigri
grill (= on cooker
→ grille)
grills
grilled
grilling
grille (= screen
→ grill)
grilse
grim
grimmer
grimmest
grimace
grimaces
grimaced
grimacing
grimacer
grimalkin
grime
✗ grimice = grimace
Grimsby
grin
grins
grinned
grinning
grind
grinds
ground
grinding
grinder
grindstone

gringo
  gringos
grip
  grips
  gripped
  gripping
gripe
  gripes
  griped
  griping
grippe
griseous
gris-gris
grisly (= horrible
  → grizzly)
  grislier
  grisliest
grison
grist
gristle
grit
  grits
  gritted
  gritting
gritter
gritty
  grittier
  grittiest
✗ griyere = Gruyère
grizzle
  grizzles
  grizzled
  grizzling
grizzly (= bear
  → grisly)
  grizzlier
  grizzliest
groan
  groans
  groaned

groaning
groat
grocer
groceries
grocery
grog
groggy
  groggier
  groggiest
groin
groom
  grooms
  groomed
  grooming
groomsman
  groomsmen
groove
  grooves
  grooved
  grooving
groovy
  groovier
  grooviest
grope
  gropes
  groped
  groping
groper
grosbeak
✗ grose = gross
grosgrain
gross
  grosses
  grossed
  grossing
grot
grotesque
grotesquely
grotesqueness
grotto

grottoes or
  grottos
grotty
  grottier
  grottiest
grouch
  grouches
  grouched
  grouching
grouchy
  grouchier
  grouchiest
ground
  grounds
  grounded
  grounding
groundage
grounding
groundless
groundnut
groundsel
groundsheet
groundsman
  groundsmen
groundwork
group
  groups
  grouped
  grouping
grouper
groupie
grouse
  grouse
grouse
  grouses
  groused
  grousing
grout
  grouts
  grouted

grouting
grove
grovel
  grovels
  grovelled
  grovelling
grow
  grows
  grew
  grown
  growing
grower
growl
  growls
  growled
  growling
growler
grown-up
  grown-ups
growth
groyne
grub
  grubs
  grubbed
  grubbing
grubby
  grubbier
  grubbiest
grudge
  grudges
  grudged
  grudging
gruel
gruelling
gruesome
gruff
  gruffly
grumble
  grumbles
  grumbled

grumbling
grummet
grump
grumpy
  grumpier
  grumpiest
grunt
  grunts
  grunted
  grunting
grunter
Gruyère (cheese)
gryphon
grysbok
G-string
G-suit
guacamole
Guadalajara
guanaco
  guanacos
guano
guar
guarantee
  guarantees
  guaranteed
  guaranteeing
guarantor
guaranty
  guaranties
guard
  guards
  guarded
  guarding
guardee
guardian
Guatemala
guava
guayule
gubbins
gubernatorial

gudgeon
guelder-rose
guerilla
guerrilla (= terrorist
  → gorilla)
guerrillaism
guess
  guesses
  guessed
  guessing
guesstimate
guesswork
guest
guffaw
  guffaws
  guffawed
  guffawing
guidance
guide
  guides
  guided
  guiding
guidebook
guideline
guild (= association
  → gild)
guilder
Guildford
guildhall
guile
guileless
guillemot
guillotine
  guillotines
  guillotined
  guillotining
guilt (= blame
  → gilt)
guiltless
guilty

guiltier
guiltiest
guimpe
guinea
Guinea
guipure
Guisborough
guise
guitar
guitarist
Gujarati
gulf
gull
gullet
gullible
gully
   gullies
gulp
   gulps
   gulped
   gulping
gum
   gums
   gummed
   gumming
gumboots
gumbotil
gummite
gummy
   gummier
   gummiest
gumption
gumshield
gumshoe
gumtree
gun
   guns
   gunned
   gunning
gunboat

gunfight
gunfire
gunge
gungey
gungier
gungiest
gunk
gunman
gunmen
gunmetal
gunnel
✗ gunnel = gunwhale
gunner
gunnery
   gunneries
gunpoint
gunpowder
gunrunning
gun-shy
gunslinger
gunsmith
gunwale
guppy
   guppies
gurgitation
gurgle
   gurgles
   gurgled
   gurgling
gurjun
✗ gurka = Ghurka
Gurkha
Gurkhali
gurnard
guru
   gurus
gush
   gushes
   gushed
   gushing

gusher
gushy
   gushier
   gushiest
gusset
gust
   gusts
   gusted
   gusting
gustation
gustatory
gusto
gusty
   gustier
   gustiest
gut
gutless
guts
gutsy
   gutsier
   gutsiest
gutta-percha
gutted
gutter
guttering
guttersnipe
guttural
guv
guy
guyot
guzzle
   guzzles
   guzzled
   guzzling
Gwent
Gwynedd
gybe
   gybes
   gybed
   gybing

gym
gymkhana
  gymkhanas
gymnasium
  gymnasiums *or*
  gymnasia
gymnast
gymnastic
gymnastically
gymnastics
gymslip
gynaecological
gynaecology
gynandrous
gynandry
✗ gynecological =
  gynaecological
✗ gynecology =
  gynaecology
✗ gynicological =
  gynaecological
✗ gynicology =
  gynaecology
gynodioecious
gynomonoecious
gyp
  gyps
  gypped
  gypping
gypsum
gypsy
gyral
gyrate
  gyrates
  gyrated
  gyrating
gyration
gyrator
gyratory
gyrfalcon

gyrocompass
gyroscope
gyroscopic

H

haberdasher
haberdashery
habiliment
habilitate
habilitation
habit
habitable
habitant
habitat
habitation
habitual
habitually
habitualness
habituate
  habituates
  habituated
  habituating
habituation
habitué
✗ habius corpus =
  habeus corpus
hack
  hacks
  hacked
  hacking
hacker
hackles
hackney
hackneyed
hacksaw
had
hadal

haddock
Hades
Haiti
hadj
  hadjes
hadji
hadjis
hadron
hadrosaur
hadst
haem
haemal
haematic
haematite
haematoid
haematology
haematoma
  haematomas *or*
  haematomata
haematuria
haemodialysis
haemoglobin
haemolysis
haemolytic
haemophile
haemophilia
haemophiliac
haemophilic
haemopoiesis
haemorrhage
  haemorrhages
haemorrhage
  haemorrhages
  haemorrhaged
  haemorrhaging
haemostasis
hafnium
haft
hag
hagfish

hagfish *or*
  hagfishes
Haggadah
haggard
haggis
haggis
haggle
haggles
haggled
haggling
hagiarchy
hagiocracy
hagiographer
hagiographic
hagiography
hagiolatry
hagiologic
hagiology
hah
ha-ha
hahnium
haiku
hail (= frozen rain
  → hale)
hails
hailed
hailing
hailstone
hair (= on the head
  → hare)
hairbrained
hairdo
hairdos
hairdresser
hairless
hairpiece
hair-raising
hair's-breadth
hairsplitting
hairstyle

hairy
hairier
hairiest
Haitian
hajj
  hajjes
hake
halal
halation
halberd
halcyon
halcyonic
hale
hales
haled
haling
haler
half (= segment
  → halve)
half-a-crown
half-baked
half-brother
half-caste
half-cock
half-cocked
half-hearted
half-hour
half-inch
half-length
half-marathon
half-mast
half-nelson
halfpenny
halfpennyworth
half-price
half-sister
half-size
half-timbered
half-truth
half-volley

halfway
halfwit
halibut
halide
halite
halitosis
hall
halleluiah
Halley (comet)
hallelujah
halliard
hallmark
hallo
　hallos
halloo
　halloos
　hallooed
　hallooing
hallow
　hallows
　hallowed
　hallowing
Halloween
Hallowe'en
hallucinate
　hallucinates
　hallucinated
　hallucinating
hallucination
hallucinator
hallucinatory
hallucinogen
hallucinogenic
hallux
hallway
halma
halo
　haloes *or*
　halos
halogen

haloid
halophyte
halophytic
halothane
halt
　halts
　halted
　halting
halter
halva
halvah
halve (= divide in
　two → half)
　halves
　halved
　halving
halves
halyard
ham
　hams
　hammed
　hamming
hamadryad
hamartiology
hamburger
hame
ham-fisted
ham-handed
Hamitic
hamlet
hammer
　hammers
　hammered
　hammering
hammertoe
hamming
hammock
hamper
　hampers
　hampered

hampering
hamster
hamstring
　hamstrings
　hamstrung
　hamstringing
hand
　hands
　handed
　handing
handbarrow
handbrake
handbreadth
handcart
handcraft
handcrafted
handcuff
handedness
Handel, George Fre-
　derick
handful
　handfuls
handicap
　handicaps
　handicapped
　handicapping
handicraft
handier
handiest
handily
handiwork
handkerchief
handle
　handles
　handled
　handling
handlebars
handler
handsaw
hand's-breadth

handshake
handshaking
handsome
hand-to-hand
hand-to-mouth
handwriting
handwritten
handy
  handier
  handiest
handyman
hang
  hangs
  hanged *or*
  hung
  hanging
hangar (= for
  planes → hanger)
hanged (= killed by
  rope → hung)
hanger (= for
  clothes → hangar)
hanger-on
  hangers-on
hangman
hangnail
hangover
  hangovers
hang-up
  hang-ups
hank
hanker
  hankers
  hankered
  hankering
hankie
  hankies
hanky
  hankies
hanky-panky

Hanoi
Hanover
Hanoverian
Hansard
Hanseatic
hansom
Hanukkah
ha'penny
haphazard
haphazardly
haphazardness
hapless
haploid
haplont
haply
ha'p'orth
happen
  happens
  happened
  happening
happenstance
happy
  happier
  happiest
happy-go-lucky
hapteron
haptic
hara-kiri
harangue
  harangues
  harangued
  haranguing
  haranguer
Harare
harass
  harasses
  harassed
  harassing
harbinger
harbour

harbours
harboured
harbouring
harbourage
hard
hard-bitten
hardboard
hard-boiled
harden
  hardens
  hardened
  hardening
hardener
hard-hitting
hardihood
hardily
hardiness
hardly
hardness
hard-pressed
hardship
hardware
hardwood
hardy
  hardier
  hardiest
hare (= animal
  → hair)
harebell
harebrained
harelip
harem
hare's-foot
✗ harf = half
haricot
hari-kari
✗ harikiri = hara kiri
hark
harken
  harkens

harkened

harkening

harl

  harls

  harled

  harling

Harlech

harlequin

harlequinade

harlot

harm

  harms

  harmed

  harming

harmattan

harmful

  harmfully

harmless

harmonic

harmonica

harmonically

harmonics

harmonious

  harmoniously

harmonisation

harmonise

  harmonises

  harmonised

  harmonising

harmoniser

harmonist

harmonium

harmonization

harmonize

  harmonizes

  harmonized

  harmonizing

harmonizer

harmony

  harmonies

harmotome

harness

  harnesses

  harnessed

  harnessing

harp

  harps

  harped

  harping

harpoon

  harpoons

  harpooned

  harpooning

harpooner

harpsichord

harpy

  harpies

harridan

harrier

harrow

  harrows

  harrowed

  harrowing

✗ harve = halve

harrumph

  harrumphs

  harrumphed

  harrumphing

harry

  harries

  harried

  harrying

harsh

  harsher

  harshest

hart try heart

hart (= deer
→ heart)

hartebeest

hartshorn

harum-scarum

harvest

  harvests

  harvested

  harvesting

harvester

Harwich

has

has-been

✗ hasen = hasten

hash

  hashes

  hashed

  hashing

hashish

Haslemere

haslet

hasn't

hasp

hassle

  hassles

  hassled

  hassling

hassock

hast

hastate

haste

hasten

  hastens

  hastened

  hastening

hasty

  hastier

  hastiest

hat

hatch

  hatches

  hatched

  hatching

hatchback

hatchery
   hatcheries
hatchet
hatchment
hatchway
hate
   hates
   hated
   hating
hateful
hath
hatred
hatted
hatter
hauberk
haughty
   haughtier
   haughtiest
haul
   hauls
   hauled
   hauling
haulage
haulier
haulm
haunch
   haunches
   haunched
haunt
   haunts
   haunted
   haunting
haustellum
haustorium
hauteur
✗ hauty = haughty
have
   has
   had
   having

✗ havec = havoc
have
haves
haven
have-not
haven't
haver
   havers
   havered
   havering
haversack
haversine
havildar
havoc
haw
   haws
   hawed
   hawing
Hawaii
Hawaiian
haw-haw
hawk
   hawks
   hawked
   hawking
hawker
hawk-eyed
hawkweed
hawse
   hawses
   hawsed
   hawsing
hawser
hawthorn
hay
haybox
haycock
✗ hayday = heyday
Haydn, Franz Josef
hayfork

haymaking
haymaker
hayseed
haystack
haywire
hazard
   hazards
   hazarded
   hazarding
hazardous
haze
hazel
hazelhen
hazelnut
hazy
   hazier
   haziest
H-bomb
he
head
   heads
   headed
   heading
headache
headband
headboard
head-butt
   head-butts
   head-butted
   head-butting
headcase
headdress
header
headfirst
headgear
head-hunting
heading
headland
headless
headlight

headline
headlock
headlong
headman
headmen
headmaster
headmistress
headmistresses
headmost
headphones
headpiece
headquarters
headrace
headrest
headroom
headscarf
headset
headship
headstone
headstrong
headwaters
headway
headwind
heady
heador
headier
headiest
heal (= get better
→ heel)
heals
healed
healing
heal-all
health
healthful
healthy
healthier
healthiest
heap
heaps
heaped

heaping
hear (= listen
→ here)
hears
heard
hearing
hearken
hearkens
hearkened
hearkening
hearsay
hearse
heart (= body organ
→ hart)
heartache
heartbeat
heartbreaking
heartbroken
heartburn
hearten
heartens
heartened
heartening
heartfelt
hearth
hearthstone
heartier
heartiest
heartily
heartland
heartless
heart-rending
heartsease
heart's-ease
heartstrings
heart-throb
heart-to-heart
hearty
heartier
heartiest

heat
heats
heated
heating
heater
heath
heathberry
heathberries
heathen
heathendom
heathenish
heather
heathfowl
heating
heatstroke
heave
heaves
heaved
heaving
heave-ho
heaven
heavenly
heaven-sent
heavenward
heavenwards
heavily
heavy
heavier
heaviest
heavy-duty
heavy-footed
heavy-handed
heavy-hearted
heavyweight
Hebraic
Hebraism
Hebraist
Hebrew
heck
heckle

heckles
heckled
heckling
hectare
hectic
hectolitre
hectometre
hector
hectors
hectored
hectoring
Hecuba
he'd
hedge
hedges
hedged
hedging
hedgehog
hedgerow
hedonic
hedonics
hedonism
heebie-jeebies
heed
heeds
heeded
heeding
heedless
heehaw
heel (= part of shoe
→ heal)
heels
heeled
heeling
heelpiece
heeltap
✗heffer = heifer
hefty
heftier
heftiest

hegemonic
hegemony
Hegira
hegumen
heh
he-he
heifer
heigh-ho
height
heighten
heightens
heightened
heightening
heinous
heir (= inheritor
→ air)
heirdom
heiress
heiresses
heirloom
heirship
Hejira
held
helenium
helianthemum
helianthus
helical
helices
helicline
helicograph
helicoid
helicopter
heliocentric
heliocentricism
heliocentricity
heliograph
heliographer
heliographic
heliolatry
heliophyte

heliosphere
heliostat
heliotactic
heliotaxis
heliotrope
heliotropic
heliotropism
helipad
heliport
helium
helix
helices or
helixes
hell
he'll
Hellas
hellbent
hellcat
hellebore
Hellenic
Hellenism
Hellenist
Hellenistic
hellfire
hellhole
hellhound
hellish
hello
hellos
✗hallucinate =
hallucinate
✗hallucinogen =
hallucinogen
helluva
helm
helminth
helminthiasis
helminthic
helminthoid
helmsman

help
  helps
  helped
  helping
helpful
helping
helpless
helpline
helpmate
helpmeet
helter-skelter
Helvetian
Helvetic
Helvetii
hem
  hems
  hemmed
  hemming
✗ hemafilia =
  haemophilia
✗ hemaglobin =
  haemoglobin
hemal
✗ hemaphilia =
  haemophilia
✗ hematologist =
  haematologist
he-man
Hemel Hempstead
✗ hemerage =
  haemorrhage
hemichordate
hemicycle
hemicyclic
hemihedral
hemihydrate
hemimorphic
Hemingway, Ernest
hemiola
hemiolic

hemiplegia
hemipteran
hemipteron
hemipterous
hemisphere
hemispheric
hemispheroid
hemistich
hemitrope
hemizygous
hemline
hemlock
hemmed
hemmer
hemming
hemo- (see haemo)
✗ homogenaity =
  homogeneity
✗ hemorage =
  haemorrhage
hemp
hen
henbane
henbit
hence
henceforth
henchman
  henchmen
hencoop
hendecagon
hendecagonal
hendecahedron
hendecasyllabic
hendecasyllable
hendiadys
henequen
henequin
heniquen
henge
henna

hennery
  henneries
henotheism
henpeck
  henpecks
  henpecked
  henpecking
henry
  henries or
  henrys
hep
heparin
hepatic
hepatica
hepatitis
Hepplewhite
heptad
heptagon
heptagonal
heptahedron
heptamerous
heptameter
heptane
heptangular
heptarchal
heptarchic
heptarchy
Heptateuch
heptathlete
heptathlon
heptavalent
heptose
her
herald
  heralds
  heralded
  heralding
heraldic
heraldically
heraldry

herb
herbs
herbed
herbing
herbaceous
herbage
herbal
herbalist
herbarial
herbarium
herbicide
herbivore
herbivorous
herbivorousness
herby
herbier
herbiest
Hercegovina
herculean
Hercules
Hercynian
herd
herds
herded
hering
herder
herdsman
herdsmen
here (= in this place
→ hear)
hereabouts
hereafter
hereat
hereby
hereditability
hereditable
hereditarily
hereditariness
hereditary
hereditist

heredity
herein
hereinafter
hereinbefore
hereinto
hereof
hereon
heresy
heresies
heretic
heretical
heretically
hereto
heretofore
hereunder
hereunto
hereupon
herewith
heritable
heritage
heritor
heritress
hermaphrodite
hermaphroditic
hermaphrodistical
hermaphroditism
hermeneutic
hermeneutics
hermetic
hermetically
hermit
hermitage
hermitic
hermitical
hermitically
hernia
hero
heroes
heroic
heroically

heroicalness
heroicness
heroics
heroin (= drug)
heroine (= hero)
heroism
heron
heronry
heronries
hero-worship
herpes
herpetic
herpetologic
herpetology
herring
herringbone
hers
herself
hertz
he's
hesitant
hesitate
hesitates
hesitated
hesitating
hesperidin
hesperidium
hessian
hetero
heterocercal
heterochromatic
heterochromosome
heterochromous
heteroclite
heterocyclic
heterodactyl
heterodont
heterodox
heterodyne
heteroecious

heterogamete	hexachord	hiccough
heterogametic	hexad	hiccoughs
heterogamy	hexadecimal	hiccoughed
heterogeneity	hexadic	hiccoughing
heterogeneous	hexaemeron	hiccup
heterogenous	hexagon	hiccups
heterogony	hexagonal	hiccuped *or*
heterogynous	hexagonally	hiccupped
heterokaryon	hexagram	hiccuping *or*
heterologous	hexahedron	hiccupping
heteromerous	hexamerism	hick
heteromorphic	hexamerous	hickey
heteronomous	hexameter	hickory
heteronym	hexametric	hickories
heteronymous	hexangular	hid
heterophony	hexapod	hidden
heterophyllous	hexapodic	hide
heterophyte	hexapody	hides
heteroploid	hexastyle	hid
heteropterous	Hexateuch	hidden
heterosexism	hexavalent	hiding
heterosexual	hexose	hide-and-seek
heterosexuality	hexyl	hideaway
heterosporous	hey	hidebound
heterostyly	heyday	hideosity
heterotaxis	HGV	hideous
heterotopic	hi *try* high	hideousness
heterotrophic	hi	hide-out
heterozygote	hiatal	hidey-hole
heterozygous	hiatus	✘hidius = hideous
heuristic	hiatuses	hie
heuristically	hibachi	hies
heuristics	hibernaculum	hied
hew (= cut down	hibernal	hieing *or*
→ hue)	hibernate	hying
hews	hibernates	✘hiefer = heifer
hewed *or*	hibernated	✘hieght = height
hewn	hibernating	hierarch
hewing	hibiscus	✘hierarcial =
hex	hic	hierarchial

✗ hierarcy = hierarchy
hierarchy
hieratic
hierocracy
hierocratic
✗ hieroglyphics =
   hieroglyphics
hieroglyphic
hieroglyphics
hieroglyphist
hierogram
hifalutin
hi-fi
higgledy-piggledy
high
   higher
   highest
highball
highbrow
higher (= further up
   → hire)
higher-up
highfalutin
high-flier
high-flown
high-flyer
Highland
Highlander
highlife
highlight
highly
highness
Highness
   Highnesses
high-octane
high-powered
high-pressure
high-rise
highroad
high-spirited

high-stepper
hight
hightail
hightails
hightailed
hightailing
high-tech
high-tension
high-up
highway
highwayman
   highwaymen
High Wycombe
hijack
hijacks
hijacked
hijacking
hijinks
hike
hikes
hiked
hiking
hilarious
hilariously
hilariousness
hilarity
Hilary
hill
hillbilly
   hillbillies
hillock
hilt
hilum
   hila
him (= male
   → hymn)
hind
   hinder
hindmost or
   hindermost

hindbrain
hinder
   hinders
   hindered
   hindering
Hindi
hindquarter
hindrance
hindsight
Hindu
Hinduism
Hindustani
hinge
   hinges
   hinged
   hinging
hinny
hint
   hints
   hinted
   hinting
hinterland
hip
   hipper
   hippest
hipbone
hip-hop
hipped
hippie
hippo
   hippos
hippocampus
hippodrome
hippogriff
hippogryph
hippopotamus
   hippopotamuses or
   hippopotami
hippy
   hippies

hipsters
hiragana
hircine
hire (= rent
    → higher)
  hires
  hired
  hiring
hireling
hire-purchase
Hiroshima
hirsute
his
Hispanic
hispid
hispidity
hiss
  hisses
  hissed
  hissing
hist
histamine
histogen
histogram
histoid
histological
histologist
histology
histolysis
histolytic
histone
historian
historiated
historic
historical
historically
historicalness
historicism
historicist
historicity

historiographer
historiographic
historiographical
historiography
history
histrionic
hit
  hits
  hit
  hitting
✗hite = height
✗hiten = heighten
hitch
  hitches
  hitched
  hitching
hitchhike
  hitchhikes
  hitchhiked
  hitchhiking
hi-tech
hither
hithermost
hitherto
hitherward
Hitlerism
hitter
HIV
HIV-positive
hive
  hives
  hived
  hiving
HMG
HMS
HNC
HND
ho try who
hoar (= frost
    → whore)

hoard (= collect
    → horde)
hoards
hoarded
hoarding
hoarfrost
hoarhound
hoarse
hoarsen
hoarsens
hoarsened
hoarsening
hoary
hoarier
hoariest
hoatzin
hoax
  hoaxes
  hoaxed
  hoaxing
hob
  hobs
  hobbed
  hobbing
hobbit
hobble
  hobbles
  hobbled
  hobbling
hobbledehoy
hobby
  hobbies
hobbyhorse
hobgoblin
hobnail
hobnob
  hobnobs
  hobnobbed
  hobnobbing
hobo

hoboes *or*
hobos
hock
hockey
hocus-pocus
hod
hodgepodge
hoe
  hoes
  hoed
  hoing
hoedown
hog
  hogs
  hogged
  hogging
hogback
hogfish
  hogfish *or*
  hogfishes
hoggish
Hogmanay
hogshead
hogwash
hogweed
ho-ho
hoicks
hoiden
hoist
  hoists
  hoisted
  hoisting
hoity-toity
hokey-pokey
hokku
Holarctic
hold
  holds
  held
  holding

holdall
holder
hold-up
  hold-ups
hole
  holes
  holed
  holing
✘holecaust =
  holocaust
✘holegram =
  hologram
hole-and-corner
holiday
  holidays
  holidayed
  holidaying
holiday-maker
holier
holiest
holily
holiness
holism
holistic
holistically
holland
holler
  hollers
  hollered
  hollering
hollo
  hollos
  holloed
  holloing
hollow
  hollows
  hollowed
  hollowing
  hollower

hollowest
hollow-eyed
hollowware
holly
hollyhock
holmic
holmium
holoblastic
holocaust
holocrine
holoenzyme
hologram
holograph
holographic
holography
holohedral
holophrastic
holophyte
holophytic
holoplankton
holothurian
holotype
holotypic
holozoic
hols
holster
✘holt = halt
✘holter = halter
holus-bolus
holy
  holier
  holiest
holystone
homage
hombre
homburg
home
  homes
  homed
  homing

homebred
home-brew
homecoming
home-grown
homeland
homely
   homelier
   homeliest
home-made
homeopath
homeopathic
homeopathy
homeostasis
homeostatic
homeotypic
Homer
Homeric
homesick
homespun
homestead
homeward
homey
   homier
   homiest
homicidal
homicide
homiletic
homiletics
homily
   homilies
✗homiopath =
   homeopath
✗homiopathy =
   homeopathy
homing
hominid
hominoid
homo
   homos
homocentric

homocercal
homochromatic
homochromatism
homochromous
homocyclic
homoeopathic
homoeopathy
homoeostasis
homoeostatic
homoeroticism
homogametic
homogamous
homogamy
homogeneity
homogeneous
homogenisation
homogenise
   homogenises
   homogenised
   homogenising
homogeniser
homogenization
homogenize
   homogenizes
   homogenized
   homogenizing
homogenizer
homogenous
homogeny
homogonous
homogony
homograft
homograph
homoiothermic
homologate
homologation
homologise
   homologises
   homologised
   homologising

homologiser
homologize
   homologizes
   homologized
   homologizing
homologizer
homologous
homolographic
homologue
homology
homolysis
homolytic
homomorphism
homonym
homonymous
homonymy
Homoousian
homophobia
homophone
homophonic
homophonous
homophony
homophyllic
homophyly
homoplastic
homopolar
homopolarity
homopterous
homosexual
homosexuality
homotaxis
homothallic
homozygote
homozygotic
homozygous
homuncular
homuncule
homunculus
homy
   homier

homiest
honcho
honchos
Honduras
hone
  hones
  honed
  honing
honest
honestly
honesty
honewort
honey
honeybee
honeycomb
honeydew
honey-eater
honeyed
honeymoon
honeysucker
honeysuckle
Hong Kong
honied
honk
  honks
  honked
  honking
honker
honky-tonk
Honolulu
honorarium
  honorariums *or*
  honoraria
honorary
honorific
honour
  honours
  honoured
  honouring
honourable

hooch
hood
  hoods
  hooded
  hooding
hoodlum
hoodoo
  hoodoos
hoodwink
  hoodwinks
  hoodwinked
  hoodwinking
hooey
hoof
  hoofs *or*
  hooves
hoofed
hoo-ha
hook
  hookd
  hooked
  hooking
hooka
hookah
hooker
hookey
hook-up
  hook-ups
hookworm
hooky
hooley
  hooleys *or*
  hoolies
hoolie
hooligan
hoop
  hooper
  hoopla
hoopoe
hooray

hoorays
hoorayed
hooraying
hoot
  hoots
  hooted
  hooting
hootch
hooter
Hoover™
hooves
hop
  hops
  hopped
  hopping
hope
  hopes
  hoped
  hoping
hopeful
hopefully
hopeless
hoplologist
hoplology
hopper
hopsack
hopscotch
horal
horary
horde (= crowd
  → hoard)
hordein
horehound
✘horescope =
  horoscope
✘hors derv =
  hors d'oeuvre
horizon
horizontal
horizontally

hormonal
hormonally
hormone
horn
  horns
  horned
  horning
hornbeam
hornbill
hornblende
hornet
hornpipe
horntail
hornwort
hornwrack
horny
  hornier
  horniest
horologic
horologion
horologist
Horologium
horology
horoscope
horoscopic
horoscopy
horrendous
horrendously
horrible
horribly
horrid
  horrider
  horriddest
horridly
horridness
horrific
horrifically
horrify
  horrifies
  horrified

horrifying
horripilation
horror
horror-struck
horse
horses
horsed
horsing
horseback
horsebox
horsefly
horseflies
horsehair
horseman
horsemen
horsemanship
horseplay
horsepower
horseradish
horseshoe
horseweed
horsewhip
  horsewhips
  horsewhipped
  horsewhipping
horsewoman
  horsewomen
horsey
horst
horsy
  horsier
  horsiest
hortation
hortatory
horticultural
horticulture
hosanna
hose
  hoses
  hosed

hosing
hosier
hosiery
hospice
hospitable
hospital
hospitalisation
hospitalise
  hospitalises
  hospitalised
  hospitalising
hospitality
hospitalization
hospitalize
  hospitalizes
  hospitalized
  hospitalizing
hospitaller
host
  hosts
  hosted
  hosting
hostage
hostel
hosteller
hostelling
hostelry
hostess
hostile
hostility
  hostilities
hostler
hot
  hotter
  hottest
hotbed
hot-blooded
hotchpotch
hotel
hotelier

hotfoot
   hotfoots
   hotfooted
   hotfooting
hothead
hot-headed
hothouse
hotplate
hotpot
hotshot
Hottentot
hotter
hottest
hottish
hot-wire
   hot-wires
   hot-wired
   hot-wiring
houdah
hough
houmous
houmus
hound
   hounds
   hounded
   hounding
hour
hourglass
houri
   houris
hourly
house
   houses
   housed
   housing
houseboat
housebound
houseboy
housebreaking
housecoat

housefather
housefly
   houseflies
household
householder
househusband
housekeep
   housekeeps
   housekept
   housekeeping
housekeeper
housekeeping
housemaid
houseman
   housemen
housemaster
housemistress
houseroom
houses
housetop
house-warming
housewife
housewifely
housewifery
housework
housey-housey
housing
hove
   hoves
   hoved
   hoving
hovel
hover
   hovers
   hovered
   hovering
hovercraft
hoverport
how
howbeit

howdah
how-do-you-do
howdy
however
howitzer
howl
   howls
   howled
   howling
howler
howsoever
hoy
hoyden
hub
hubble-bubble
hubbub
hubby
   hubbies
hubcap
Hubble (telescope)
hubris
hubristic
huck
huckaback
huckleberry
huckster
huddle
   huddles
   huddled
   huddling
hudibrastic
hue (= colour
   → hew)
huff
huffish
hug
   hugs
   hugged
   hugging
huge

hugely
hugeous
huggermugger
Hugh
Huguenot
huh
hula
hula-hoop
hulk
hulks
hulked
hulking
hull
hulls
hulled
hulling
hullaballoo
hullabaloo
hullo
hullos
hum
hums
hummed
humming
human
humane
humanely
humaneness
humanise
humanises
humanised
humanising
humanism
humanitarian
humanitarianism
humanitarianist
humanity
humanize
humanizes
humanized

humanizing
humankind
humanly
humanoid
humble
humbler
humblest
humbug
humdinger
humdrum
humectant
humeral
✗ humerist = humorist
humerus
humic
humid
humidification
humidifier
humidify
humidifies
humified
humidifying
humidistat
humidity
humidor
humify
humifies
humified
humifying
humiliate
humiliates
humiliated
humiliating
humiliatingly
humiliation
humiliative
humiliator
humiliatory
humility
hummed

humming
hummingbird
hummock
hummus
humongous
humoral
humoresque
humorist
humorous
humour
humoursome
hump
humpback
humph
humpy
humpier
humpiest
humungous
humungously
humus
Hun
hunch
hunches
hunched
hunching
hunchback
hundred
hundredth
hundredweight
hung (= suspended,
put up → hanged)
Hungary
Hungarian
hunger
hungers
hungered
hungering
hungry
hungrier
hungriest

hunk
hunker
  hunkers
  hunkered
  hunkering
hunky-dory
hunt
  hunts
  hunted
  hunting
hunter
huntress
  huntresses
huntsman
  huntsmen
hurdle
  hurdles
  hurdled
  hurdling
hurdy-gurdy
hurl
  hurls
  hurled
  hurling
hurley
hurly-burly
  hurly-burlies
hurrah
  hurrahs
  hurrahed
  hurrahing
hurricane
hurry
  hurries
  hurried
  hurrying
✗ hurse = hearse
hurt
  hurts
  hurt

hurting
hurter
hurtful
hurtle
  hurtles
  hurtled
  hurtling
husband
husbandry
hush
  hushes
  hushed
  hushing
hushaby
hush-hush
husk
  husks
  husked
  husking
husky
  huskier
  huskiest
husky
  huskies
huss
hussar
hussy
  hussies
hustings
hustle
  hustles
  hustled
  hustling
hut
hutch
hutzpah
hyacinth
hyacinthine
hyaena
hyaline

hyalite
hyaloid
hyaloplasm
hybrid
hybridise
  hybridises
  hybridised
  hybridising
hybridity
hybridize
  hybridizes
  hybridized
  hybridizing
hybris
hybristic
hydathode
hydatid
hydra
hydracid
hydrangea
  hydrangeas
hydrant
hydranth
hydrargyria
hydrargyric
hydrastine
hydrastinine
hydrastis
hydrate
  hydrates
  hydrated
  hydrating
hydration
hydraulic
hydraulically
hydraulics
hydrazide
hydrazine
hydric
hydride

hydrilla
hydro
hydros
hydrocarbon
hydrocele
hydrocephalic
hydrocephalus
hydrochloride
hydrocortisone
hydrodynamic
hydrodynamics
hydroelectric
hydroelectricity
hydrofoil
hydrogel
hydrogen
hydrogenate
hydrogenates
hydrogenated
hydrogenating
hydrogenise
hydrogenises
hydrogenised
hydrogenising
hydrogenize
hydrogenizes
hydrogenized
hydrogenizing
hydrogenolysis
hydrogenous
hydrograph
hydrographer
hydrographic
hydrography
hydroid
hydrologic
hydrologist
hydrology
hydrolyse
hydrolyses

hydrolysed
hydrolysing
hydrolysis
hydrolyte
hydrolytic
hydromancy
hydrometeor
hydrometer
hydrometric
hydrometry
hydropathic
hydropathist
hydropathy
hydrophane
hydrophanous
hydrophilic
hydrophilous
hydrophily
hydrophobia
hydrophobic
hydrophyte
hydrophytic
hydroplane
hydroponics
hydropower
hydroscope
hydroscopic
hydrosome
hydrosphere
hydrostat
hydrostatic
hydrostatics
hydrosulphide
hydrosulphite
hydrotaxis
hydrothermal
hydrotropic
hydrotropism
hydrous
hydroxide

hydroxy
hydroxyl
hydroxylamine
hydrozoan
hyena
hyenic
hygiene
hygienic
hygienically
hygienics
hygienist
hygrograph
hygrometer
hygrometric
hygrometry
hygrophile
hygrophilous
hygrophyte
hygrophytic
hygroscope
hygroscopic
hygrostat
hying
hyla
hylomorphism
hylophagous
hylotheism
hylozoism
hymen
hymeneal
hymenopteran
hymenopterous
hymn (= song
→ him)
hymnal
hymnic
hymnist
hymnodical
hymnody
hymnologic

hymnologist
hymnology
hyoid
hyoscine
hyoscyamine
hypaesthesia
hypalgesia
hypallage
hype
  hypes
  hyped
  hyping
hyper
hyperacidity
hyperactive
hyperaemia
hyperaesthesia
hyperbaric
hyperbaton
hyperbola
hyperbole
hyperbolic
hyperbolise
  hyperbolises
  hyperbolised
  hyperbolising
hyperbolism
hyperbolize
  hyperbolizes
  hyperbolized
  hyperbolizing
hyperboloid
Hyperborean
hypercapnia
hypercritical
hypergamy
hyperglycaemia
hypericum
hyperinflation
Hyperion

hyperkinesia
hyperkinetic
hypermania
hypermarket
hypermeter
hypermetric
hypermnesia
hyperon
hyperphagia
hyperphysical
hyperplane
hyperplasia
hyperplastic
hyperploid
hyperpnoea
hyperpyretic
hyperpyrexia
hypersensitive
hypersonic
hyperspace
hyperspatial
hypersthene
hypersthenic
hypertension
hypertensive
hypertext
hyperthermia
hyperthyroidism
hypertonic
hypertrophic
hypertrophy
hyperventilate
  hyperventilates
  hyperventilated
  hyperventilating
hyperventilation
hypha
  hyphae
hyphen
hyphenate

hyphenates
hyphenated
hyphenating
hypnagogic
hypnogenesis
hypnogenetic
hypnoid
hypnologic
hypnologist
hypnology
hypnosis
hypnotherapy
hypnotic
hypnotically
hypnotise
  hypnotises
  hypnotised
  hypnotising
hypnotism
hypnotist
hypnotize
  hypnotizes
  hypnotized
  hypnotizing
hypoacidity
hypoallergenic
hypocentre
hypochondria
hypochondriac
hypochondriasis
hypochondrium
hypocrisy
hypocrite
hypocycloid
hypodermic
hypodermis
hypoglycaemia
hypognathism
hypognathous
hypogynous

hypogyny
hypomania
hypomanic
hyponym
hyponymy
hypophysial
hypophysis
hypopituitarism
hypoplasia
hypoplastic
hypoploid
hypopnoea
hyposensitise
   hyposensitises
   hyposensitised
   hyposensitising
hyposensitize
   hyposensitizes
   hyposensitized
   hyposensitizing
hypostasis
hypostasisation
hypostasise
   hypostasises
   hypostasised
   hypostasising
hypostasization
hypostasize
   hypostasizes
   hypostasized
   hypostasizing
hypostatic
hypostatisation
hypostatise
   hypostasises
   hypostised
   hypostising
hypostatization
hypostatize
   hypostatizes

hypostatized
hypostatizing
hyposthenia
hyposthenic
hypostyle
hypotactic
hypotension
hypotensive
hypotenuse
hypothalamic
hypothalamus
hypothermal
hypothermia
hypothesis
   hypotheses
hypothesise
   hypothesises
   hypothesized
   hypothesizing
hypothesiser
hypothesist
hypothesize
   hypothesizes
   hypothesized
   hypothesizing
hypothesizer
hypothetical
hypothetically
hypothymia
hypothyroidism
hypotonic
hypoxia
hypoxic
hypsographic
hypsography
hypsometer
hypsometric
hypsometrist
hypsometry
hyracoid

hyrax
   hyraxes *or*
   hyraces
hyson
hyssop
hysterectomy
hysteresis
hysteretic
hysteria
hysteric
hysterical
hysterically
hysterics
Hywel

I

lain
iambic
lan
✗ ian = eon
✗ iatola = ayatollah
iatrogenic
Iberian
ibex
  ibexes
ibid.
ibis *or*
  ibises
ICA
ice
  ices
  iced
  icing
iceberg
icebound
icebox
icebreaker
icecap
ice-cream
iced
icefall
Iceland
Icelander
Icelandic
✗ ictheology =
  ichthyology
ichneumon

ichor
ichthyic
ichthyoid
ichthyology
ichthyophagous
ichthyornis
ichthyosaur
ichthysaurus
  ichthysauruses
  ichthysauri
ichthyosis
icicle
icier
iciest
icily
iciness
icing
icon
iconic
iconoclasm
iconoclast
iconographical
iconography
iconolatry
iconology
iconomatic
iconoscope
icterus
icy
id
I'd
idea
ideal
idealisation
idealise
  idealises
  idealised
  idealising
idealism
idealization

idealize
idealizes
idealized
idealizing
identical
identification
identify
identifies
identified
identifying
Identikit™
identity
  identifies
ideogram
ideologist
ideology
  ideologies
✗ ider = eider
✗ iderdown =
  eiderdown
ides
idioblast
idiocy
  idiocies
✗ idiogram = ideogram
idiol try ideol
idiolect
idiom
idiopathy
idiophone
idiosyncrasy
  idiosyncratic
  idiosyncratically
idiot
idiotic
idle
  idles
  idled
  idling
idler

idocrase
idol (= something
  or someone wor-
  shipped → idle)
idolatry
idolise
  idolises
  idolised
  idiolising
idolize
  idolizes
  idolized
  idolizing
idyll
idyllic
  idyllically
i.e.
if
iffy
  iffier
  iffiest
igloo
  igloos
igneous
ignescent
ignite
  ignites
  ignited
  igniting
igniter
ignitibility
ignitible
ignition
✗ ignius = igneous
ignoble
ignobleness
ignominy
  ignominies
ignoramus
  ignoramuses

ignorance
ignorant
ignore
  ignores
  ignored
  ignoring
iguana
iguanid
iguanodon
ikebana
ikon
✗ iland = island
ileac
ileostomy
ileum (= part of the
  small intestine
  → ilium)
ilex
  ilexes
Ilia
iliac
Iliad
ilium (= part of the
  hipbone → ileum)
ilk
✗ ilet = islet
llkley
ill
  worse
  worst
I'll
ill-advised
ill-assorted
ill-behaved
ill-bred
ill-considered
ill-defined
ill-disposed
illegal
illegalise

illegalises
illegalised
illegalising
illegalize
  illegalizes
  illegalized
  illegalizing
illegally
illegible
illegibleness
illegitimate
ill-fated
ill-favoured
ill-founded
ill-gotten
illiberal
illiberalism
illicit (= not lawful
  → elicit)
illimitable
illimitableness
Illinois
illiquid
illiterate
illiterateness
ill-judged
ill-mannered
ill-natured
illness
  illnesses
illogic
illogical
illogicalness
ill-omened
ill-starred
ill-treat
  ill-treats
  ill-treated
  ill-treating
illuminance

illuminant
illuminate
  illuminates
  illuminated
  illuminating
illuminati
illuminating
illumination
illumine
  illumines
  illumined
  illumining
ill-use
  ill-uses
  ill-used
  ill-using
illusion (= false
  impression → al-
  lusion)
illusionism
illusionist
illusive (= unreal/
  deceptive → elu-
  sive)
illusively
illusiveness
illusory
illustrate
  illustrates
  illustrated
  illustrating
illustration
illustrious
illuviation
illuvium
I'm
image
imagery
  imageries
imaginal

imaginary
imagination
imaginative
imagine
  imagines
  imagined
  imagining
imagism
imago
  imagoes *or*
  imagines
imam
imbalance
imbecile
imbed
  imbeds
  imbedded
  imbedding
imbibe
  imbibes
  imbiibed
  imbibing
imbricate
imbroglio
  imbroglios
imbue
  imbues
  imbued
  imbuing
imitate
  imitates
  imitated
  imitating
imitation
imitative
immaculate
immaculateness
immanent (= exist-
  ing/inherent →
  imminent)

immaterial
immaterialise
  immaterialises
  immaterialised
  immaterialising
immaterialism
immaterialize
  immaterializes
  immaterialized
  immaterializing
immature
immeasurable
immeasurableness
immediate
immediately
immediateness
immemorial
immense
immensity
  immensities
immerse
  immerses
  immersed
  immersing
immerser
immersion
immethodical
immigrant
immigrate
  immigrates
  immigrated
  immigrating
imminent (= about
  to happen → im-
  manent)
immiscible
immobile
immobilisation
immobilise
  immobilises

impeller

immobilised
immobilising
immobilise
immobilism
immobilize
immobilizes
immoblized
immobilizing
immoderate
immoderateness
immodest
immolate
immolates
immolated
immolating
immoral
immorality
immortal
immortalisation
immortalise
immortalises
immortalised
immortalising
immortalize
immortalizes
immortalized
immortalizing
immortelle
immotile
immovable
immovably
immovableness
immoveable
immoveably
immoveableness
immune
immunise
immunises
immunised
immunising

immunity
immunize
immunizes
immunized
immunizing
immunodeficiency
immunogen
immunogenic
immunoglobulin
immunological
immunology
immunosuppression
immunosuppressive
immunotherapeutic
immunotherapy
immure
immures
immured
immuring
immutable
immutably
immutableness
imp
impact
impacts
impacted
impacting
impactive
impair
impairs
impaired
impairing
impala
impalas or
impala
impale
impales
impaled
impaling
impalpable

imparity
imparities
impart
imparts
imparted
imparting
impartial
impartialness
impassable
impassableness
impasse
impassioned
impassive
impassivity
impatience
impatiens
impatient
impeach
impeaches
impeached
impeaching
impeachable
impeachment
impeccable
impeccably
impecuniosity
impecunious
impedance
impede
impedes
impeded
impeding
impediment
impedimenta
impedimentary
impel
impels
impelled
impelling
impeller

impend
  impends
  impended
  impending
impenetrable
  impenetrably
impenitent
impenitentness
imperative
  imperatively
imperceptible
  imperceptibly
imperceptive
  imperceptively
imperfect
imperfection
imperfective
imperial
imperialism
imperil
  imperils
  imperilled
  imperilling
imperious
imperishable
imperishableness
✗ imperitive =
  imperative
impermanency
impermanent
impermeable
impermeableness
impermissible
impersonal
  impersonally
impersonalisation
impersonalise
  impersonalises
  impersonalised
  impersonalising

impersonalize
  impersonalizes
  impersonalized
  impersonalizing
impersonate
  impersonates
  impersonated
  impersonating
impersonation
impersonator
impertinence
impertinent
  impertinently
imperturbable
imperturbation
impervious
  imperviously
  imperviousness
impetigo
impetuosity
impetuous
  impetuously
  impetuousness
impetus
impiety
impinge
  impinges
  impinged
  impinging
impingement
impinger
impious
impish
implacability
implacable
implacableness
implacably
implant
  implants
  implanted

implanting
implantation
implanter
implausibility
implausible
implausibleness
implausibly
implement
  implements
  implemented
  implementing
implicate
  implicates
  implicated
  implicating
implication
implicit
  implicitly
  implicitness
implicity
implied
implode
  implodes
  imploded
  imploding
imploratory
implore
  implores
  implored
  imploring
implorer
imploringly
implosion
implosive
imply
  implies
  implied
  implying
impolite
impolitic

impoliticness
imponderability
imponderable
imponderableness
imponderably
import
  imports
  imported
  importing
importance
important
importantly
importation
importer
importunacy
importunate
importunately
importunateness
importune
  importunes
  importuned
  importuning
importuner
imposable
impose
  imposes
  imposed
  imposing
imposer
imposingly
imposingness
imposition
impossibility
  impossibilities
impossible
impossibleness
impossibly
impostor
imposture

impotent
impound
  impounds
  impounded
  impounding
impoundage
impounder
impoverish
  impoverishes
  impoverished
  impoverishing
impoverishment
impracticability
impracticable
  impracticabilities
impracticableness
impracticably
impractical
impracticality
  impracticalities
impractically
impracticalness
imprecate
  imprecates
  imprecated
  imprecating
imprecation
imprecise
imprecision
impregnability
impregnable
impregnableness
impregnably
impregnate
  impregnates
  impregnated
  impregnating
impregnator
impresario
  impresarios

impress
  impresses
  impressed
  impressing
impresser
impressible
impression
impressionability
impressionable
impressionableness
impressionism
impressionist
impressionistic
impressive
impressively
impressiveness
imprimatur
imprint
  imprints
  imprinted
  imprinting
imprinter
imprinting
imprison
  imprisons
  imprisoned
  imprisoning
imprisonment
improbability
  improbabilities
improbable
improbableness
improbably
impromptu
improper
improperly
improperness
impropriety
  improprieties
improve

improves
improved
improving
improvement
improver
improvidence
improvident
improvidently
improvingly
improvisation
improvise
  improvises
  improvised
  improvising
imprudence
imprudent
imprudently
impudence
impudent
impugn
  impugns
  impugned
  impugning
impugner
impugnment
✗ impune = impugn
impulse
impulsive
impulsively
impulsiveness
impunity
impure
impurely
impureness
impurity
imputability
imputable
imputableness
impute
  imputes

imputed
  imputing
imputer
in
inability
inaccessible
inaccuracy
inaccurate
inaccurately
inaccurateness
✗ inacsessible =
  inaccessible
inaction
inactivate
  inactivates
  inactivated
  inactivating
inactivation
inactive
inactively
inactiveness
inadequacy
  inadequacies
inadequate
inadequately
inadmissible
inadvertence
inadvertent
inadvisable
inalienability
inalienable
inalienableness
inalienably
inalterability
inalterable
inalterableness
inalterably
inamorata
  inamoratas
inamorato

inamoratos
inane
inanely
inanimate
inanimately
inanimateness
inanition
inanity
  inanities
inapplicability
inapplicable
inapplicableness
inapplicably
inapposite
inappositely
inappositeness
inappreciable
inappreciably
inappreciative
inappreciatively
inappropriate
inappropriately
inapt
inaptitude
inaptly
inaptness
inarticulate
inarticulately
inarticulateness
inartistic
inartistically
inattentive
inattentively
inaudibility
inaudible
inaudibleness
inaudibly
inaugural
inaugurate
  inaugurates

inaugurated
inaugurating
inauguration
inaugurator
inauguratory
inauspicious
✗ inaxessible =
inaccessible
inborn
inbred
✗ inbilt = inbuilt
inbuilt
incalculability
incalculable
incalculableness
incalculably
incandesce
incandesces
incandesced
incandescing
incandescence
incandescent
incantation
incapability
incapable
incapableness
incapably
incapacitate
incapacitates
incapacitated
incapacitating
incapacity
incarcerate
incarcerates
incarcerated
incarcerating
incarceration
incarcerator
incarnate
incarnation

incaution
incautious
incautiously
incautiousness
incendiary
incendiary
incendiaries
incense
incentive
inception
incessancy
incessant
incessantly
incessantness
incest
incestuous
incestuously
incestuousness
inch
inches
inched
inching
inchoate
inchoateness
inchoative
incidence
incident
incidental
incidentally
incinerate
incinerates
incinerated
incinerating
incineration
incinerator
incipience
incipiency
incipient
incipiently
incise

incision
incisive
incisively
incisiveness
incisor
incite
incites
incited
inciting
incitement
inciter
incivility
incivilities
inclemency
inclement
inclemently
inclementness
inclination
incline
inclines
inclined
inclining
include
includes
included
including
inclusion
inclusive
inclusiveness
✗ incoate = inchoate
incognito
incoherent
incoherence
incombustible
income
incomer
incoming
incommensurate
incommode
incommodes

incommoded
incommoding
incommodious
incommunicable
incommunicado
incommunicative
incommutable
incomparability
incomparable
incomparableness
incomparably
incompatible
incompatibly
incompetence
incompetency
incompetent
incompetently
incomplete
incomprehensible
incomprehensibly
incomprehension
inconceivable
inconceivably
✗ inconceivable =
  inconceivable
inconclusive
incongruence
incongruently
incongruity
incongruous
incongruously
incongruousness
inconsequential
inconsiderable
inconsiderate
inconsistency
inconsistent
inconsolable
inconsolably
inconspicuous

inconstancy
inconstant
inconstantly
incontestable
incontinence
incontinency
incontinent
incontinently
incontrovertible
incontrovertibly
inconvenience
incorporate
  incorporates
  incorporated
  incorporating
incorporation
incorporator
incorporeal
incorrect
incorrigibility
incorrigible
incorrigibleness
incorrigibly
incorruptible
increase
  increases
  increased
  increasing
increaser
incredibility
incredible
incredibleness
incredibly
incredulity
incredulous
incredulously
incredulousness
increment
incremental
increscent

incriminate
incriminates
incriminated
incriminating
incrimination
incriminator
incriminatory
incubate
incubates
incubated
incubating
incubator
incubus
incubuses or
incubi
inculcate
inculcates
inculcated
inculcating
incumbency
incumbent
incunabula
incur
incurs
incurred
incurring
incurability
incurable
incurableness
incurably
incurrence
incursion
incursive
incurvate
incurvature
incus
indebted
indebtedness
indecency
indecent

indecipherable
  indecipherably
indecisive
indeclinable
indecorously
indecorousness
indecorum
indeed
indefatigable
  indefatigably
indefensible
indefensibly
indefinable
indefinably
indefinite
indefinitely
indefiniteness
indehiscent
indelibility
indelible
indelibleness
indelibly
indelicacy
indelicate
indelicately
indelicateness
indemnification
indemnifier
indemnify
  indemnifies
  indemnified
  indemnifying
indemnity
indent
  indents
  indented
  indenting
indentation
indenture
independence

independency
independent
in-depth
indescribable
  indescribably
indestructible
indeterminable
indefeminably
indeterminate
✗ indeted = indebted
index
  index or
  indices
indexation
India
Indian
indicate
  indicates
  indicated
  indicating
indication
indicative
indicator
indices
✗ indicision =
  indecision
✗ indicisive =
  indecisive
indict
  indicts
  indicted
  indicting
indictable
indicter
indictment
indictor
indifference
indifferent
indifferently
indigenous

indigent
indigestible
indigestion
✗ indiginous =
  indigenous
indignant
indignantly
indignation
indignity
  indignities
indigo
indirect
indiscipline
indiscreet (= tact-
  less → indiscrete)
indiscrete (= not
  divisible → indis-
  creet)
indiscretion
indiscriminate
indispensable
indispensably
indisposed
indisposition
indisputable
indisputably
indissoluble
indistinct
indistinctive
indistinguishable
indistinguishably
✗ inditable =
  indictable
✗ indite = indict
✗ inditement =
  indictment
indium
individual
individualise
  individualises

individualised
individualising
individualism
individualist
individuality
individualize
individualizes
individualized
individualizing
individuate
individuates
individuated
individuating
individuation
indivisible
indoctrinate
indoctrinates
indoctrinated
indoctrinating
indoctrination
indoctrinator
indolent
indomitability
indomitable
indomitableness
indomitably
Indonesia
Indonesian
indoor
indoors
indorsable
indorse
indorsee
indorsement
indorser
indorsor
indrawn
indubitability
indubitable
indubitableness

indubitably
induce
induces
induced
inducing
inducement
inducer
inducible
induct
inducts
inducted
inducting
inductance
induction
inductive
inductor
indulge
indulges
indulged
indulging
indulgence
indulgent
indulgently
indulger
indusium
industrial
industrialisation
industrialise
industrialises
industrialised
industrialising
industrialism
industrialist
industrialization
industrialize
industrializes
industrialized
industrializing
industrially
industrious

industriously
industriousness
industry
industries
inebriant
inebriate
inebriation
inebriety
inedibility
inedible
ineducability
ineducable
ineffability
ineffable
ineffableness
ineffably
ineffective
ineffectual
inefficacious
inefficacy
inefficient
inefficiency
✗ inegsorstible =
inexhaustible
inelegance
inelegancy
inelegant
inelegantly
ineligibility
ineligible
ineligibleness
ineligibly
ineloquence
ineloquent
ineloquently
ineluctable
ineluctably
inept
ineptitude
ineptly

ineptness
inequable
inequality
 inequalities
inequitable
inequitableness
inequitably
inequity
ineradicable
ineradicably
inert
inertia
inertly
inertness
inescapable
 inescapably
inescutcheon
inessential
inessive
inestimability
inestimable
inestimableness
inestimably
inevitability
inevitable
inevitableness
inevitably
inexact
✗inexhaustible =
 inexhaustible
inexcusable
inexcusably
inexhaustible
inexorability
inexorable
inexorableness
inexorably
inexpensive
inexperience
inexpert

inexpertly
inexpertness
inexpiable
inexplicable
inexplicably
inexplicit
inexpressible
inexpressibly
inexpressive
inexpungible
inextinguishable
inextirpable
inextricable
inextricably
infallibility
infallible
infallibleness
infallibly
infamous
infamy
infancy
 infancies
infant
infanticidal
infanticide
infantile
infantry
 infantries
infantryman
 infantrymen
infarct
infarcted
infarction
infatuate
infatuates
infatuated
infatuating
infatuation
infeasibility
infeasible

infeasibleness
infect
 infects
 infected
 infecting
infecter
infection
infectious
infectiously
infectiousness
infective
infector
infecund
infecundity
infelicitous
 infelicities
infelicity
✗infamous =
 infamous
✗infemy = infamy
infen try infan
infer
 infers
 inferred
 inferring
inference
inferential
inferior
inferiority
inferiorly
infernal
infernally
inferno
 infernos
inferrer
infertile
infertility
infest
 infests
 infested

infesting
infester
infidel
infidelity
infidelities
infielder
infighting
infill
infills
infilled
infilling
infiltrate
infiltrates
infiltrated
infiltrating
infinite
infinitesimal
infinitive
infinity
infirm
infirmary
infirmaries
infirmity
infirmities
infirmness
inflame
inflames
inflamed
inflaming
inflammability
inflammable
inflammableness
inflammably
inflammation
inflammatorily
inflammatory
inflatable
inflate
inflates
inflated

inflating
inflation
inflationary
inflationism
inflationist
inflect
inflects
inflected
inflecting
inflection
inflectional
inflective
inflexed
inflexibility
inflexibleness
inflexibly
inflexionless
inflict
inflicts
inflicted
infliction
inflicter
infliction
inflictor
in-flight
inflorescence
inflow
influence
influential
influenza
influx
inform
informs
informed
informing
informal
informality
informally
informant
informatics

information
informative
informatively
informativeness
informed
informedly
informer
infotainment
infract
infracts
infracted
infraction
infractor
infrangibility
infrangible
infrangibleness
infrared
infrasonic
infrasound
infrastructure
infrequence
infrequency
infrequent
infrequently
infringe
infringes
infringed
infringing
infringement
infringer
infundibular
infuriate
infuriates
infuriated
infuriating
infuriating
infuriatingly
infuse
infuses

infused
infusing
infuser
infusion
ingenious
ingeniously
ingeniousness
ingénue
ingenuity
ingenuous
ingenuously
ingenuousness
ingest
  ingests
  ingested
  ingesting
ingestible
ingestion
ingestive
ingle
inglenook
inglorious
ingloriously
ingloriousness
ingoing
ingot
ingrain
  ingrains
  ingrained
  ingraining
ingrate
ingratiate
  ingratiates
  ingratiated
  ingratiating
ingratiating
ingratiatingly
ingratitude
ingredient
ingress

ingrowing
ingrown
inguinal
inhabit
  inhabits
  inhabited
  inhabiting
inhabitability
inhabitable
inhabitance
inhabitancy
inhabitant
inhabitation
inhalant
inhalation
inhale
  inhales
  inhaled
  inhaling
inhaler
inhere
  inheres
  inhered
  inhering
inherence
inherent
inherently
inherit
  inherits
  inherited
  inheriting
inheritability
inheritable
inheritableness
inheritance
inheritor
inhibit
  inhibits
  inhibited
  inhibiting

inhibition
inhibitive
inhospitable
inhospitableness
inhospitably
inhospitality
inhuman
inhumane
inhumanity
inhumanly
inhumanness
inimical
inimicality
inimically
inimicalness
inimitability
inimitable
inimitableness
inimitably
iniquitous
iniquity
  iniquities
✗ iniscapable =
  inescapable
initial
  initials
  initialled
  initialling
  initially
initiate
  initiates
  initiated
  initiating
initiation
initiative
initiator
initiatory
inject
  injects
  injected

injecting
injection
injector
✗ injer = injure
✗ injered = injured
✗ injery = injery
injudicious
injunction
injure
  injures
  injured
  injuring
injurious
injury
  injuries
injustice
ink
inkling
inky
  inkier
  inkiest
inlaid
inland
in-law
  in-laws
inlay
  inlays
  inlaid
  inlaying
inlet
inlying
inmate
inmost
inn
innards
innate
innately
innateness
inner
innermost

innings
innkeeper
innocence
innocent
innocuous
innocuously
innocuousness
innovate
  innovates
  innovated
  innovating
innovation
innoxious
innoxiously
innoxiousness
innuendo
  innuendoes
Innuit
innumerability
innumerable
innumerableness
innumerably
innumeracy
innumerate
inoculate
  inoculates
  inoculated
  inoculation
inoffensive
inofficious
inoperability
inoperable
inoperableness
inoperably
inoperative
inoperativeness
inopportune
inopportunely
inopportuneness
inordinate

inordinately
inordinateness
inorganic
inpatient
input
  inputs
  input
  inputting
inquest
inquietude
inquiline
inquire
  inquires
  inquired
  inquiring
inquirer
inquiring
inquiringly
inquiry
  inquiries
inquisition
inquisitive
inquisitively
inquisitiveness
inquisitor
inquisitorial
inroad
inrush
insalubrious
insalubrity
insane
insanely
insaneness
insanitariness
insanitary
insanity
insatiability
insatiable
insatiableness
insatiably

inscribe
  inscribes
  inscribed
  inscribing
inscriber
inscription
inscrutability
inscrutable
inscrutableness
inscrutably
inse try insu
insect
insectarium
  insectariums *or*
  insectaria
insecticidal
insecticide
insectivore
insectivorous
insecure
inseminate
  inseminates
  inseminated
  inseminating
insemination
inseminator
insensate
insensately
insensateness
insensibility
insensible
insensibleness
insensibly
insensitive
insensitively
insensitiveness
insensitivity
insentience
insentient
inseparability

inseparable
inseparableness
inseparably
insert
  inserts
  inserted
  inserting
inserter
insertion
inset
✗ inshorance =
  insurance
inshore
✗ inshored = insured
inside
insider
insidious
insidiously
insidiousness
insight
insignia
insignificant
insincere
insincerity
insinuate
  insinuates
  insinuated
  insinuating
insinuation
insinuator
insipid
insipidly
insipidness
insist
  insists
  insisted
  insisting
insistence
insistency
insistent

insistently
insister
insobriety
insole
insolent
insolubility
insoluble
insolubleness
insolubly
insolvability
insolvable
insolvency
insolvent
insomnia
insomniac
insomuch
insouciance
insouciant
insouciantly
inspect
  inspects
  inspected
  inspecting
inspection
inspector
inspectorate
inspiration
inspirational
inspire
  inspires
  inspired
  inspiring
inspirer
inst
instability
instable
install
installant
installer
instalment

instance
instancy
instantaneity
instantaneous
instantly
instate
  instates
  instated
  instating
instatement
instead
instep
instigate
  instigates
  instigated
  instigating
instil
  instils
  instilled
  instilling
instiller
instilment
instinct
instinctive
instinctively
institute
  institutes
  instituted
  instituting
institution
institutional
institutionalise
  institutionalises
  institutionalised
  institutionalising
institutionalism
institutionalize
  institutionalizes
  institutionalized
  institutionalizing

✗ instrement =
✗ instremental =
  instrumental
instruct
  instructs
  instructed
  instructing
instructible
instruction
instructional
instructive
instructively
instructiveness
instructor
instrument
instrumental
instrumentalism
instrumentalist
instrumentation
insubordinate
insubstantial
insufferable
insufferableness
insufferably
insufficiency
insufficient
insufflate
  insufflates
  insufflated
  insufflating
insular
insularity
insulate
  insulates
  insulated
  insulating
insulation
insulator
insulin

insult
  insults
  insulted
  insulting
insulter
insuperability
insuperable
insuperableness
insuperably
insupportable
insuppressible
insurability
insurable
insurance
insure
  insures
  insured
  insuring
insurer
insurgence
insurgency
insurgent
insurmountable
insurrection
intact
intactness
intaglio
  intaglios
intake
intangibility
intangible
intangibleness
intangibly
intarsia
integer
integral
integrand
integrant
integrate
  integrates

integrated
integrating
integration
integrator
integrity
integument
integumental
integumentary
intellect
intellectual
intellectualise
 intellectualises
 intellectualised
 intellectualising
intellectualism
intellectualize
 intellectualizes
 intellectualized
 intellectualizing
intelligence
intelligent
intelligently
intelligentsia
intelligibility
intelligible
intelligibleness
intelligibly
intemperance
intemperate
intemperately
intemperateness
✗ intenation =
 intonation
intend
 intends
 intended
 intending
intense
intensely
intenseness

intensification
intensifier
intensify
 intensifies
 intensified
 intensifying
intensity
intensive
intensively
intensiveness
intent
intention
intentional
intentionally
intently
intentness
inter
 inters
 interred
 interring
interact
 interacts
 interacted
 interacting
interaction
interactive
intercede
 intercedes
 interceded
 interceding
intercept
 intercepts
 intercepted
 intercepting
interceptor
intercession
interchange
 interchanges
 interchanged
 interchanging

intercity
intercom
intercourse
interdict
 interdicts
 interdicted
 interdicting
interdiction
interdisciplinary
interest
 interests
 intrested
 interesting
interface
 interfacing
interfere
 interferes
 interfered
 interfering
interference
interim
interior
interiorly
interject
 interjects
 interjected
 interjection
interlace
interlay
 interlays
 interlaid
 interlaying
interleave
 interleaves
 interleaved
 interleaving
interlock
 interlocks
 interlocked
 interlocking

interlocution
interlocutor
interlocutory
interloper
interlude
intermarry
  intermarries
  intermarried
  intermarrying
intermediary
intermediate
  intermediates
  intermediated
  intermediating
intermezzo
interminability
interminable
interminableness
interminably
intermission
intermittent
intern
internal
internalisation
internalise
  internalises
  internalised
  internalising
internalization
internalize
  internalizes
  internalized
  internalizing
internally
internalness
international
internationalise
  internationalises
  internationalised
  internationalising

internationalism
internationalist
internationalize
  internationalizes
  internationalized
  internationalizing
internee
internuncio
internuncios
interplay
Interpol
interpolate
  interpolates
  interpolated
  interpolating
interpolater
interpolation
interpolative
interpolator
interpose
interposition
interpret
  interprets
  interpreted
  interpreting
interpretability
interpretable
interpretableness
interpretably
interpretation
interpretational
interpretatively
interpreter
interpretive
interregnum
interrelate
  interrelates
  interrelated
  interrelating
interrogate

interrogates
interrogated
interrogating
interrogatingly
interrogation
interrogational
interrogative
interrogator
interrogatory
interrupt
  interrupts
  interrupted
  interrupting
interrupter
interruption
interruptor
intersect
  intersects
  intersected
  intersecting
intersection
interspace
  interspaces
  interspaced
  interspacing
intersperse
  intersperses
  interspersed
  interspersing
interspersedly
interstate
interstice
interstitial
intertidal
intertwine
  intertwines
  intertwined
  intertwining
intertwist
  intertwists

intertwisted
intertwisting
intervene
  intervenes
  intervened
  intervening
intervention
interventionist
interview
interweave
  interweaves
  interweaved
  interweaving
intestacy
intestate
intestinal
intestine
✗ intiger = integer
intimacy
  intimacies
intimate
intimation
intimidate
  intimidates
  intimidated
  intimidating
intimidation
intimidator
into
intolerability
intolerable
intolerableness
intolerably
intolerance
intolerant
intolerantly
intonation
intone
  intones

intoned
intoning
intoner
intorsion
intoxicant
intoxicate
  intoxicates
  intoxicated
  intoxicating
intoxicatingly
intoxication
intoxicative
intractability
intractable
intractableness
intractably
intrados
  intrados or
  intradoses
intramuscular
intransigence
intransigency
intransigent
intransigently
intransitive
intransitively
intransitiveness
intransitivity
intrauterine
intravasation
intravenous
✗ intrecacy = intricacy
✗ intrecate = intricate
intrepid
intrepidly
intrepidness
intricate
intriguer
intriguing

intriguingly
✗ intrim = interim
intrinsic
intrinsically
intro
introduce
  introduces
  introduced
  introducing
introduction
introductory
introit
introspection
introspective
introversion
introvert
introverted
intrude
intruder
intrusion
intrusive
intrusiveness
intubate
intuit
  intuits
  intuited
  intuiting
intuition
intuitive
intuitiveness
intumescence
intussuscept
  intussuscepts
  intussuscepted
  intussuscepting
intussusception
Inuit
inulin
inundate
  inundates

inundated
inundating
inundatory
inurbane
inurbanity
inure
inurement
invadable
invade
   invades
   invaded
   invading
invader
invalid
invalidate
   invalidates
   invalidated
   invalidating
invalidation
invalidism
invalidity
invalidness
invaluable
invaluableness
invaluably
invariability
invariable
invariableness
invariably
invariance
invariancy
invariant
invasion
invasive
✗ invay = inveigh
invective
invectiveness
inveigh
   inveighs

inveighed
inveighing
inveigher
inveigle
inveiglement
inveigler
invent
invention
inventive
inventively
inventiveness
inventor
inventory
   inventories
Inverness
inverse
inversely
inversion
inversive
invert
inverts
inverted
inverting
invertebrate
invertible
invest
invests
invested
investing
investigable
investigate
investigates
investigated
investigating
investigation
investigational
investigator
investigatory
investitive
investiture

investment
investor
inveteracy
inveterate
inveterately
inveterateness
inviability
inviable
inviableness
inviably
invidious
invidiously
invidiousness
invigilate
   invigilates
   invigilated
   invigilating
invigilation
invigilator
invigorate
   invigorates
   invigorated
   invigorating
invigoratingly
invigoration
invincibility
invincible
invincibleness
invincibly
inviolability
inviolable
inviolableness
inviolably
inviolacy
inviolate
inviolateness
invisibility
invisible
invisibleness
invitation

✗ invegle = inveigle

invite
  invites
  invited
  inviting
inviter
invitingly
invitingness
invoke
  invokes
  invoked
  invoking
invoker
involuntarily
involuntariness
involuntary
involute
involution
involve
  involves
  involved
  involving
involvement
involver
invulnerability
invulnerable
invulnerableness
invulnerably
inward
inwardly
inwards
iodate
iodide
iodise
  iodises
  iodised
  iodising
iodism
iodize
  iodizes
  iodized

iodizing
iodous
ion
Ionesco, Eugene
Ionian
Ionic
✗ ioning = ironing
ionisation
ionise
  ionises
  ionised
  ionising
ionosphere
ionotropy
iota
IOU
Iowa
ipecac
ipecacuanla
IQ
Iran
Iranian
Iraq
Iraqi
irascibility
irascible
irascibleness
irascibly
irate
irately
ire
Ireland
irenic
irenically
irenics
iridescent
iridium
iridology
iris
  irises

Irish
Irishman
irk
  irks
  irked
  irking
irksome
✗ irobic = aerobic
iron
  irons
  ironed
  ironing
ironic
ironically
ironing
ironmonger
ironware
ironwork
irony
irradiance
irradiant
irradiate
  irradiates
  irradiated
  irradiating
irradiation
irrational
irrationality
irrationally
irrationalness
irreclaimable
irreconcilability
irreconcilable
irreconcilableness
irreconcilably
irrecoverable
irredeemable
irredeemably
irreducible
irrefragability

irrefragable
irrefragableness
irrefragably
irrefrangible
irrefutability
irrefutable
irrefutableness
irrefutably
irregular
irregularity
  irregularities
irregularly
irrelative
irrelatively
irrelevance
irrelevancy
irrelevant
irrelevantly
irreligious
irremediable
irremovable
irreparability
irreparable
irreparableness
irreparably
irreplaceable
irrepressible
irrepressibly
irreproachable
irreproachably
irresistible
irresistibily
irresolute
irresolutely
irresoluteness
irresolution
irresolvable
irrespective
irresponsible
irresponisbly

irretrievable
irretrievably
irreverence
irreverent
irreverential
irreverently
irreversible
irrevocability
irrevocable
irrevocableness
irrevocably
irrigate
  irrigates
  irrigated
  irrigation
irritable
irritant
irritate
  irriates
  irritated
  irriating
  irritation
irrupt (= enter
  abruptly → erupt)
irruption
irruptive
is
isatin
ischaemia
ischaemic
ischium
Islam
Islamic
island
islander
Islay
isle (= small island
  → aisle)
islet
isn't

isobar
isobaric
isobath
isochromatic
isochronal
isoclinal
isocline
isocracy
isocratic
isogamete
isogametic
isogamous
isogamy
isogenic
isogenous
isogeny
isogon
isogonic
isogram
isolate
  isolates
  isolated
  isolating
isolation
isolationism
isomer
isomerism
isomerous
isometric
isometrics
isonomy
isopod
isoprene
isosceles
isothere
isothermal
isotone
isotonic
isotope
isotopic

isotopy
isotron
isotropic
isotropy
Israel
Israeli
issue
  issues
  issued
  issuing
Istanbul
✗ istedfod =
  eisteddfod
isthmian
isthmus
it
Italian
italic
italicisation
italicise
  italicises
  italicised
  italicising
italicization
italicize
  italicizes
  italicized
  italicizing
Italy
itch
  itches
  itched
  itching
item
itemise
  itemises
  itemised
  itemising
itemize
  itemizes

itemized
  itemizing
iterate
  iterises
  interised
  interising
iterative
✗ ither = either
itinerancy
itinerant
itinerary
it'll
its (= of it (its
  cover) → its)
it's (= it is → its)
itself
itsy-bitsy
I've
ivied
ivory
  ivories
ivy
  ivies

J

jab
  jabs
  jabbed
  jabbing
jabber
  jabbers
  jabbed
  jabbing
jabberwocky
  jabberwockies
jabot
jacaranda
  jacarandas
jack
  jacks
  jacked
  jacking
jackal
jackanapes
jackass
  jackasses
jackdaw
jacket
  jackets
  jacketed
  jacketing
jack-in-the-box
  jack-in-the-boxes
jackknife
  jacknives
  jacknifs
  jacknifed

jacknifing
jackpot
jacks-in-the-box
Jacobean
Jacqueline
jactitation
Jacuzzi ™
jade
  jades
  jaded
  jading
jag
  jags
  jagged
  jagging
jaggery
  jaggier
  jaggiest
jaggy
jaguar
jail
  jails
  jailed
  jailing
jailbird
jailer
jailor
Jakarta
jalopy
  jalopies
jam (= sweet
  spread/to stick →
  jamb)
  jams
  jammed
  jamming
Jamaica
jamb (= door-post
  → jam)
jambalaya

jambalayas
jamboree
jammy
jangle
jangles
jangled
jangling
January
japan
  japans
  japanned
  japanning
Japan
Japanese
jape
  japes
  japed
  japing
japonica
jar
  jars
  jarred
  jarring
jardinière
jargon
jasmine
jasper
jaundice
  jaundices
  jaundiced
  jaundicing
jaunt
  jaunts
  jaunted
  jaunting
jaunty
  jauntier
  jauntiest
Javanese
javelin

jaw
jaws
jawed
jawing
jawbone
jay
jaywalk
  jaywalks
  jaywalked
  jaywalking
jazz
jazzy
  jazzes
  jazzed
  jazzing
  jazzier
  jazziest
JCB ™
jealous
jealousy
  jealousies
Jeanette
jeans
Jedburgh
Jeep ™
jeer
  jeers
  jeered
  jeering
Jeffrey
Jehovah
jejunum
jell
  jells
  jelled
  jelling
jelly
  jellies
  jelled
  jellying

jellybean
jellyfish
  jellyfish *or*
  jellyfishes
jemmy
  jemmies
jennet
Jennifer
jeopardise
  jeoardises
  jeopardised
  jeopardising
jeopardize
  jeaprdizes
  jeapordized
  jeopordizing
jeopardy
✗ jeperdize =
  jeopardize
✗ jeperdy = jeopardy
jerboa
jeremiad
jerk
  jerks
  jerked
  jerking
jerkin
jerky
  jerkier
  jerkiest
jeroboam
jerry-built
jersey
Jerusalem
jessamine
jest
  jests
  jested
  jesting
jester

Jesuit
jet
  jets
  jetted
  jetting
jetsam
jettison
  jettisons
  jettisoned
  jettisoning
jetty
  jetties
Jew
jewel
✗ jewelry = jewellery
jeweller
jewellery
Jewish
Jewry
jew's-harp
jezebel
jib
  jibs
  jibbed
  jibbing
jibe
  jibes
  jibed
  jibing
jiffy
  jiffies
jig
  jigs
  jigged
  jigging
jigger
jiggery-pokery
jiggle
  jiggles
  jiggled

jiggling
jigsaw
jilt
  jilts
  jilted
  jilting
jingle
  jingles
  jingled
  jingling
jingoism
jingoistic
jingoistically
jinnee
jinn
jinni
jinn
jitter
  jitters
  jittered
  jittering
jitterbug
  jitterbugs
  jitterbugged
  jitterbugging
jiujitsu
jiujutsu
jive
  jives
  jived
  jiving
job
  jobs
  jobbed
  jobbing
jobber
jobbing
Jobcentre
jobless
joblessness

jockey
  jockeys
  jockeyed
  jockeying
jockstrap
jocose
jocosely
jocoseness
jocosity
jocular
jocularity
jocund
jocundity
jodhpurs
jog
  jogs
  jogged
  jogging
jogger
joggle
  joggles
  joggled
  joggling
Johannesburg
John
johnny
  johnnies
Johnsonian
join
  joins
  joined
  joining
joiner
joinery
joint
  joints
  jointed
  jointing
jointer
jointure

joist
  joists
  joisted
  joisting
jojoba
joke
  jokes
  joked
  joking
joker
jollification
jollify
  jollifies
  jollified
  jollifying
jollities
jollity
jolly
  jollies
  jollied
  jollying
jolt
  jolts
  jolted
  jolting
Jonathan
✗ jondarm =
  gendarme
jonquil
Jordan
✗ jorgen = Georgian
jorum
Joseph
jostle
  jostles
  jostled
  jostling
jot
  jots
  jotted
  jotting
joule
journal

journalese
journalism
journalist
journalistic
journey
  jouneys
  journeyed
  journeying
journeyman
joust
  jousts
  jousted
  jousting
jovial
jowl
  jowled
joy
  joys
  joyed
  joying
Joyce
Joycean
joyful
joyless
joyous
joyride
  joyrides
  joyrode
  joyriding
joystick
jubilant
jubilation
jubilee
Judaic
judder
  judders
  juddered
  juddering
judge
  judges

judged
judging
judgement
judgemental
judgment
judgmental
judicature
judicial
judicially
judiciary
judicious
judiciously
judiciousness
judo
jug
  jugs
  jugged
  jugging
jugful
  jugfuls
juggernaut
juggins
juggle
  juggles
  juggled
  juggling
juggler
jugular
juice
juicy
  juicier
  juiciest
jujitsu
jujube
jujutsu
jukebox
julep
julienne
July
jumble

jumbles
jumbled
jumbling
jumbo
jumbos
jump
jumps
jumped
jumping
jumper
jumpy
jumpier
jumpiest
junction
juncture
June
Jungian
jungle
junior
juniper
junk
  junks
  junked
  junking
junket
junkie
  junkies
junky
  junkies
Junoesque
junta
junto
Jupiter
Jurassic
jurisdiction
jurisprudence
jurisprudent
jurisprudential
jurist
✗ jurnal = journal

✗ jurnalism =
  journalism
✗ jurnelist = journalist
✗ jurney = journey
juror
jury
  juries
jussive
just
justice
justiciary
justiciary
justifiable
justification
justificatory
justify
  justifies
  justified
  justifying
jut
  juts
  jutted
  jutting
jute
juvenescence
juvenescent
juvenile
juvenilia
juvenility
juxtapose
  juxtaposes
  juxtaposed
  juxtaposing

K

Kabul
Kafka, Franz
kaftan
kagoul
kagoule
kail
kailyard
✗kaki = khaki
kala-azar
kale
kaleidoscope
kaleidoscopic
kaleidoscopically
kalends
kaleyard
kalif
Kamasutra
kamikaze
kanga
kangaroo
   kangaroos
kangha
Kantian
kaolin
kaoline
kaolinite
kaon
kapok
kaput
karaoke
karate
karma

karri
kart
karting
kasbah
Kathmandu
katydid
kauri
kayak
kayo
   kayoes or
   kayos
   kayoed
   kayoing
Kazakhstan
kebab
ked
kedge
kedgeree
✗kee = key or quay
✗keebord = keyboard
keef
keel
   keels
   keeled
   keeling
keelhaul
   keelhauls
   keelhauled
   keelhauling
✗keelo = kilo
keelson
keen
   keens
   keened
   keening
✗keenote = keynote
keep
   keeps
   kept
   keeping

keeper
keeping
keepsake
keeshond
✗keeside = quayside
✗keestone = keystone
kef
keg
Keighley
Keith
✗kelidascope =
   kaleidoscope
keloid
kelp
kelpie
kelvin
kemp
kempt
ken
Kendal
kendo
kennel
   kennels
   kennelled
   kennelling
kenosis
kenotic
Kenya
kepi
kepis
kept
keratin
keratoid
keratose
keratosis
kerb
kerbstone
kerchief
kerfuffle
kermes

kernel
kerogen
kerosene
kerosine
kesh
kestrel
ketch
ketchup
ketone
ketonic
kettle
kettledrum
key (= opener of
  doors → quay)
  keys
  keyed
  keying
keyboard
  keyboards
  keyboarded
  keyboarding
keyhole
keynote
keystone
khaki
khalif
khanga
Khartoum
kiang
✗kibab = kebab
kibble
  kibbles
  kibbled
  kibbling
kibbutz
  kibbutzim
kibosh
kick
kickshaw
kid

kids
kidded
kidding
kiddie
kiddy
  kiddies
kidnap
  kidnaps
  kidnapped
  kidnapping
kidney
kidology
kief
kif
kilim
Kilimanjaro
kill
  kills
  killed
  killing
killick
killjoy
kiln
kilo
  kilos
kilobyte
kilocalorie
kilocycle
kilogram
kilogramme
kilohertz
kilometre
kilometric
kilos
kiloton
kilovolt
kilowatt
kilt
  kilts
  kilted

kilting
kilter
kimberlite
kimono
  kimonos
kimonoed
kin
kinaesthesia
kinaesthetic
kinase
kind
kindergarten
kindle
  kindles
  kindled
  kindling
kindling
kindly
  kindlier
  kindliest
kindness
  kindnesses
kindred
kinematics
kinesics
kinesiology
kinesis
kinetic
kinetically
kinetics
king
kingdom
kingfisher
kingly
kingpin
king-size
king-sized
Kingussie
kink
kinks

kinked
kinking
kinky
  kinkier
  kiniest
kino
kinsfolk
kinship
kinsman
  kinsmen
  kinswoman
  kinswomen
kiosk
kip
  kips
  kipped
  kipping
kippa
kipper
kir
Kircudbright
kirigami
Kirkby Lonsdale
kirmess
kirpan
Kirsch
Kirundi
kish
kismet
kiss
  kisses
  kissed
  kissing
kissagram
kit
  kits
  kitted
  kitting
kitbag
✘ kitch = kitsch

kitchen
kitchenette
kite
kith
kitsch
kitten
kittenish
kittiwake
kitty
  kitties
kiwis
klaxon
kleptomania
klystron
knack
knacker
  knackers
  knackered
  knackering
knapsack
knapweed
Knaresborough
knave (= rogue
  → nave)
knavery
knead (= press with
  hands → kneed)
  kneads
  kneaded
  kneading
knee
  knees
  kneed (= hit with
    knee → knead)
  kneeing
kneecap
  kneecaps
  kneecapped
  kneecapping
knee-deep

knee-high
kneel
  kneels
  kneeled or
  knelt
  kneeling
knee-length
knees-ups
knell
  knells
  knelled
  knelling
knew
knickerbockers
knickers
knick-knack
knife
  knives
  knifes
  knifed
  knifing
knight (= person of
  rank → night)
knighthood
knightly (= of a
  knight → night)
knit (= make from
  wool → nit)
  knits
  knitted
  knitting
knitwear
knives
knob
knobbly
  knobblier
  knobbliest
knock
  knocks
  knocked

knocking
knocker
knock-knee
knockout
✗ knoledge =
 knowledge
knoll
knot (= tangle in
 string etc → not)
 knots
 knotted
 knotting
knotty (= tangled
 → naughty)
 knottier
 knottiest
know (= have
 knowledge of
 → no)
 knows
 knew (= had
 knowledge of
 → new)
 known
 knowning
know-all
know-how
knowledgable
knowledge
knowledgeable
knuckle
knuckle-duster
KO
 KO's
 KO'ed
 KO'ing
koala
kofta
kohl
✗ kole = kohl

konimeter
koniology
kookaburra
koppa
✗ kopy = kopje
Koran
Korea
Korean
korma
kosher
koumis
koumiss
koumyss
kowtow
 kowtows
 kowtowed
 kowtowing
kraal
kremlin
krill
kris
krypton
Kuala Lumpur
kudos
kumiss
kümmel
kumquat
Kurdish
kurfuffle
kurtosis
Kuwait
kwashiorkor
kyphosis
kyphotic
Kyrgystan

L

label
labelloid
labellum
labella
labia
labial
labiate
labile
lability
✗ labirinth = labyrinth
✗ labirinthine =
 labyrinthine
labium
 labia
laboratory
 laboratories
laborious
laboriously
laboriousness
labour
 labours
 laboured
 labouring
labourer
Labourite
labradorite
labroid
laburnum
 laburnums
labyrinth
labyrinthine
labyrinthitis

laccolith
lace
  laces
  laced
  lacing
Lacedaemonian
lacerate
  lacerates
  lacerated
  lacerating
lace-up
  lace-ups
lachrymal
lachrymose
lachrymosity
lacing
lack
  lacks
  lacked
  lacking
lackadaisical
✗ lacker = lacquer
lackey
  lackeys
lacklustre
laconic
laconically
laconism
lacquer
lacrosse
✗ lacrymose =
  lachrymose
lactam
lactase
lactate
  lactates
  lactated
  lactating
lactation
lacteal

lactic
lactiferous
lactone
lactonic
lactose
lacuna
  lacunae
lacunal
lacunary
lacustrine
lacy
  lacier
  laciest
lad
ladder
laddie
laden
la-di-da
ladies
ladies-in-waiting
ladle
  ladles
  ladled
  ladling
lady
  ladies
lady-in-waiting
  ladies-in-waiting
ladylike
laevnlin
✗ laf = laugh
✗ lafable = laughable
✗ lafter = laughter
lag
  lags
  lagged
  lagging
lager
laggard
laggardly

lagging
lagomorph
lagoon
lah
lahar
lah-di-dah
laic
laicise
  laicises
  laicised
  laicising
laicize
  laicizes
  laicized
  laicizing
laid (= put down
  → lade)
lain (= been hor-
  izontal → lane)
lair (= animal's den
  → layer)
laird
laity
lake
lam (= thrash
  → lamb)
lams
lammed
lamming
✗ lama = llama
lama (= Tibetan
  priest → llama)
Lamaism
lamb
  lambs
  lambed
  lambing
lambada
lambaste
  lambastes

lambasted
lambasting
lambda
lambdoid
lambent
lambert
lambkin
lame
  lames
  lamed
  laming
lamella
  lammelae *or*
  lamellas
lamellar
lamellate
lamellicorn
lamelliform
lamellose
lamellosity
lament
  laments
  lamented
  lamenting
lamentable
lamentation
lamenter
lamina
  laminae *or*
  laminas
laminaria
laminate
  laminates
  laminated
  laminating
lamination
laminose
Lammas
lamp
lampoon

lampoons
lampooned
lampooning
lampooner
lampoonist
lamppost
lamprey
lanate
Lancashire
lance
  lances
  lanced
  lancing
lanceolate
lancer
lancers
lancet
lanceted
lancinate
land
  lands
  landed
  landing
landau
  landaus
landfall
landfill
landform
landing
landlady
  landladies
landlocked
landlord
landlubber
landmark
landmass
✗ landow = landau
landowner
landrace
landscape

landscapist
landside
landslide
landslip
landsman
landward
landwards
lane (= path
  → lain)
✗ langer = languor
✗ langerous =
  languorous
✗ langery = lingerie
langouste
langoustine
langrage
language
languid
languish
  languishes
  languished
  languishing
languor
languorous
laniary
laniferous
lank
lanky
  lankier
  lankiest
lanner
lanneret
lanolated
lanolin
lanose
lanosity
lantern
lanthanum
lanuginose
lanuginous

lanuginousness
lanugo
  lanugos
lanyard
laodicean
Laos
lap
  laps
  lapped
  lapping
laparoscopy
laparotomy
lap-chart
lapdog
lapel
lapelled
lapidarian
lapidary
  lapidaries
lapidicolous
lapillus
lapis lazuli
lappet
lapse
  lapses
  lapsed
  lapsing
lapsus
lapwing
larceny
  larcenies
larch
  larches
lard
  lards
  larded
  larding
larder
large
large-hearted

largely
largen
largens
largened
largening
large-scale
largess
largesse
largish
largo
lariat
lark
  larks
  larked
  larking
larkspur
larva
  larvae
laryngeal
larynges
laryngitic
laryngitis
laryngologic
laryngological
laryngologically
laryngoscope
laryngotomy
larynx
  larynges
lasagna
lasagne
lascivious
lasciviously
lasciviousness
laser
lash
  lashes
  lashed
  lashing
✗ lasivious =

lascivious
lass
  lasses
✗ lassay fare =
  laissez faire
lassitude
lasso
  lassos *or*
  lassoes
lassoer
last
  lasts
  lasted
  lasting
lastly
latch
  latches
  latched
  latching
latchet
latchkey
late
latecomer
lately
latency
latent
later
lateral
laterally (= side-
  ways → latterly)
laterality
laterigrade
laterite
lateritic
latest
latex
lath
lathe
lather
lathers

lathered
lathering
laticiferous
Latin
Latinate
Latino
latish
latitude
latitudinarian
latria
latrine
latter
latter-day
latterly (= lately
  → laterally)
lattermost
lattice
Latvia
Latvian
laud
  lauds
  lauded
  lauding
laudable
laudanum
laudation
laudatory
laugh
  laughs
  laughed
  laughing
laughable
laughter
launch
  launches
  launched
  launching
launcher
launder
  launders

laundered
laundering
laundress
launderette
laundrette
laundry
laundries
laundryman
lauraceous
laureate
laurel
Laurentian
lava
lavabo
  lavaboes or
  lavabos
lavage
lava-lava
lavatorial
lavatory
  lavatories
lavender
laver
lavish
  lavishes
  lavished
  lavishing
law
law-and-order
lawbreaker
lawful
lawless
lawmaker
lawn
Lawrence
lawrencium
Lawrentian
lawsuit
lawyer
lax

laxative
laxity
laxness
lay (= put down
  → lies)
lays
laid
laying
layabout
lay-by
lay-bys
layer (= coating
  → lair)
layers
layered
layering
layette
layman
laymen
lay-off
lay-offs
layout
lays
laze
  lazes
  lazed
  lazing
lazuli
lazy
  lazier
  laziest
lazybones
lbw
LCD
L-driver
lea
LEA
leach
  leaches
  leached

leaching
lead (= metal
→ led)
leads
led (= guided
→ lead)
leading
leaden
leader
leadership
leading
leaf
leaves
leaflet
leafy
leafier
leafiest
league
leak (= drip
→ leek)
leaks
leaked
leaking
leakage
leaky
leakier
leakiest
Leamington
lean
leans
leant or
leaned
leaning
lean-to
lean-tos
leap
leap
leaps
leaped
leaping

leapfrog
leapfrogs
leapfrogged
leapfrogging
learn
learns
learnt or
learned
learning
lease
leases
leased
leasing
leasehold
leaseholder
leash
leashes
leashed
leashing
least
leastways
leather
leathers
leathered
leathering
leathery
leatherier
leatheriest
leave
leaves
left
leaving
leaved
leaven
leavings
Lebanon
lecher
lecherous
lecherously
lechery

lecithin
✗ lecross = lacrosse
lectern
lectin
lector
lecture
lectures
lectured
lecturing
lecturer
lectureship
led (= guided
→ lead)
ledger
lee
leeboard
leech
leeches
Leeds (town)
leek (= vegetable
→ leak)
leer
leers
leered
leering
lees
✗ leetmotive =
leitmotif or
leitmotiv
leeward
leeway
left
✗ leftenant =
lieutenant
left-handed
left-hander
lefties
leftist
leftover
leftovers

lent

leftward
leftwards
left-wing
lefty
　lefties
leg
　legs
　legged
　legging
legacy
　legacies
legal
legalese
legalise
　legalises
　legalised
　legalising
legality
legalize
　legalizes
　legalized
　legalizing
legally
legate
legatee
legation
legationary
legend
legendary
legerdemain
✗ leget = legate
　legged
　legging
　leggings
leggy
　leggier
　leggiest
leghorn
legible
　legibly

legion
legionnaire
legislate
　legislates
　legislated
　legislating
legislation
legislative
legislatively
legislator
legislatorial
legislature
legit
legitimacy
legitimate
　legitimates
　legitimated
　legitimating
legitimately
legitimateness
legitimisation
legitimatise
　legitimises
　legitimised
　legitimising
legitimatization
legitimatize
　legitimatizes
　legitimatized
　legitimatizing
legless
legman
　legmen
Lego ™
leg-pull
legroom
legume
legumin
leguminous
legwarmer

legwork
lei
Leicester
Leicestershire
leisure
leisured
leisurely
leitmotif
leitmotiv
lek
lemma
lemming
lemniscate
lemniscus
　lemnisci
lemon
lemonade
lemony
lemonier
lemoniest
lemur
lend
　lends
　lended
　lending
length
lengthen
　lengthens
　lengthened
　lengthening
lengthways
lengthy
　lengthier
　lengthiest
lenient
Leninism
lenitive
lenity
lens
lent

Lent (= before
Easter)
lentic
lenticel
lenticle
lenticular
lentil
lentissimo
lentivirus
lento
lentoid
Leo
Leominster
Leonardo da Vinci
leone
Leonid
leonine
leopard
leotard
✗ lepard = leopard
leper
lepidopteran
  lepidopterans *or*
  lepidoptera
lepidopterist
lepidopteron
lepidote
leporid
leporine
leprechaun
leprose
leprosy
leprous
lepton
leptophyllous
leptosomatic
leptosome
leptospirosis
✗ lern = learn
✗ lerner = learner

lesbian
lesbianism
lese-majesty
lesion
Lesley (female)
Leslie (male)
less
lessee
lessen (= grow/
  become less
  → lesson)
lesser (= not so
  great → lessor)
lesson (= instruc-
  tion → lessen)
lessor (= one who
  leases → lesser)
lest
✗ lesure = leisure
let
  lets
  let
  letting
letch
lethal
lethally
lethargic
lethargically
lethargy
let-out
  let-outs
let's (= let us, as in
  let's go → lets)
letter
lettered
letterhead
lettering
letting
✗ lettice = lettuce
lettuce

let-up
  let-ups
leucocyte
leucocytic
leukaemia
leukocyte
Levant
levee
level
  levels
  levelled
  levelling
level-headed
leveller
lever
  levers
  levered
  levering
leverage
leveret
leviathan
levied
levies
levitate
  levitates
  levitated
  levitating
levity
levy
  levies
  levied
  levying
lewd
Lewes (town)
Lewis (island; name)
lexeme
lexical
lexicographic
lexicographically
lexicographer

lexicography
lexicon
lexis
liabilities
liability
liable
liaise
  liaises
  liaised
  liaising
liaison
liana
lianoid
liar (= teller of lies
  → lyre)
✗ liase = liaise
✗ liason = liaison
✗ libary = library
libation
✗ libeedinous =
  libidinous
libel
  libels
  libelled
  libelling
libellant
libellee
libellous
liberal
Liberal
liberalise
  liberalises
  liberalised
  liberalising
liberalism
liberality
liberalize
  liberalizes
  liberalized
  liberalizing

liberate
  liberates
  liberated
  liberating
liberation
Liberia
libertarian
libertine
liberty
  liberties
libidinal
libidinous
libidinousness
libido
Libra
librarian
librarianship
library
  libraries
  libraries
librettist
libretto
  librettos or
  libretti
Libya
Libyan
lice
licence (= offical
  permission
  → license
license (= to give
  official permission
  → licence)
  licenses
  licensed
  licensing
licensee
licentiate
licentious
licentiously

licentiousness
lichee
lichen
Lichfield
licit
lick
  licks
  licked
  licking
✗ lickor = liquor
✗ licorice = liquorice
✗ licyeur = liqueur
lid
  lidded
lido
  lidos
lie (= be in a
  horizontal position
  → lay)
  lies
  lay
  lain
  lying
lie (= tell untruths)
  lies
  lied
  lying
lieder
liege
lieu
lieutenancy
lieutenant
life
  lives
lifeboat
lifeguard
lifeless
lifelike
lifelong
lifer

life-size
life-sized
lifestyle
lifetime
lift
  lifts
  lifted
  lifting
liftoff
ligament
ligamentous
ligase
ligature
ligger
light
  lights
  lit *or*
  lighted
  lighting
lighten (= getting
  lighter)
  lightens
  lightened
  lightening
lightening
lighter
lighterage
light-headed
light-hearted
lighthouse
lightness
lightning (= flash
  off)
lightweight
ligneous
lignicolous
ligniform
lignify
  lignifies
  lignified

lignifying
lignin
lignite
lignitic
lignivorous
likable
like
  likes
  liked
  liking
likeable
likelihood
likely
liken
  likens
  likened
  likening
likeness
likenesses
likewise
liking
lilac
✗ lile = lisle
liliaceous
lilies
Lilliputian
Lilo℠
  Lilos
lilt
  lilts
  lilted
  lilting
lily
  lilies
lily-livered
limaciform
limacine
Limassol
limb
limbed

limber
limbers
limbered
limbering
limbos
lime
limeade
limekiln
limelight
limerick
✗ limerzine =
limousine
limestone
limicoline
limicolous
limit
  limits
  limited
  limiting
limitation
limiter
limitrophe
limivorous
limn
  limns
  limned
  limning
limnetic
limnological
limnologist
limnology
limnophilous
limo
  limos
Limoges
limousine
limp
  limps
  limped
  limping

limpet
limpid
limpidity
Limpopo
limulus
limy
  limier
  limiest
linage
linchpin
Lincoln
linctus
  lictuses
linden
line
  lines
  lined
  lining
lineage
lineal
lineament
lineamental
linear
linearity
lineate
lineation
linen
liner
linesman
line-up
ling
linger
  lingers
  lingered
  lingering
lingerie
lingo
  lingoes
lingual
linguini

linguist
linguistic
linguistically
linguistics
lingulate
✗ liniage = lineage
✗ liniament =
  lineament
liniment
lining
link
  links
  linked
  linking
linkage
linker
linkup
Linnaean
Linnean
linnet
lino
linocut
linoleate
linoleum
linseed
lint
lintel
linum
lion
lioness
lion-hearted
lionise
  lionises
  lionised
  lionising
lionize
  lionizes
  lionized
  lionizing
lip

lipaemia
lipase
lipid
lipide
lipogenesis
lipoid
lipoma
lipomatous
liposome
liposuction
lipped
lip-synch
lipuria
✗ liquedate = liquidate
✗ liquedize = liquidize
✗ liquedizer =
  liquidizer
liquefacient
liquefaction
liquefy
  liquefies
  liquefied
  liquefying
liquesce
  liquesces
  liquesced
  liquescing
liquescence
liquescency
liquescent
liqueur
liquid
liquidate
  liquidates
  liquidated
  liquidating
liquidation
liquidator
liquidise
  liquidises

liquidised
liquidising
liquidiser
liquidity
liquidize
  liquidizes
  liquidized
  liquidizing
liquidizer
liquor
liquorice
Liskeard
lisle
lisp
  lisps
  lisped
  lisping
lissom
lissome
list
  lists
  listed
  listing
listen
  listens
  listened
  listening
listeria
listeriosis
listless
lit
litany
  litanies
litchi
literacy
literal (= word for
  word → littoral)
literally
literary
literate

literati
literatim
literation
literature
lithe
lithesome
lithic
lithification
lithium
litho
lithograph
lithographer
lithographic
lithography
lithoid
lithologic
lithologist
lithology
lithophyte
lithophytic
lithosphere
Lithuania
Lithuanian
litigant
litigate
  litigates
  litigated
  litigating
litigation
litigious
litmus
litotes
litre
litter
  litters
  littered
  littering
little
littler
littlest

littoral (= of the
  shore → literal)
liturgical
liturgically
liturgics
liturgy
  liturgies
livable
live
  lives
  lived
  living
liveable
live-in
livelihood
livelong
lively
  livelier
  liveliest
liven
  livens
  livened
  livening
liver
liveried
liverish
Liverpudlian
liverwort
liverwurst
livery
  liveries
livestock
livid
lividity
living
lizard
Ljubljana
llama (= animal
  → lama)
Llanelli

Llangollen
llano
  llanos
Lloyd's
lo
loach
  loach *or*
  loaches
load (= place goods
  on → lode)
  loads
  loaded
  loading
loader
loadstar
loadstone
loaf
  loaves
  loafs
  loafed
  loafing
loafer
loam
loan (= lent
  → lone)
  loans
  loaned
  loaning
loath
loathe
  loathes
  loathed
  loathing
loathing
loathly
  loathlier
  loathliest
loathsome
loaves
lob

lobs
lobbed
lobbing
lobar
lobate
lobby
  lobbies
  lobbyist
lobe
lobectomy
lobelia
lobotomised
lobotomized
lobotomy
  lobotomies
lobster
lobular
lobule
lobworm
local
locale
localise
  localises
  localised
  localising
localism
locality
  localities
localize
  localizes
  localized
  localizing
locally
✗ locarl = locale
locatable
locate
  locates
  located
  locating
locater

location
locative
loch
lochia
loci
lock
  locks
  locked
  locking
locker
locket
lockjaw
lockout
locksmith
lockup
loco
locomotion
locomotive
locomotor
locular
locule
  locules *or*
  loculi
locum
locus
  loci
locust
locution
locutionary
lode (= metal
  → load)
lodestar
lodestone
lodge
  lodges
  lodged
  lodging
lodgement
lodger
lodgings

lodgment
loess
loessal
loessial
loft
  lofts
  lofted
  lofting
lofter
lofty
  loftier
  loftiest
log
  logs
  logged
  logging
logagraphia
loganberry
logarithm
logarithmic
logbook
loge
logger
loggerheads
loggia
logia
logical
logically
logician
logicism
logistically
logistician
logistics
loglog
logo
  logos
logogram
logogrammatic
logographer
logography

logogriph
logomachist
logomachy
logorrhoea
logotype
loin
loincloth
loiter
  loiters
  loitered
  loitering
Loki
loll
  lolls
  lolled
  lolling
Lollard
lollipop
lollop
  lollops
  lolloped
  lolloping
lolly
  lollies
Lomond, Loch
London
lone (= alone
  → loan)
lonely
  lonelier
  loneliest
loner
lonesome
long
  longs
  longed
  longing
longboat
longbow
long-drawn-out

✗ longery = lingerie
longevity
longevous
longing
longish
longitude
longitudinal
longitudinally
long-legged
long-lived
longship
long-sighted
long-suffering
longueur
longways
long-winded
loo
loofa
loofah
look
  looks
  looked
  looking
lookalike
looker
look-in
lookout
loom
  looms
  loomed
  looming
loon
loony
  loonier
  looniest
loop
  loops
  looped
  looping
loophole

loopy
  loopier
  loopiest
loose
  looses
  loosed
  loosing
loose-leaf
loosen
  loosens
  loosened
  loosening
loosestrife
loot (= money
  → lute)
lop
  lops
  lopped
  lopping
lope
  lopes
  loped
  loping
lopsided
loquacious
loquaciously
loquaciousness
loquacity
loquat
loran
lord
lordly
  lordlier
  lordliest
lordosis
lordotic
lordship
lore
✗ lorel = laurel
lorgnette

✗ loriet = laureate
loris
✗ lorniette = lorgnette
✗ lornyette = lorgnette
lorry
  lorries
lose
  loses
  lost
  losing
loser
loss
lossmaker
lossy
lost
lot
loth
Lothario
lotic
lotion
lots
lottery
  lotteries
lotto
lotus
louche
loud
louden
  loudens
  loudened
  loudening
loud-hailer
loudish
loudmouth
loudmouthed
loudspeaker
lough (= lake)
Loughborough
Louis
lounge

lounges
lounged
lounging
lounger
loupe
lour
  lours
  loured
  louring
louse
  lice
lousewort
lousy
  lousier
  lousiest
lout
loutish
louvre
louvred
lovable
lovage
lovat
love
  loves
  loved
  loving
lovebird
lovebite
love-in-a-mist
loveless
lovelorn
lovely
  lovelier
  loveliest
lovemaking
lover
lovesick
lovey-dovey
loving
low

lows
lowed
lowing
lowbrow
lowdown
lower
  lowers
  lowered
  lowering
lowermost
Lowestoft
low-key
low-keyed
lowland
lowly
  lowlier
  lowliest
low-necked
low-rise
low-tech
lox
loyal
loyalist
loyally
loyalty
  loyalties
lozenge
LP
  LPs
L-plate
LSD
Ltd
lubber
lubricant
lubricate
  lubricates
  lubricated
  lubricating
lubricator
lubricious

lubriciously
lubricity
luce
lucent
lucerne
lucid
lucidity
lucidly
Lucifer
luck
luckily
luckless
lucky
  luckier
  luckiest
lucrative
lucre
✗ lucocyte = leucocyte
✗ lucshery = luxury
Luddite
ludicrous
ludo
✗ lue = lieu
luff
luffa
lug
  lugs
  lugged
  lugging
luge
Luger
luggage
lugger
lugsail
lugubrious
lugubriously
lugubriousness
lugworm
✗ lukemia = leukaemia
lukewarm

lull
lulls
lulled
lulling
lullaby
  lullabies
lulu
lumbago
lumbar (= of the
  lower back
  → lumber)
lumber (= move
  clumsily → lumbar)
lumbers
lumbered
lumbering
lumberjack
lumberjacket
lumen
  lumens or
  lumina
luminance
luminary
  luminaries
luminesce
  luminesces
  luminesced
  luminescing
luminescence
luminosity
luminous
lummox
lump
lumpectomy
lumpen
lumpfish
lumpy
  lumpier
  lumpiest
lunacy

lunacies
lunar
lunate
lunatic
lunatically
lunch
lunches
lunched
lunching
luncheon
lune
lunette
lung
lunge
  lunges
  lunged
  lunging
lungfish
lungworm
lungwort
lunula
  lunulae
lunular
lunulate
lupin
lupine
lupus
lurch
  lurches
  lurched
  lurching
lurcher
lure
  lures
  lured
  luring
Lurex™
lurid
lurk
  lurks

lurked
lurking
luscious
lusciously
lush
✗ lushus = luscious
lust
lusts
lusted
lusting
lusterware
lustful
lustfully
lustral
lustrate
lustrates
lustrated
lustrating
lustration
lustrative
lustre
lusty
  lustier
  lustiest
lute (= musical
  instrument → loot)
luteal
lutein
lutenist
luteolin
Lutheran
lux
  lux
Luxembourg
luxuriance
luxuriant
luxuriantly
luxuriate
luxuriates
luxuriated

luxuriating
luxuriation
luxurious
luxuriously
luxuriousness
luxury
  luxuries
lyase
lycanthrope
lycanthropic
lycanthropy
lychee
lye
lying
Lyme Regis
Lymington
lymph
lymphangial
lymphatic
lymphoblast
lymphocyte
lymphocytic
lymphoid
lymphoma
  lymphomas or
  lymphomata
lyncean
lynch
✗ lynchpin = linchpin
lynx
  lynx or
  lynxes
lyre (= musical
  instrument → liar)
lyrebird
lyric
lyrical
lyrically
lyricism
lyricist

M

lyrist		Machynlleth
lyse		macho
lyses		macintosh
lysed		mackerel
lysing		mackintosh
lysin		macramé
lysine		macrobiotics
lysis		macrocosm
lysosome	ma	macroeconomics
Lytham	ma′am	macroscopic
lythraceous	mac (= mackintosh	mad
lytic	→ Mach)	madder
	macabre	maddest
	macadam	Madagascar
	macadamia	madam
	macaque	madame
	macaroni	madcap
	macaroon	madden
	macaw	maddens
	mace	maddened
	Macedonia	maddening
	macerate	madder
	macerates	maddest
	macerated	madding
	macerating	Madeira
	✗macaroni = macaroni	made (= manufac-
	Mach (= Mach	tured → maid)
	number → mac)	mademoiselle
	machete	mesdemoiselles
	Machiavellian	madrigal
	machinable	maelstrom
	machination	Maesteg
	machine	maestro
	machines	maestri or
	machined	maestros
	machining	Mafia
	machineable	mafioso
	machinery	mafiosos or
	machinist	mafiosi
	machismo	magazine

mage
magenta
maggot
maggoty
magi
magic
magician
magisterial
magistracy
magistral
magistrate
maglev
magma
magmatic
magnanimity
magnanimous
magnate
magnesia
magnesium
magnet
magnetic
magnetically
magnetise
  magnetises
  magnetised
  magnetising
magnetism
magnetite
magnetize
  magnetizes
  magnetized
  magnetizing
magneto
magneton
magnetron
magnification
magnificence
magnificent
magnifier
magnify

magnifies
magnified
magnifying
magniloquence
magniloquent
magnitude
magnolia
magnox
magnum
magpie
magus
  magi
maharaja
maharajah
maharanee
maharani
maharishi
mahjong
mah-jongg
mahogany
Mahometan
mahout
maid (= girl
  → made)
maiden
maidenhair
maidenhead
maidenhood
maidservant
mail (= post
  → male)
mails
mailed
mailing
mailcoach
mailshot
maim
maims
maimed
maiming

main (= most im-
  portant → mane)
mainbrace
mainframe
mainland
mainline
mainsail
mainstay
mainstream
maintain
  maintains
  maintained
  maintaining
maintainable
maintenance
maisonette
maize (= corn
  → maze)
majestic
majestically
majesty
  majesties
✗ majong =
  mahjong
major
  majors
  majored
  majoring
major-domo
  major-domos
majorette
majority
  majorities
make
  makes
  made
  making
makeover
maker (= manufac-
  turer)

Maker (= God)
makes
makeshift
makeweight
making
mako
  makos
malachite
maladjusted
maladjustment
maladroit
malady
  maladies
malaise
malapropism
malapropos
malaria
malarial
malarkey
malarky
malate
Malawi
Malaysia
malcontent
male (= opposite of
female → mail)
maleate
malediction
malefactor
maleficence
maleficent
✗ malestrom =
maelstrom
malevolence
malevolent
malformation
malformed
malfunction
Mali
malice

malicious
malign
maligns
maligned
maligning
malignancy
malignant
malignity
✗ maline = malign
malinger
malingers
malingered
malingering
malingerer
mall
mallard
malleable
mallet
mallow
Malmesbury
malmsey
malnourished
malnutrition
malodorous
malpractice
malpractitioner
malt (= grain
→ moult)
maltase
Malthusian
maltier
maltiest
malting
maltose
maltreat
maltreats
maltreated
maltreating
maltreatment
malty

maltier
maltiest
mam
mama
mamba
mambo
  mambos
mamma
mammal
mammalian
mammalogy
mammary
mammography
mammon
Mammon
mammoth
man
  men
  mans
  manned
  manning
manacle
manacles
manacled
manacling
manage
  manages
  managed
  managing
manageable
management
manager
manageress
managerial
Manchester
mandala
mandarin
mandate
mandatorily
mandatory

mandible	manhole	manning
mandolin	manhood	mannequin
mandoline	manhunt	manner (= way →
mandrake	mania	manna; manor)
mandrel	maniac	mannered
mandril	maniacal	mannerism
mandrill	manic	mannerless
mane (= of a horse	manicotti	mannikin
→ main)	manicure	mannish
maned	manicurist	manoeuvrability
manful	manifest	manoeuvrable
manganate	manifestation	manoeuvre
manganese	manifesto	manoeuvres
manganite	manifold	manoeuvred
mange	✗ manigement =	manoeuvring
mangelwurzel	management	manoeuvrer
manger	✗ maniger = manager	✗ manooverable =
mangetout	✗ manigerial =	manoeuvrable
mangey	managerial	✗ manoovre =
mangier	manikin	manoeuvre
mangiest	Manila (city)	manor (= house
mangily	manilla	→ manna; manner)
manginess	manipulate	manorial
mangle	manipulates	manpower
mangles	manipulated	manse
mangled	manipulating	mansion
mangling	manipulation	manslaughter
mango	manipulative	mantel (= frame
mangoes or	manipulator	→ mantle)
mangos	manipulatory	mantelpiece
mangosteen	mankind	mantis
mangrove	manky	mantises or
mangy	mankier	mantes
mangier	mankiest	mantle (= cloak
mangiest	manlike	→ mantel)
manhandle	manna (= food →	✗ mantlepiece =
manhandles	manner; manor)	mantelpiece
manhandled	manned	mantra
manhandling	✗ mannikin =	manual
Manhattan	mannequin	manufacture

manufactures
manufactured
manufacturing
manufacturer
manure
manuscript
Manx
Manxman
  Manxmen
many
many-sided
manzanilla
Maoism
Maori
  Maoris *or*
  Maori
map
  maps
  mapped
  mapping
maple
maquis
mar
  mars
  marred
  marring
marabou
marabout
maraca
maraschino
marathon
maraud
  marauds
  marauded
  marauding
marauder
marble
marbling
march (= walk)
  marches

marched
marching
March (= month)
marcher
marchioness
mardy
mare
margarine
margarita
margarite
margay
marge
✗margerine =
  margarine
✗margerite =
  marguerite
margin
marginal
marginalise
  marginalises
  marginalised
  marginalising
marginality
marginalize
  marginalizes
  marginalized
  marginalizing
marguerite
mariachi
✗marianette =
  marionette
mariculture
marigold
marihuana
marijuana
marina
marinade
  marinades
  marinaded
  marinading

marinate
  marinates
  marinated
  marinating
marine
mariner
maritime
marionette
marital
maritime
marjoram
mark (= spot,
  symbol etc →
  marque)
marks
marked
marking
markdown
✗markee = marquee
marker
market
✗marketry =
  marquetry
marketable
marketing
marketplace
marking
marksman
marksmen
marl
marlin
marline
marmalade
marmoreal
marmoset
marmot
✗marmsy = malmsey
maroon
  maroons
  marooned
  marooning

marque (= product
brand → mark)
marquee
marquess
marquetry
marquetries
marquis
marquises or
marquis
marquise
Marrakesh
marred
marriage
marriageable
✗marridge = marriage
marring
marrow
marry
marries
married
marrying
Marseilles
marsh
marshal (= officer
→ martial)
marshals
marshalled
marshalling
marshland
marshmallow
marshwort
marshy
marshier
marshiest
marsupial
mart
marten
✗marter = martyr
martial (= military
→ marshal)

Martian
martin
martinet
martini
martinis
martyr
martyrdom
marvel
marvels
marvelled
marvelling
Marvell, Andrew
marvellous
✗maruana =
marijuana
Marxism
Marxist
marzipan
mascara
mascot
masculine
maser
mash
mashes
mashed
mashing
✗mashetty = machete
✗mashine = machine
✗mashinery =
machinery
mask (= disguise
→ masque)
masks
masked
masking
masochism
mason
masonic

masonry
masque (= enter-
tainment → mask)
masquerade
mass (= large
amount)
masses
massed
massing
Mass (= church
service)
Massachusetts
massacre
massacres
massacred
massacring
massacrer
massage
massages
massaged
massaging
masseur
masseuse
massif (= moun-
tains)
massive (= huge)
mast
mastectomy
mastectomies
master
masters
mastered
mastering
masterful
masterpiece
mastery
masticate
masticates
masticated
masticating

✗marker = martyr

✗maskerade =
masquerade

mastiff
mastitis
mastodon
masturbate
  masturbates
  masturbated
  masturbating
masturbatory
mat
  mats
  matted
  matting
matador
match
  matches
  matched
  matching
matchbox
matchmaker
matchstick
mate
  mates
  mated
  mating
mater
materfamilias
material
materialisation
materialise
  materialises
  materialised
  materialising
materialism
materialist
materialistic
materialistically
materialization
materialize
  materializes
  materialized

  materializing
matériel
maternal
maternalism
maternalistic
maternally
maternity
matey
  matier
  matiest
mathematical
mathematics
maths
matily
matiness or
mateyness
matin
matinée
matins
matriarch
matriarchy
  matriarchies
matric
matrices
matricide
matriculate
  matriculates
  matriculated
  matriculating
matriculation
matriculator
matrilineal
matrimonial
matrimony
matrix
  matrices or
  matrixes
matron
matronage
matronymic

matt
matte
✗ matteck = mattock
matter
  matters
  mattered
  mattering
matting
mattins
mattress
maturation
mature
  matures
  matured
  maturing
maturity
maty
  matier
  matiest
maudlin
maul
  mauls
  mauled
  mauling
Mauritania
Mauritius
mausoleum
  mausoleums or
  mausolea
mauve
maven
maverick
maw (= mouth →
  more; moor; Moor)
mawkish
maxim
maxima
maximal
maximin
maximise

maximises
maximised
maximising
maximize
  maximizes
  maximized
  maximizing
maximum
may (= might)
May (= month)
maybe
✗ mayenase =
  mayonnaise
mayfly
  mayflies
mayhem
mayn't
mayonnaise
mayor
mayoralty
mayoress
maypole
maze (= paths
  → maize)
mazourka
mazuma
mazurka
me
mead
meadow
meagre
meal
mealworm
mean (= average, or
  stingy → mien)
  means
  meant
  meaning
meander
  meanders

meandered
meandering
meandrous
meanie
meaning
meaningful
meaningless
meantime
meanwhile
meany
  meanies
measles
measly
measurable
measure
  measures
  measured
  measuring
measurement
meat (= beef etc
  → meet; mete)
meatball
meaty
  meatier
  meatiest
meca try mecha
Meccano™
mechanic
mechanical
mechanics
mechanise
  mechanises
  mechanised
  mechanising
mechanism
mechanistic
mechanize
  mechanizes
  mechanized
  mechanizing

medal (= award →
  meddle)
medallion
medallist
✗ medcine =
  medicine
meddle (= interfere
  → medal)
  meddles
  meddled
  meddling
meddler (= some-
  one who meddles
  → medlar)
✗ medecine =
  medicine
meddlesome
media
mediacy
mediaeval
mediaevalism
mediaevalist
medial
median
mediate
  mediates
  mediated
  mediating
mediation
medic
medical
medicament
medicate
  medicates
  medicated
  medicating
medication
medicinal
medicine
medick (= plant)

medico
medicos
medieval
medievalism
medievalist
mediocre
mediocrity
meditate
meditates
meditated
meditating
meditation
medium
media *or*
mediums
medlar (= tree
  → meddler)
medley
medusa (= jellyfish)
Medusa (= in Greek
  myth)
meek
meerkat
meerschaum
meet (= join
  → meat; mete)
meets
met
meeting
mega
megabit
megabyte
megacycle
megadeath
megaflop
megahertz
megalith
megalomania
megalomaniacal
megalosaur

megaphone
megascopic
megastar
megaton
megavolt
megawatt
megohm
✗megrain = migraine
meiosis
meiotic
Meirionnydd
melamine
melancholia
melancholic
melancholically
melancholiness
melancholy
melange *or*
mélange
melanin
melanoma
melatonin
✗melay = mélée
Melbourne
meld
melds
melded
melding
melee *or*
mélée
✗meline = malign
✗melinger = malinger
✗melingerer =
  malingerer
mellifluous
mellow
mellows
mellowed
mellowing
melodeon

melodic
melodically
melodion
melodious
melodist
melodrama
melodramatic
melody
  melodies
melon
✗melonge = mélange
melt
  melts
  melted
  melting
meltdown
Melton Mowbray
member
membership
membrane
membranous
✗membrenous =
  membranous
memento
  mementos *or*
  mementoes
memo
  memos
memoir
memoirs
memorabilia
memorable
memorandum
  memorandums *or*
  memoranda
memorial
memorise
  memorises
  memorised
  memorising

memorize
  memorizes
  memorized
  memorizing
memory
  memories
memos
memsahib
men
menace
  menaces
  menaced
  menacing
ménage
menagerie
menarche
mend
  mends
  mended
  mending
mendacious
mendacity
mendelevium
mendicant
menhir
menial
meningeal
meningitis
✗ menir = menhir
✗ menogomy =
  monogamy
menopause
menorah
✗ menotonous =
  monotonous
✗ menotony =
  monotony
menses
menstrual

menstruate
  menstruates
  menstruated
  menstruating
menstruation
mensurable
mensuration
mensurative
menswear
mental
mentalism
mentality
  mentalities
menthol
mentholated
mention
  mentions
  mentioned
  mentioning
mentor
mentorial
mentoring
menu
  menus
meow
  meows
  meowed
  meowing
✗ mer = myrrh
✗ merang = meringue
mercantile
mercantilism
Mercator (projec-
  tion)
mercenary
  mercenaries
mercer
merchandise
merchandising
merchant

merchantable
mercies
merciful
merciless
mercurial
mercury
mercy
  mercies
mere
meretricious
merge
  merges
  merged
  merging
merger
meridian
meridional
meringue
Merioneth
merit
  merits
  merited
  meriting
meritocracy
  meritocracies
meritocratic
meritorious
merlin
mermaid
merman
  mermen
meroblastic
merocrine
✗ meronic = moronic
✗ merose = morose
merriment
merry
  merrier
  merriest
merrymaking

Merthyr Tydfil
✗ mertle = myrtle
mesa
mésalliance
mesarch
mescal
mescalin
mescaline
mesdames
mesdemoiselles
mesh
  meshes
  meshed
  meshing
mesmeric
mesmerise
  mesmerises
  mesmerised
  mesmerising
mesmerism
mesmerize
  mesmerizes
  mesmerized
  mesmerizing
Mesolithic
meson
Mesozoic
mesquit
mesquite
mess
  messes
  messed
  messing
message
messenger
messianic
messianism
messieurs
messily
messiness

messmate
Messrs
messy
messier
messiest
met
metabolic
metabolisable
metabolise
metabolises
metabolised
metabolising
metabolizable
metabolize
metabolizes
metabolized
metabolizing
→ mettle)
metallic
metallically
metallurgist
metallurgy
metalwork
metamorphic
metamorphism
metamorphose
  metamorphoses
  metamorphosed
  metamorphosing
  metamorphosis
metaphor
metaphoric
metaphysical
metaphysics
metastasis
metastatic
metathesis
metazoan
mete (= distribute

→ meat, meet)
metes
meted
meting
meteor
✗ metea = meteor
✗ metemorphose =
  metamorphose
✗ metemorphosis =
  metamorphosis
meteoric
meteorite
meteoritic
meteoroid
meteorological
meteorology
meter (= parking
  etc → metre)
meters
metered
metering
methadone
methane
methanol
method
methodical
Methodism
Methodist
methodological
methodology
  methodologies
meths
methyl
meticulous
métier
metonym
metonymical
metonymy
metonymies
metre (= measure

metal (= iron etc

→ meter)
metric
metrical
metro
  metros
metrological
metrologist
metrology
metronome
metronomic
metronymic
metropolis
metropolitan
mettle (= courage
  → metal)
mettled
meunière
mew
  mews (= like a
    cat → muse;
    Muse)
  mewed
  mewing
mewl
  mewls
  mewled
  mewling
mews (= building
  → muse; Muse)
Mexico
mezuzah
  mezuzahs or
  mezuzoth
mezzanine
mezzo
  mezzos
mezzotint
miaou
  miaous
  miaoued

miaouing
miaow
  miaows
  miaowed
  miaowing
miasma
miasmal
mica
mice
Michael
Michelangelo
mickey
micra
microbe
microbiological
microbiology
microchemistry
microchip
microcircuit
microcomputer
microcosm
microeconomics
microfauna
microfiche
microfilm
microlight
micrometer
micron
microorganism
microphone
microprocessor
microscope
microscopic
microsecond
microsurgery
microtechnology
microwave
  microwaves
  microwaved
  microwaving

micturate
  micturates
  micturated
  micturating
micturition
midair
midday
middle
middlebrow
middleman
  middlemen
middleweight
middling
midfield
midge
midget
midnight
mid-off
mid-on
midpoint
midrash
  midrashim
midriff
midst
midsummer
midterm
midway
midweek
midwife
  midwives
midwifery
midwinter
mien (= manner
  → mean)
miff
  miffs
  miffed
  miffing
might (= may;
  strength → mite)

mightily
mightiness
mighty
  mightier
  mightiest
migraine
migrant
migrate
  migrates
  migrated
  migrating
migration
migrator
migratory
mikado
  mikados
milady
✗ milage = mileage
mild
mildew
mile
mileage
mileometer
milepost
miler
milestone
milieu
militant
militaria
militarise
  militarises
  militarised
  militarising
militarism
militarize
  militarizes
  militarized
  militarizing
military
militate

militates
militated
militating
militia
milk
milks
milked
milking
milkily
milkiness
milky
milkier
milkiest
mill
mills
milled
milling
millefleurs
millenary (= to do
  with a thousand
  → millinery)
millennial
millennium
millepede
miller
millet
milliampere
milliard
millibar
millieme
milligram
milligramme
millilitre
millimetre
millimicron
milliner
millinery (= hats →
  millenary)
million
millionaire

millionth
millipede
millisecond
✗ millit = millet
millpond
millstone
millstream
millwheel
Milngavie
milo
milometer
milquetoast
mime
mimes
mimed
miming
Mimeograph™
mimesis
mimetic
mimetically
mimic
  mimics
  mimicked
  mimicking
mimicry
miminy-piminy
mimosa
mina (= bird
  → miner; minor)
minaret
✗ minastroni =
  minestrone
✗ minature = miniature
✗ minaturize =
  miniaturize
mince
  minces
  minced
  mincing
mincemeat

mind (= care about
→ mined)
  minds
  minded
  minding
minder
mindful
mindless
mine
  mines
  mined (= dug out
  → mind)
  mining
minefield
minelayer
miner (= coalminer
→ mynah; minor)
mineral
mineralogical
mineralogy
minestrone
minesweeper
mingle
  mingles
  mingled
  mingling
mingy
  mingier
  mingiest
mini
  minis
miniature
miniaturise
  miniaturises
  miniaturised
  miniaturising
miniaturist
miniaturize
  miniaturizes
  miniaturized

miniaturizing
minibus
minicab
minicomputer
minim
minimal
minimalism
minimax
minimise
  minimises
  minimised
  minimising
minimize
  minimizes
  minimized
  minimizing
minimum
minion
minipill
✗ miniscule = minus-
  cule
miniseries
miniskirt
minister
  ministers
  ministered
  ministering
  ministerial
  ministerialist
  ministration
  ministry
  ministries
✗ miniture = miniature
✗ miniturize =
  miniaturize
mink
minneola
minnow
Minoan
minor (= not major

→ miner; mynah)
minority
minster
minstrel
mint
  mints
  minted
  minting
mintage
minuend
minuet
minus
minuscular
minuscule
minute
  minutes
  minuted
  minuting
minutiae
minx
Miocene
miosis
miotic
✗ miow = miaow or
  meow
miracle
miraculous
mirage
mire
mirk
mirkily
mirkiness
mirky
  mirkier
  mirkiest
mirror
  mirrors
  mirrored
  mirroring
mirth

misadventure
misanthrope
misanthropic
misanthropy
misapprehend
  misapprehends
  misapprehended
  misapprehending
misapprehension
misbehave
  misbehaves
  misbehaved
  misbehaving
misbehaviour
misbelief
miscalculate
  miscalculates
  miscalculated
  miscalculating
miscarriage
miscarry
  miscarries
  miscarried
  miscarrying
miscegenation
miscellanea
miscellaneous
miscellanist
miscellany
  miscellanies
mischance
mischief
mischievous
miscible (= capable
  of mixing → mis-
  sable)
✗ mischif = mischief
✗ mischifous =
  mischievous
misconceive

misconceives
misconceived
misconceiving
misconception
misconduct
misconstrue
  misconstrues
  misconstrued
  misconstruing
miscount
  miscounts
  miscounted
  miscounting
miscreant
misdeed
misdemeanour
miser
miserable
misère
misericord
misericorde
misery
  miseries
misfire
  misfires
  misfired
  misfiring
misfit
  misfits
  misfitted
  misfitting
misfortune
misgiving
misguided
mishandle
  mishandles
  mishandled
  mishandling
mishap
mishear

mishears
misheard
mishearing
mishit
mishits
mishit
mishitting
mishmash
misinform
  misinforms
misinformed
misinforming
misinformation
misinterpret
  misinterprets
misinterpreted
misinterpreting
misjudge
  misjudges
misjudged
misjudging
mislay
  mislays
mislaid
mislaying
mislead
  misleads
misled
misleading
mismatch
misnomer
miso
misogamist
misogamy
misogynist
misogynous
misogyny
misplace
  misplaces
misplaced

misplacing
misprint
mispronounce
  mispronounces
  mispronounced
  mispronouncing
mispronunciation
misquote
  misquotes
  misquoted
  misquoting
misread
  misreads
  misread
  misreading
misrepresent
  misrepresents
  misrepresented
  misrepresenting
misrule
  misrules
  misruled
  misruling
miss
  misses
  missed (= failed
    to hit → mist)
  missing
missable (= can be
  missed → miscible)
missal
✗ misselanious =
  miscellaneous
✗ misselany =
  miscellany
✗ misseltoe =
  mistletoe
misshapen
  misshapenly
missile

missing
mission
missionary
  missionaries
missis
Mississippi
missive
misspell
  misspells
  misspelled *or*
  misspelt
  misspelling
misspend
  misspends
  misspent
  misspending
misstate
  misstates
  misstated
  misstating
misstep
missus
mist (= fog →
  missed)
  mists
  misted
  misting
mistakable
mistakably
mistake
  mistakes
  mistook
  mistaken
  mistaking
mistakeable
mistakeably
mister
mistier
mistiest
mistily

mistiness
mistime
  mistimes
  mistimed
  mistiming
mistletoe
mistral
mistreat
  mistreats
  mistreated
  mistreating
mistress
mistrial
✗ mistro = maestro
mistrust
  mistrusts
  mistrusted
  mistrusting
misty
  mistier
  mistiest
misunderstand
  misunderstands
  misunderstood
  misunderstanding
misuse
  misuses
  misused
  misusing
mite (= small crea-
  ture etc → might)
mither
mitigate
  mitigates
  mitigated
  mitigating
mitochondrion
mitosis
mitotic
mitotically

mitre
mitt
mitten
mitzvah
  mitzvahs or
  mitzvoth
mix
  mixes
  mixed
  mixing
mixer
mixture
m'lud
mnemonic
mnemonically
mnemonics
mo
moa
moan (= complain
  → mown)
  moans
  moaned
  moaning
moat (= round a
castle → mote)
✗moave = mauve
mob
  mobs
  mobbed
  mobbing
mobcap
mobile
mobilise
  mobilises
  mobilised
  mobilising
mobility
mobilize
  mobilizes
  mobilized

mobilizing
moccasin
mocha (= coffee
  → mocker)
mock
  mocks
  mocked
  mocking
mocker (= person
  who mocks
  → mocha)
mockers
mockery
mockeries
mockingbird
mod
modal
modality
  modalities
mode (= fashion
  → mowed)
model
  models
  modelled
  modelling
modem
moderate
  moderates
  moderated
  moderating
moderation
moderator
modern
modernise
  modernises
  modernised
  modernising
modernism
modernity
modernize

modernizes
modernized
modernizing
modest
modesty
modicum
modification
modifier
modify
  modifies
  modified
  modifying
modish
modular
modulate
  modulates
  modulated
  modulating
modulation
module
modulus
moduli
mogul
mohair
Mohammedan
Mohammedanism
mohel
Mohican
moiety
  moieties
moire or
  moiré
moist
moisten
  moistens
  moistened
  moistening
moisture
moisturise
  moisturises

moisturised
moisturising
moisturize
moisturizes
moisturized
moisturizing
molal
molar
molarity
molasses
✗ mold = mould
✗ molding = moulding
Moldova
✗ moldy = mouldy
mole
molecular
molecularity
molecule
molehill
moleskin
moleskins
molest
molests
molested
molesting
molestation
molester
Molière
moll
mollify
mollifies
mollified
mollifying
mollusc
molluscs
mollycoddle
mollycoddles
mollycoddled
mollycoddling
✗ molt = malt or moult

molten
moment
momentarily
momentariness
momentary
momentous
momentum
momenta or
momentums
momma
✗ monacle = monocle
monarch
monarchic
monarchical
monarchy
monarchies
monasterial
monastery
monasteries
monastic
monastically
monasticism
✗ moncay = manqué
Monday
✗ monerc = monarch
✗ monercy =
monarchy
Monet, Claude
monetarism
monetary
money
moneys or
monies
moneybags
moneychanger
moneyed
moneylender
monger
✗ mongetou =
mangetout

mongol (= person
with Down's syn-
drome)
Mongol (= of or
from Mongolia)
Mongolia
mongolism
mongoloid (= hav-
ing Down's syn-
drome)
Mongoloid (= a
racial group)
mongoose
mongooses
mongrel
monicker
monied
monies
moniker
monitor
monitors
monitored
monitoring
monk
monkery
monkey
monkeys
monkeyed
monkeying
monkfish
monkhood
monochrome
monocle
monocotyledon
✗ monocrome =
monochrome
monogamist
monogamous
monogamy
monogram

monograph
monolingual
monolith
monolithic
monologue
monomania
monomaniacal
monomer
monoplane
 monopolies
monopolisation
monopolise
 monopolises
 monopolised
 monopolising
monopolization
monopolize
 monopolizes
 monopolized
 monopolizing
monopoly
 monopolies
monorail
monoski
monosodium
monosyllabic
monosyllable
monotheism
monotone
monotonous
monotony
 monotonies
monounsaturated
✗ Monsaineur =
 Monseigneur
monsieur
 messieurs
Monsignor
 Monsignors or
 Monsignori

monsoon
monster
monstrosity
monstrous
montage
montbretia
month
Montreal
monument
monumental
moo
 moos
 mooed (= like a
 cow → mood)
 mooing
mooch
 mooches
 mooched
 mooching
mood (= state of
 mind → mooed)
moodily
moodiness
moody
 moodier
 moodiest
moon
 moons
 mooned
 mooning
moonbeam
Moonie
moonlight
 moonlights
 moonlighted
 moonlighting
moonlit
moonquake
moonrise
moonscape

moonshine
moonshot
moonstone
moonstruck
moor (waste ground;
 tie a boat up →
 maw; more; Moor)
moors
moored
mooring
Moor (= a North
 African Muslim →
 maw; moor; more)
moorage
moorcock
moorfowl
moorhen
moorings
Moorish (= to do
 with the Moors
 → moreish)
moorland
moose (= animal
 → mousse)
moose
moot
mop
 mops
 mopped
 mopping
mope
 mopes
 moped
 moping
moped
moraine
morainic
moral (= behaviour)
morale (= opti-
 mism)

moralise
　moralises
　moralised
　moralising
moralism
moralist
morality
　moralities
moralize
　moralizes
　moralized
　moralizing
morass
moratorium
　moratoria *or*
　moratoriums
moratory
moray
Moray (in Scotland)
✗ morays = mores
morbid
morbidity
mordant
more (= opposite of
　less → maw; moor;
　Moor)
moreish (= making
　you want more →
　Moorish)
morel
morello
　morellos
moreover
mores
morgue
✗ morhen = moorhen
moribund
✗ moring = mooring
morish (= making
　you want more

　→ Moorish)
✗ morland = moorland
Mormon
morn (= morning
　→ mourn)
mornay
✗ morner = mourner
✗ mornful = mournful
morning (= before
　noon → mourning)
Morocco
moron
moronic
moronically
moronity
morose
morph
morpheme
morphemic
morphine
morphology
morrow
morsel
mortal
mortality
　mortalities
mortar
mortarboard
mortgage
　mortgages
　mortgaged
　mortgaging
mortgagee
mortgagor
mortice
mortician
mortification
mortify
　mortifies
　mortified

mortifying
mortise
mortuary
　mortuaries
mosaic (= pattern)
Mosaic (= to do
　with Moses)
mosasaur
Moscow
Moselle
✗ mosk = mosque
Moslem
mosque
mosquito
　mosquitos *or*
　mosquitoes
moss
most
MOT
mote (= small speck
　→ moat)
motel
motet
moth
mothball
mother
　mothers
　mothered
　mothering
motherboard
motherhood
motherland
motherliness
motherly
motif
motile
motility
motion
　motions
　motioned

motioning
motionless
motivate
  motivates
  motivated
  motivating
motivation
motive
motivity
motley
motocross
motoneuron
motor
  motors
  motored
  motoring
motorbicycle
motorbike
motorboat
motorcade
motorcar
motorcoach
motorcycle
motorise
  motorises
  motorised
  motorising
motorist
motorize
  motorizes
  motorized
  motorizing
motorway
motte
mottle
  mottles
  mottled
  mottling
motto
  mottoes *or*

mottos
mouillé
mould
mouldboard
mouldily
mouldiness
moulding
mouldy
  mouldier
  mouldiest
moulin
moult (= lose hair
  → malt)
  moults
  moulted
  moulting
mound
mount
  mounts
  mounted
  mounting
mountain
mountaineer
mountainous
mountebank
✗ mountin = mountain
  mounting
mourn (= grieve
  → morn)
  mourns
  mourned
  mourning
mourner
mournful
mourning (= griev-
  ing → morning)
mouse
  mice
mouser
mousetail

mousetrap
mousey
  mousier
  mousiest
mousily
mousiness
moussaka
mousse (= cream
  → moose)
mousseline
moustache
moustached
mousy
  mousier
  mousiest
mouth
  mouths
  mouthed
  mouthing
mouthful
mouthpart
mouthpiece
mouthwash
mouthwatering
mouthy
  mouthier
  mouthiest
movable
move
  moves
  moved
  moving
moveable
movement
mover
movie
mow (= cut grass
  → mo)
  mows
  mowed (= cut

grass → mode)
mowing
mown (= grass
→ moan)
Mozambique
Mozart, Wolfgang
Amadeus
mozzarella
mu
much
mucid
mucidity
mucigen
mucilage
mucilaginous
mucin
muck
mucks
mucked
mucking
mucky
muckier
muckiest
mucoid
mucoprotein
mucosa
mucosal
mucosity
mucous (= of or like
mucus)
mucro
mucrones
mucronate
mucus (= slime →
mucous)
mud
muddily
muddiness
muddle
muddles

muddled
muddling
muddleheaded
muddler
muddy
muddier
muddiest
mudguard
mudlark
mudpack
mudslinging
muesli
muezzin
muff
muffin
muffle
muffles
muffled
muffling
muffler
mufti
mug
mugs
mugged
mugging
mugful
mugger
muggily
mugginess
muggins
muggy
muggier
muggiest
Muhammadan
Muhammedan
mujaheddin
mujahedeen
mujahideen
mukluk
mulatto

mulattos *or*
mulattoes
mulberry
mulberries
mulch
mulches
mulched
mulching
mule
muleteer
mulish
mull
mulls
mulled
mulling
mulla
mullah
mullet
mulligatawny
mullion
mullite
multi-angular
multicoloured
multicultural
multiculturalism
multidisciplinary
multiethnic
multifaceted
multifactorial
multifarious
multilateral
multilingual
multimillionaire
multinational
multinomial
multinuclear
multipartite
multiparty
multipath
multiped

multiple
multiplet
multiplex
multiplicand
multiplication
multiplicative
multiplicity
   multiplicities
multiplier
multiply
   multiplies
   multiplied
   multiplying
multiprocessor
multiprogramming
multipurpose
multiracial
multistorey
multitude
multitudinous
mum
mumble
   mumbles
   mumbled
   mumbling
mummer
mummery
   mummeries
mummify
   mummifies
   mummified
   mummifying
mummy
   mummies
mumps
munch
   munches
   munched
   munching
Munch, Edvard

mundane
municipal
municipality
   municipalities
munificence
munificent
muniment
muniments
munition
munitioner
munitions
muntjac
muntjak
muon
mural
murder
   murders
   murdered
   murdering
murderous
murk
murkily
murkiness
murky
   murkier
   murkiest
murmur
murmurs
murmured
murmuring
murrain
✗ mus = mousse
✗ musaka = moussaka
muscadel
muscadelle
muscat
muscatel
muscavado
muscle (= body part
   → mussel)

muscles
muscled
muscling
muscovado
muscovite (= a
   mineral)
Muscovite (= of or
   from Moscow)
muscular
muscularity
musculature
musculocutaneous
muse (= think about
   → mews; Muse)
muses
mused
musing
Muse (= goddess
   → mews; muse)
museology
museum
mush
   mushes
   mushed
   mushing
mushily
mushiness
mushroom
mushy
   mushier
   mushiest
music
musical
musically
musicassette
musician
musicianship
musicological
musicology
musk

musket
musketeer
muskiness
muskmelon
muskrat
  muskrats *or*
  muskrat
musky
  muskier
  muskiest
✗ musli = muesli
Muslim
muslin
musquash
muss
  musses
  mussed (=
    messed up →
    must)
  mussing
mussel (= shellfish
  → muscle)
must (= has to →
  mussed)
mustache
mustached
mustachio
mustachioed
mustang
mustard
✗ mustash =
  moustache
muster
mustily
mustiness
musty
  mustier
  mustiest
mutable
mutagen

mutagenic
mutant
mutate
  mutates
  mutated
  mutating
mutation
mutational
mutative
mute
  mutes
  muted
  muting
mutilate
  mutilates
  mutilated
  mutilating
mutineer
mutinous
mutiny
  mutinies
  mutinied
  mutinying
mutism
mutt
mutter
  mutters
  muttered
  muttering
mutton
mutual
mutualism
mutuality
muu-muu
Muzak℠
muzhik
muzzily
muzziness
muzzle
  muzzles

muzzled
  muzzling
muzzy
  muzzier
  muzziest
my
myalgia
myalgic
myasthenia
myasthenic
mycelial
mycelium
  mycelia
myceloid
Mycenaean
mycology
mycosis
myelin
myelinated
myelitis
myeloblast
myeloblastic
myeloid
myeloma
myna (= bird →
  miner; minor)
mynah (= bird →
  miner; minor)
myoma
  myomas *or*
  myomata
myopia
myopic
myopically
myriad
myrrh
myrtle
myself
✗ mysteek = mystique
mysterious

mystery
  mysteries
mystic
mystical
mysticism
mystify
  mystifies
  mystified
  mystifying
mystique
myth
mythical
mythological
mythology
  mythologies
myxomatosis

N

na try kna
naan
nab
  nabs
  nabbed
  nabbing
nabob
nacre
nadir
naff
✗ naftha = naphtha
nag
  nags
  nagged
  nagging
naiad
✗ naiborhood =
  neighbourhood
✗ naibour = neighbour
✗ naibourly =
  neighbourly
naïf
nail
  nails
  nailed
  nailing
nailbrush
nailfile
Nairobi
naive *or*
  naïve
naively

naivety
naked
namby-pamby
name
  names
  named
  naming
nameless
namely
nameplate
namesake
nametape
Namibia
nan
nana
nancy
  nancies
nanny
  nannies
nanometre
nanosecond
nap
  naps
  napped
  napping
napalm
nape
napery
naphtha
napkin
Napoleonic
napping
nappy
  nappies
narcissism
narcissus
narcotic
nark
✗ narled = gnarled
narrate

narrates

narrated

narrating

narration

narrative

narrator

narrow

✗ narsisism =

narcissism

✗ narsisus = narcissus

narwal

narwhal

nary

NASA

nasal

nasalise

nasalises

nasalised

nasalising

nasality

nasalize

nasalizes

nazalized

nasalizing

nascent

✗ nasent = nascent

✗ nash = gnash

nasogastric

nasopharyngeal

nasopharynx

nasturtium

nastily

nastiness

nasty

nastier

nastiest

✗ nat = gnat

natal

natality

nation

nationalise

nationalises

nationalised

nationalising

nationality

nationalities

nationalize

nationalizes

nationalized

nationalizing

nationwide

native

Nativity

Nato

NATO

natter

natters

nattered

nattering

nattily

nattiness

natty

nattier

nattiest

natural

naturalise

naturalises

naturalised

naturalising

naturalist

naturalize

naturalizes

naturalized

naturalizing

naturally

nature

naturism

naturopath

naturopathic

naturopathy

naught (= nothing

→ nought)

naughtily

naughtiness

naughty

naughtier

naughtiest

nausea

nauseate

nauseates

nauseated

nauseating

nauseous

✗ nausius = nauseous

nautical

naval (= to do with

a navy → navel)

nave (= in a church

→ knave)

navel (= tummy

button → naval)

navigable

navigate

navigates

navigated

navigating

navigation

navigator

navvy

navvies

navy

navies

✗ naw = gnaw

nawab

✗ nawing = gnawing

nay (= no → née;

neigh)

✗ nazal = nasal

Nazi

ne try kne

Neagh, Lough
✗ nean = neon
Neanderthal
neap
near
   nears
   neared
   nearing
nearby
nearly
nearside
neat
neaten
   neatens
   neatened
   neatening
Neath
nebula
   nebulae or
   nebulas
nebulous
necessarily
necessary
necessitate
   necessitates
   necessitated
   necessitating
necessitous
necessity
   necessities
neck
   necks
   necked
   necking
neckband
neckerchief
necklace
neckline
necktie
necrology

necromancy
necrophilia
necrophobia
nectar
nectarine
nee or
née (= born → nay;
   neigh)
need
   needs
   needed
   needing
needful
neediness
needle
   needles
   needled
   needling
needlecord
needlecraft
needlepoint
needlework
needs
needy
   needier
   neediest
ne'er
✗ neesh = niche
✗ neevus = naevus
nefarious
negate
   negates
   negated
   negating
negation
negative
negator
neglect
   neglects
   neglected

neglecting
neglectful
negligee or
negligée
negligence
negligent
negligible
negligibly
negotiable
negotiate
   negotiates
   negotiated
   negotiating
negotiation
negotiator
Negro
✗ neice = niece
neigh (= horse
   noise → nay; née)
neighs
neighed
neighing
neighbour
neighbourhood
neighbourly
neither
nematode
✗ nemonic =
   mnemonic
✗ neofite = neophyte
Neolithic
neologism
neon
neonate
Nepal
nephew
nephrectomy
nephrectomies
nephritic
nephritis

nephrosis
nepotism
nerd
✗ nervana = nirvana
nerve
  nerves
  nerved
  nerving
nerve-racking
nerve-wracking
nervily
nerviness
nervous
nervously
nervy
  nervier
  nerviest
nest
  nests
  nested
  nesting
nestle
  nestles
  nestled
  nestling
net (= for fishing
  etc → nett)
  nets
  netted
  netting
netball
nether
Netherlands
nethermost
nett (= nett profit
  → net)
  netting
nettle
network
networking

✗ neumatic =
pneumatic
✗ neumonia =
pneumonia
neural
neuralgia
neuralgic
neurasthenia
neurasthenic
neurological
neurologist
neurology
neuromuscular
neuron
neurosis
  neuroses
neurosurgery
neurotic
neurotically
neuroticism
neurovascular
neuter
  neuters
  neutered
  neutering
neutral
neutralise
  neutralises
  neutralised
  neutralising
neutrality
neutralize
  neutralizes
  neutralized
  neutralizing
neutrino
  neutrinos
neutron
never
nevermore

nevertheless
new (= opposite of
  old → knew)
Newark
newborn
newcomer
newfangled
newly
newlywed
news
newsagent
newsflash
newsier
newsiest
newsletter
newspaper
newspeak
newsprint
newsreader
newsreel
newsroom
newsstand
newsworthy
newsy
  newsier
  newsiest
newt
newton
New Zealand
next
nexus
  nexuses
NHS
ni try kni
niacin
Niagara
nib
nibble
  nibbles
  nibbled

nibbling
NICAM
Nicaragua
nice (= good
  → gneiss)
nicety
  niceties
niche
nick
  nicks
  nicked
  nicking
nickel
nickelodeon
nick-nack
nickname
nicotine
niece
✘nieve = naive
✘nievely = naively
✘nievity = naivety
niff
niftily
niftiness
nifty
  niftier
  niftiest
nigella
Niger
Nigeria
niggardly
nigger
niggle
  niggles
  niggled
  niggling
nigh
night (= opposite of
  day → knight)
nightcap

nightclothes
nightclub
nightdress
nightfall
nightgown
nighthawk
nightie
nightingale
nightjar
nightlife
nightlong
nightly
nightmare
nightshade
nightshirt
nightspot
nightwear
nighty
  nighties
nihilism
nil
nimble
nimbostratus
  nimbostrati
nimbus
  nimbi or
  nimbuses
NIMBY
niminy-piminy
✘nimonic =
  mnemonic
nincompoop
nine
ninefold
ninepins
nineteen
nineteenth
ninetieth
ninety
  nineties

ninny
  ninnies
ninth
ninthly
nip
  nips
  nipped
  nipping
nipper
nippily
nipple
nippy
  nippier
  nippiest
nirvana
✘nish = niche
nisi
nit (= louse egg
  → knit)
✘nither = neither
nitrate
nitration
nitric
nitride
nitrite
nitrogen
nitroglycerine
nitrous
nitty-gritty
nitwit
✘nixt = next
no try kno
no (= opposite of
  yes → know)
  noes or
  nos (= negatives
  → nose; knows)
nobble
  nobbles
  nobbled

nobbling
nobility
nobilities
noble
nobleman
noblemen
noblesse
noblewoman
noblewomen
nobody
nobodies
✗ nocshus = noxious
✗ noctious = noxious
nocturnal
nocturnally
nocturne
nod
nods
nodded
nodding
nodal
nodality
noddle
noddy
node
nodule
Noel *or*
Noël
noes (= negatives
→ knows; nose)
nog
noggin
noir
noise
noiseless
noisily
noisiness
noisome
noisy
noisier

noisiest
nomad
nomadic
✗ nome = gnome
nomenclature
nominal
nominally
nominate
nominates
nominated
nominating
nomination
nominative
nominee
nonagenarian
nonaggression
nonagon
nonagonal
nonaligned
✗ nonalined =
nonaligned
✗ nonalinement =
nonalignment
nonappearance
nonce
nonchalant
noncommittal
nonconductor
nonconformist
noncontributory
noncooperation
noncooperative
nondescript
nondrip
none (= not any
→ nun)
nonentity
nonentities
nonequivalence
nonessential

nonesuch
nonetheless
nonevent
nonferrous
nonfiction
nonflammable
nonintervention
noniron
nonjudgemental
nonjudgmental
nonmetal
nonpareil
nonparticipating
nonpartisan
nonplus
nonplusses
nonplussed
nonplussing
nonproductive
nonproliferation
nonresident
nonreturnable
nonscheduled
nonsense
nonsensical
✗ nonshalence =
nonchalance
nonslip
nonsmoker
nonsmoking
nonstandard
nonstarter
nonstick
nonstop
non-U
nonunion
nonviolent
✗ noo = gnu
noodle
nook

nooky
noon
noonday
noontime
noose
nope
nor (= neither
  → gnaw)
noradrenaline
Nordic
Norfolk
norm
normal
normalisation
normalise
  normalises
  normalised
  normalising
normality
normalization
normalize
  normalizes
  normalized
  normalizing
normally
Norman
normative
Norse
north
Northampton
northbound
northeast
northeasterly
northeastern
northeastward
northeastwards
northerly
northern
Northerner
northernmost

Northumberland
northward
northwards
northwest
northwesterly
northwestward
northwestwards
Norway
Norwegian
Norwich
nos (= negatives
  → knows; nose)
nose (= part of the
  face → knows;
  noes; nos; nose)
noses
nosed
nosing
nosebag
nosebleed
nosepiece
nosey
nosier
nosiest
nosh
nosily
nosiness
nostalgia
nostalgic
nostalgically
✗nostic = gnostic
nostril
nostrum
nosy
nosier
nosiest
not (= negative
  → knot)
notability
notable

notably
notarise
  notarises
  notarised
  notarising
notarize
  notarizes
  notarized
  notarizing
notary
notaries
notate
  notates
  notated
  notating
notation
notch
  notches
  notched
  notching
note
  notes
  noted
  noting
notebook
notecase
notelet
notepaper
notes
noteworthily
noteworthiness
noteworthy
nothing
nothingness
notice
  notices
  noticed
  noticing
noticeable
noticeably

notifiable
notification
notify
  notifies
  notified
  notifying
notion
notional
notionally
notions
notoriety
notorious
notwithstanding
nougat
nought (= zero
  → naught)
noun
nourish
  nourishes
  nourished
  nourishing
nourishment
nous
nouveau riche
  nouveaux riches
nova
  novae or
  novas
novel
novelette
novelise
  novelises
  novelised
  novelising
novelist
novelize
  novelizes
  novelized
  novelizing
novella

novelty
  novelties
November
novena
novice
noviciate
novitiate
now
nowadays
nowhere
nowt
noxious
nozzle
nu
nuance
nub
nubile
nuclear
nuclease
nucleate
nuclei
nuclein
nucleon
nucleoplasm
nucleoprotein
nucleosynthesis
nucleotide
nucleus
  nuclei or
  nucleuses
nude
nudge
  nudges
  nudged
  nudging
nudism
nudity
  nudities
✗ nuga = nought
nugatory

nugget
nuisance
nuke
  nukes
  nuked
  nuking
null
nullify
  nullifies
  nullified
  nullifying
nullity
  nullities
✗ numatic = pneumatic
numb
number
  numbers
  numbered
  numbering
numberless
numberplate
numbskull
numerable
numeracy
numeral
numerary
numerate
numeration
numerator
numerical
numerological
numerology
numerous
numismatics
numismatist
✗ numly = numbly
✗ numness =
  numbness
✗ numonia =
  pneumonia

numskull
nun (= in a convent
  → none)
Nuneaton
nunnery
  nunneries
✗ nuonce = nuance
nuptial
nuptials
nur try neur
✗ nurish = nourish
nurse
  nurses
  nursed
  nursing
nursemaid
nursery
  nurseries
nurture
  nurtures
  nurtured
  nurturing
✗ nusance = nuisance
nut try neut
nut
nutcase
nutcracker
nuthatch
nuthouse
nutlet
nutmeg
nutrient
nutrition
nutritional
nutritionally
nutritionary
nutritionist
nutritious
nutritiously
nutritive

nutshell
nutter
nuttily
nuttiness
nutty
  nuttier
  nuttiest
✗ nuvo reesh =
  nouveau riche
nuzzle
  nuzzles
  nuzzled
  nuzzling
nyala
  nyala or
  nyalas
nylon
nylons
nymph
nymphet
nympho
nymphos
nymphomania
nymphomaniacal

O

o try au
oak
OAP
oar (= on a boat
  → or; ore)
  oars
  oared
  oaring
oarlock
oasis
  oases
oast
oat
oatcake
oath
oatmeal
✗ obaisance =
  obeisance
✗ obay =
  obey
obdurate
OBE
obedience
obedient
obeisance
obeisant
obelisk
✗ obergine =
  aubergine
obese
obesity
obey

obeys
obeyed
obeying
obfuscate
obfuscates
obfuscated
obfuscating
obituarist
obituary
obituaries
✘ objay dar =
obet d'art
object
objects
objected
objecting
objection
objective
✘ obleek = oblique
obligate
obligates
obligated
obligating
obligation
obligatorily
obligatory
oblige
obliges
obliged
obliging
oblique
obliterate
obliterates
obliterated
obliterating
obliteration
oblivion
oblivious
oblong
obloquy

obloquies
✘ obnocshus =
obnoxious
✘ obnoctious =
obnoxious
obnoxious
oboe
oboes
obscene
obscenity
obscenities
obscure
obscures
obscured
obscuring
obscurity
obscurities
obsequious
observable
observably
observance
observant
observation
observatory
observatories
observe
observes
observed
observing
observer
obsess
obsesses
obsessed
obsessing
obsession
obsessive
obsessively
obsolescent
obsolete
obstacle

obstetric
obstetrically
obstetrician
obstetrics
✘ obsticle = obstacle
obstinacy
obstinacies
obstinate
obstreperous
obstreperously
obstruct
obstructs
obstructed
obstructing
obstruction
obstructive
obstructively
obstructor
obtain
obtains
obtained
obtaining
obtainable
obtrude
obtrudes
obtruded
obtruding
obtruder
obtrusion
obtrusive
obtuse
obverse
obviate
obviates
obviated
obviating
obvious
obviously
ocarina
occasion

occasional
occasionally
occident
occidental
occidentally
occlude
  occludes
  occluded
  occluding
occult
occultism
occupancy
  occupancies
occupant
occupation
occupational
occupier
occupy
  occupies
  occupied
  occupying
occur
  occurs
  occurred
  occurring
occurrence
ocean
oceanic
oceanography
ocelot
✗ ocer = ochre
och
ochre
o'clock
ocs try ox
✗ ocsident = occident
octagon
octagonal
octagonally
octahedral

octahedron
  octahedrons or
    octahedra
octal
octane
octangular
octave
octavo
✗ octepus = octopus
octet
octette
octillion
octillionth
October
octogenarian
octopus
  octopuses or
    octopi
octuple
ocular
odd
oddball
oddity
  oddities
oddly
ode (= poem
  → owed)
✗ oder = odour
odious
odium
odorous
odour
Odysseus
Odyssey
Oedipus
oenologist
oenology
o'er (= over
  → ower)
oesophageal

oesophagus
  oesophagi
oestrogen
oestrus
oeuvre
of
off
offal
offbeat
offcut
✗ offen = often
offence
offend
  offends
  offended
  offending
offender
offensive
offer
  offers
  offered
  offering
offertory
  offertories
offhand
office
officer
official
officially
officiate
  officiates
  officiated
  officiating
officiation
officiator
officious
officiously
offing
offish
offprint

offset
  offsets
  offset
  offsetting
offshoot
offshore
offside
offspring
offstage
oft
often
ogle
  ogles
  ogled
  ogling
ogre
ogress
oh (= exclamation
  → owe)
ohm
ohmage
ohmmeter
oho
✗ oh per = au pair
oik
oil
  oils
  oiled
  oiling
oilcan
oilcloth
oilfield
oilfired
oilily
oiliness
oilskin
oily
  oilier
  oiliest
oink

ointment
O.K.
okapi
  okapis or
  okapi
okay
  okays
  okayed
  okaying
O'Keeffe, Georgia
Okehampton
okey-doke
Oklahoma
okra
✗ olay = olé
old
olden
olde-worlde
oldfangled
oldie
oldster
olé
oleaginous
oleander
oleaster
olfaction
olfactory
  olfactories
oligarch
oligarchy
  oligarchies
Oligocene
oligopoly
  oligopolies
olive
Oliver
oloroso
Olympiad
Olympian
Olympic

Olympus
Oman
ombudsman
  ombudsmen
omega
omelet
omelette
omen
omicron
✗ omiga = omega
ominous
omission
omit
  omits
  omitted
  omitting
✗ omlet = omelet
omnibus
  omnibuses
omnipotence
omnipotent
omnipresent
omniscience
omniscient
omnisciently
omnivore
omnivorous
on
onanism
onanistic
✗ on bloc = en bloc
once
oncogene
oncogenic
oncological
oncologist
oncology
oncoming
one (= number
  → won)

✗ oner = honour
✗ onerable =
  honourable
onerous
oneself
✗ onest = honest
✗ onestly = honestly
one-upmanship
✗ onfont terrible =
  enfant terrible
ongoing
ongoingly
onion
onionskin
onlooker
only
✗ on mas = en masse
onomatopoeia
onomatopoeic
onomatopoeically
✗ onorable =
  honourable
✗ onour = honour
✗ onpassion = en
  passant
onrush
onset
onshore
onside
onslaught
on-stage
onto
✗ ontont = entente
✗ ontray = entrée
✗ ontrepener =
  entrepreneur
onus
  onuses
onward
onwards

✗ onwy = ennui
onyx
oodles
ooh
oompah
oomph
oops
✗ ootray = outré
ooze
oozes
oozed
oozing
oozily
ooziness
✗ oozo = ouzo
oozy
oozier
ooziest
opacity
opacities
✗ opake = opaque
opal
opaque
open
opens
opened
opening
opener
opening
openly
opera
operable
operate
operates
operated
operating
operatic
operatically
operation
operational

operationally
operative
operator
operetta
  operettas
ophthalmic
ophthalmological
ophthalmologist
ophthalmology
ophthalmoscope
opiate
opine
opines
opined
opining
opinion
opinionated
opinionatedly
opium
opossum
  opossums or
  opossum
opponent
opportune
opportunist
opportunistic
opportunistically
opportunity
  opportunities
oppose
opposes
opposed
opposing
opposite
opposition
oppress
oppresses
oppressed
oppressing
oppression

oppressive
oppressor
opprobrious
opprobrium
opt
  opts
  opted
  opting
✗ opthalmic =
  ophthalmic
optic
optical
optically
optician
optics
optimal
optimise
  optimises
  optimised
  optimising
optimism
optimize
  optimizes
  optimized
  optimizing
optimum
  optima *or*
  optimums
option
optional
optionally
✗ optishen = optician
optometrist
optometry
opulent
opus
  opuses *or*
  opera
or (= either . . . or
  → oar; ore)

oracle
oracy
oral
orally
orange
orangeade
orangery
  orangeries
orangewood
orang-utan
  orang-utans
orate
  orates
  orated
  orating
oration
orator
oratorio
  oratorios
oratory
orb
orbit
orbital
orbiter
orc
✗ orcestra = orchestra
orchard
orchestra
  orchestras
orchestral
orchestrally
orchestrate
  orchestrates
  orchestrated
  orchestrating
orchid
✗ orcid = orchid
ordain
  ordains
  ordained

ordaining
ordeal
✗ or de combat =
  hors de combat
✗ ordenary = ordinary
✗ ordenarly =
  ordinarily
order
  orders
  ordered
  ordering
orderliness
orderly
  orderlies
✗ or derv =
  hors d'oeuvre
ordinal
ordinance
ordinand
ordinarily
ordinary
ordinate
ordination
ordnance
ordure
ore (= metal
  → oar; ore)
oregano
organ
organdie
organic
organically
organisation
organise
  organises
  organised
  organising
organiser
organism
organist

organization
organize
  organizes
  organized
  organizing
organizer
orgasm
orgasmic
orgy
  orgies
✗ oricle = oracle
oriel
orient
oriental
orientalism
orientalist
orientally
orientate
  orientates
  orientated
  orientating
orientation
orienteering
orifice
origami
origin
original
originality
originally
originate
  originates
  originated
  originating
origination
originator
✗ oringade = orangeade
✗ oringe = orange
oriole
Orion

Orkney
✗ ormelu = ormolu
ormolu
ornament
ornamental
ornamentally
ornate
ornithological
ornithologically
ornithology
orotund
orphan
orphanage
orthodontist
orthodontics
orthodox
orthodoxy
orthogonal
orthography
  orthographies
orthopaedics
orthopaedist
orthoptic
orthoptics
orthoptist
oryx
  oryxes or
  oryx
oscillate
  oscillates
  oscillated
  oscillating
oscillation
oscillator
oscillatory
oscillogram
oscillograph
oscilloscope
✗ oshen = ocean
✗ oshenographer =

oceanographer
✗ oshianic = oceanic
osier
Oslo
osmiridium
osmium
osmosis
osmotic
osmotically
osprey
ossification
ossify
  ossifies
  ossified
  ossifying
✗ ossilate = oscillate
ossuary
  ossuaries
✗ ossy = Aussie
ostensible
ostensibly
ostentation
ostentatious
osteoarthritic
osteoarthritis
osteomyelitis
osteopath
osteopathic
osteopathy
osteoporosis
ostler
Ostpolitik
ostracise
  ostracises
  ostracised
  ostracising
ostracize
  ostracizes
  ostracized
  ostracizing

ostrich
  ostriches *or*
  ostrich
Ostrogoth
Oswestry
otalgia
other
otherwise
otherworldly
otiose
otiosity
otitis
otolaryngology
otology
otter
ottoman (= seat or
  stool)
  ottomans
Ottoman (= Turkish
  empire)
ouch
ought
Ouija™
ounce
Oundle
our (= belonging to
  us → hour)
✗ourly = hourly
ourself
  ourselves
oust
  ousts
  ousted
  ousting
out (= not in
  → owt)
  outs
  outed
  outing
outback

outboard
outbreak
outbuilding
outburst
outcast
outclass
  outclasses
  outclassed
  outclassing
outcome
outcrop
outcry
  outcries
outdated
outdistance
  outdistances
  outdistanced
  outdistancing
outdo
  outdoes
  outdid
  outdone
  outdoing
outdoor
outdoors
outer
outermost
outfield
outfit
outfitter
outflank
  outflanks
  outflanked
  outflanking
outflow
outfoot
  outfoots
  outfooted
  outfooting
outgoing

outgoings
outgrow
  outgrows
  outgrew
  outgrown
  outgrowing
outgrowth
outgun
  outguns
  outgunned
  outgunning
outhouse
outing
outlandish
outlaw
  outlaws
  outlawed
  outlawing
outlay
  outlays
  outlaid
  outlaying
outlet
outlier
outline
  outlines
  outlined
  outlining
outlive
  outlives
  outlived
  outliving
outlook
outlying
outmanoeuvre
  outmanoeuvring
outmoded
outnumber
  outnumbers
  outnumbered

outnumbering
outpatient
outpost
outpour
outpouring
output
outrageous
outrageously
outré
outreach
outrider
outrigger
outright
outrun
  outruns
  outran
  outrun
  outrunning
outset
outside
outsider
outsize
outsized
outskirts
outspoken
outstanding
outstandingly
outstay
  outstays
  outstayed
  outstaying
outstretched
outtake
outward
outwards
outweigh
  outweighs
  outweighed
  outweighing
outwit

outwits
outwitted
outwitting
outwork
outworker
outworn
ouzo
ova
oval
ovally
ovalness
ovarian
ovary
  ovaries
ovation
oven
ovenware
over
overachieve
overachiever
overact
  overacts
  overacted
  overacting
overage
overall
overarm
overawe
  overawes
  overawed
  overawing
overbalance
  overbalances
  overbalanced
  overbalancing
overbearing
overbearingly
overboard
overcast
overcharge

overcharges
overcharged
overcharging
overcoat
overcome
overcomes
overcame
overcome
overcoming
overcompensate
overcompensates
overcompensated
overcompensating
overdo
overdoes
overdid
overdone
overdoing
overdose
overdraft
overdrive
overdue
overestimate
overflow
overflows
overflowed
overflown
overflowing
overgarment
overground
overgrow
overgrows
overgrew
overgrown
overgrowing
overhang
overhaul
overhauls
overhauled
overhauling

overhead
overheads
overhear
overhears
overheard
overhearing
overheat
overheats
overheated
overheating
overindulge
overindulges
overindulged
overindulging
overkill
overlap
overlaps
overlapped
overlapping
overleaf
overload
overloads
overloaded
overloading
overlong
overlook
overlooks
overlooked
overlooking
overly
overmuch
overnight
overpass
overpopulated
overpower
overpowers
overpowered
overpowering
overpoweringly

overqualified
overrated
✗ overrawt =
overwrought
overreact
overreacts
overreacted
overreacting
overreaction
override
overrides
overrode
overridden
overriding
✗ overrought =
overwrought
overrule
overrules
overruled
overruling
overrun
overruns
overran
overrun
overrunning
overseas
oversee
oversees
oversaw
overseen
overseeing
overseer
oversensitive
oversensitively
oversensitivity
overshadow
overshadows
overshadowed
overshadowing
oversight

oversimplify
oversimplifies
oversimplified
oversimplifying
oversize
oversleep
oversleeps
overslept
oversleeping
overspill
overstatement
overt
overtake
overtakes
overtook
overtaken
overtaking
overtime
overtone
overture
overturn
overturns
overturned
overturning
overvalued
overview
overweening
overweight
overwhelming
overwhelmingly
overwrought
oviduct
ovine
oviparous
ovoid
ovulate
ovulates
ovulated
ovulating
ovule

ovum
  ova
ow
owe (= owe money
  → oh)
  owes
  owed (= owed
    money → ode)
  owing
ower (= person who
  owes → o'er)
owl
owlet
owlish
owlishly
own
  owns
  owned
  owning
owner
ownership
owt (= anything
  → out)
ox
  oxen
oxbow
oxeye
oxhide
oxidant
oxidase
oxidation
oxide
oxidise
  oxidises
  oxidised
  oxidising
oxidiser
oxidize
  oxidizes
  oxidized

oxidizing
oxidizer
oxlip
oxtail
oxtongue
oxyacetylene
oxygen
oxygenate
  oxygenates
  oxygenated
  oxygenating
oxygenator
oxyhaemoglobin
oxymoron
oyes
oyez
oyster
oystercatcher
ozone

P

pa
✗ pa = de = der =
  pas = de = deux
pace
  paces
  paced (= walked
    → paste)
  pacing
pacemaker
pacesetter
pachouli
pachyderm
✗ paciderm =
  pachyderm
pacifism
pacifist
pacify
  pacifies
  pacified
  pacifying
pack
  packs
  packed (= full
    → pact)
  packing
package
  packages
  packaged
  packaging
packer
packet
packhorse

palpitate

pact (= bargain
   → packed)
pad
   pads
   padded
   padding
paddle
   paddles
   paddled
   paddling
paddock
paddy
   paddies
padlock
padre
paean
paediatrician
paedophile
paedophilia
paella
pagan
page
   pages
   paged
   paging
pageant
pageantry
pageboy
pagoda
paid
pail (= bucket
   → pale)
pain (= hurt
   → pane)
   pains
   pained
   paining
painful
painfully
painkiller

painstaking
paint
   paints
   painted
   painting
paintbox
paintbrush
painter
painting
paintwork
pair (= two
   → pare; pear)
   pairs
   paired
   pairing
paisley
Pakistan
pakora
pal
palace
Palaeocene
Palaeolithic
palatable
palatal
palate (= part of
   the mouth
   → pallet; palette)
palatial
palatinate
palaver
pale
   pales
   paled
   paling
paleface
Palestinian
palette (= for
   paints → palate;
   pallet)
✗ palice = palace

palimony
palindrome
palindromic
paling
✗ paliolithic =
   Palaeolithic
✗ paliontology =
   palaeontology
palisade
palish
✗ palitable = palatable
pall
   palls
   palled
   palling
pallbearer
pallet (= bed or
   platform → palate;
   palette)
palliative
pallid
pallor
pally
   pallier
   palliest
palm
   palms
   palmed
   palming
palmate
palmistry
palomino
   palominos
palpable
palpate
   palpates
   palpated
   palpating
palpation
palpitate

palpitates
palpitated
palpitating
palsy
palsies
paltrily
paltriness
paltry (= insignif-
  icant → poultry)
paltrier
paltriest
pampas (= grass
  → pampers)
pamper
pampers (=
  indulges
  → pampas)
pampered
pampering
pamphlet
pamphleteer
pan
  pans
  panned
  panning
panacea
panache
Panama
✗ panash = panache
pancake
pancreas
pancreatic
✗ pancromatic =
  panchromatic
panda (= animal
  → pander)
pandemic
pandemonium
pander (= gratify
  → panda)

panders
pandered
pandering
✗ pandimonium =
  pandemonium
pane (= window etc
  → pain)
panel
panelling
panellist
panettone
  panettones or
  pannetoni
pang
pangolin
panic
  panics
  panicked
  panicking
panicky
panned
pannier
panning
panoply
  panoplies
panorama
panoramic
pans
pansy
  pansies
pant
  pants
  panted
  panting
pantaloons
pantechnicon
pantheism
pantheon
panther
panties

pantihose
pantile
panto
  pantos
pantograph
pantomime
pantry
  pantries
pants
pantyhose
panzer
pap
papa
papacy
  papacies
papal
paparazzo
  paparazzi
papaw
papaya
paper
  papers
  papered
  papering
paperback
paperboy
paperclip
papergirl
paperweight
paperwork
papier-mâché
papillote
papist
papoose
pappoose
paprika
Papua New Guinea
papyrus
  papyri or
  papyruses

par
para
parable
parabola
parabolic
paracetamol
parachute
  parachutes
  parachuted
  parachuting
parade
  parades
  paraded
  parading
paradigm
paradigmatic
paradise
paradisiacal
paradox
paraffin
paragliding
paragon
paragraph
Paraguay
parakeet
parallax
parallel
  parallels
  paralleled
  paralleling
parallelogram
paralyse
  paralyses
  paralysed
  paralysing
paralysis
paralytic
paramedic
parameter
paramilitary

paramount
paramour
paranoia
paranoid
paranormal
parapet
paraphernalia
paraphrase
  paraphrases
  paraphrased
  paraphrasing
paraplegia
parasailing
parascending
✗ parashute =
  parachute
✗ parasicology =
  parapsychology
parasite
parasitic
paraskiing
parasol
paratroops
parboil
  parboils
  parboiled
  parboiling
parcel
  parcels
  parcelled
  parcelling
parch
  parches
  parched
  parching
parchment
pardon
  pardons
  pardoned
  pardoning

pardoner
pare (= peel →
  pair; pear)
parent
  parents
  parented
  parenting
parentage
parental
parentally
parenteral
parenterally
parenthesis
  parentheses
parenthetic
parenting
parfait
pariah
parietal
paring
parish
parishioner
parity
  parities
park
  parks
  parked
  parking
parka
✗ parkay = parquet
parkin
parkland
parky
  parkier
  parkiest
✗ parlament =
  parliament
parlance
parley
parliament

parliamentarian
parliamentarianism
parliamentary
parlour
parlous
✗ parm = palm
Parmesan
✗ parmistry =
palmistry
parochial
parochialism
parochially
parody
　parodies
parole
paroxysm
parquet
parquetry
parricide
parrot
　parrots
　parroted
　parroting
parry
　parries
　parried
　parrying
parse (= in gram-
　mar → pass)
　parses
　parsed
　parsing
parsec
Parsee
parsimonious
parsimony
parsley
parsnip
parson
parsonage

part
parts
parted
parting
partake
partakes
partook
partaken
partaking
partial
partiality
partially
participant
participate
participates
participated
participating
participation
participator
participatory
participial
participle
particle
parti-coloured
particular
parting
partisan
partition
partly
partner
　partners
　partnered
　partnering
partnership
partook
partridge
parts
parturition
partway
party

parties
parve
pascal
pasha
✗ pashense = patience
pass (= pass a test
　→ parse)
passes
passed (=
　passed by
　→ past)
passing
passable
passably
passage
passageway
✗ passay = passé
passé
passenger
passer-by
　passers-by
passing
passion
passionate
passionflower
passive
passivity
Passover
passport
password
past (= long ago →
　passed)
pasta
paste (= wallpaper
　paste → paced)
pastes
pasted
pasting
✗ pasteel = pastille
pastel

pasteurisation
pasteurise
  pasteurises
  pasteurised
  pasteurising
pasteurization
pasteurize
  pasteurizes
  pasteurized
  pasteurizing
pastiche
pastier
pasties
pastiest
pastil
pastille
pastime
pasting
pastis
✗ pastishe = pastiche
pastitsio
pastor
pastoral
pastrami
pastry
  pastries
pasturage
pasture
✗ pasturization =
  pasteurization
✗ pasturize =
  pasteurize
pasty
  pasties
  pastier
  pastiest
pat
  pats
  patted
  patting

patch
  patches
  patched
  patching
patchily
patchiness
patchouli
patchwork
patchy
  patchier
  patchiest
pate
pâté
patella
patent
patentee
patentor
pater
paterfamilias
  patresfamilias
paternal
paternalism
paternalist
paternalistic
paternalistically
paternity
paternoster
path
pathetic
pathetically
pathogen
pathogenic
pathological
pathologist
pathology
pathos
pathway
patience
patient
patina

patio
  patios
patisserie
patois
  patois
patresfamilias
patriarch
patriarchy
  patriarchies
patrician
patricide
patrilineal
patrimonial
patrimony
  patrimonies
patriot
patriotic
patriotism
patrol
  patrols
  patrolled
  patrolling
patron
patronage
patronise
  patronises
  patronised
  patronising
patronize
  patronizes
  patronized
  patronizing
patronymic
pats
✗ pattay = pâté
patted
patter
  patters

patten (= clog
  → pattern)

pattered
pattering
pattern (= style or
   decoration → pat-
   ten)
patty
patties
paucity
paunch
pauper
pause (= wait
   → paws)
pauses
paused
pausing
pave
paves
paved
paving
pavement
pavilion
paw (= animal's
   hand → pore; poor;
   pour)
paws (= touches
   → pause)
pawed
pawing
✗pawlsied = palsied
✗pawlsy = palsy
pawn (= chess
   piece; leave with a
   pawnbroker
   → porn)
pawns
pawned
pawning
pawnbroker
pawnshop
pawpaw

pax
pay
pays
paid
paying
payable
payday
PAYE
payee
payer
payload
paymaster
payment
payoff
payout
payphone
payroll
pays
pazazz
pazzazz
PE
pea (= vegetable
   → pee)
peace (= not war
   → piece)
peaceable
peaceful
peacekeeping
peacemaker
peacetime
peach
peachiness
peachy
   peachier
   peachiest
peacock
   peacocks or
   peacock
peafowl
   peafowls or

peafowl
peak (= summit
   → peek; peke;
   pique)
peaks
peaked
peaking
peaked
peal (= bells
   → peel)
peals
pealed
pealing
✗pean = paean
peanut
pear (= fruit
   → pair; pare)
pearl (= necklace
   → purl)
pearliness
pearlised
pearlized
pearly
   pearlier
   pearliest
pearmain
peasant
peasantry
pease
peasouper
peat
pebble
pecan
peccadillo
   peccadillos or
   peccadilloes or
peccary
   peccaries or
   peccary
peck

pecks
pecked
pecking
pecker
peckish
✗ peconcy = piquancy
pectase
pectin
pectoral
peculiar
peculiarity
  peculiarities
pecuniary
pedagogic
pedagogue
pedagogy
pedal (= on a bike
  → peddle)
  pedals
  pedalled
  pedalling
pedalo
  pedalos or
  pedaloes
pedant
pedantic
pedantically
pedantry
  pedantries
peddle (= sell
  → pedal)
peddler
✗ pedent = pedant
pedestal
pedestrian
pedestrianisation
pedestrianization
✗ pediatrician =
  paediatrician
✗ pediatrics =

paediatrics
pedicure
pedigree
✗ pedistal = pedestal
pedlar
pedometer
✗ pedophile =
  paedophile
pee (= urinate
  → pea)
pees
peed
peeing
peek (= peep
  → peak; peke;
  pique)
peekaboo
peel (= remove skin
  → peal)
  peels
  peeled
  peeling
peeler
  peeling
peep
  peeps
  peeped
  peeping
peephole
✗ peeple = people
peepshow
peer (= look or
  nobleman → pier)
peerage
peeress
pees
peeve
  peeves
  peeved
  peeving

peevish
peewit
peg
  pegs
  pegged
  pegging
pegboard
peignoir
pejoration
pejorative
peke (= dog →
  peak; peek; pique)
Peking
Pekingese
pekoe
pel try pol
pelican
pellagra
✗ pellergonium =
  pelargonium
pellet
pell-mell
pelmet
pelt
  pelts
  pelted
  pelting
pelvic
pelvis
pemican
pemmican
pen
  pens
  penned
  penning
penal
penalise
  penalises
  penalised
  penalising

penalize
  penalizes
  penalized
  penalizing
penalty
  penalties
penance
pence
penchant
pencil
pendant (= neck-\
  lace)
pendent (= hang-\
  ing)
pending
pendulous
pendulum
✗penecilin =
  penicillin
Penelope
✗penelty = penalty
✗penence = penance
✗penent = pennant
penetrate
  penetrates
  penetrated
  penetrating
penetration
penguin
penicillin
penile
peninsula
peninsular
penis
penitent
penitential
penitentiary
  penitentiaries
penknife
  penknives

pennant
penned
pennies
penniless
penning
pennon
penny
  pennies *or*
  pence
Pennicuik
✗pennife = penknife
Pennines
Pennsylvania
pennyworth
pens
pension
pensioner
pensive
pent
pentagon
pentagonal
pentagram
pentahedron
  pentahedrons *or*
  pentahedra
pentameter
pentathlon
penthouse
penultimate
penurious
penury
Penzance
peony
  peonies
people
pep
peps
pepped
pepping
pepper

peppers
peppered
peppering
peppercorn
peppermint
pepperoni
peppery
pepping
peptic
peptide
per try pur
per
peradventure
perambulation
perambulator
percale
perceivable
perceivably
perceive
  perceives
  perceived
  perceiving
percentage
percentile
perceptible
perceptibly
perception
perceptive
perceptual
perch
  perches
  perched
  perching
perchance
percipience
percipient
percolate
  percolates
  percolated
  percolating

percolator	pericardium	perks
percussion	pericardia	perked
percussionist	pericarp	perking
percussive	peril	perkily
perdition	perilous	perkiness
peregrine	perimeter	perky
peremptorily	perinatal	perkier
peremptoriness	perineum	perkiest
peremptory	perinea	perm
perennial	period	perms
perennially	periodic	permed
✗ pereration =	periodical	perming
peroration	periodically	permafrost
perfect	periodontal	permanence
perfection	periodontics	permanent
perfectionist	peripatetic	permanganate
perfidious	peripheral	permeability
perfidy	periphery	permeable
perfidies	peripheries	permeate
perforate	periscope	permeates
perforates	periscopic	permeated
perforated	perish	permeating
perforating	perishes	permissible
perforation	perished	permissibly
perforce	perishing	permission
perform	perishable	permissive
performs	peristalsis	permit
performed	peritoneum	permits
performing	peritonea *or*	permitted
performance	peritoneums	permitting
performer	periwig	permutability
perfume	periwinkle	permutable
perfumer	perjure	permutably
perfumery	perjures	permutation
perfunctorily	perjured	permute
perfunctoriness	perjuring	permutes
perfunctory	perjurious	permuted
✗ perger = perjure	perjury	permuting
pergola	perjuries	pernicious
perhaps	perk	pernickety

peroneal
peroration
peroxide
perpendicular
perpetrate
  perpetrates
  perpetrated
  perpetrating
perpetrator
perpetual
perpetually
perpetuate
  perpetuates
  perpetuated
  perpetuating
perpetuation
perpetuity
perplex
  perplexes
  perplexed
  perplexing
perquisite
persecute
  persecutes
  persecuted
  persecuting
persecution
perseverance
persevere
  perseveres
  persevered
  persevering
persimmon
persist
  persists
  persisted
  persisting
persistence
persistent
person

persons *or*
  people
persona
  personae
personable
personage
personal
personalise
  personalises
  personalised
  personalising
personality
  personalities
personalize
  personalizes
  personalized
  personalizing
personally
personification
personify
  personifies
  personified
  personifying
personnel
persons
perspective
Perspex®
perspicacious
perspicacity
perspicuity
perspicuous
perspiration
perspire
  perspires
  perspired
  perspiring
persuade
  persuades
  persuaded
  persuading

persuader
persuasible
persuasion
persuasive
pert
pertain
  pertains
  pertained
  pertaining
pertinacious
pertinent
perturb
  perturbs
  perturbed
  perturbing
perturbable
perturbably
perturbation
  perturbing
pertussis
Peru
peruke
perusal
peruse
  peruses
  perused
  perusing
pervade
  pervades
  pervaded
  pervading
pervasive
perverse
perversion
perversive
pervert
  perverts
  perverted
  perverting
  perverted

pervertible
pervious
peseta
peskily
peskiness
pesky
  peskier
  peskiest
peso
  pesos
pessary
  pessaries
pessimism
pessimist
pest
pester
  pesters
  pestered
  pestering
pesticide
pestilence
pestilent
pestilential
pestle
pesto
pet
  pets
  petted
  petting
petal
petard
✗ peteet = petite
peter
  peters
  petered
  petering
Peterborough
petersham
pethidine
✗ peticular =

particular
✗ peticularly =
  particularly
petiole
petit
petite
petition
  petitions
  petitioned
  petitioning
petitioner
petrel (= sea bird
  → petrol)
petrifies
petrified
petrifying
petrochemical
petrochemistry
petrodollar
petrol (= for vehi-
  cles → petrel)
petroleum
pets
petted
petticoat
petting
pettily
pettiness
petty
  pettier
  pettiest
petulant
petunia
Pevensey
pew
pewee
pewit
pewter
peyote

✗ pezazz = pizazz
pfennig
  pfennigs or
  pfennige
pH
phaeton
phagocyte
phalange
phalangeal
phalanx
phalanxes
  phalanxes or
  phalanges
phallic
phallus
  phalli or
  phalluses
phantasm
phantasmagoria
phantasmagoric
phantasmal
phantasmic
phantasmically
phantom
Pharaoh
Pharisee
pharmaceutical
pharmacist
pharmacological
pharmacology
pharmacopoeia
✗ pharmacutical =
  pharmaceutical
pharmacy
  pharmacies
pharynx
  pharynges or
  pharynxes
phase
  phases

phased
phasing
PhD
pheasant
✗ pheenix = phoenix
phenobarbitone
phenol
phenomena
phenomenal
phenomenon
  phenomena
phenotype
phenyl
pheromone
phew (= exclama-
  tion → few)
phi
phial
Philadelphia
philanderer
philanthropic
philanthropist
philanthropy
philatelic
philatelist
philately
✗ phile = phial
philharmonic
Philippines
philologist
philology
philosopher
philosophical
philosophise
  philosophises
  philosophised
  philosophising
philosophize
  philosophizes
  philosophized

philosophizing
philosophy
  philosophies
philtre (= love
  potion → filter)
phiz
phizog
phlegm
phlegmatic
✗ phlem = phlegm
phlox
  phlox or
  phloxes
phobia
phobic
Phoebe
phoenix
phone
  phones
  phoned
  phoning
phonecard
phoneme
phonemic
phonetic
phonetically
phonetics
phoney
phonier
phoniest
phonics
phonily
phoniness
phonograph
phonology
phony
phonier
phoniest
phooey
phosphate

phosphor
phosphorescence
phosphorescent
phosphorous (adj.)
phosphorus (noun)
photo
  photos
photocell
photocopier
photocopy
  photocopies
  photocopied
  photocopying
Photofit™
photogenic
photograph
photographer
photographic
photography
photogravure
photojournalism
photomontage
photon
photosensitive
Photostat™
photosynthesis
photosynthesise
  photosynthesises
  photosynthesised
  photosynthesising
photosynthesize
  photosynthesizes
  photosynthesized
  photosynthesizing
phototropic
phototropism
phrasal
phrase
  phrases
  phrased

phrasing
phraseology
 phraseologies
phrenology
phut
phylactery
 phylacteries
phylum
 phyla
Phyllis
✗physeek = physique
physic
physical
physician
physicist
physics
physiognomy
physiological
physiology
✗physionomy =
 physiognomy
physiotherapy
physique
pi (= number or
 Greek letter → pie)
pis
pianissimo
pianist
piano
 pianos
pianoforte
piazza
✗picancy = piquancy
✗picant piquant
picaresque
piccalilli
piccolo
 piccolos
pick
 picks

picked
picking
pickaxe
picket
pickets
picketed
picketing
pickier
pickiest
pickily
pickiness
pickings
pickle
pickles
pickled
pickling
pickled
pickpocket
picky
 pickier
 pickiest
picnic
picnics
picnicked
picnicking
pictogram
pictograph
pictorial
picture
pictures
pictured
picturing
picturesque
piddling
pidgin (= language
 → pigeon)
pie (= food
 → pi)
pies
piebald

piece (= part →
 peace)
pieces
pieced
piecing
piecemeal
piecework
pied
pied-à-terre
 pieds-à-terre
✗piella = paella
pier (= at the
 seaside → peer)
pierce
pierces
pierced
piercing
pies
piety
 pieties
piffle
piffling
pig
 pigs
 pigged
 pigging
pigeon (= bird
 → pidgin)
pigeonhole
 pigeonholes
 pigeonholed
 pigeonholing
piggish
piggy
 piggies
piggyback
piglet
pigment
pigmentation
pigmy

pigmies
pigpen
pigskin
pigsty
   pigsties
pigswill
pike
pikelet
pikestaff
✗ pikinese = Peking-
   ese
pilau
pilchard
pile
   piles
   piled
   piling
piles
pilfer
   pilfers
   pilfered
   pilfering
pilgrim
pilgrimage
pill
pillar
pillbox
pillion
pillock
pillory
   pillories
   pilloried
   pillorying
pillow
   pillows
   pillowed
   pillowing
pillowcase
pilot
   pilots

piloted
piloting
pilotage
pilule
pimento
   pimentos
pimiento
   pimientos
pimp
pimpernel
pimple
pin
   pins
   pinned
   pinning
pinafore
pinball
pince-nez
   pince-nez
pincers
pinch
   pinches
   pinched
   pinching
pincushion
pine
   pines
   pined
   pining
pineapple
ping
   pings
   pinged
   pinging
pinger
Ping-Pong™
✗ pinicle = pinnacle
pinion
pink
   pinks

pinked
   pinking
pinkeye
pinnacle
pinned
pinning
pinny
   pinnies
pinochle
pinpoint
   pinpoints
   pinpointed
   pinpointing
pinprick
pins
pinstripe
pint
pinto
   pintos
pioneer
pious
pip
   pips
   pipped
   pipping
pipe
   pipes
   piped
   piping
pipefish
pipeline
piper
pipette
piping
pipistrelle
pipped
pippin
pipping
pips
pipsqueak

piquancy
piquant
pique (= resent-
  ment → peak;
  peek)
  piques
  piqued
  piquing
piquet
piquing
piracy
  piracies
pirana
piranha
pirate
  pirates
  pirated
  pirating
piratic
piratical
pirouette
  pirouettes
  pirouetted
  pirouetting
Pisa
piscatorial
Pisces
pish
piss
  pisses
  pissed (= uri-
    nated → piste)
  pissing
pissed (= drunk →
  piste)
pistachio
  pistachios
piste (= ski slope
  → pissed)
pistil (= part of a

flower)
pistol (= gun)
piston
pit
  pits
  pitted
  pitting
pitch
  pitches
  pitched
  pitching
pitcher
pitchfork
piteous
piteously
pitfall
pith
pithead
pithily
pithiness
pithy
  pithier
  pithiest
pitiable
pitied
pities
pitiful
pitifully
pitiless
✗pitius = piteous
piton
pits
pitta
pittance
pitter-patter
pituitary
  pituitaries
pity
  pities
  pitied

pitying
✗pius = pious
pivot
  pivots
  pivoted
  pivoting
pivotal
pixel
pixie
  pixies
pixy
  pixies
pizazz
pizza
pizzazz
pizzeria
pizzicato
pizzle
placard
placate
  placates
  placated
  placating
placatory
place (= put →
  plaice)
  places
  placed
  placing
placebo
  placebos or
  placebos
placement
placenta
  placentas or
  placentae
placid
placidity
placing
✗plack = plaque

✗ plad = plaid
plagiarise
  plagiarises
  plagiarised
  plagiarising
plagiarism
plagiarize
  plagiarizes
  plagiarized
  plagiarizing
plague
  plagues
  plagued
  plaguing
plaice (= fish
  → place)
  plaice *or*
  plaices
plaid
plain (= flat ground,
  or simple → plane)
  plains
plaint
plaintiff
plait
plan
  plans
  planned
  planning
plane (= flat sur-
  face or aeroplane
  → plain)
planet
planetarium
  planetariums *or*
  planetaria
planetary
plangent
plank
plankton

planned
planning
plant
  plants
  planted
  planting
plantain
plantation
planter
plaque
plasma
plaster
  plasters
  plastered
  plastering
plasterboard
plastic
Plasticine™
plasticiser
plasticity
plasticizer
✗ plat = plait
plate
  plates
  plated
  plating
plateau
  plateaus *or*
  plateaux
platelet
platform
platinum
platitude
✗ plato = plateau
Platonic
platoon
platter
platypus
plaudit
plausible

play
  plays
  played
  playing
playback
playboy
player
playful
playgoer
playground
playgroup
playhouse
playlet
playmate
playpen
✗ playright =
  playwright
✗ playrite = playwright
playroom
playschool
plaything
playtime
playwright
plaza
plc *or*
  PLC
plea
plead
  pleads
  pleaded
  plead *or*
  pled
  pleading
pleadings
pleasant
pleasantry
please
  pleases
  pleased
  pleasing

pleased
pleasurable
pleasure
pleat
  pleats
  pleated
  pleating
plebeian
plebiscite
plectrum
  plectra *or*
  plectrums
pled
pledge
  pledges
  pledged
  pledging
Pleistocene
plenary
plenipotentiary
  plenipotentiaries
plenitude
plenteous
plenteously
plentiful
plentifully
plenty
plenum
  plenums *or*
  plena
plethora
pleura
  pleurae
pleurisy
plexus
  plexuses *or*
  plexus
pliable
pliant
plié

plied
pliers
plies
plight
plimsoll
plink
plinth
Pliocene
PLO
plod
  plods
  plodded
  plodding
plonk
  plonks
  plonked
  plonking
plonker
plop
  plops
  plopped
  plopping
plosion
plosive
plot
  plots
  plotted
  plotting
plotter
plough
  ploughs
  ploughed
  ploughing
plover
✗plow = plough
ploy
pluck
  plucks
  plucked
  plucking

pluckily
pluckiness
plucky
  pluckier
  pluckiest
plug
  plugs
  plugged
  plugging
plughole
plum (= fruit)
plumage
plumb (= weight)
  plumbs
  plumbed
  plumbing
plumbing
plume
✗plummer = plumber
plummet
  plummets
  plummeted
  plummeting
plummy
  plummier
  plummiest
plump
  plumps
  plumped
  plumping
plunder
  plunders
  plundered
  plundering
plunge
  plunges
  plunged
  plunging
plunger
plunk

plunks
plunked
plunking
pluperfect
plural
pluralism
✗ plurisy = pleurisy
plus
plush
Pluto
plutocracy
plutocrat
plutocratic
plutonium
ply
　plies
　plied
　plying
ply
plying
Plymouth
plywood
pm
PM
p.m.
P.M.
PMS
PMT
pneumatic
pneumatically
pneumonia
Pnom Penh
poach
　poaches
　poached
　poaching
poacher
pock
pocket
　pockets

pocketed
pocketing
pocketful
pocketknife
　pocketknives
pockmark
pod
　pods
　podded
　podding
podge
podgily
podginess
podgy
　podgier
　podgiest
podium
　podiums or
　podia
pods
poem
poesy
　poesies
poet
poetaster
poetic
poetically
poetry
po-faced
pogo
pogoes
pogoed
pogoing
pogrom
poignant
poinsettia
point
　points
　pointed
　pointing

pointed
pointer
poise
poised
poison
　poisons
　poisoned
　poisoning
poisonous
poke
　pokes
　poked
　poking
poker
pokerwork
pokey
　pokier
　pokiest
pokily
pokiness
poky
　pokier
　pokiest
Poland
polar
polarisation
polarise
　polarises
　polarised
　polarising
polarity
　polarities
polarization
polarize
　polarizes
　polarized
　polarizing
Polaroid(TM)
polder

pole (= stick
→ poll)
poleaxe
polecat
polemic
polemically
polemicist
polemics
polenta
police
  polices
  policed
  policing
policeman
  policemen
policewoman
  policewomen
policy
  policies
policyholder
polio
poliomyelitis
polish
  polishes
  polished
  polishing
Polish
polite
politic
political
politically
politician
politicise
  politicises
  politicised
  politicising
politicize
  politicizes
  politicized
  politicizing

politicking
politico
  politicos
politics
polity
  polities
polka
poll (= vote
→ pole)
  polls
  polled
  polling
pollard
pollen
pollinate
  pollinates
  pollinated
  pollinating
pollster
pollutant
pollute
  pollutes
  polluted
  polluting
polluter
pollution
polo
polonaise
polony
poltergeist
✗ poltice = poultice
polyanthus
polyester
polygamist
polygamous
polygamy
polyglot
polygon
polygonal
polygraph

polyhedron
  polyhedrons *or*
  polyhedra
polymath
polymer
polymorphous
polynomial
polyp
polypropylene
polystyrene
polysyllabic
polysyllable
polytechnic
polytheism
polythene
polyunsaturated
polyurethane
pomade
pomander
pomegranate
pomelo
  pomelos
pommel
pommy
  pommies
pomp
pompadour
pompom
pompon
pomposity
pompous
pompously
ponce
poncey
poncho
  ponchos
pond
ponder
  ponders
  pondered

pondering
ponderous
pondweed
pong
  pongs
  ponged
  ponging
ponies
pontiff
pontifical
pontificate
  pontificates
  pontificated
  pontificating
pontoon
pony
  ponies
Pontypridd
ponytail
✗ poo = pooh
pooch
poodle
poof (= homosexual → pouf; pouffe)
poofter
pooh
pool
  pools
  pooled
  pooling
Poona
poop
pooper-scooper
✗ poopoo = pooh = pooh
poor (= not rich → pore; pour)
poorhouse
poorly
pop

pops
popped
popping
popcorn
pope
popedom
popgun
poplar
poplin
popliteal
poppadom
poppadum
popped
popper
poppet
popping
poppy
  poppies
poppycock
pops
populace
popular
popularise
  popularises
  popularised
  popularising
popularity
popularize
  popularizes
  popularized
  popularizing
popularly
populate
  populates
  populated
  populating
population
populous
✗ popuri = potpourri
porcelain

porch
porcine
porcupine
pore (pore over a book, or pore in the skin → poor; pour)
pores
pored
poring
pork
porker
porky
  porkier
  porkiest
  porkies
porn (= pornography → pawn)
porno
pornographic
pornography
porosity
  porosities
porous
porpoise
  porpoises or
  porpoise
porridge
porringer
port
portable
portal
portcullis
portend
  portends
  portended
  portending
portent
portentous
porter
portfolio

portfolios
porthole
portico
  porticos *or*
  porticoes
portion
portliness
portly
  portlier
  portliest
portmanteau
  portmanteaus *or*
  portmanteaux
portrait
portraiture
portray
  portrays
  portrayed
  portraying
portrayal
Port-Salut
Portugal
Portuguese
pose
  poses
  posed
  posing
poser
poseur
posh
posit
  posits
  posited
  positing
position
positive
positron
posse
possess
  possesses

possessed
possessing
possessed
possession
possessive
possessor
posset
possibility
  possibilities
possible
possibly
possum
✗ possy = posse
post
  posts
  posted
  posting
postage
postal
postbag
postbox
postcard
postcode
poster
posterior
posterity
postern
postgraduate
posthaste
posthumous
postilion
postillion
posting
postman
  postmen
postmark
postmaster
postmortem
postpone
  postpones

postponed
postponing
postponement
postscript
postulant
postulate
postulates
postulated
postulating
✗ postumous =
  posthumous
posture
postwoman
postwomen
posy
  posies
pot
  pots
  potted
  potting
potable
potash
potassic
potassium
potato
  potatoes
potboiler
potency
  potencies
potent
potentate
potential
pother
pothole
potholing
potion
potluck
potpourri
  potpourris
pots

potsherd
pottage
potted
potter
  potters
  pottered
  pottering
pottery
  potteries
pottiness
potty
  potties
  pottier
  pottiest
pouch
pouf (= seat
  → poof)
pouffe (= seat
  → poof)
poultice
poultry (= chickens
  → paltry)
pounce
  pounces
  pounced
  pouncing
pounce
pound
  pounds
  pounded
  pounding
pour (= pour the tea
  → poor; pore)
  pours
  poured
  pouring
poussin
pout
  pouts
  pouted

pouting
poverty
pow
POW
powder
  powders
  powdered
  powdering
power
powerboat
powerboating
powerful
powerhouse
Powys
powwow
pox
poxy
  poxier
  poxiest
practicable
practical
practice (noun)
practise (verb)
  practises
  practised
  practising
practitioner
✗ pracy = précis
pragmatic
pragmatism
prairie
praise
  praises
  praised
  praising
praiseworthy
praline
pram
prance
  prances

pranced
prancing
prandial
prang
  prangs
  pranged
  pranging
prank
prankster
prat
prattle
  prattles
  prattled
  prattling
prawn
pray (= talk to God
  → prey)
  prays
  prayed
  praying
prayer
pre try pro
preach
  preaches
  preached
  preaching
preacher
preamble
prebend
prebendary
precancerous
precarious
precaution
precautionary
precede
  precedes
  preceded
  preceding
precedence
precedent

precept
preceptor
precinct
precious
precipice
precipitance
precipitancy
precipitant
precipitate
   precipitates
   precipitated
   precipitating
precipitation
precipitous
precis
   precis
precise
precision
preclude
   precludes
   precluded
   precluding
preclusion
preclusive
precocious
preconception
precondition
✗ precoshus =
   precocious
precursor
predator
predatory
predecessor
predestination
predeterminate
predicament
predicate
predict
   predicts
   predicted

predicting
predictability
predictable
predictably
prediction
predictor
predilection
predisposition
predominance
predominant
predominate
pre-empt
   pre-empts
   pre-empted
   pre-empting
   pre-emption
   pre-emptive
   pre-emptively
preen
   preens
   preened
   preening
prefab
preface
prefatory
prefect
prefer
   prefers
   preferred
   preferring
preferable
preference
preferential
✗ prefice = preface
prefix
pregnancy
   pregnancies
pregnant
prehensile
prehistoric

prehistory
prejudice
prejudicial
prelate
preliminary
   preliminaries
prelude
premature
premeditate
   premeditates
   premeditated
   premeditating
premenstrual
premier
premiere
premise
premises
premium
   premiums
premonition
preoccupation
preoccupied
prep
preparation
preparatory
prepare
   prepares
   prepared
   preparing
preponderance
preposition
prepossessing
preposterous
prequel
prerequisite
prerogative
presage
   presages
   presaged
   presaging

Presbyterian
presbytery
  presbyteries
preschool
prescience
prescribe (= give
  medicine → pro-
  scribe)
  prescribes
  prescribed
  prescribing
prescription
prescriptive
presence
present
  presents
  presented
  presenting
presentability
presentable
presentably
presentation
presenter
presently
presents
preservation
preservative
preserve
  preserves
  preserved
  preserving
preserver
preset
✗ presher = pressure
✗ presherize =
  pressurize
preshrunk
✗ preshus = precious
preside
  presides

presided
presiding
presidency
president
presidential
✗ presience =
  prescience
✗ present = prescient
press
  presses
  pressed
  pressing
pressure
pressurise
  pressurises
  pressurised
  pressurising
pressurize
  pressurizes
  pressurized
  pressurizing
✗ presteege = prestige
prestidigitation
prestige
prestigious
presto
presumable
presumably
presume
  presumes
  presumed
  presuming
presumption
presumptuous
presuppose
  presupposes
  presupposed
  presupposing
presupposition
pretence

pretend
  pretends
  pretended
  pretending
pretender
pretentious
preterite
preternatural
pretext
prettify
  prettifies
  prettified
  prettifying
prettily
prettiness
pretty
pretzel
prevail
  prevails
  prevailed
  prevailing
prevalent
prevaricate
  prevaricates
  prevaricated
  prevaricating
prevarication
prevaricator
✗ prevelent =
  prevalent
prevent
  prevents
  prevented
  preventing
preventable
preventably
preventative
preventible
preventibly
prevention

preventive
preview
previous
previously
✗ prevue = preview
prewar
prey (= bird of prey
　→ pray)
　preys
　preyed
　preying
price
　prices
　priced
　pricing
priceless
pricey
　pricier
　priciest
prick
　pricks
　pricked
　pricking
prickle
　prickles
　prickled
　prickling
prickliness
prickly
　pricklier
　prickliest
pride (= vanity
　→ pried)
pried (= was nosy
　→ pride)
pries (= is nosy
　→ prise; prize)
priest
priesthood

prig
prim
　primmer
　primmest
primacy
　primacies
primaeval
primarily
primary
　primaries
primate
prime
　primes
　primed
　priming
primer
primetime
primeval
primitive
primmer
primmest
primogenitor
primogeniture
primordial
primp
　primps
　primped
　primping
primrose
prims
primula
Primus℠
prince
princely
princess
principal (= chief
　→ principle)
　principalities
principle (= moral

rule → principal)
principled
print
　prints
　printed
　printing
printable
printer
prior
prioress
prioritise
　prioritises
　prioritised
　prioritising
prioritize
　prioritizes
　prioritized
　prioritizing
priority
　priorities
priory
　priories
prise (= force open
　→ prize)
　prises
　prised
　prising
✗ prisidium =
　praesidium
prism
prison
prisoner
prissily
prissiness
prissy
　prissier
　prissiest
pristine
privacy
private

✗ prier = prior

privation
privatise
  privatises
  privatised
  privatising
privatize
  privatizes
  privatized
  privatizing
privet
privilege
privileged
prize (= reward
  → pries; prise)
  prizes
  prized
  prizing
prize (= reward
  → pries; prise)
prizefight
prizewinner
pro
  pros (profes-
    sionals
    → prose)
probability
  probabilities
probable
probably
probate
probation
probationary
probationer
probe
  probes
  probed
  probing
probity
problem
problematic

problematically
proboscis
  proboscises
procedural
procedure
proceed
  proceeds
  proceeded
  proceeding
  proceeds
process
  processes
  processed
  processing
procession
processional
processor
proclaim
  proclaims
  proclaimed
  proclaiming
proclamation
proclivity
  proclivities
procrastinate
  procrastinates
  procrastinated
  procrastinating
procrastination
procrastinator
procreate
  procreates
  procreated
  procreating
proctor
procurator
procure
  procures
  procured
  procuring

prod
  prods
  prodded
  prodding
prodigal
prodigious
prodigy
  prodigies
produce
  produces
  produced
  producing
producer
product
production
productive
productivity
profane
profanity
  profanities
profess
  professes
  professed
  professing
profession
professional
professionalism
professor
professorial
proffer
  proffers
  proffered
  proffering
proficiency
proficient
profile
✗ profishency =
  proficiency
profit (= make
  money → prophet)

profits
profited
profiting
profitable
profiterole
profligacy
profligate
profound
profundity
profuse
profusion
progenitor
progeny
  progenies
progesterone
progestogen
prognosis
  prognoses
prognostic
program (= computer → programme)
  programs
  programmed
  programming
programmable
programme (= TV or radio → program)
  programmes
  programmed
  programming
programmer
progress
  progresses
  progressed
  progressing
progression
progressive
prohibit
  prohibits
  prohibited

prohibiting
prohibition
prohibitive
project
  projects
  projected
  projecting
projectile
projection
projectionist
projector
prolapse
proletarian
proletariat
proliferate
  proliferates
  proliferated
  proliferating
proliferation
prolific
prolifically
✗ prolitarian = proletarian
prologue
prolong
  prolongs
  prolonged
  prolonging
prom
promenade
prominence
prominent
promiscuity
promiscuous
promise
  promises
  promised
  promising
promissory
promontory

promontories
promote
promotes
promoted
promoting
promoter
promotion
promotional
prompt
prompts
prompted
prompting
prone
prong
pronged
pronominal
pronoun
pronounce
pronounces
pronounced
pronouncing
pronounceable
pronounced
pronouncement
pronto
pronunciation
proof
proofread
proofreads
proofread
proofreading
prop
props
propped
propping
propaganda
propagate
propagates
propagated
propagating

propagator
propane
propel
  propels
  propelled
  propelling
propellant
propellent
propeller
propensity
  propensities
proper
propertied
property
  properties
prophecy (noun)
  prophecies
prophesy (verb)
  prophesies
  prophesied
  prophesying
prophet (= religion
  → profit)
prophetic
prophetically
prophylactic
prophylaxis
propinquity
propitiate
  propitiates
  propitiated
  propitiating
propitiation
propitious
proponent
proportion
proportional
proportionate
proposal
propose

proposes
proposed
proposing
proposer
proposition
propound
  propounds
  propounded
  propounding
propping
proprietary
proprietor
proprietress
propriety
props
propulsion
pros (= profes-
  sionals → prose)
prosaic
prosaically
proscenium
  prosceniums or
  proscenia
prosciutto
proscribe (= prohi-
  bit → prescribe)
  proscribes
  proscribed
  proscribing
proscription
proscriptive
prose (= writing
  → pros)
prosecute
  prosecutes
  prosecuted
  prosecuting
prosecution
prosecutor

proselytism
✗ prosenium =
  proscenium
prosodic
prosody
prospect
prospective
prospectively
prospector
prospectus
  prospectuses
prosper
  prospers
  prospered
  prospering
prosperity
prosperous
prostaglandin
prostate
prosthesis
  prostheses
prostitute
  prostitutes
  prostituted
  prostituting
prostrate
  prostrates
  prostrated
  prostrating
prostration
protagonist
protect
  protects
  protected
  protecting
protection
protectionism
protectionist
protective
protector

protectorate
protégé
protein
protest
  protests
  protested
  protesting
Protestant
protestation
protester
protocol
proton
protoplasm
prototype
protozoan
protozoon
  protozoa
protract
  protracts
  protracted
  protracting
protractedly
protractile
protractor
protrude
  protrudes
  protruded
  protruding
protrusion
protuberance
protuberant
protuberantly
proud
prove
  proves
  proved
  proved or
  proven
  proving
provenance

Provençal (= from
  Provence)
Provençale (= style
  of cooking)
proverb
proverbial
proves
provide
  provides
  provided
  providing
providence
provident
providential
provider
province
provincial
proving
provision
provisional
proviso
  provisos or
  provisoes
provisorily
provisory
provocation
provocative
provoke
  provokes
  provoked
  provoking
provolone
provost
prow
prowess
prowl
  prowls
  prowled
  prowling
proximity

proxy
  proxies
prude
prudence
prudent
prudential
prudish
prudishly
prune
  prunes
  pruned
  pruning
prurient
pruritus
Prussian
pry
  pries (= is nosy
    → prise; prize)
  pried (= was
    nosy → pride)
  prying
PS
psalm
psephologist
psephology
pseud
pseudo
pseudocarp
pseudonym
pseudonymous
pseudopodium
  pseudopodia
psittacosis
psoriasis
psych
  psyches
  psyched
  psyching
psyche
psychedelia

psychedelic	pubic	puerperal
psychedelically	pubis	puff
psychiatric	public	puffs
psychiatrist	publican	puffed
psychiatry	publication	puffing
psychic	publicise	puffball
psycho	publicises	puffily
psychos	publicised	puffin
psychoanalyse	publicising	puffiness
psychoanalyses	publicist	puffy
psychoanalysed	publicity	puffier
psychoanalysing	publicize	puffiest
psychoanalysis	publicizes	pug
psychoanalyst	publicized	pugilism
psychoanalytic	publicizing	pugnacious
psychobabble	publicly	pugnacity
psychological	publish	puke
psychologically	publishes	pukes
psychologist	published	puked
psychology	publishing	puking
psychopath	publisher	pukka
psychosis	puce	pull
psychoses	puck	pulls
psychosocial	pucker	pulled
psychosomatic	puckers	pulling
psychotherapy	puckered	pullet
psychotic	puckering	pulley
psychotically	pud	pullover
PT	pudding	pulmonary
PTA	puddle	pulp
ptarmigan	pudendum	pulps
pterodactyl	pudenda	pulped
pto *or*	pudgily	pulping
PTO	pudginess	pulpit
Ptolemy	pudgy	pulsar
pub	pudgier	pulsate
puberty	pudgiest	pulsates
pubes	pueblo	pulsated
pubescence	pueblos	pulsating
pubescent	puerile	pulsation

pulse
pulverise
  pulverises
  pulverised
  pulverising
pulverize
  pulverizes
  pulverized
  pulverizing
puma
pumice
pummel
  pummels
  pummelled
  pummelling
pump
  pumps
  pumped
  pumping
pumpernickel
pumpkin
pun
  puns
  punned
  punning
punch
  punches
  punched
  punching
punchball
punchbowl
punchily
punchiness
punchy
  punchier
  punchiest
punctilious
punctual
punctuate
  punctuates

punctuated
punctuating
punctuation
puncture
  punctures
  punctured
  puncturing
pundit
pungent
punish
  punishes
  punished
  punishing
  punishable
  punishment
punitive
Punjabi
punk
punned
punnet
punning
puns
punt
punter
puniness
puny
  punier
  puniest
pup
pupa
  pupae *or*
  pupas
pupate
  pupates
  pupated
  pupating
pupation
pupil
puppet
puppeteer

puppetry
puppy
  puppies
✗ puray = purée
purchase
  purchases
  purchased
  purchasing
purda
purdah
pure
purebred
puree
purée
  purées
  puréed
  puréeing
purely
purgative
purgatorial
purgatory
purge
  purges
  purged
  purging
puri
purify
  purifies
  purified
  purifying
Purim
puritan
puritanical
purity
purl (= stitch →
  pearl)
purloin
  purloins
  purloined
  purloining

purple
purport
  purports
  purported
  purporting
purportedly
purpose
purposeful
purposefully
purposely
purposive
purr
  purrs
  purred
  purring
purse
  purses
  pursed
  pursing
purser
pursue
  pursues
  pursued
  pursuing
pursuit
purveyor
pus
push
  pushes
  pushed
  pushing
pushcart
pushchair
pusher
pushily
pushiness
pushover
pushy
  pushier
  pushiest

pusillanimous
puss
pussy
  pussies
pussycat
pussyfoot
  pussyfoots
  pussyfooted
  pussyfooting
pustular
pustule
put
  puts
  put
  putting
putative
✗ putch = putsch
putrefaction
putrefy
  putrefies
  putrefied
  putrefying
putrid
puts
putsch
putt
putter
putting
putty
  putties
puzzle
  puzzles
  puzzled
  puzzling
puzzlement
puzzler
PVC
Pwhlheli
pygmy
  pygmies

pyjama
pyjamas
pylon
pyramid
pyramidal
pyre
Pyrex™
pyrotechnics
Pythagoras (theo-
  rem)
python
pzazz

Q

Qatar
quack
  quacks
  quacked
  quacking
quackery
quad
quadrangle
quadrant
quadraphonic
quadrat
quadrate
quadratic
quadrilateral
quadrille
quadrillion
quadrillionth
quadriplegia
quadriplegic
quadruped
quadruple
quadruplet
quaff
  quaffs
  quaffed
  quaffing
✗ quafure = coiffure
quagga
  quaggas *or*
  quagga
quagmire
quail

quails *or*
quail
quaint
quake
  quakes
  quaked
  quaking
Quaker
quakily
quakiness
quaky
  quakier
  quakiest
qualification
qualifier
qualify
  qualifies
  qualified
  qualifying
qualitative
quality
  qualities
qualm
quandary
  quandaries
quango
  quangos
quantifier
quantify
  quantifies
  quantified
  quantifying
quantitative
quantity
  quantities
quantum
quarantine
quark
quarrel
  quarrels

quarrelled
quarrelling
quarrelsome
quarrier
quarry
  quarries
  quarried
  quarrying
quart
quarter
  quarters
  quartered
  quartering
quarterback
quarterdeck
quarterfinal
quarterly
quartermaster
quarters
quartet
quartile
quarto
quartz
quartzite
quasar
quash
  quashes
  quashed
  quashing
quatercentenary
  quatercentenaries
quaternary
  quaternaries
quatrain
quatrefoil
quaver
  quavers
  quavered
  quavering
quay (= for boats

→ key)
quayside
queasily
queasiness
queasy
  queasier
  queasiest
queen
queenly
queer
quell
  quells
  quelled
  quelling
quench
  quenches
  quenched
  quenching
quenelle
✗ querty = qwerty
querulous
query
  queries
quest
question
  questions
  questioned
  questioning
questionable
questionnaire
queue (= line
  → cue)
  queues
  queued
  queuing
quibble
  quibbles
  quibbled
  quibbling
quiche

quick
quicken
  quickens
  quickened
  quickening
quickie
quickly
quicklime
quicksand
quickset
quicksilver
quicksilver
quickstep
quid
quiescence
quiescent
quiet
quieten
  quietens
  quietened
  quietening
quietly
quietude
quietus
quiff
quill
quilling
quilt
quilting
quince
quincentenary
  quincentenaries
quincentennial
quinine
quinquagenarian
quinquecentenary
  quinquecentenar-
    ies
quinquennial
quintessence

quintessential
quintet
quintuple
quintuplet
quintuplicate
quip
  quips
  quipped
  quipping
quire (= of paper
  → choir; coir)
quirk
✗ cuisine = cuisine
quisling
quit
  quits
  quit or
  quitted
  quitting
quite
quitter
quiver
  quivers
  quivered
  quivering
quiverful
quixotic
quiz
  quizzes
  quizzed
  quizzing
quizmaster
quizzical
quo try qua
quoit
quoits
quorate
quorum
quotable
quotation

quote
  quotes
  quoted
  quoting
quotidian
quotient
Qur'an

R

ra try wra
rabbi
  rabbis
rabbinate
rabbinic
rabbit
  rabbits
  rabbited
  rabbiting
rabble
✗ rabese = rabies
rabid
rabidity
rabies
RAC
raccoon
  raccoons
race
  races
  raced
  racing
racecard
racecourse
racegoer
racehorse
raceme
racer
races
racetrack
racial
racialism
racialist

racially
racier
raciest
racily
raciness
racing
racism
racist
rack
  racks
  racked
  racking
racket (= noise
  → racquet)
racketeer
racoon
  racoons
  racoon
racquet (= for
  tennis → racket)
racy
  racier
  raciest
rad
radar
raddled
✗ radei = radii
radial
radian
radiance
radiant
radiate
  radiates
  radiated
  radiating
radiation
radiator
radical (= funda-
  mental → radicle)
radicalism

radically
radicchio
radicle (= root
→ radical)
radii
radio
  radios
radioactive
radioactivity
radiocarbon
radiochemistry
radiocommunication
radiogram
radiograph
radiographic
radiography
radio-immuno-assay
radioisotope
radioisotopic
radiological
radiology
radioluminescence
radiopager
radiophone
radiophonic
radiophony
radioscope
radioscopic
radioscopy
radiosensitive
radiosonde
radiotelegram
radiotelegraph
radiotelegraphy
radiotelemetry
radiotelephone
radiotelephony
radioteletype
radiotherapy
radiothermy

radiotoxic
radish
  radishes
radium
radius
  radii or
  radiuses
radix
  radices or
  radixes
radon
RAF
raffia
raffish
raffle
  raffles
  raffled
  raffling
raft
rafter
rag
  rags
  ragged
  ragging
ragbag
rage
  rages
  raged
  raging
ragged
raggedy
ragging
raggle-taggle
raglan
✗ragoo = ragout
ragout
ragtag
ragtime
raid
  raids

raided
raiding
rail
  rails
  railed
  railing
railcar
railcard
railhead
railing
raillery
  railleries
railroad
  railroads
  railroaded
  railroading
railway
railwayman
  railwaymen
raiment
rain (= weather
  → reign; rein)
  rains
  rained
  raining
rainbow
raincoat
✗raindeer = reindeer
rainfall
rainforest
rainier
rainiest
rainily
raininess
rainmaker
rainproof
rains
rainstorm
rainwater
rainwear

rainy
  rainier
  rainiest
raise (= lift
  → raze)
  raises
  raised
  raising
raisin
raita
raj
raja
rajah
rake
  rakes
  raked
  raking
rakee
raki
rakish
Raleigh, Sir Walter
rallentando
rally
  rallies
  rallied
  rallying
rally
  rallies
rallycross
ram
  rams
  rammed
  ramming
Ramadan
ramble
  rambles
  rambled
  rambling
rambler
rambunctious

rambutan
ramekin
ramequin
ramification
✗ ramikin = ramekin
ramjet
ramming
ramp
rampage
  rampages
  rampaged
  rampaging
rampant
rampart
ramrod
rams
ramshackle
ran
ranch
rancher
ranchero
  rancheros
rancho
  ranchos
rancid
rancidity
rancour
rand
randier
randiest
randily
randiness
random
randomise
  randomises
  randomised
  randomising
randomize
  randomizes
  randomized

randomizing
randy
  randier
  randiest
ranee
rang
range
  ranges
  ranged
  ranging
rangefinder
ranger
rangily
ranginess
rangy
  rangier
  rangiest
rani
rank
  ranks
  ranked
  ranking
rankle
  rankles
  rankled
  rankling
ransack
  ransacks
  ransacked
  ransacking
ransom
rant
  rants
  ranted
  ranting
rap
  raps
  rapped (= hit →
    rapt; wrapped)
  rapping

rapacious
rapacity
rape
  rapes
  raped
  raping
rapeseed
Raphael
rapid
rapidity
rapids
rapier
rapine
rapist
rapped (= hit
  → rapt; wrapped)
rappel
  rappels
  rappelled
  rappelling
rapper
rapping
✗rappore = rapport
rapport
rapporteur
raps
rapscallion
✗rapsodic = rhapsodic
✗rapsodize =
  rhapsodize
✗rapsody = rhapsody
rapt (= rapt atten-
  tion → rapped;
  wrapped)
rapture
rapturous
rare
rarebit
rarefaction
rarefied

rarely
raring
rarity
  rarities
rascal
rash
✗rashel = racial
✗rashelist = racialist
✗rashelly = racially
rasher
rasp
  rasps
  rasped
  rasping
raspberry
  raspberries
Rasta
Rastafarian
raster
rat
  rats
  ratted
  ratting
ratable
ratafia
ratatouille
ratbag
ratchet
rate
  rates
  rated
  rating
rateable
ratepayer
rates
✗ratefia = ratafia
rather
ratify
  ratifies

ratified
ratifying
rating
ratio
  ratios
ration
  rations
rationed
rationing
rational
rationale
rationalise
  rationalises
  rationalised
  rationalising
rationalism
rationality
rationalize
  rationalizes
  rationalized
  rationalizing
rationally
rats
ratsbane
rattan
ratted
ratter
rattily
rattiness
ratting
rattle
  rattles
  rattled
  rattling
rattler
rattlesnake
rattly
rattlier
rattliest
ratty

rattier
rattiest
raucous
raunchiness
raunchily
raunchy
 raunchier
 raunchiest
ravage
 ravages
 ravaged
 ravaging
rave
 raves
 raved
 raving
ravel
 ravels
 ravelled
 ravelling
raven
ravening
ravenous
raver
ravine
raving
ravioli
ravish
 ravishes
 ravished
 ravishing
raw
rawboned
rawhide
Rawlplug™
ray
rayon
raze (= demolish a
 building → raise)
 razes

razed
razing
razee
razor
razzle-dazzle
re try wre
re
RE
✗ rea = rhea
reach
 reaches
 reached
 reaching
react
 reacts
 reacted
 reacting
reactance
reactant
reaction
 reactionary
 reactionaries
reactivate
 reactivates
 reactivated
 reactivating
reactivation
reactive
reactivity
reactor
read (= read a book
 → reed)
 reads
 read
 reading
readable
readably
reader
readership
readier

readies
readiest
readily
readiness
reading
readjust
 readjusts
 readjusted
 readjusting
reads
ready
 readier
 readiest
reagent
real (= true → reel)
realise
 realises
 realised
 realising
realism
realist
realistic
realistically
reality
 realities
realize
 realizes
 realized
 realizing
really
realm
realpolitik
realtor
ream
reap
 reaps
 reaped
 reaping
 reaper
rear

rears
reared
rearing
rearguard
rearm
rearms
rearmed
rearming
rearmament
rearmost
rearrange
rearranges
rearranged
rearranging
rearward
rearwards
reason
reasons
reasoned
reasoning
reasonable
reasoning
reassure
reassures
reassured
reassuring
✗ reath = wreath
✗ reathe = wreathe
rebarbative
rebate
rebec
rebeck
rebel
rebels
rebelled
rebelling
rebellion
rebellious
rebelliously
rebirth

reborn
rebound
rebuff
rebuffs
rebuffed
rebuffing
rebuke
rebukes
rebuked
rebuking
rebus
rebut
rebuts
rebutted
rebutting
rebuttal
recalcitrance
recalcitrant
recall
recalls
recalled
recalling
recant
recants
recanted
recanting
recantation
recap
recaps
recapped
recapping
recapitulate
recapitulates
recapitulated
recapitulating
recapitulation
recapture
recaptures
recaptured
recapturing

✗ recawse = recourse
recce
recces
recceing
recede
recedes
receded
receding
receipt
✗ receit = receipt
receivable
receive
receives
received
receiving
receiver
receivership
recent
receptacle
reception
receptionist
receptive
receptivity
receptor
recess
recession
recessional
recessionary
recessive
recharge
recharges
recharged
recharging
rechargeable
recherché
recidivism
recidivist
recipe
recipience
recipient

reciprocal
reciprocality
reciprocally
reciprocate
    reciprocates
    reciprocated
    reciprocating
reciprocation
reciprocative
reciprocator
reciprocatory
reciprocity
✗ recipy = recipe
recitable
recital
recitation
recite
    recites
    recited
    reciting
reckless
reckon
    reckons
    reckoned
    reckoning
reckoner
✗ recky = recce
reclaim
    reclaims
    reclaimed
    reclaiming
reclaimable
reclamation
reclinable
recline
    reclines
    reclined
    reclining
recliner
recluse

reclusion
reclusive
recognise
    recognises
    recognised
    recognising
recognition
recognitive
recognitory
recognize
    recognizes
    recognized
    recognizing
recoil
    recoils
    recoiled
    recoiling
recollect
    recollects
    recollected
    recollecting
recollection
recommend
    recommends
    recommended
    recommending
recommendation
recommendatory
recompense
reconcilable
reconcile
    reconciles
    reconciled
    reconciling
reconciliation
reconciliatory
recondite
recondition
    reconditions
    reconditioned

    reconditioning
reconnaissance
reconnoitre
    reconnoitres
    reconnoitred
    reconnoitring
reconsider
    reconsiders
    reconsidered
    reconsidering
reconsideration
reconstituent
reconstitute
    reconstitutes
    reconstituted
    reconstituting
reconstruct
    reconstructs
    reconstructed
    reconstructing
record
    records
    recorded
    recording
recordable
recorder
recording
recount
    recounts
    recounted
    recounting
recoup
    recoups
    recouped
    recouping
recoupable
recoupment
recourse
recover
    recovers

recovered
recovering
recoverability
recoverable
recoverer
recovery
recoveries
recreation
recreational
recriminate
recriminates
recriminated
recriminating
recrimination
recriminative
recriminatory
recruit
recruits
recruited
recruiting
recruitable
recruiter
recruitment
rectal
rectangle
rectangular
rectangularity
rectify
rectifies
rectified
rectifying
rectilinear
rectitude
recto
rectos
rector
rectory
rectories
rectum
rectums *or*

recta
✗ recue = recoup
recumbent
recuperate
recuperates
recuperated
recuperating
recuperation
recur
recurs
recurred
recurring
recurrence
recurrent
recurrently
recycle
recycles
recycled
recycling
recyclable
red
redbreast
redbrick
redcoat
redcurrant
redden
reddens
reddened
reddening
redder
reddest
reddish
Redditch
redeem
redeems
redeemed
redeeming
redeemability
redeemable
redeemably

Redeemer
redemption
redeploy
redeploys
redeployed
redeploying
redevelop
redevelops
redeveloped
redeveloping
redhead
redneck
redo
redoes
redid
redone
redoing
redolent
redouble
redoubles
redoubled
redoubling
✗ redout = redoubt
redoubt
redoubtable
redoubtably
✗ redoutable =
redoubtable
redraft
redress
redresses
redressed
redressing
reds
redshank
redskin
redstart
✗ reduble = redouble
reduce
reduces

reduced
reducing
reducibility
reducible
reducibly
reductase
reduction
reductive
✗ redue = redo
redundancy
  redundancies
redundant
reduplication
reduplicative
redwing
redwood
reed (= grass
  → read)
reediness
reedy
  reedier
  reediest
reef
reefer
reek (= smell
  → wreak)
  reeks
  reeked
  reeking
reel (= dance or
  cotton reel → real)
  reels
  reeled
  reeling
reeve
ref
refectory
  refectories
refer
  refers

referred
referring
referee
reference
referendum
  referenda or
  referendums
referent
referential
referral
refill
refillable
refinancing
refine
  refines
  refined
  refining
refined
refinement
refiner
refinery
  refineries
refit
reflation
reflect
  reflects
  reflected
  reflecting
reflection
reflective
reflectivity
reflector
reflex
reflexive
reflexivity
reflexology
reflux
reform
  reforms
  reformed

reforming
reformer
refractable
refraction
refractive
refractivity
refractor
refractory
refrain
  refrains
  refrained
  refraining
refresh
  refreshes
  refreshed
  refreshing
refresher
refreshment
refrigerant
refrigerate
  refrigerates
  refrigerated
  refrigerating
refrigeration
refrigerator
refuel
  refuels
  refuelled
  refuelling
refuge
refugee
refulgence
refulgent
refund
  refunds
  refunded
  refunding
refundable
✗ refur = refer
refurbish

refurbishes
refurbished
refurbishing
refurbishment
✗ referee = referee
✗ refurral = referral
refusal
refuse
refuses
refused
refusing
refusenik
refutability
refutable
refutation
refute
refutes
refuted
refuting
regain
regains
regained
regaining
regal
regale
regales
regaled
regaling
regalia
regality
regard
regards
regarded
regarding
regardless
regatta
✗ regay = reggae
✗ regen = region
regency

regencies
✗ regenel = regional
regenerate
regenerates
regenerated
regenerating
regeneration
regenerative
regenerator
regent
reggae
regicide
regime
regimen
regiment
region
regional
regionalism
register
registers
registered
registering
registrant
registrar
registration
registry
registries
regress
regresses
regressed
regressing
regression
regressive
regret
regrets
regretted
regretting
regretful
regrettable
regrettably

regroup
regroups
regrouped
regrouping
regular
regularly
regulate
regulates
regulated
regulating
regulation
regulator
regulo
regurgitate
regurgitates
regurgitated
regurgitating
regurgitation
rehabilitate
rehabilitates
rehabilitated
rehabilitating
rehabilitation
rehash
rehashes
rehashed
rehashing
rehearsal
rehearse
rehearses
rehearsed
rehearsing
reheat
reheats
reheated
reheating
rehoboam
✗ rehursal = rehearsal
✗ rehurse = rehearse
Reich

Reigate
reign (= rule
→ rain; rein)
reigns
reigned
reigning
reimburse
reimburses
reimbursed
reimbursing
rein (= straps
→ rain; reign)
reincarnation
reindeer
reindeer
reinforce
reinforces
reinforced
reinforcing
reinstate
reinstates
reinstated
reinstating
reiterate
reiterates
reiterated
reiterating
reiteration
reiterative
reject
rejects
rejected
rejecting
rejection
rejig
rejigs
rejigged
rejigging
rejoice
rejoices

rejoiced
rejoicing
rejoin
rejoins
rejoined
rejoining
rejoinder
rejuvenate
rejuvenates
rejuvenated
rejuvenating
rejuvenation
relapse
relapses
relapsed
relapsing
relate
relates
related
relating
relation
relational
relations
relationship
relative
relatively
relativity
relax
relaxes
relaxed
relaxing
relaxant
relaxation
relaxed
relay
relays
relayed
relaying
release
releases

released
releasing
relegate
relegates
relegated
relegating
relent
relents
relented
relenting
relentless
relentlessly
relevant
reliability
reliable
reliably
reliance
reliant
relic
relict
relief
relieve
relieves
relieved
relieving
religion
religionist
religiosity
religious
religiously
relinquish
relinquishes
relinquished
relinquishing
reliquary
reliquaries
relish
relishes
relished
relishing

relivable
relive
  relives
  relived
  reliving
relocate
  relocates
  relocated
  relocating
reluctance
reluctant
rely
  relies
  relied
  relying
rem
remain
  remains
  remained
  remaining
remainder
remains
remake
  remakes
  remade
  remaking
remand
  remands
  remanded
  remanding
remark
  remarks
  remarked
  remarking
remarkable
remarkably
rematch
Rembrandt van Rijn
remediable
remediably

remedial
remedially
remedy
  remedies
remember
  remembers
  remembered
  remembering
  remembrance
remind
  reminds
  reminded
  reminding
  reminder
reminisce
  reminisces
  reminisced
  reminiscing
  reminiscence
  reminiscent
remiss
remission
remit
  remits
  remitted
  remitting
  remittance
remnant
✗remold = remould
remonstrance
remonstrate
  remonstrates
  remonstrated
  remonstrating
remonstrative
remorse
remorseful
remorseless
remote
remould

remount
  remounts
  remounted
  remounting
removable
removably
removal
remove
  removes
  removed
  removing
remunerate
  remunerates
  remunerated
  remunerating
remuneration
remunerative
remunerator
✗renaig = renege
renaissance
renal
renascence
renascent
rend
  rends
  rent
  rending
render
  renders
  rendered
  rendering
rendezvous
rendition
rends
renegade
renege
  reneges
  reneged
  reneging
renew

renews
renewed
renewing
renewable
renewal
rennet
renounce
renounces
renounced
renouncing
renovate
renovates
renovated
renovating
renown
renowned
rent
rents
rented
renting
rental
x rentgen = roentgen
renter
renunciation
reorganise
reorganises
reorganised
reorganising
x reostate = rheostat
rep
repair
repairs
repaired
repairing
repairable
repairer
reparable
reparation
repartee
repast

repatriate
repatriates
repatriated
repatriating
repatriation
repay
repays
repaid
repaying
repayable
repayment
repeal
repeals
repealed
repealing
repeat
repeats
repeated
repeating
repeatability
repeatable
repeated
repeatedly
repeater
repel
repels
repelled
repelling
repellent
repeller
repent
repents
repented
repenting
repentance
repentant
repenter
repercussion
repertoire
repertory

repertories
repetition
repetitious
repetitive
rephrase
rephrases
rephrased
rephrasing
repine
repines
repined
repining
replace
replaces
replaced
replacing
replaceable
replacement
replay
replenish
replenishes
replenished
replenishing
replenishment
replete
replica
replicate
replicates
replicated
replicating
replication
replier
reply
replies
replied
replying
report
reports
reported
reporting

reportable
reportage
reportedly
reporter
repose
  reposes
  reposed
  reposing
repository
  repositories
repossess
  repossesses
  repossessed
  repossessing
repossession
reprehensible
represent
  represents
  represented
  representing
representation
representational
representative
repress
  represses
  repressed
  repressing
repression
repressive
reprieve
  reprieves
  reprieved
  reprieving
reprimand
  reprimands
  reprimanded
  reprimanding
reprint
  reprints
  reprinted

reprinting
reprisal
reprise
repro
  repros
reproach
  reproaches
  reproached
  reproaching
reproachful
reprobate
reproduce
  reproduces
  reproduced
  reproducing
reproduction
reproductive
reprographic
reprography
reproof
reproval
reprove
  reproves
  reproved
  reproving
reptile
reptilian
republic
republican
repudiate
  repudiates
  repudiated
  repudiating
repudiation
repugnance
repugnant
repulse
repulsion
repulsive
reputable

reputation
repute
reputed
reputedly
request
  requests
  requested
  requesting
requiem
require
  requires
  required
  requiring
requirement
requisite
requisition
reredos
✗ rerite = rewrite
rerun
  reruns
  reran
  rerunning
resalable
resale
resaleable
rescind
  rescinds
  rescinded
  rescinding
rescue
  rescues
  rescued
  rescuing
research
  researches
  researched
  researching
researcher
resemblance
resemble

resembles
resembled
resembling
resent
resents
resented
resenting
resentful
resentment
✗reserch = research
reservable
reservation
reserve
reserves
reserved
reserving
reserved
reservist
reservoir
reset
resets
reset
resetting
✗resevoir = reservoir
✗reshershay =
recherché
reshuffle
reside
resides
resided
residing
residence
residency
residencies
resident
residential
residual
residue
residuum
residua

resign
resigns
resigned
resigning
resignation
resigned
resilience
resilient
resin
✗resind = rescind
✗resine = resign
resist
resists
resisted
resisting
resistance
resistant
resistible
resistibly
resistor
resit
resits
resat
resitting
resoluble
resolute
resolution
resolvable
resolve
resolves
resolved
resolving
resonance
resonant
resonate
resonates
resonated
resonating
resonator
resorption

resort
resound
resounds
resounded
resounding
resource
resourceful
respect
respects
respected
respecting
respectability
respectable
respectably
respectful
respective
respiration
respirator
respiratory
respire
respires
respired
respiring
respite
resplendence
resplendent
respond
responds
responded
responding
respondent
response
responsibility
responsible
responsibly
responsive
rest
rests
rested
resting

restate
  restates
  restated
  restating
restatement
restaurant
restaurateur
✗ resteront =
  restaurant
restful
resting
restitution
restive
restless
restoration
restorative
restore
  restores
  restored
  restoring
restorer
✗ restoront =
  restaurant
restrain
  restrains
  restrained
  restraining
restrained
restraint
restrict
  restricts
  restricted
  restricting
restriction
restrictive
result
  results
  resulted
  resulting
resultant

resume (= carry on
  → résumé)
  resumes
  resumed
  resuming
résumé (= summary
  → resume)
resumption
resurgence
resurgent
resurrect
  resurrects
  resurrected
  resurrecting
resurrection
✗ resus = rhesus
resuscitate
  resuscitates
  resuscitated
  resuscitating
resuscitation
retail
  retails
  retailed
  retailing
retain
  retains
  retained
  retaining
retainable
retainer
retake
  retakes
  retook
  retaken
  retaking
retaliate
  retaliates
  retaliated
  retaliating

retaliation
retaliative
retaliatory
retard
  retards
  retarded
  retarding
retardant
retarded
retarder
retch (= vomit
  → wretch)
  retches
  retched
  retching
retention
retentive
rethink
  rethinks
  rethought
  rethinking
reticent
retina
  retinas or
  retinae
retinue
retire
  retires
  retired
  retiring
retirement
retiring
✗ retoric = rhetoric
✗ retorical = rhetorical
✗ retorician =
  rhetorician
retort
  retorts
  retorted
  retorting

retrace
　retraces
　retraced
　retracing
retract
　retracts
　retracted
　retracting
retractability
retractable
retraction
retractor
retread
retreat
　retreats
　retreated
　retreating
retrenchment
retrial
retribution
retrievable
retrievably
retrieval
retrieve
　retrieves
　retrieved
　retrieving
retriever
retroactive
retroflex
retrograde
retrorocket
retrospect
retrospection
retrospective
retrospectively
retroussé
retrovirus
retsina
✗ retuch = retouch

return
　returns
　returned
　returning
returnable
returner
✗ reumatic =
　rheumatic
✗ reumatism =
　rheumatism
reunion
reunite
　reunites
　reunited
　reuniting
rev
　revs
　revved
　revving
✗ revally = reveille
revaluation
revalue
　revalues
　revalued
　revaluing
revamp
　revamps
　revamped
　revamping
reveal
　reveals
　revealed
　revealing
reveille
revel
　revels
　revelled
　revelling
revelation
revelry

revelries
revenge
　revenges
　revenged
　revenging
revengeful
revenue
reverberate
　reverberates
　reverberated
　reverberating
reverberation
revere
　reveres
　revered
　revering
reverence
reverend
reverent
reverential
reverie
reversal
reverse
　reverses
　reversed
　reversing
reversi
reversibility
reversible
reversibly
reversion
revert
　reverts
　reverted
　reverting
review (= look
　again → revue)
　reviews
　reviewed
　reviewing

reviewer
revile
 reviles
 reviled
 reviling
revise
 revises
 revised
 revising
revision
revisionism
revisionist
revitalisation
revitalise
 revitalises
 revitalised
 revitalising
revitalization
revitalize
 revitalizes
 revitalized
 revitalizing
revival
revivalism
revivalist
revive
 revives
 revived
 reviving
revocable
revocation
revokably
revoke
 revokes
 revoked
 revoking
revolt
 revolts
 revolted
 revolting

revolution
revolutionary
revolutionise
 revolutionises
 revolutionised
 revolutionising
revolutionize
 revolutionizes
 revolutionized
 revolutionizing
revolve
 revolves
 revolved
 revolving
revolver
revs
revue (= a show →
 review)
✗ revuer = reviewer
revulsion
revved
revving
reward
 rewards
 rewarded
 rewarding
rewind
 rewinds
 rewound
 rewinding
rewrite
 rewrites
 rewrote
 rewritten
 rewriting
Reykjavik
Rhamadhan
rhapsodic
rhapsodically
rhapsodise

rhapsodises
rhapsodised
rhapsodizing
rhapsodize
rhapsodizes
rhapsodized
rhapsodizing
rhapsody
 rhapsodies
rhea
rheostat
rheotropic
rheotropism
rhesus
rhetoric
rhetorical
rhetorically
rhetorician
rheumatic
rheumatically
rheumatics
rheumatism
rheumatoid
rheumy (watery
 → roomy)
Rhine
rhinestone
rhinitis
rhino
 rhinos or
 rhino
rhinoceros
 rhinoceroses or
 rhinoceros
rhinoplasty
rhizome
rho (= Greek letter
 → roe; row)
rhos (= Greek
 letters → rose;

rows)
rhododendron
rhombic
rhombohedral
rhombohedron
rhomboid
rhombus
  rhombuses *or*
  rhombi
Rhondda
rhubarb
rhyme (= sound like
  → rime)
  rhymes
  rhymed
  rhyming
rhythm
rhythmical
rhythmically
ri *try* wri
✗ ria = rhea
rib
  ribs
  ribbed
  ribbing
ribald
ribaldry
riband
ribband
  ribbed
  ribbing
ribbon
ribcage
riboflavin
riboflavine
ribs
rice
ricer
✗ riceshay = ricochet
rich

richer
richest
riches
rick
  ricks
  ricked
  ricking
rickets
rickety
rickshaw
ricochet
  ricochets
  ricocheted *or*
  ricochetted
  ricocheting *or*
  ricochetting
ricotta
rictus
  rictus *or*
  rictuses
rid
  rids
  rid *or*
  ridded
  ridding
riddance
ridden
riddle
ride
  rides
  rode (= rode a
  horse → road)
  ridden
  riding
rider
rides
ridge
ridicule
  ridicules
  ridiculed

ridiculing
ridiculous
ridiculously
riding
✗ rie = rye
riesling
rife
riff
riffle
  riffles
  riffled
  riffling
riffraff
rifle
  rifles
  rifled
  rifling
rift
rig
  rigs
  rigged
  rigging
rigadoon
rigamarole
rigatoni
rigger (= workman
  → rigor; rigour)
right (= opposite of
  left, or correct →
  rite; write)
  rights
  righted
  righting
rightable
righten
  rightens
  rightened
  rightening
righteous
righteously

rightful
rightfully
rightish
rightist
rightly
righto
rightward
rightwards
rigid
rigidity
rigmarole
rigor (= rigidity
  → rigger; rigour)
rigorous
rigorously
rigour (= harshness
  → rigger; rigor)
rile
  riles
  riled
  riling
rim
Rimbaud, Arthur
rime (= frost →
  rhyme)
rimmed
rind
✗ rinestone =
  rhinestone
ring
  rings
  rang
  rung
  ringing
ringdove
ringed
ringer
ringleader
ringlet
ringmaster

ringside
ringworm
rink
✗ rino = rhino
✗ rinoceros =
  rhinoceros
✗ rinoserus =
  rhinoceros
rinse
  rinses
  rinsed
  rinsing
Rio de Janeiro
rioja
riot
  riots
  rioted
  rioting
riotous
riotously
rip
  rips
  ripped
  ripping
RIP
ripcord
ripe
ripen
  ripens
  ripened
  ripening
riposte
ripped
ripper
ripping
ripple
  ripples
  rippled
  rippling
ripsnorter

riptide
rise
  rises
  rose (= got up
    → rhos; rows)
  risen
  rising
riser
risibility
risible
risibly
risk
  risks
  risked
  risking
✗ riskay = risqué
riskily
riskiness
risky
  riskier
  riskiest
risotto
risqué
rissole
rite (= ceremony
  → right; write)
ritual
ritually
ritzily
ritziness
ritzy
  ritzier
  ritziest
rival
✗ rivally = reveille
rivalry
river
rivet
riveting
rivulet

rood

Riyadh
✗rizome = rhizome
roach
road (= street
→ rode)
roadblock
roadhouse
roadie
roadroller
roadrunner
roadster
roadway
roadworthy
roam
roams
roamed
roaming
roan
roar
roars
roared
roaring
roast
roasts
roasted
roasting
rob
robs
robbed
robbing
robbery
robberies
robe
robin
robot
robotic
robs
robust
roc (= legendary
bird)

rock (= stone, or
sway)
rocks
rocked
rocking
rockabilly
rocker
rockery
rockeries
rocket
rockets
rocketed
rocketing
rockily
rockiness
rock'n'roll
rock'n'roller
rocky
rockier
rockiest
rococo
rod
rode (= rode a
horse → road)
rodent
rodeo
rodeos
roe (= deer, or fish
eggs → rho; row)
roebuck
roentgen
rogue
roguish
roguishly
roil
roils
roiled
roiling
roister
roisters

roistered
roistering
role or
rôle (= part)
roll (= bread, or
turn over)
rolls
rolled
rolling
rollbar
roller
rollicking
rollmop
rollneck
roly-poly
roman (= type)
Roman (= of or from
Rome)
romance
Romania
romantic
romantically
romanticise
romanticises
romanticised
romanticising
romanticize
romanticizes
romanticized
romanticizing
✗rombus = rhombus
romp
romps
romped
romping
rompers
röntgen
roo (= baby kan-
garoo → roux; rue)
rood (= in a church

→ rude; rued)
roof
roofing
roofs
rooftop
rook
rookery
  rookeries
rookie
room
roomful
roomily
roominess
roommate
roomy (= spacious
  → rheumy)
  roomier
  roomiest
✗rong = wrong
✗roon = rune
roost
  roosts
  roosted
  roosting
rooster
root (= part of a
  plant → route)
  roots
  rooted
  rooting
rootle
  rootles
  rootled
  rootling
rootless
rope
  ropes
  roped
  roping
ropey

ropier
ropiest
ropily
ropiness
ropy
  ropier
  ropiest
Roquefort
rosary
  rosaries
rose (= flower
  → rhos; rows)
rosé (= wine)
roseate
rosebud
rosehip
rosemary
roseola
rosery
  roseries
rosette
rosewood
✗rosiate = roseate
rosier
rosiest
rosily
rosin
rosiness
roster
rostrum
  rostrums or
  rostra
rosy
  rosier
  rosiest
rot
  rots
  rotted
  rotting
✗roth = wrath

rotary
rotatable
rotate
  rotates
  rotated
  rotating
rotation
rotational
rotator
rotatory
rote (= learn by rote
  → wrote)
rotgut
rotisserie
rotogravure
rotted
rotten
rotter
rotting
Rottweiler
rotund
rotunda
rotundity
rouble
roué
rouge
rough (= not
  smooth → ruff)
roughage
roughen
  roughens
  roughened
  roughening
roughly
roughneck
roughshod
✗rought = wrought
roulade
roulette
round

rounds
rounded
rounding
roundabout
rounded
rounder
rounders
roundly
roundup
roundworm
rouse
  rouses
  roused
  rousing
roust
  rousts
  rousted
  rousting
rout
  routs
  routed
  routing
route (= road
  → root)
  routes
  routed
  routeing
routemarch
routine
roux (= sauce
  → roo; rue)
rove
  roves
  roved
  roving
rover
row (= row a boat
  etc → rho; roe)
  rows (= rows a
    boat etc → rhos;

rose)
rowed (= rowed
  a boat → road;
  rode)
rowing
rowan
rowboat
rowdily
rowdiness
rowdy
  rowdier
  rowdiest
rowdyism
rowlock
royal
royalist
royalty
  royalties
rozzer
RSJ
RSVP
rub
  rubs
  rubbed
  rubbing
✗ rubarb = rhubarb
rubber
rubbery
rubbing
rubbish
rubble
rubdown
rubella
rubicund
rubric
rubs
ruby
  rubies
ruche
ruching

ruck
  rucks
  rucked
  rucking
rucksack
ruckus
  ruckuses
ruction
rudder
ruddily
ruddiness
ruddy
  ruddier
  ruddiest
rude
rudely
rudiment
rudimentary
rue (= regret
  → roo; roux)
  rues (= regrets
    → ruse)
  rued (= regretted
    → rood; rude)
  ruing
rueful
ruff
ruffian
ruffle
  ruffles
  ruffled
  ruffling
rufous
rug
rugby
rugged
rugger
ruin
  ruins
  ruined

ruining
ruination
ruing
ruinous
rule
  rules
  ruled
  ruling
ruler
rum
✗ rumatic = rheumatic
✗ rumatism =
  rheumatism
✗ rumba = rhumba
rumble
  rumbles
  rumbled
  rumbling
rumbustious
ruminant
ruminate
  ruminates
  ruminated
  ruminating
rummage
rummer
rummest
rummy
rumour
rump
rumple
  rumples
  rumpled
  rumpling
rumpus
  rumpuses
run
  runs
  ran
  run

running
runabout
runaway
rundown
rune
rung (= rung of a
  ladder → wrung)
runner
running
runny
  runnier
  runniest
runoff
runs
runt
runway
rupee
rupture
rural
ruse (= plan
  → rues)
rush
  rushes
  rushed
  rushing
rushes
rusk
russet
Russia
Russian
rust
rustic
rusticity
rustier
rustiest
rustily
rustiness
rustle
  rustles
  rustled

rustling
rustler
rustproof
rusty
rustier
rustiest
rut
ruts
rutted
rutting
rutabaga
ruthless
Rwanda
rye (= grass
  → wry)
✗ ryly = wryly
✗ ryme = rhyme
✗ rythm = rhythm
✗ rythmic = rhythmic

salaried

S

Sabbath
sabbatical
sabin
sable
sabot
sabotage
  sabotages
  sabotaged
  sabotaging
saboteur
sabra
sabre
sac
saccharin
saccharine
sacerdotal
sacerdotalism
sachet (= envelope
  → sashay)
sack
  sacks
  sacked
  sacking
sackbut
sackcloth
sacral
sacrament
sacramental
sacramentalism
sacramentality
sacred
sacrifice

sacrificial
sacrilege
sacrilegious
sacristan
sacristy
  sacristies
sacroiliac
sacrosanct
sacrum
  sacra
sad
sadden
sadder
saddest
saddle
  saddles
  saddled
  saddling
saddleback
saddlebag
saddlecloth
saddler
saddlery
sadism
sadistic
sadistically
sadomasochism
SAE
✗ saence = seance or
  séance
safari
safe
safeguard
safekeeping
safety
safflower
saffron
sag
  sags
  sagged

sagging
saga
sagacious
sagacity
sage
sagebrush
sagittal
Sagittarius
sago
saguaro
  saguaros
Sahara
sahib
said
sail (= boat
  → sale)
  sails
  sailed
  sailing
sailboard
sailboarding
sailboat
sailcloth
sailfish
sailor
sailplane
saint
sainted
Saint-Émilion
sainthood
sake (= for her
  sake)
saké (= rice wine)
saki
salaam
salacious
salad
salamander
salami
salaried

salary
  salaries
sale (= in a shop →
  sail)
saleable
salesclerk
salesgirl
saleslady
  salesladies
salesman
  salesmen
salesmanship
saleswoman
  saleswomen
salic
salient
saline
salinity
Salisbury
saliva
salivary
salivate
  salivates
  salivated
  salivating
sallow
sally
  sallies
  sallied
  sallying
salmagundi
salmagundy
salmon
salmonella
salmonellosis
salon
saloon
salopettes
salsa
salsify

salt
  salts
  salted
  salting
saltcellar
saltier
saltiest
saltiness
saltpetre
saltwater
saltworks
salty
  saltier
  saltiest
salubrious
salutary
salutation
salutatory
salute
  salutes
  saluted
  saluting
salvable
salvage
  salvages
  salvaged
  salvaging
salvation
salve
  salves
  salved
  salving
salver
salvo
  salvos or
  salvoes
Salzburg
Samaritan
samarium
samba

same
samey
samizdat
✗ samon = salmon
Samoan
samosa
samovar
Samoyed
sampan
samphire
sample
  samples
  sampled
  sampling
sampler
samurai
  samurai
sanatorium
  sanatoriums or
  sanatoria
sancta
sanctify
  sanctifies
  sanctified
  sanctifying
sanctimonious
sanction
  sanctions
  sanctioned
  sanctioning
sanctitude
sanctity
sanctuary
  sanctuaries
sanctum
  sanctums or
  sancta
sand
sandal
sandalwood

sandbank
sandblast
  sandblasts
  sandblasted
  sandblasting
sandbox
✗ sandel = sandal
sandfly
  sandflies
sandier
sandiest
sandiness
Sandinista
sandman
sandpaper
sandpiper
sandpit
sandshoe
sandstone
sandstorm
sandwich
  sandwiches
sandworm
sandy
  sandier
  sandiest
sane
sang
sang-froid
sangria
sanguine
sanguineous
sanguinity
sanitarily
sanitariness
sanitary
sanitation
sanitise
  sanitises
  sanitised

sanitising
sanitize
  sanitizes
  sanitized
  sanitizing
sanity
sank
sans-culotte
sansevieria
Sanskrit
sans serif
Santa
✗ sanwich = sandwich
✗ saonce = seance or
  séance
sap
  saps
  sapped
  sapping
sapient
sapling
sapper
Sapphic
sapphire
sapphism
sapping
Sappho
saps
✗ sar = czar or
  tsar or tzar
Saracen
Sarajevo
sarcasm
sarcastic
sarcastically
sarcoma
sarcophagus
sardine
Sardinian
sardonic

sardonically
sardonicism
✗ sargent = sergeant
sari
saris
sarnie
✗ sarm = psalm
sarong
sarsaparilla
sarsen
sartorial
Sartre, Jean-Paul
sash
sashay (= walk
  along → sachet)
  sashays
  sashayed
  sashaying
sashimi
Saskatchewan
  (state)
Saskatoon (city)
sassafras
sassily
sassiness
sassy
  sassier
  sassiest
sat
satai
Satan
satanic
satanically
Satanism
satay
satchel
sate
  sates
  sated
  sating

sateen
satellite
satiable
satiate
  satiates
  satiated
  satiating
satin
satinet
satinette
satinwood
satire
satirical
satirise
  satirises
  satirised
  satirising
satirist
satirize
  satirizes
  satirized
  satirizing
satisfaction
satisfactory
satisfy
  satisfies
  satisfied
  satisfying
satrap
satsuma
saturable
saturant
saturate
  saturates
  saturated
  saturating
saturation
Saturday
Saturn
saturnine

satyr
sauce (= tomato
  sauce → source)
saucepan
saucer
saucily
sauciness
saucy
saucier
sauciest
Saudi Arabia
sauerbraten
sauerkraut
sauna
saunter
  saunters
  sauntered
  sauntering
saurian
saurischian
sauropod
sauropodous
sausage
sauté
  sautés
  sautéed
  sautéing *or*
  sautéeing
Sauternes
savage
savagery
savanna
savannah
savant
save
  saves
  saved
  saving
saver (= person

who saves
✗ savery = savoury
saviour (= rescuer)
Saviour (= Jesus
  Christ)
savoir-faire
savour (= enjoy
  → saver)
savours
savoured
savouring
savoury
savoy
savvy
savvier
savviest
saw (= cut → soar;
  sore)
saws
sawed
sawn
sawing
sawbill
sawdust
sawfly
sawhorse
sawmill
sawtooth
sawyer
sax
saxifrage
Saxon
saxophone
saxophonist
say
says
said
saying
scab

scabs
scabbed
scabbing
scabbard
scabbily
scabbiness
scabby
  scabbier
  scabbiest
scabese = scabies
scabies
scabious
scabrous
scad
  scads *or*
  scad
scaffold
scaffolding
scalable
scalar
scald
  scalds
  scalded
  scalding
scale
  scales
  scaled
  scaling
scalene
scalier
scaliest
scaliness
scallawag
scallion
scallop
scallywag
scaloppine
  scaloppini
scalp
  scalps

scalped
scalping
scalpel
scaly
  scalier
  scaliest
scam
scamp
scamper
scampers
scampered
scampering
scampi
scan
  scans
  scanned
  scanning
scandal
scandalise
  scandalises
  scandalised
  scandalising
scandalize
  scandalizes
  scandalized
  scandalizing
scandalmonger
Scandinavian
scandium
scanned
scanner
scanning
scans
scansion
scant
scantily
scantiness
scantling
  scantlings
scanty

scantier
scantiest
scape
scapegoat
scapegrace
scapula
scapular
scar
  scars
  scarred
  scarring
scarab
scarce
scarcity
scare
  scares
  scared
  scaring
scarecrow
scaredy-cat
scaremonger
scarf
  scarves *or*
  scarfs
scarier
scariest
scarlatina
scarlet
scarp
scarper
  scarpers
  scarpered
  scarpering
scarring
scars
scarves
scary
  scarier
  scariest
scat

scats
scatted
scatting
scathe
scathing
scatological
scatologist
scatology
scatter
scatters
scattered
scattering
scatterbrain
scattering
scattily
scattiness
scatty
scattier
scattiest
scavenge
scavenges
scavenged
scavenging
scavenger
✗ scema = schema
✗ sceme = scheme
scenario
scenarios
scene (= view →
seen)
scenery
scenic
scent (= smell →
sent)
sceptic
sceptre
✗ scerzo = scherzo
schedule
schedules
scheduled

scheduling
schema (= plan →
schemer)
schemata
schematic
schematically
schematise
schematises
schematised
schematising
schematize
schematizes
schematized
schematizing
scheme
schemes
schemed
scheming
schemer (= person
who schemes
→ schema)
scherzando
scherzo
schism
schismatic
schizoid
schizophrenia
schizophrenic
schlep
schleps
schlepped
schlepping
schmaltz
schmalz
schnapps
schnaps
schnauzer
schnitzel
scholar
scholarship

scholastic
scholastically
school
schools
schooled
schooling
schoolboy
schoolgirl
schoolhouse
schoolmarm
schoolmaster
schoolmistress
schoolteacher
schooner
schuss
sciatic
sciatica
science
scientific
scientist
Scientology
sci-fi
scimitar
scintillate
scintillates
scintillated
scintillating
scintillation
scion
✗ scism = schism
scissor
scissors
scissored
scissoring
scissors
✗ scizophrenia =
schizophrenia
✗ scizophrenic =
schizophrenic
sclera

sclerite
scleritic
sclerotic
scoff
  scoffs
  scoffed
  scoffing
scolar = scholar
scold
  scolds
  scolded
  scolding
scollop
sconce
scone
scool = school
scooner = schooner
scoop
  scoops
  scooped
  scooping
scoot
  scoots
  scooted
  scooting
scooter
scope
scorbutic
scorch
  scorches
  scorched
  scorching
scorcher
score
  scores
  scored
  scoring
scoreboard
scorecard
scorld = scald

scorn
  scorns
  scorned
  scorning
Scorpio
scorpion
Scot
scotch
  scotches
  scotched
  scotching
scot-free
Scottish
scoundrel
scour
  scours
  scoured
  scouring
scourge
Scouse
scout
  scouts
  scouted
  scouting
scoutmaster
scowl
  scowls
  scowled
  scowling
scrabble
  scrabbles
  scrabbled
  scrabbling
scrag
  scraggly
  scraggy
  scraggier
  scraggiest
scram
scramble

scrambles
scrambled
scrambling
scrambler
scrap
  scraps
  scrapped
  scrapping
scrapbook
scrape
  scrapes
  scraped
  scraping
scrapheap
scrapie
  scrapped
  scrapping
scrappy
  scrappier
  scrappiest
  scraps
scratch
  scratches
  scratched
  scratching
scrawl
  scrawls
  scrawled
  scrawling
scrawnily
scrawniness
scrawny
  scrawnier
  scrawniest
scream
  screams
  screamed
  screaming
scree
screech

screeches
screeched
screeching
screed
screen
screens
screened
screening
screenplay
screenwriter
screw
screws
screwed
screwing
screwball
screwdriver
screwworm
screwy
screwier
screwiest
scribble
scribbles
scribbled
scribbling
scribe
scrimmage
scrimp
scrimps
scrimped
scrimping
scrimshank
scrimshaw
script
scriptural
scripture
scriptwriter
scrivener
scrofula
scrofulous
scroll

scrolls
scrolled
scrolling
scrollwork
scrotum
scrota *or*
scrotums
scrounge
scrounges
scrounged
scrounging
scrub
scrubs
scrubbed
scrubbing
scrubby
scrubbier
scrubbiest
scrubbiness
scrubland
scruff
scruffily
scruffiness
scruffy
scruffier
scruffiest
scrum
scrummage
scrumptious
scrumpy
scrunch
scrunches
scrunched
scrunching
scruple
scrupulous
scrutable
scrutineer
scrutinise
scrutinises

scrutinised
scrutinising
scrutinize
scrutinizes
scrutinized
scrutinizing
scrutiny
scrutinies
scry
scries
scried
scrying
scuba
scud
scuds
scudded
scudding
scuff
scuffs
scuffed
scuffing
scuffle
scuffles
scuffled
scuffling
scull
scullery
sculleries
scullion
sculpt
sculpts
sculpted
sculpting
sculptor
sculpture
scum
scumbag
✗ scurge = scourge
scurrility

scurrilous
scurry
  scurries
  scurried
  scurrying
scurvy
scuttle
scuzziness
scuzzy
  scuzzier
  scuzziest
scythe
  scythes
  scythed
  scything
se try sce
sea (= ocean
  → see)
seaboard
seaborne
seacoast
seadog
seafarer
seafaring
seafood
seafront
seagoing
seagull
seal
  seals
  sealed
  sealing
sealant
sealer
sealskin
seam (= join
  → seem)
seaman
  seamen
seamanship

seaminess
seamstress
  seamstresses
seamy
  seamier
  seamiest
seance or
  séance
seaplane
seaport
seaquake
sear (burn → sere)
  sears
  seared
  searing
search
  searches
  searched
  searching
searchlight
seascape
seashell
seashore
seasick
seaside
season
  seasons
  seasoned
  seasoning
seasonable
seasonably
seasonal
seat
  seats
  seated
  seating
seaward
seawards
seaweed
seaworthiness

seaworthy
sebaceous
✗ sebashes = sebaceous
✗ sebatious = sebaceous
seborrhoea
sebum
sec
secant
secateurs
secede
  secedes
  seceded
  seceding
secession
secessionism
secessionist
secluded
seclusion
seclusive
✗ secoia = sequoia
second
secondarily
secondary
  secondaries
secondly
secondment
secrecy
secret
secretarial
secretariat
secretary
  secretaries
secrete
  secretes
  secreted
  secreting
secretin
secretion

secretive
secretor
secretory
sect
sectarian
section
sector
sectorial
secular
securable
secure
  secures
  secured
  securing
security
  securities
✗ sed = said
sedan
sedate
sedation
sedative
Sedbergh
sedentary
Seder
sedge
sediment
sedimentary
sedimentation
sedition
seditionary
seditious
seduce
  seduces
  seduced
  seducing
seducer
seduction
seductive
sedulity
sedulous

see (= look at
  → sea)
sees
saw (= looked at
  → sore)
seen (= sighted
  → scene)
seeing
seed (= of a plant
  → cede)
seedbed
seedcake
seedcase
seedily
seediness
seedling
seedy
  seedier
  seediest
seeing
seek (= look for
  → Sikh)
seeks
sought (= looked
  for → sort)
seeking
✗ seelacanth =
  coelacanth
seem (= appear
  → seam)
seems
seemed
seeming
seen (= looked at
  → scene)
seep
seeps
seeped
seeping
seepage

seer
seersucker
sees (= looks at →
  seize)
seesaw
seethe
seethes
seethed
seething
segment
segmental
segmentary
segmentation
segregable
segregate
  segregates
  segregated
  segregating
segregation
segregationist
seigneur
seismic
seismograph
seismography
seismologic
seismological
seismologist
seismology
seize (= grab
  → sees)
seizes
seized
seizing
seizure
seldom
select
selects
selected
selecting
selection
selective

selectivity
selector
selenite
selenium
self
  selves
selfish
selfless
selfsame
sell
  sells
  sold
  selling
seller
Sellotape℠
sellout
selvage
selvedge
selves
semantic
semantically
semantics
semaphore
semblable
semblance
semen
semester
semi
  semis
semiannual
semiaquatic
semiarid
semiautomatic
semibreve
semicentennial
semicircle
semicircular
semiconductor
semiconscious
semidetached

semidiurnal
semifinal
semifinalist
semifluid
semiliquid
semiliterate
semilunar
seminal
seminar
seminarian
seminary
  seminaries
semiology
semiotic
semiotician
semiotics
semipermeable
semiporcelain
semiprecious
semiprofessional
semiquaver
semirigid
semis
semiskilled
semisolid
Semite
Semitic
semitone
semitropical
semivocal
semivowel
semiyearly
semolina
sempstress
senate
senator
senatorial
send
  sends
  sent (= posted

→ scent)
sending
Senegal
senile
senility
senior
seniority
senna
señor
  señors *or*
  señores
señora
señorita
sensate
sensation
sensational
sensationalise
  sensationalises
  sensationalised
  sensationalising
sensationalism
sensationalist
sensationalistic
sensationalize
  sensationalizes
  sensationalized
  sensationalizing
sensationally
sense
  senses
  sensed
  sensing
senseless
sensibility
  sensibilities
sensible
sensitise
  sensitises
  sensitised
  sensitising

sensitive
sensitivity
  sensitivities
sensitize
  sensitizes
  sensitized
  sensitizing
sensor
sensorimotor
sensory
sensual
sensualism
sensualist
sensuality
sensuous
sent (= posted
  → scent)
sentence
  sentences
  sentenced
  sentencing
sententious
sentience
sentient
sentiment
sentimental
sentimentalise
  sentimentalises
  sentimentalised
  sentimentalising
sentimentalism
sentimentality
sentimentalize
  sentimentalizes
  sentimentalized
  sentimentalizing
sentinel
sentry
  sentries
sepal

sepaloid
sepalous
  separable
separate
  separates
  separated
  separating
separation
separatist
separator
✗ sephology =
  psephology
sepia
sepsis
September
septet
septette
septic
septicaemia
septicemia
septuagenarian
sepulchral
sepulchre
sequel
sequence
sequencer
sequencing
sequential
sequester
  sequesters
  sequestered
  sequestering
sequestrable
sequestrate
  sequestrates
  sequestrated
  sequestrating
sequestration
sequestrator
sequin

sequoia
sera
seraph
Serb
Serbian
Serbo-Croat
Serbo-Croatian
✗ serca = circa
✗ serch = search
sere (= dried up
  → sear)
serenade
  serenades
  serenaded
  serenading
serendipity
serene
serenely
serenity
serf
serge (= fabric
  → surge)
sergeant
serial (= TV serial
  → cereal)
serialise
  serialises
  serialised
  serialising
serialize
  serializes
  serialized
  serializing
series
  series
serif
sermon
serpent
serrate
serrated

serried
serum
 sera
servant
serve
 serves
 served
 serving
server
service
 services
 serviced
 servicing
serviceable
services
serviette
servile
servility
serving
servitude
servo
 servos
servomechanical
servomechanism
servomotor
sesame
session
set
 sets
 set
 setting
setback
setoff
setscrew
sett
settee
setter
setting
settle
 settles

settled
settling
settlement
settler
setup
seven
Sevenoaks
seventeen
seventeenth
seventh
seventhly
seventieth
seventy
 seventies
sever
 severs
 severed
 severing
severable
several
severance
severe
severely
severity
sew (= stitch → so;
 sow)
 sews
 sewed
 sewn
 sewing
sewage
sewer
sewerage
sex
sexagenarian
sexagesimal
sexangular
sexcentenary
 sexcentenaries
sexed

sexier
sexiest
sexily
sexiness
sexism
sexist
sexless
sextant
sextet
sextette
sexton
sextuple
sextuplet
sexual
sexuality
sexy
 sexier
 sexiest
Seychelles
✗ sha = shah
shabby
 shabbier
 shabbiest
shack
shackle
shade
 shades
 shaded
 shading
shadily
shadiness
shadow
 shadows
 shadowed
 shadowing
shadowy
shady
 shadier
 shadiest
shaft

shafts
shafted
shafting
shag
shags
shagged
shagging
✘ shagrin = chagrin
shaggy
shaggier
shaggiest
shah
✘ shaise = chaise
shake (= shake
hands → sheik;
sheikh)
shakes
shook
shaken
shaking
shakedown
shaken
shaker
shakes
Shakespeare, William
Shakespearean
Shakespearian
shakily
shakiness
shaking
shaky
shakier
shakiest
shale
✘ shalet = chalet
shall
shallot
shallow
shalt

sham
shaman
shamanic
shamanism
shamble
shambles
shambled
shambling
shambolic
shame
shames
shamed
shaming
shameful
shameless
✘ shampane =
champagne
shampoo
shamrock
✘ shandelier =
chandelier
shandy
shandies
shank
shan't
shanty
shanties
shantytown
shape
shapes
shaped
shaping
shapeless
✘ shaperone =
chaperone
✘ shar = shah
✘ sharabang =
charabanc
✘ sharade = charade

shard
share
shares
shared
sharing
sharecropper
sharefarmer
shareholder
shareware
shark
sharkskin
sharp
sharpen
sharpens
sharpened
sharpening
sharpshooter
shashlick
shashlik
✘ shato = château
shatter
shatters
shattered
shattering
shatterproof
shave
shaves
shaved
shaven
shaving
shaver
shawl
she
sheaf
sheaves
shear (= cut
→ sheer)
shears
sheared
sheared or

shorn
shearing
shearling
shears
shearwater
sheath
sheathe
sheathes
sheathed
sheathing
sheaves
shed
sheds
shed
shedding
she'd
✗ shedule = schedule
✗ sheek = chic
sheep
sheep
sheepdog
sheepfold
sheepish
sheepskin
sheer (= steep →
shear)
sheet
✗ shef = chef
Sheffield
sheik (= head of
tribe → shake)
sheikdom
sheikh (= head of
tribe → shake)
sheikhdom
Sheila
shekel
shelf
shelves
shell

shells
shelled
shelling
she'll
shellac
shellfire
shellfish
shellproof
shelter
shelters
sheltered
sheltering
shelve
shelves
shelved
shelving
✗ sheneel = chenille
shepherd
shepherdess
sherbet
sheriff
Sherpa
Sherpas *or*
Sherpa
sherry
sherries
she's
✗ shewawa =
chihuahua
shiatsu
shibboleth
shied
shield
shields
shielded
shielding
shier
shies
shiest
shift

shifts
shifted
shifting
shiftily
shiftiness
shiftless
shiftwork
shifty
shiftier
shiftiest
Shiite
✗ shikanery =
chicanery
shiksa
✗ shilaly = shillelagh
shillelagh
shilling
shillyshally
shillyshallies
shillyshallied
shillyshallying
shily
shimmer
shimmers
shimmered
shimmering
shin
shinbone
shindig
shine
shines
shone *or*
shined
shining
shingle
shingles
shininess
shiny
shinier
shiniest

✗shinyon = chignon
ship
  ships
  shipped
  shipping
shipboard
shipbuilder
shipload
shipmaster
shipmate
shipment
shipowner
shipped
shipper
shipping
ships
shipshape
shipway
shipworm
shipwreck
shipwright
shipyard
shire
shirk
  shirks
  shirked
  shirking
✗shiropodist =
  chiropodist
shirr
  shirrs
  shirred
  shirring
shirt
shirtsleeve
shirty
  shirtier
  shirtiest
shit
  shits

shit or
  shitted
  shitting
✗shivalrous =
  chivalrous
shiver
  shivers
  shivered
  shivering
  shivery
✗shmaltz = schmaltz
✗shmoltz = schmaltz
✗shnapps = schnapps
✗shnitzel = schnitzel
shoal
shoat
shock
  shocks
  shocked
  shocking
shocker
shockheaded
shockproof
shod
shoddily
shoddiness
shoddy
  shoddier
  shoddiest
shoe (= footwear
  → shoo)
  shoes
  shod
shoeing
shoeblack
Shoeburyness
shoehorn
shoelace
shoeshine
shoestring

shoetree
shofar
shofars or
  shofroth
✗shofer = chauffeur
shogun
✗sholder = shoulder
shone
shoo (= go away!
  → shoe)
  shoos
  shooed
  shooing
✗shood = should
shook
shoot (= with a gun
  → chute)
  shoots
  shot
  shooting
shop
  shops
  shopped
  shopping
shopkeeper
shoplifter
shopper
shopsoiled
shoptalk
shopwalker
shopworn
shore (= sea
  → sure)
shoreless
shoreline
shoreward
shoreweed
✗shorely = surely
shorn
short

shortage
shortbread
shortcake
✗ shortcercit =
  shortcircuit
shortcircuit
shortcoming
shorten
  shortens
  shortened
  shortening
shortening
shortfall
shorthand
shorthorn
shortly
shorts
shortstop
shot
shotgun
should
shoulder
  shoulders
  shouldered
  shouldering
shouldn't
shout
  shouts
  shouted
  shouting
shove
  shoves
  shoved
  shoving
shovel
  shovels
  shovelled
  shovelling
shovelful
✗ shovinism =

chauvinism
show
  shows
  showed
  shown
  showing
showcase
showdown
shower
  showers
  showered
  showering
showerproof
showgirl
showground
showier
showiest
showily
showiness
showing
showjumping
showman
  showmen
shown
showpiece
showroom
shows
showy
  showier
  showiest
shrank
shrapnel
shred
  shreds
  shredded *or*
  shred
  shredding
shrew
shrewd
Shrewsbury

shriek
  shrieks
  shrieked
  shrieking
shrift
shrike
shrill
shrimp
shrink
  shrinks
  shrunk *or*
  shrank
  shrunk *or*
  shrunken
  shrinking
shrinkage
shrivel
  shrivels
  shrivelled
  shrivelling
Shropshire
shroud
  shrouds
  shrouded
  shrouding
Shrove Tuesday
shrub
shrubbery
  shrubberies
shrug
  shrugs
  shrugged
  shrugging
shrunk
shrunken
shudder
  shudders
  shuddered
  shuddering
shuffle

shuffles
shuffled
shuffling
✗ shugar = sugar
shun
shuns
shunned
shunning
shunt
shunts
shunted
shunting
shush
shushes
shushed
shushing
shut
shuts
shut
shutting
shutdown
shuteye
shutout
shutter
shuttle
shuttlecock
shy
shies
shied
shying
si try sci
Siamese
sibling
sic (= as written)
six try psych
sick (= ill)
sickbay
sicken
sickens
sickened

sickening
sickle
sickliness
sickly
sicklier
sickliest
sickroom
✗ sicoia = sequoia
side (= left side →
    sighed)
sideband
sideboard
sideboards
sideburns
sidecar
sidekick
sidelight
sideline
sidelines
sidelined
sidelining
sidelong
sidereal
sideroad
sideshow
sideslip
sidestep
sidestroke
sideswipe
sidetrack
sidetracks
sidetracked
sidetracking
sidewalk
sideways
sidewinder
siding
sidle
sidles

sidled
sidling
Sidney
siege
siemens
sienna
sierra
Sierra Leone
siesta
sieve
sieves
sieved
sieving
sift
sifts
sifted
sifting
sigh
sighs (=
    breathes a sigh
    → size)
sighed
sighing
sight (= seeing
    → cite; site)
sights
sighted
sighting
sightless
sightliness
sightly
sightlier
sightliest
sightsee
sightsees
sightsaw
sightseen
sightseeing
sightseer
sigma

sign (= road sign
→ sine)
　signs
　signed
　signing
signal
　signals
　signalled
　signalling
signatory
　signatories
signature
signet (= ring or
　seal → cygnet)
significance
significant
signification
signify
　signifies
　signified
　signifying
signor
　signors *or*
　signori
signora
　signoras *or*
　signore
signorina
　signorinas *or*
　signorine
signpost
Sikh (= religion →
　seek)
silage
sild
silence
　silences
　silenced
　silencing
silencer

silent
silhouette
silica
silicon
silicone
silk
silken
silkily
silkiness
silkweed
silkworm
silky
　silkier
　silkiest
sill
sillabub
silliness
silly
　sillier
　silliest
silo
　silos
silt
✗ siluette = silhouette
silver
silverfish
silverside
silversmith
silverware
silverweed
silvery
✗ simelar = similar
✗ simely = simile
simian
similar
similarity
simile
　similes
similitude
simitar

simmer
　simmers
　simmered
　simmering
simper
　simpers
　simpered
　simpering
simple
simpleton
simplicity
simplify
　simplifies
　simplified
　simplifying
simplistic
simplistically
simply
simulate
　simulates
　simulated
　simulating
simulation
simulcast
simultaneity
simultaneous
sin
　sins
　sinned
　sinning
since
sincere
sincerely
sincerity
sine (= of an angle
　→ sign)
sinecure
sinew
sinewy
sinful

sing
  sings
  sang
  sung
  singing
Singapore
singe
  singes
  singed
  singeing
singer
single
singlet
singleton
singly
sings
singsong
singular
singularity
sinister
sink
  sinks
  sank *or*
  sunk
  sunk *or*
  sunken
  sinking
sinkhole
sinks
sinuous
sinus
sinusitis
Sioux
sip
  sips
  sipped
  sipping
siphon
sir
sire

siren
sis
sisal
✗ sismic = seismic
✗ sismograph =
  seismograph
✗ sismology =
  seismology
sissy
  sissies
sister
sisterhood
sisterliness
sisterly
sit
  sits
  sat
  sitting
sitar
sitcom
site (= place
  → cite; sight)
  sites
  sited
  siting
✗ sithe = scythe
✗ siticosis =
  psittacosis
✗ sittacosis =
  psittacosis
situate
  situates
  situated
  situating
situation
✗ siv = sieve
six
sixfold
sixpence
sixteen

sixteenth
sixth
sixthly
sixtieth
sixty
  sixties
sizable
size (= big or little
  → sighs)
  sizes
  sized
  sizing
sizeable
✗ sizmic = seismic
✗ sizmograph =
  seismograph
✗ sizmology =
  seismology
sizzle
  sizzles
  sizzled
  sizzling
ska
✗ skane = skein
skate
  skates
  skated
  skating
skateboard
skater
skedaddle
Skegness
skein
skeleton
sketch
  sketches
  sketched
  sketching
sketchbook
sketchily

sketchiness
sketchy
  sketchier
  sketchiest
skew
skewbald
skewer
skewwhiff
ski
  skis
  skied
  skiing
skid
  skids
  skidded
  skidding
✗skidaddle =
  skedaddle
skidlid
skidpan
skidproof
skied
skier
skies
skiff
skiffle
skiing
skilful
skill
skilled
skillet
skim
  skims
  skimmed
  skimming
skimp
  skimps
  skimped
  skimping
skimpily

skimpiness
skimpy
  skimpier
  skimpiest
skims
skin
  skins
  skinned
  skinning
skinflint
skinful
skinhead
skinny
  skinnier
  skinniest
skint
skintight
skip
  skips
  skipped
  skiping
skipjack
skiplane
skipper
skirmish
skirt
  skirts
  skirted
  skirting
skis
skit
skittle
skive
  skives
  skived
  skiving
skiver
skivvy
  skivvies
skua

skulduggery
skulk
  skulks
  skulked
  skulking
skull
skullcap
skunk
sky
  skies
skydive
  skydives
  skydived
  skydiving
skydiver
skydiving
skyjack
skylark
skylight
skyline
skyrocket
skysail
skyscape
skyscraper
skyward
skywards
skywriting
slab
slack
slacken
  slackens
  slackened
  slackening
slacks
slag
  slags
  slagged
  slagging
slain
slalom

slam
slams
slammed
slamming
slammer
slander
slanders
slandered
slandering
slang
slant
slants
slanted
slanting
slantwise
slap
slaps
slapped
slapping
slapdash
slaphappy
slapshot
slapstick
slash
slashes
slashed
slashing
slat
slate
slatted
slattern
slaughter
slaughters
slaughtered
slaughtering
slaughterhouse
✗ slauter = slaughter
slave
slaves
slaved

slaving
slaver
slavery
slavish
slay (= kill
    → sleigh)
slays
slew
slain
slaying
Sleaford
sleaze
sleazy
sledge
sledges
sledged
sledging
sledgehammer
sleek
sleep
sleeps
slept
sleeping
sleeper
sleepily
sleepiness
sleepwalk
sleepwalks
sleepwalked
sleepwalking
sleepy
sleepier
sleepiest
sleepyhead
sleet
sleeve
sleigh (= sledge
    → slay)
sleight (= of hand
    → slight)

slender
slept
sleuth
slew
slewed
✗ slewth = sleuth
slice
slices
sliced
slicing
slicer
slick
slide
slides
slid
sliding
slight (= small
    → sleight)
slily
slim
slims
slimmed
slimming
slime
slimily
sliminess
slimmer
slimy
slimier
slimiest
sling
slings
slung
slinging
slingback
slingshot
slink
slinks
slunk
slinking

slinkily
slinkiness
slinky
  slinkier
  slinkiest
slip
  slips
  slipped
  slipping
slipcase
slipcover
slipknot
slipnoose
slipover
slippage
slipped
slipper
slipperiness
slippery
slippiness
slipping
slippy
  slippier
  slippiest
slipsheet
slipshod
slipstream
slipway
slit
  slits
  slit
  slitting
slither
  slithers
  slithered
  slithering
sliver
slob
slobber
  slobbers

slobbered
slobbering
sloe (= berries
  → slow)
slog
  slogs
  slogged
  slogging
slogan
sloop
slop
  slops
  slopped
  slopping
slope
  slopes
  sloped
  sloping
sloppily
sloppiness
sloppy
  sloppier
  sloppiest
slosh
  sloshes
  sloshed
  sloshing
slot
  slots
  slotted
  slotting
sloth
slothful
slouch
  slouches
  slouched
  slouching
slough
  sloughs
  sloughed

sloughing
Slovak
Slovakia
Slovenia
slovenly
slow (= not fast
  → sloe)
  slows
  slowed
  slowing
slowcoach
slowpoke
slowworm
✗ sluce = sluice
sludge
✗ sluff = slough
slug
sluggish
sluice
  sluices
  sluiced
  sluicing
sluicegate
sluiceway
slum
  slums
  slummed
  slumming
slumber
  slumbers
  slumbered
  slumbering
slump
  slumps
  slumped
  slumping
slung
slunk
slur
  slurs

slurred
slurring
slurp
slurps
slurped
slurping
slurry
slush
slushiness
slushy
slushier
slushiest
slut
sly
slyer
slyest
smack
smacks
smacked
smacking
smacker
smacking
small
smallholding
smallpox
smarmily
smarminess
smarmy
smarmier
smarmiest
smart
smarts
smarted
smarting
smarty-pants
smash
smashes
smashed
smashing
smashing

smattering
smear
smears
smeared
smearing
smell
smells
smelled *or*
smelt
smelling
smelliness
smelly
smellier
smelliest
smelt
smelts
smelted
smelting
smelter
smile
smiles
smiled
smiling
smiler
smirk
smirks
smirked
smirking
smithereens
smithy
smithies
smitten
smock
smocking
smog
smoke
smokes
smoked
smoking
smokehouse

smokeless
smoker
smokestack
smokily
smokiness
smoky
smokier
smokiest
✗ smolder = smoulder
smooth
smooths
smoothed
smoothing
smoothly
smoothy
smoothies
smorgasbord
smother
smothers
smothered
smothering
smoulder
smoulders
smouldered
smouldering
smudge
smudges
smudged
smudging
smug
smugger
smuggest
smuggle
smuggles
smuggled
smuggling
smuggler
smut
snack
snaffle

snag
snags
snagged
snagging
snail
snake
snakes
snaked
snaking
snakebite
snakeskin
snakily
snakiness
snaky
snakier
snakiest
snap
snaps
snapped
snapping
snapdragon
snappy
snappier
snappiest
snapshot
snare
snares
snared
snaring
snarl
snarls
snarled
snarling
snatch
snatches
snatched
snatching
snazzily
snazziness
snazzy

snazzier
snazziest
sneak
sneaks
sneaked
sneaking
sneakily
sneakiness
sneakers
sneer
sneers
sneered
sneering
sneeze
sneezes
sneezed
sneezing
snide
sniff
sniffs
sniffed
sniffing
sniffle
sniffles
snifter
snigger
sniggers
sniggered
sniggering
snip
snips
snipped
snipping
snipe
snipes
sniped
sniping
sniper
snippet
snivel

snivels
snivelled
snivelling
snob
snog
snogs
snogged
snogging
snook
snooker
snoop
snoops
snooped
snooping
snooper
snooty
snootier
snootiest
snooze
snoozes
snoozed
snoozing
snore
snores
snored
snoring
snorkel
snort
snorts
snorted
snorting
snot
snotty
snout
snow
snows
snowed
snowing
snowball
snowberry

snowberries
snowcap
Snowdon
snowdrift
snowdrop
snowfall
snowfield
snowflake
snowman
snowmen
snowmobile
snowplough
snowshoe
snowstorm
snowy
snowier
snowiest
snub
snubs
snubbed
snubbing
snuff
snuffs
snuffed
snuffing
snuffbox
snuffle
snug
snugger
snuggest
snuggle
snuggles
snuggled
snuggling
so (= Is that so?
→ sew; sow)
soak
soaks
soaked
soaking

soap
soapbark
soapberry
soapberries
soapbox
soapily
soapiness
soapstone
soapsuds
soapy
soapier
soapiest
soar (= fly → saw;
sore)
soars
soared
soaring
sob
sobs
sobbed
sobbing
sobeit
sober
sobriety
sobriquet
soccer
sociable
social
socialisation
socialise
socialises
socialised
socialising
socialism
socialist
socialite
socialization
socialize
socializes
socialized

socializing
societal
society
societies
sociobiology
socioeconomic
sociolinguistics
sociological
sociology
sociometric
sociometry
sociopolitical
sock
socket
sod
soda
sodden
sodium
sodomy
sofa
soft
softball
soften
softens
softened
softening
softener
softhearted
softie
softness
software
softwood
softy
softies
soggily
sogginess
soggy
soggier
soggiest
soigné

soil
 soils
 soiled
 soiling
soirée
sojourn
solace
solar
sold
solder
 solders
 soldered
 soldering
soldier
sole (= only
 → soul)
solecism
solely
solemn
✗ solice = solace
solicit
 solicits
 solicited
 soliciting
solicitor
solicitous
solicitude
solid
solidarity
solidify
 solidifies
 solidified
 solidifying
solidus
 solidi
soliloquise
 soliloquised
 soliloquising
soliloquist
soliloquize

soliloquizes
soliloquized
soliloquizing
soliloquy
 soliloquies
solitaire
solitarily
solitariness
solitary
solitude
solo
 solos
soloist
solstice
✗ solt = salt
✗ solty = salty
solubility
 solubilities
soluble
solution
solve
 solves
 solved
 solving
solvency
solvent
Somalia
sombre
sombrero
some (= a few
 → sum)
somebody
someday
somehow
someone
somersault
Somerset
something
sometime
sometimes

somewhat
somewhere
somnambulist
somnolent
son (= child → sun)
sonar
sonata
✗ sonerous = sonorous
song
songster
songwriter
sonic
sonics
sonnet
sonny (= boy
 → sunny)
 sonnies
sonorous
soon
✗ soopson = soupçon
soot
soothe
 soothes
 soothed
 soothing
soothsayer
sootily
sootiness
sooty
 sootier
 sootiest
sop
sophisticated
sophistication
soporific
soppily
soppiness
sopping
soppy
 soppier

soppiest
soprano
sorbet
✗ sorce = source
sorcerer
sorcery
✗ sord = sword
sordid
sore (= hurting →
 saw; soar)
sorghum
sorrel
sorrow
sorry
sort (= kind →
 sought)
 sorts
 sorted
 sorting
sortie
sosh try soci
SOS
✗ sossage = sausage
sot
✗ sotay = sauté
sou
✗ soubricay =
 soubriquet
soubriquet
soufflé
souffléed
sough
sought (= looked
 for → sort)
souk
soul (= spirit →
 sole)
soulful
soulless
✗ souna = sauna

sound
sounds
sounded
sounding
soundboard
soundbox
soundings
soundless
soundproof
soundtrack
soup
soupçon
sour
 sours
 soured
 souring
source (= origin
 → sauce)
sourdough
sourpuss
sourwood
sousaphone
souse
 souses
 soused
 sousing
south
South Africa
Southampton
southeast
southeasterly
southerly
southern
southernly
southward
southwards
southwest
southwesterly
souvenir
sou'wester

sovereign
sovereignty
 sovereignties
Soviet
sow (= crops etc
 → sew; so)
sows
sowed
sown or
 sowed
 sowing
Soweto
sozzled
spa
space
 spaces
 spaced
 spacing
spacecraft
spacelab
spaceless
spaceman
spacemen
spaceship
spacesuit
spacewalk
spacial
spacious
spade
spadework
spaghetti
Spain
span
 spans
 spanned
 spanning
spangle
Spaniard
spaniel
Spanish

spank
  spanked
  spanks
  spanking
spanned
spanner
spanning
spar
  spars
  sparred
  sparring
spare
  spares
  spared
  sparing
sparerib
spark
  sparks
  sparked
  sparking
sparkle
  sparkles
  sparkled
  sparkling
sparkler
sparrow
sparrowgrass
sparrowhawk
sparse
✗ spashus = spacious
spasm
spasmodic
spastic
spat
spate
spatial
spatter
  spatters
  spattered
  spattering

spatula
spawn
  spawns
  spawned
  spawning
spay
  spays
  spayed
  spaying
speak
  speaks
  spoke
  spoken
  speaking
speakeasy
  speakeasies
speaker
spear
  spears
  speared
  spearing
spearfish
spearhead
spearmint
special
specialise
  specialises
  specialised
  specialising
specialism
specialist
speciality
  specialities
specialize
  specializes
  specialized
  specializing
species
  species
specific

specifically
specification
specify
  specifies
  specified
  specifying
specimen
specious
speck
speckle
specs
spectacle
spectacles
spectacular
spectacularly
spectate
  spectates
  spectated
  spectating
spectator
spectre
spectrum
  spectra
speculate
  speculates
  speculated
  speculating
speculation
speculative
speculator
speculum
  speculums *or*
  specula
speech
speechify
  speechifies
  speechified
  speechifying
speed
  speeds

sped *or*
speeded
speeding
speedboat
speedily
speediness
speedo
speedos
speedometer
speedway
speedwell
speedy
  speedier
  speediest
spell
  spells
  spelled *or*
  spelt
  spelling
spellbind
  spellbinds
  spellbound
  spellbinding
spellbound
spelled
speller
spells
spelt
spend
  spends
  spent
  spending
spendthrift
Spenserian
sperm
spermaceti
spermatozoon
  spermatozoa
spesh try speci
spew

spews
spewed
spewing
sphagnum
sphere
spherical
spheroid
sphincter
sphingomyelin
sphingosine
sphinx
  sphinxes *or*
  sphinges
spic
spice
  spices
  spiced
  spicing
spicily
spiciness
spick-and-span
spicy
  spicier
  spiciest
spider
spied
spiel
spies
spigot
spike
  spikes
  spiked
  spiking
spikily
spikiness
spiky
  spikier
  spikiest
spill
  spills

spilled *or*
spilt
spilling
spillage
spin
  spins
  spun
  spinning
spinach
spinal
spindle
spindly
  spindlier
  spindliest
spindrift
spine
spineless
✗ spinich = spinach
spininess
spinney
spinster
spiny
  spinier
  spiniest
spiracle
spiral
spire
spirit
spirited
spiritless
spiritous
spiritual
spiritualism
spirituality
spit
  spits
  spat *or*
  spit
  spitting
spite

spiteful
spittle
spittoon
spiv
splash
  splashes
  splashed
  splashing
splashback
splashboard
splashdown
splashily
splashiness
splashy
  splashier
  splashiest
splat
splatter
  splatters
  splattered
  splattering
splay
spleen
splendid
splendour
splice
  splices
  spliced
  splicing
splint
splinter
  splinters
  splintered
  splintering
split
  splits
  split
  splitting
splodge
splurge

splurges
splurged
splurging
splutter
  splutters
  spluttered
  spluttering
spoil
  spoils
  spoiled *or*
  spoilt
  spoiling
spoilage
spoiler
spoils
spoilsport
spoilt
spoke
spoken
sponge
  sponges
  sponged
  sponging
sponger
spongily
sponginess
spongy
  spongier
  spongiest
sponsor
spontaneity
spontaneous
spontaneously
spoof
spook
spookily
spookiness
spooky
  spookier
  spookiest

spool
spools
spooled
spooling
spoon
spoons
spooned
spooning
spoonbill
spoonerism
spoonful
spoor
sporadic
sporadically
sporangium
sporangia
spore
sporran
sport
sports
sported
sporting
sportily
sportiness
sportscast
sportsman
sportsmen
sportsperson
sportspeople
sportswear
sportswoman
sportswomen
sporty
sportier
sportiest
spot
spots
spotted
spotting
spotless

spotlight
spotter
spottily
spottiness
spotty
  spottier
  spottiness
spouse
spout
  spouts
  spouted
  spouting
sprain
  sprains
  sprained
  spraining
sprang
sprat
sprawl
  sprawls
  sprawled
  sprawling
spray
  sprays
  sprayed
  spraying
spread
  spreads
  spread
  spreading
spreadsheet
spree
sprig
sprightliness
sprightly
  sprightlier
  sprightliest
spring
  springs
  sprang or

sprung
springing
springboard
springbok
springily
springiness
springtime
springy
  springier
  springiest
sprinkle
  sprinkles
  sprinkled
  sprinkling
sprinkler
sprint
  sprints
  sprinted
  sprinting
sprite
spritzer
sprocket
sprout
  sprouts
  sprouted
  sprouting
spruce
sprung
spry
spud
spume
spun
spunk
spur
  spurs
  spurred
  spurring
spurious
spurn
  spurns

spurned
spurning
spurs
spurt
  spurts
  spurted
  spurting
Sputnik
sputum
spy
  spies
  spied
  spying
spyglass
spyhole
squab
  squab or
  squabs
squabble
  squabbles
  squabbled
  squabbling
squad
squadron
squalid
squall
squalor
squander
  squanders
  squandered
  squandering
square
  squares
  squared
  squaring
squarely
squash
  squashes
  squashed
  squashing

squashily
squashiness
squashy
  squashier
  squashiest
squat
  squats
  squatted
  squatting
  squatter
squaw
squawk
  squawks
  squawked
  squawking
squeak
  squeaks
  squeaked
  squeaking
squeal
  squeals
  squealed
  squealing
squeamish
squeegee
squeeze
  squeezes
  squeezed
  squeezing
squelch
  squelches
  squelched
  squelching
squib
squid
  squid or
  squids
squiggle
squint
  squints

squinted
squinting
squire
squirm
  squirms
  squirmed
  squirming
squirrel
squirt
  squirts
  squirted
  squirting
squish
  squishes
  squished
  squishing
squo try squa
Sri Lanka
St Neots
St Petersburg
stab
  stabs
  stabbed
  stabbing
stabilise
  stabilises
  stabilised
  stabilising
stabiliser
stability
stabilize
  stabilizes
  stabilized
  stabilizing
stabilizer
stable
stabling
stabs
staccato
✗ stachue = statue

stack
  stacks
  stacked
  stacking
stadium
  stadia or
  stadiums
staff
  staffs or
  staves
stag
stage
  stages
  staged
  staging
stagecoach
stagecraft
stagehand
stager
stagflation
stagger
  staggers
  staggered
  staggering
stagnant
stagnate
  stagnates
  stagnated
  stagnating
stagnation
staid (= sedate
  → stayed)
stain
  stains
  stained
  staining
Staines (town)
stainless
stair (= steps
  → stare)

staircase
stairway
stairwell
stake (= bet, or
  fence → steak)
  stakes
  staked
  staking
stakeout
stalactite
stalagmite
stale
stalemate
Stalinism
stalk (= part of a
  plant → stork)
  stalks
  stalked
  stalking
stall
  stalls
  stalled
  stalling
stallholder
stallion
stalwart
✗ stallwert = stalwart
stamen
  stamens *or*
  stamina
stamina
stammer
  stammers
  stammered
  stammering
stamp
  stamps
  stamped
  stamping
stampede

stance
stanch
  stanches
  stanched
  stanching
stand
  stands
  stood
  standing
standard
standardise
  standardises
  standardised
  standardising
standardize
  standardizes
  standardized
  standardizing
standing
standoffish
  standoffishly
standpipe
standpoint
stands
standstill
stank
Stanley
stanza
stapes
  stapes *or*
  stapedes
staphylococcus
  staphylococci
staple
  staples
  stapled
  stapling
stapler
star
  stars

starred
starring
starboard
starch
  starches
  starched
  starching
starchily
starchiness
starchy
  starchier
  starchiest
stardom
stardust
stare (= look hard
  at → stair)
  stares
  stared
  staring
starfish
starflower
stargaze
  stargazes
  stargazed
  stargazing
stargazer
stark
starkers
starlet
starlight
starling
starlit
starred
starrily
starriness
starring
starry
  starrier
  starriest
stars

start
  starts
  started
  starting
starter
startle
  startles
  startled
  startling
starvation
starve
  starves
  starved
  starving
stash
stasis
state
  states
  stated
  stating
statecraft
stateless
stateliness
stately
  statelier
  stateliest
statement
stateroom
stateside
static
station
stationary (= not moving)
stationer
stationery (= writing paper etc)
statistic
statistical
statistician
statistics

statue
statuesque
statuette
stature
status
statute
statutory
staunch
  staunches
  staunched
  staunching
stave
  staves
  staved *or*
  stove
  staving
staves
stay
  stays
  stayed (= stayed at home
  → staid)
  staying
stayer
stead
steadfast
steadily
steadiness
steady
  steadies
  steadied
  steadying
  steadier
  steadiest
steak (= meat → stake)
steakhouse
steal (take property → steel)
  steals

stole
stolen
stealing
stealth
stealthily
stealthiness
stealthy
  stealthier
  stealthiest
steam
  steams
  steamed
  steaming
steamboat
steamer
steamily
steaminess
steamroller
steamship
steamy
  steamier
  steamiest
steed
steel (= metal → steal)
  steels
  steeled
  steeling
steeliness
steelworks
steelyard
steep
  steeps
  steeped
  steeping
steeple
steeplechase
steeplejack
steer
  steers

steered
steering
steerage
stegosaur
stellar
stellate
stem
  stems
  stemmed
  stemming
stench
stencil
stenography
stentorian
step (= footstep
  → steppe)
  steps
  stepped
  stepping
stepbrother
stepchild
  stepchildren
stepdaughter
stepfather
Stephen
Stephenson, George
stepladder
stepmother
steppe (= plain
  → step)
stepsister
stepson
stereo
  stereos
stereophonic
stereophonically
stereoscopic
stereoscopically
stereotype
sterile

sterilisation
sterilise
  sterilises
  sterilised
  sterilising
sterility
sterilization
sterilize
  sterilizes
  sterilized
  sterilizing
✗ sterio = stereo
✗ steriotype =
  stereotype
sterling
stern
sternum
  sterna *or*
  sternums
steroid
stethoscope
stetson
stevedore
Steven
Stevenson, R.L.
stew
  stews
  stewed
  stewing
steward
stewardess
stick
  sticks
  stuck
  sticking
sticker
stickily
stickiness
stickleback
stickler

sticky
  stickier
  stickiest
sties
stiff
stiffen
  stiffens
  stiffened
  stiffening
stifle
  stifles
  stifled
  stifling
stigma
  stigmas *or*
  stigmata
stigmatise
  stigmatises
  stigmatised
  stigmatising
stigmatize
  stigmatizes
  stigmatized
  stigmatizing
stile (= steps
  → style)
stiletto
  stilettos
still
  stills
  stilled
  stilling
stillbirth
stillborn
stilly
stilt
stilted
Stilton
stimulant
stimulate

stimulates
stimulated
stimulating
stimulus
  stimuli
sting
  stings
  stung
  stinging
stingily
stinginess
stingray
stingy
  stingier
  stingiest
stink
  stinks
  stank *or*
  stunk
  stinking
stinkweed
stint
stipend
stipendiary
stipulate
  stipulates
  stipulated
  stipulating
stir
  stirs
  stirred
  stirring
Stirling
stirrer
stirrup
stitch
  stitches
  stitched
  stitching
stoat

stock
  stocks
  stocked
  stocking
stockade
stockbreeder
stockbroker
stockfish
stockholder
Stockholm
stockier
stockiest
stockily
stockiness
stocking
stockist
stockjobber
stockpile
  stockpiles
  stockpiled
  stockpiling
stockpot
stockroom
stocks
stocktaking
stocky
  stockier
  stockiest
stockyard
stodge
stodginess
stodgy
  stodgier
  stodgiest
stoic
stoke
  stokes
  stoked
  stoking
stoker

stole
stolen
stolid
stoma
  stomata
stomach
  stomachs
  stomached
  stomaching
stomachache
stomp
  stomps
  stomped
  stomping
stone
  stones
  stoned
  stoning
stonechat
stonecrop
stonecutter
stonefish
stonefly
  stoneflies
stoneground
stonemason
stonewall
  stonewalls
  stonewalled
  stonewalling
stoneware
stonewashed
stonework
stonily
stoniness
stony
  stonier
  stoniest
stood
stooge

stook
stool
stoop
  stoops
  stooped
  stooping
stop
  stops
  stopped
  stopping
stopcock
stopgap
stoplight
stopoff
stopover
stoppage
stopper
stopping
stops
stopwatch
storage
store
  stores
  stored
  storing
storehouse
storekeeper
storeroom
storey (= of a
  building → story)
storeyed
stork (= bird
  → stalk)
storm
  storms
  stormed
  storming
stormbound
stormproof
stormily

storminess
stormy
  stormier
  stormiest
story (= tale
  → storey)
  stories
storyboard
storybook
storyteller
stout
stouthearted
stove
stovepipe
stow
  stows
  stowed
  stowing
stowage
stowaway
straddle
  straddles
  straddled
  straddling
strafe
  strafes
  strafed
  strafing
straggle
  straggles
  straggled
  straggling
straight (= not
  crooked → strait)
straightaway
straighten
  straightens
  straightened
  straightening
straightforward

straightjacket
strain
  strains
  strained
  straining
strainer
strait (= sea
  → straight)
✗ strait = straight
straitjacket
strand
strange
stranger
strangle
  strangles
  strangled
  strangling
stranglehold
strap
  straps
  strapped
  strapping
straphanger
strapless
Strasbourg
strata
stratagem
✗ stratasphere =
  stratosphere
strategic
strategically
strategist
strategy
  strategies
stratocumulus
  stratocumuli
stratosphere
stratum
  strata *or*
  stratums

straw
strawberry
strawberries
strawflower
stray
strays
strayed
straying
streak
streaks
streaked
streaking
streakily
streakiness
streaky
streakier
streakiest
stream
streams
streamed
streaming
streamer
streamlined
street
streetcar
streetlight
streetwalker
streetwise
strength
strengthen
strengthens
strengthened
strengthening
strenuous
strenuously
streptococcus
streptococci
stress
stresses
stressed

stressing
stressful
stressfully
stretch
stretches
stretched
stretching
stretcher
stretchiness
stretchmarks
stretchy
stretchier
stretchiest
strewn
stricken
strict
stricture
stride
strides
strode
stridden
striding
strident
strife
strike
strikes
struck
striking
striker
striking
string
strings
strung
stringing
stringed
stringent
stringiness
stringy
stringier
stringiest

strip
strips
stripped
stripping
stripe
striped
stripling
stripper
striptease
stripy
stripier
stripiest
strive
strives
strove
striven
striving
strobe
strode
stroganoff
stroke
strokes
stroked
stroking
stroll
strolls
strolled
strolling
strong
strongbox
stronghold
strongman
strongmen
strongpoint
strongroom
strontium
stroppy
stroppier
stroppiest
strove

struck
structural
structure
structured
strudel
struggle
  struggles
  struggled
  struggling
strum
  strums
  strummed
  strumming
strumpet
strung
strut
  struts
  strutted
  strutting
strychnine
✗ strycnine =
  strychnine
stub
  stubs
  stubbed
  stubbing
stubble
stubborn
stucco
stuck
stud
studded
student
studio
  studios
studious
study
  studies
  studied
  studying

stuff
stuffs
stuffed
stuffing
stuffily
stuffiness
stuffy
stuffier
stuffiest
stultify
stultifies
stultified
stultifying
✗ stumack =
  stomach
stumble
  stumbles
  stumbled
  stumbling
stump
stun
  stuns
  stunned
  stunning
stung
stunk
stunt
stupefaction
stupefy
  stupefies
  stupefied
  stupefying
stupendous
stupid
stupidity
stupor
sturdily
sturdiness
sturdy
  sturdier

sturdiest
sturgeon
stutter
  stutters
  stuttered
  stuttering
sty
  sties (= pigs)
stye (= in your
  eye)
style (= fashion
  → stile)
  styles
  styled
  styling
stylish
stylist
stylus
  styli or
  styluses
styrene
✗ suade = suede
suave
sub
  subs
  subbed
  subbing
subalpine
subaltern
subantarctic
subaqua
subaquatic
subaqueous
subarctic
subatomic
subbed
subbing
subconscious
subconsciously
subcontinent

subsolar

subcontinental
subcontract
  subcontracts
  subcontracted
  subcontracting
subcontractor
subcortex
subcortical
subculture
subcutaneous
subdivide
  subdivides
  subdivided
  subdividing
subdivision
subdue
  subdues
  subdued
  subdueing
subedit
  subedits
  subedited
  subediting
subeditor
subgroup
subheading
subhuman
subject
  subjects
  subjected
  subjecting
subjection
subjective
subjugate
  subjugates
  subjugated
  subjugating
subjunctive
✗ subleftenant =
  sublieutenant

sublet
  sublets
  sublet
  subletting
sublieutenant
sublimate
  sublimates
  sublimated
  sublimating
sublimation
sublime
subliminal
subliminally
submarine
submariner
submerge
  submerges
  submerged
  submerging
submersible
submersion
submission
submissive
submit
  submits
  submitted
  submitting
subnormal
subnuclear
suboceanic
✗ suboltern =
  subaltern
subordinate
  subordinates
  subordinated
  subordinating
subordination
✗ subpeena =
  subpoena
subplot

subpoena
  subpoenas
  subpoened
  subpoenaing
subpopulation
subregion
subscribe
  subscribes
  subscribed
  subscribing
subscriber
subscription
subsequent
subservience
subservient
subset
subside
  subsides
  subsided
  subsiding
subsidence
subsidiary
  subsidiaries
subsidise
  subsidises
  subsidising
  subsidised
subsidize
  subsidizes
  subsidized
  subsidizing
subsidy
  subsidies
subsist
  subsists
  subsisted
  subsisting
subsistence
subsoil
subsolar

subsonic
substance
substandard
substantial
substantially
substitute
  substitutes
  substituted
  substituting
substitution
substrate
subsume
  subsumes
  subsumed
  subsuming
subtenant
subterfuge
subterranean
subtitle
subtle
subtlety
subtotal
subtract
  subtracts
  subtracted
  subtracting
subtracter
subtraction
subtropical
suburb
suburban
suburbia
subversion
subversive
subway
subzero
succeed
  succeeds
  succeeded
  succeeding

success
successful
successfully
successfulness
succession
successive
successively
successor
succinct
Succoth
succour (= help
  → sucker)
succulent
succumb
  succumbs
  succumbed
  succumbing
such
suck
  sucks
  sucked
  sucking
sucker (= some-
  thing that sucks
  → succour)
suckle
  suckles
  suckled
  suckling
sucrose
✗ sucseed = succeed
✗ sucsess = success
✗ sucsession =
  succession
✗ sucsessive =
  successive
✗ sucsessor =
  successor
✗ sucsinct = succinct
suction

Sudan
sudden
✗ sude = pseud
suds
sue
  sues
  sued
  suing
suede
suet
✗ suff = sough
✗ suffecate =
  suffocate
suffer
  suffers
  suffered
  suffering
sufferable
sufferance
suffice
sufficiency
sufficient
suffix
suffocate
  suffocates
  suffocated
  suffocating
Suffolk
suffrage
suffragette
suffragist
suffused
sugar
sugary
suggest
  suggests
  suggested
  suggesting
suggestible
suggestion

suggestive
suggestively
suicidal
suicide
suing
suit
  suits
  suited
  suiting
suitable
suitcase
suite (= furniture → sweet)
suitor
sukiyaki
Sukkoth
sulk
  sulks
  sulked
  sulking
sulkily
sulkiness
sulky
  sulkier
  sulkiest
sullen
sully
  sullies
  sullied
  sullying
sulphate
sulphide
sulphite
sulphur
sultan
sultana
sultrily
sultriness
sultry
  sultrier

sultriest
sum (= addition → some)
sums
summed
summing
summarise
summarises
summarised
summarising
summarize
summarizes
summarized
summarizing
summary
summaries
summarily
summed
summer
summerhouse
summertime
summery
summing
summit
summon
summons
summoned
summoning
summons
summonses
sumo
sump
sumptuous
sun (= star → son)
suns
sunned
sunning
sunbathe
sunbathes

sunbathed
sunbathing
sunbeam
sunbird
sunbonnet
sunbow
sunburn
sunburned or
sunburnt
sunburst
sundae (= ice-cream)
sundaes
Sunday (= day of the week)
sunder
sundew
sundial
sundown
sundowner
sundress
sundry
  sundries
sunfast
sunfish
sunflower
sung
sunglass
sunglasses
sunglow
sungrebe
sunhat
sunk
sunken
sunken
sunlight
sunned
sunnily
sunniness
sunning

sunny (= warm
→ sonny)
sunnier
sunniest
sunrise
sunroof
suns
sunset
sunshade
sunshine
sunspot
sunstar
sunstone
sunstroke
sunsuit
suntan
suntrap
sunup
sunward
sunwards
sup
sups
supped
supping
super
superannuation
superb
supercharge
supercharges
supercharged
supercharging
supercharger
supercilious
supercomputer
super-duper
superficial
superficiality
superfluity
superfluous
superglue

supergrass
superhero
superheros
superhuman
superimpose
superimposes
superimposed
superimposing
superintendent
superior
superiority
superlative
superlatively
superman
supermen
supermarket
supernatural
supernova
supernovas or
supernovae
superordinate
superpower
supersede
supersedes
superseded
superseding
supersonic
superstar
superstition
superstitious
superstore
supertanker
supertax
supervise
supervised
supervises
supervising
supervision
supervisor
superwoman

superwomen
supine
supped
supper
supping
supplant
supplants
supplanted
supplanting
supple
supplement
supplementary
supplier
supply
supplies
supplied
supplying
support
supports
supported
supporting
supporter
supportive
suppose
supposes
supposed
supposing
supposition
suppository
suppositories
suppress
suppresses
suppressed
suppressing
suppression
supremacy
supreme
suprême
supremo
supremos

sups
surcharge
  surcharges
  surcharged
  surcharging
sure (= certain
  → shore)
surely
surety
  sureties
surf
  surfs
  surfed
  surfing
surface
  surfaces
  surfaced
  surfacing
surfactant
surfboard
surfeit
surfing
✗ surfit = surfeit
surge (= move
  forward → serge)
surgeon
surgery
  surgeries
surgical
surlily
surliness
surly
  surlier
  surliest
surmise
  surmises
  surmised
  surmising
surmount
  surmounts

surmounted
surmounting
surmountable
surname
surpass
  surpasses
  surpassed
  surpassing
surplice
surplus
surprise
  surprises
  surprised
  surprising
  surprisedly
  surprisingly
surreal
surrealism
surrealist
surrender
  surrenders
  surrendered
  surrendering
surreptitious
surrogacy
surrogate
surround
  surrounds
  surrounded
  surrounding
  surroundings
✗ survalence =
  surveillance
surveillance
survey
  surveys
  surveyed
  surveying
surveyor
survivable

survival
survive
  survives
  survived
  surviving
survivor
susceptible
susceptibly
sushi
suspect
  suspects
  suspected
  suspecting
suspend
  suspends
  suspended
  suspending
suspender
suspense
suspension
suspicion
suspicious
suspiciously
suss
  susses
  sussed
  sussing
sustain
  sustains
  sustained
  sustaining
sustainable
sustenance
✗ sutherly = southerly
✗ suthern = southern
✗ sutlety = subtlety
suttee
✗ suttle = subtle
suture
svelte

swab
swabs
swabbed
swabbing
swaddle
swaddles
swaddled
swaddling
Swaffham
swag
swagger
swaggers
swaggered
swaggering
swallow
swallows
swallowed
swallowing
swam
swami
swamies *or*
swamis
swamp
swamps
swamped
swamping
swan
✘ swaniay = soigné
swank
swanky
swankier
swankiest
Swansea
swap
swaps
swapped
swapping
✘ sware = swear
swarm
swarms

swarmed
swarming
swarthily
swarthiness
swarthy
swarthier
swarthiest
swashbuckling
swastika
swat
swats
swatted
swatting
swatch
swath
swaths
swathe
swathes
swatter
sway
sways
swayed
swaying
Swaziland
swear
swears
swore
sworn
swearing
swearword
sweat
sweats
sweated
sweating
sweatband
sweater
sweatily
sweatiness
sweatshirt
sweatshop

sweaty
sweatier
sweatiest
swede
Sweden
Swedish
sweep
sweeps
swept
sweeping
sweepstake
sweet
sweetbread
sweetbrier
sweeten
sweetens
sweetened
sweetening
sweetener
sweetheart
sweetie
sweetmeat
swell
swells
swelled
swollen
swelling
sweltering
swerve
swerves
swerved
swerving
swift
swig
swigs
swigged
swigging
swill
swills

swilled
swilling
swim
swims
swam
swum
swimming
swimmingly
swimsuit
swindle
swindles
swindled
swindling
swine
swines *or*
swine
swineherd
swing
swings
swung
swinging
swingeing
swipe
swipes
swiped
swiping
swirl
swirls
swirled
swirling
swish
switch
switches
switched
switching
switchblade
Switzerland
swivel
swivels
swivelled

swivelling
swizzle
swollen
swoon
swoons
swooned
swooning
swoop
swoops
swooped
swooping
swoosh
swop
swops
swopped
swopping
sword
swordfish
swore
sworn
swot
swum
swung
sycamore
sycophant
sycophantic
Sydney (city)
syllable
syllabub
syllabus
    syllabuses *or*
    syllabi
syllogism
sylph
sylvan
symbiosis
✗ symble = symbol
symbol
symbolic
symbolise

symbolises
symbolised
symbolising
symbolism
symbolize
symbolizes
symbolized
symbolizing
symmetric
symmetrical
symmetry
symmetries
sympathetic
sympathise
sympathises
sympathised
sympathising
sympathize
sympathizes
sympathized
sympathizing
sympathy
sympathies
symphony
symphonies
symposium
symptom
synagogue
synapse
✗ syncapate =
    syncopate
✗ syncepy = syncope
syncromesh
synchronise
synchronises
synchronised
synchronising
synchronize
synchronizes
synchronized

synchronizing
syncopate
syncope
✗ syncromesh =
    synchromesh
✗ syncronize =
    synchronize
syndicate
syndrome
synod
synonym
synonymous
synopsis
    synopses
syntax
synthesizer
synthetic
syphilis
syphon
Syria
Syrian
syringe
syrup
system
systematic
systemic
systole
systolic

T

ta
tab
tabard
Tabasco™
tabby
    tabbies
tabernacle
tabla
tablature
table
    tables
    tabled
    tabling
tableau *or*
    tableaux *or*
    tableaus
tablecloth
tablespoon
tablespoonful
tablet
tableware
✗ tablo = tableau
tabloid
taboo
    taboos
tabor
tabour
tabu
    tabus
tabular
tabulate
    tabulates

tabulated
    tabulating
tabulator
tacheometer
tacheometric
tacheometry
tachogram
tachograph
tachometer
tachometric
tachometry
tachycardia
tachycardiac
tachymeter
tachymetry
tacit
taciturn
tack
    tacks
    tacked
    tacking
tackier
tackiest
tackiness
tackle
    tackles
    tackled
    tackling
tacky
    tackier
    tackiest
taco
    tacos
tact
tactic
tactical
tactician
tactics
tactile
tad

tadpole
tael
taffeta
tag
  tags
  tagged
  tagging
tagliatelle
tahini
Tahiti
taiga
tail (= dog's tail
  → tale)
  tails
  tailed
  tailing
tailback
tailboard
tailgate
taillight
tailor
tailorbird
tailpiece
tailpipe
tailplane
tails
tailskid
tailspin
tailwind
taint
  taints
  tainted
  tainting
Taipei
Taiwan
Tajikstan
take
  takes
  took
  taken

taking
takeaway
takeoff
takeout
takeover
taker
takes
taking
talc
  talcs
  talced or
  talcked
  talcing or
  talcking
tale (= story
  → tail)
talent
talipes
talisman
✗taliatelli =
  tagliatelle
talk (= speak
  → torc; torque)
  talks
  talked
  talking
talkative
talkie
tall
tallboy
tallis
tallith
  tallithes or
  tallitoth
tallow
tally
  tallies
  tallied
  tallying
tally-ho

Talmud
Talmudist
talon
talus
  tali or
  taluses
tam
tamale
tamarind
tamarisk
tambour
tambourine
✗tambre = timbre
tame
  tames
  tamed
  taming
Tamil
  Tamils or
  Tamil
tam-o'-shanter
tamp
  tamps
  tamped
  tamping
tamper
tampion
tampon
tan
  tans
  tanned
  tanning
tandem
tandoori
tang
tangelo
  tangelos
tangent
tangentally
tangential

tangentially
tangerine
tangible
tangier
tangiest
tangle
  tangles
  tangled
  tangling
tango
  tangos
  tangoes
  tangoed
  tangoing
tangram
tangy
  tangier
  tangiest
tank
tankage
tankard
tanker
tankful
tanned
tanner
tannery
  tanneries
tannic
tannin
tanning
tansy
  tansies
tantalise
  tantalises
  tantalised
  tantalising
tantalize
  tantalizes
  tantalized
  tantalizing

tantalum
tantalus
tantamount
tantara
tantrum
Tanzania
Tao
Taoiseach
Taoism
tap
  taps
  tapped
  tapping
tapa
tape
  tapes
  taped
  taping
taper
  tapers
  tapered
  tapering
tapestry
  tapestries
tapeworm
tapioca
tapir
tapped
tappet
tapping
taproom
taproot
taps
tar
  tars
  tarred
  tarring
taradiddle
taramasalata
tarantella

tarantula
  tarantulas or
  tarantulae
tardily
tardiness
tardy
  tardier
  tardiest
tare (= weight
  → tear)
✗ taremeselata =
  taramasalata
✗ tarentella =
  tarantella
target
  targets
  targeted
  targeting
tariff
Tarmac
✗ tarmigan =
  ptarmigan
tarn
tarnish
  tarnished
  tarnished
  tarnishing
taro
  taros (= plant)
tarot (= cards)
tarpaulin
tarpon
  tarpons or
  tarpon
tarradiddle
tarragon
tarring
tarry
  tarries
  tarried

tarrying
tars
tarsal
tarsus
tarsi
tart
tartan
tartar
tartare
Tartarean
tartaric
tartlet
tartrate
tartrazine
task
Tasmania
tassel
taste
tastes
tasted
tasting
tasteful
tasteless
taster
tastily
tastiness
tasty
tastier
tastiest
tat
ta-ta
tatami
Tatar
tatter
tattiness
tatting
tattle
tattles
tattled
tattling

tattoo
tattoos
tattooed
tattooing
tattooer
tattooist
tatty
tattier
tattiest
tau
taught (= I taught
him → taut; tort)
✗ tauk = talk
taunt
taunts
taunted
taunting
taupe
Taurus
taut (= tense
→ taught; tort)
tauten
tautens
tautened
tautening
tautological
tautologous
tautology
tautologies
tavern
taverna
taw
tawdrily
tawdriness
tawdry
tawdrier
tawdriest
tawniness
tawny
taws

tawse
tax
taxes
taxed
taxing
taxable
taxation
taxi
taxis or
taxies
taxies
taxied
taxiing or
taxying
taxicab
taxidermy
taximeter
taxing
taxis
taxiway
taxonomic
taxonomist
taxonomy
taxpayer
taxying
tayberry
tayberries
TB
Tchaikovsky
TCP℠
tea (= drink → tee)
teabread
teacake
teach
teaches
taught
teaching
teacher
teacup
teacupful

teahouse
teak
teakettle
teal
　teals *or*
　teal
team (= group
　→ teem)
　teams
　teamed
　teaming
teamster
teamwork
teapot
tear (= teardrop, or
　rip → tare; tier)
　tears
　tore
　torn
　tearing
tearaway
teardrop
tearful
tear-jerker
tearoom
tears
tease
　teases
　teased
　teasing
teasel
teaser
teashop
teaspoon
teaspoonful
teat
teazel
teazle
✗ tecela = tequila
tech.

technic
technical
technicality
　technicalities
technician
Technicolor (TM)
technicolour
technics
technique
technocracy
　technocracies
technocrat
technography
technological
technologist
technology
　technologies
technophobia
technostructure
tectonic
tectonics
teddy
　teddies
tedious
tedium
tee (= in golf
　→ tea)
　tees
　teed
　teeing
teem (= pour with
　rain → team)
　teems
　teemed
　teeming
teem
teenage
teenager
teens
teensy-weensy

teeny
teenybopper
teeny-weeny
teepee
tees
teeter
　teeters
　teetered
　teetering
teeth
teethe
　teethes
　teethed
　teething
teetotal
teetotalism
teetotaller
teetotally
te-hee
Teignmouth
telecast
　telecasts
　telecasted
　telecasting
telecommunication
telecommunications
telecommuting
telegenic
telegram
telegrammatic
telegraph
telegrapher
telegraphic
telegraphically
telegraphist
telegraphy
telekinesis
telekinetic
telemark
telemarketing

telemeter
telemetric
telemetry
telencephalic
telencephalon
teleology
telepathic
telepathy
telephone
  telephones
  telephoned
  telephoning
telephonic
telephonist
telephony
teleport
teleprinter
teleprocessing
telesales
telescience
telescope
telescopic
telescopy
telesoftware
telethon
teletypewriter
televangelist
televise
  televises
  televised
  televising
television
televisual
teleworking
telewriter
telex
tell
  tells
  told
  telling

teller
telltale
tellurian
telly
  tellies
temerity
temp
temper
  tempers
  tempered
  tempering
tempera
temperament
temperamental
temperance
temperate
temperature
tempered
tempest
tempestuous
tempi
template
temple
tempo
  tempos *or*
  tempi
temporal
temporary
temporise
  temporises
  temporised
  temporising
temporize
  temporizes
  temporized
  temporizing
tempt
  tempts
  tempted
  tempting

temptation
temptress
tempura
ten
tenable
tenacious
tenacity
tenancy
  tenancies
tenant
tench
tend
  tends
  tended
  tending
tendencious
tendency
  tendencies
tendentious
tender
  tenders
  tendered
  tendering
tenderfoot
tenderhearted
tenderise
  tenderises
  tenderised
  tenderising
tenderiser
tenderize
  tenderizes
  tenderized
  tenderizing
tenderizer
tenderloin
tendon
tendril
tenement
Tenerife

tenet
tenfold
tenner (= ten-pound
 note → tenor)
Tennessee
tennis
tenon
tenor (= voice etc
 → tenner)
tenpin
 tenpins
tense
 tenses
 tensed
 tensing
tensile
tensimeter
tensiometer
tension
tensor
tent
tentacle
tentative
tenterhook
tenth
tenthly
tenuous
tenure
tepee
tepid
tequila
terbium
tercentenary
 tercentenaries
tercentennial
teriyaki
term
termagant
terminable
terminal

terminate
 terminates
 terminated
 terminating
termination
terminator
terminological
terminology
 terminologies
terminus
 termini or
 terminuses
termite
tern (= bird
 → turn)
ternary
✗terodactyl =
 pterodactyl
terra
terrace
 terracing
terracotta
terrain
terrapin
terrazzo
terrestrial
terrible
terribly
✗terrice = terrace
terrier
terrific
terrifically
terrify
 terrifies
 terrified
 terrifying
terrine
territorial
territory
 territories

terror
terrorise
 terrorises
 terrorised
 terrorising
terrorism
terrorist
terrorize
 terrorizes
 terrorized
 terrorizing
terry
terse
tertial
tertiary
tesla
tessellate
 tessellates
 tessellated
 tessellating
tessellation
tessera
 tesserae
test
 tests
 tested
 testing
testa
 testae
testament
testate
testator
tester
testes
testicle
testicular
testify
 testifies
 testified
 testifying

testimonial
testimony
  testimonies
testiness
testis
  testes
testosterone
testy
  testier
  testiest
tetanus
tetchily
tetchiness
tetchy
  tetchier
  tetchiest
tête-à-tête
tether
  tethers
  tethered
  tethering
tetragon
tetragonal
tetragram
tetrahedron
  tetrahedrons or
  tetrahedra
tetralogy
  tetralogies
tetraplegia
tetse = tsetse
tetsy = tsetse
Teutonic
Tewkesbury
text
textbook
textile
textual
texture
Thai

Thailand
thalamus
  thalami
thalidomide
Thames
than
thank
  thanks
  thanked
  thanking
thankful
thankless
thanksgiving
that
thatch
  thatches
  thatched
  thatching
thaw
  thaws
  thawed
  thawing
the
theatre
theatrical
theatricality
theatricals
theatrics
thee
theft
their (= belonging
  to them → there;
  they're)
theirs
theism
theistic
them
thematic
thematically
theme

themself
themselves
then
thence
thenceforth
thenceforward
theocracy
  theocracies
theodolite
theologian
theological
theologist
theology
  theologies
theorem
theoretical
theoretician
theorise
  theorises
  theorised
  theorising
theorize
  theorizes
  theorized
  theorizing
theory
  theories
theosophical
theosophism
theosophist
theosophy
therapeutic
therapeutics
therapist
therapy
  therapies
there (= over there
  → their; they're)
thereabouts
thereafter

thereby
therefore
therein
thereof
thereon
thereto
thereupon
therewith
therm
thermal
thermistor
thermocouple
thermodynamic
thermodynamics
thermometer
thermonuclear
thermoplastic
Thermos℠
thermostat
thermotropism
thesaurus
  thesauruses *or*
  thesauri
these
thesis
  theses
theta
they
they'd
they'll
they're (= they are
  → their; there)
they've
thiamine
thick
thicken
  thickens
  thickened
  thickening
thicket

thickness
thickset
thief
  thieves
thieve
  thieves
  thieved
  thieving
thigh
thighbone
thimble
thimbleful
thin
  thins
  thinned
  thinning
thine
thing
thingamabob
thingumabob
thingumajig
thingummy
think
  thinks
  thought
  thinking
thinned
thinner
thinnest
thinning
thins
third
thirdly
thirst
thirstily
thirstiness
thirsty
  thirstier
  thirstiest
thirteen

thirteenth
thirtieth
thirty
  thirties
this
thistle
thistledown
thither
Thomas
thong
thoracic
thorax
  thoraxes *or*
  thoraces
thorn
thornily
thorniness
thorny
  thornier
  thorniest
thorough
thoroughbred
thoroughfare
thoroughgoing
thoroughly
those
thou
though
thought
thoughtful
thoughtless
thousand
thousandth
✗ thow = though
thrall
thrash
  thrashes
  thrashed
  thrashing
thread

threads
threaded
threading
threadbare
threadworm
threat
threaten
  threatens
  threatened
  threatening
three
three-D
threefold
threescore
threesome
threnodies
threnodist
threnody
  threnodies
thresh
  threshes
  threshed
  threshing
thresher
threshold
threw (= threw a
  ball → through)
✗threwout =
  throughout
✗threwput =
  throughput
thrice
thrift
thriftily
thriftiness
thrifty
  thriftier
  thriftiest
thrill
  thrills

thrilled
thrilling
thriller
thrive
  thrives
  thrived or
  throve
  thrived or
  thriven
  thriving
throat
throatily
throatiness
throaty
  throatier
  throatiest
throb
  throbs
  throbbed
  throbbing
throes (= death
  throes → throws)
thrombosis
throne (= king's
  chair → thrown)
throng
  throngs
  thronged
  thronging
throttle
  throttles
  throttled
  throttling
through
throughout
throughput
throve
throw
  throws (= throws
  a ball → throes)

threw
thrown (=
  thrown out
  → throne)
throwing
throwaway
throwback
thrum
  thrums
  thrummed
  thrumming
thrush
thrust
  thrusts
  thrust
  thrusting
thud
  thuds
  thudded
  thudding
thug
thumb
  thumbs
  thumbed
  thumbing
thumbnail
thumbscrew
thumbtack
thump
  thumps
  thumped
  thumping
thunder
  thunders
  thundered
  thundering
thunderbolt
thunderclap
thundercloud
thunderous

thundershower
thunderstorm
thunderstruck
✗ thurrebred =
thoroughbred
✗ thurrefare =
thoroughfare
✗ thurrely = thoroughly
✗ thurrer = thorough
Thursday
thus
thwack
thwart
  thwarts
  thwarted
  thwarting
thy
thyme (= herb
  → time)
thymus
  thymuses or
  thymi
thyroid
thyself
tiara
tiaraed
tibia
  tibiae or
  tibias
tic (= twitch)
tick (= of a clock)
  ticks
  ticked
  ticking
ticker
ticket
ticking
tickle
  tickles
  tickled

tickling
tickler
ticklish
ticktack
tick-tack-toe
ticktock
tidal
tidbit
tiddler
tiddly
tiddlywink
tiddlywinks
tide
  tides
  tided
  tiding
tidemark
tidewater
tidily
tidiness
tidings
tidy
  tidies
  tidied
  tidying
  tidier
  tidiest
tie
  ties
  tied
  tying
tieback
tiebreaker
tiepin
tier (= layer
  → tear)
ties
tiff
tiffin
tig

tiger
tight
tighten
tightens
tightened
tightening
tightfisted
tightknit
tightrope
tights
tigon
tigress
tike
tikka
tilde
tile
  tiles
  tiled
  tiling
till
  tills
  tilled
  tilling
tillage
tiller
tilt
  tilts
  tilted
  tilting
timbal
timbale
timber (= wood
  → timbre)
timbered
timberyard
timbre (= tone
  → timber)
time
  times
  timed

timing
timecard
timekeeper
timeless
timeliness
timely
  timelier
  timeliest
timepiece
timer
timesaving
timescale
timetable
timeworn
timid
timidity
timing
timorous
timpani
tin
  tins
  tinned
  tinning
tincture
tinder
tinderbox
tine
tined
tinfoil
ting
ting-a-ling
tinge
  tinges
  tinged
  tingeing *or*
  tinging
tingle
  tingles
  tingled
  tingling

tinier
tiniest
tinker
tinkers
tinkered
tinkering
tinkle
tinkles
tinkled
tinkling
tinned
tinner
tinnily
tinniness
tinning
tinnitus
tinny
  tinnier
  tinniest
tinpot
tins
tinsel
tinsmith
tint
  tints
  tinted
  tinting
tintype
tinware
tinwork
tinworks
tiny
  tinier
  tiniest
tip
  tips
  tipped
  tipping
  tipper
Tipperary

tipple
tipples
tippled
tippling
tippler
tips
tipsily
tipsiness
tipstaff
tipster
tipsy
  tipsier
  tipsiest
tiptoe
  tiptoes
  tiptoed
  tiptoeing
tiptop
tirade
tire (= get tired of
  → tyre)
  tires
  tired
  tiring
tireless
tiresome
tisane
tissue
tit
titanic
titanium
titbit
titchy
  titchier
  titchiest
titfer
tithe
tithing
Titian
titillate

titillates
titillated
titillating
titivate
titivates
titivated
titivating
title
titles
titled
titling
titleholder
titmouse
titmice
titrant
titrate
titration
titre
titter
titters
tittered
tittering
tittivate
tittivates
tittivated
tittivating
tittle-tattle
titular
tizz
tizzy
tizzies
T-junction
TNT
to (= opposite of from → too; two)
toad
toadflax
toadstool
toady
toadies

toadied
toadying
toast
toasts
toasted
toasting
toaster
toastmaster
toastmistress
toasty
tobacco
tobaccos *or* tobaccoes
tobacconist
toboggan
toboggans
tobogganed
tobogganing
tobogganer
tobogganist
toby
toccata
tocsin
tod
today
toddle
toddles
toddled
toddling
toddler
toddy
toddies
toe (= part of the foot → tow)
toes
toed
toeing
toecap
toehold
toenail

toerag
toff
toffee
toft
tofu
tog
togs
togged
togging
toga
togaed
together
togetherness
toggle
Togo
togs
toil
toils
toiled
toiling
toile
toilet
toiletry
toiletries
toilette
token
tokenism
Tokyo
tolbutamide
told
tolerable
tolerance
tolerant
tolerate
tolerates
tolerated
tolerating
toleration
toll
tolls

tolled
tolling
tollbooth
tollgate
tollhouse
Tolstoy, Leo
toluene
tom
tomahawk
tomato
  tomatoes
tomb
tombola
tomboy
tombstone
tome
tomfoolery
tommy
  tommies
tommyrot
tomography
tomorrow
tomtit
ton (= weight
  → tonne; tun)
tonal
tonality
tone
  tones
  toned
  toning
toneless
toner
tong
tongs
tongue
  tongues
  tongued
  tonguing
tonic

tonicity
tonight
tonnage
tonne (= metric ton
  → ton; tun)
tonsil
tonsillectomy
  tonsillectomies
tonsillitis
tonsorial
tonsure
too (= also → to;
  two)
toodle-oo
took
tool (= hammer etc
  → tulle)
tooling
✗ toom = tomb
✗ toomstone =
  tombstone
✗ toor = tour
✗ toorism = tourism
✗ toorist = tourist
✗ toornament =
  tournament
✗ toornicay =
  tourniquet
toot
  toots
  tooted
  tooting
tooth
toothache
toothbrush
toothed
toothily
toothiness
toothpaste
toothpick

toothsome
toothy
toothier
toothiest
✗ tootifrooti =
  tutti-frutti
tootle
  tootles
  tootled
  tootling
✗ tootoo = tutu
tootsies
top
  tops
  topped
  topping
topaz
topcoat
tope
  topes
  toped
  toping
topiary
topic
topical
topicality
topknot
topless
topnotch
topographer
topographic
topography
topological
topologist
topology
topped
topper
topping
topple
  topples

toppled
toppling
tops
topside
topsoil
topspin
topsy-turvy
toque
tor
Torah
torc (= metal band
→ talk; torque)
torch
  torches
  torched
  torching
torchbearer
tore
toreador
torment
  torments
  tormented
  tormenting
tormenter
tormentor
torn
tornado
  tornadoes *or*
  tornados
torpedo
  torpedoes
  torpedoed
  torpedoing
torpid
torpidity
torpor
Torquay
torque (= force
→ talk; torc)
torrent

torrential
torrid
torsion
torso
  torsos *or*
  torsi
tort (= in law
→ taught; taut)
torte (= cake)
tortellini
tortoise
tortoiseshell
tortuous
torture
  tortures
  tortured
  torturing
Tory
  Tories
tosh
toss
  tosses
  tossed
  tossing
tosser
tot
  tots
  totted
  totting
total
  totals
  totalled
  totalling
totaliser
totalitarian
totalitarianism
totality
  totalities
totalizator
totalizer

tote
totes
toted
toting
totem
tots
totted
totter
totting
toucan
touch
touches
touched
touching
touchdown
touché
touchily
touchiness
touching
touchline
touchpaper
touchstone
touchy
  touchier
  touchiest
tough
toughen
  toughens
  toughened
  toughening
toughness
Toulouse-Lautrec
toupee
tour
  tours
  toured
  touring
tourer
tourism
tourist

touristic
touristy
tournament
tournedos
  tournedos
tourniquet
tousle
  tousles
  tousled
  tousling
tout
  touts
  touted
  touting
tow (= pull → toe)
  tows
  towed
  towing
toward
towards
towbar
towboat
Towcester
towel
  towels
  towelled
  towelling
  towelling
tower
  towers
  towered
  towering
towhead
towing
town
township
townspeople
towpath
towrope
toxaemia

toxaemic
toxic
toxicity
toxicological
toxicology
toxin
toxoplasmosis
toy
  toys
  toyed
  toying
trace
  traces
  traced
  tracing
✗ tracea = trachea
  tracer
  tracery
  traceries
trachea
  tracheae
tracheostomy
  tracheostomies
tracheotomy
  tracheotomies
tracing
track
  tracks
  tracked
  tracking
tracksuit
tract
tractable
tractate
traction
tractor
trad
trade
  trades
  traded

trading
trademark
trader
tradescantia
tradesman
  tradesmen
tradespeople
tradeswoman
  tradeswomen
trading
✗ tradiscantia =
  tradescantia
tradition
traditional
traditionalism
traditionalist
traditionalistic
traditionally
traduce
  traduces
  traduced
  traducing
traducement
traducer
traffic
tragacanth
tragedian
tragedy
  tragedies
tragic
tragically
tragicomedy
  tragicomedies
trail
  trails
  trailed
  trailing
trailblazer
trailer
train

trains
trained
training
trainee
trainer
trainers
traipse
traipses
traipsed
traipsing
trait (= character-
istic → tray)
traitor
trajectory
trajectories
tra-la
tra-la-la
tram
tramcar
tramline
trammel
trammels
trammelled
trammelling
tramp
tramps
tramped
tramping
trample
tramples
trampled
trampling
trampoline
trance
tranche
tranquil
tranquillise
tranquillises
tranquillised
tranquillising

tranquilliser
tranquillity
tranquillize
tranquillizes
tranquillized
tranquillizing
tranquillizer
transact
transacts
transacted
transacting
transaction
transactional
transactor
transalpine
transatlantic
transceiver
transcend
transcends
transcended
transcending
transcendence
transcendency
transcendent
transcendental
transcendentalism
transcendingly
transcontinental
transcribe
transcribes
transcribed
transcibing
transcriber
transcript
transcription
transducer
transept
transfer
transfers
transferred

transferring
transferable
transferase
transference
transferential
transferrable
transferrer
transfiguration
transfigure
transfigures
transfigured
transfiguring
transfigurement
transfix
transfixes
transfixed
transfixing
transfixion
transform
transforms
transformed
transforming
transformable
transformation
transformer
transfuse
transfuses
transfused
transfusing
transfuser
transfusion
transgress
transgresses
transgressed
transgressing
transgression
transgressor
transhipment
transhumance
transient

traumatized

transistor
transit
transition
transitional
transitive
transitorily
transitoriness
transitory
translatable
translate
  translates
  translated
  translating
translation
translator
transliterate
  transliterates
  transliterated
  transliterating
translucence
translucency
translucent
transmissibility
transmissible
transmission
transmit
  transmits
  transmitted
  transmitting
transmittable
transmittance
transmittancy
transmitter
transmittible
transmogrification
transmogrify
  transmogrifies
  transmogrified
  transmogrifying
transmutability

transmutable
transmutably
transmutation
transmutative
transmute
  transmutes
  transmuted
  transmuting
transmuter
transom
transparence
transparency
  transparencies
transparent
transpire
  transpires
  transpired
  transpiring
transplant
  transplants
  transplanted
  transplanting
transplantable
transponder
transport
  transports
  transported
  transporting
transportable
transportation
transporter
transpose
  transposes
  transposed
  transposing
transsexual
transshipment
transubstantiation
transversal
transversally

transverse
transvestism
transvestite
transvestitism
trap
  traps
  trapped
  trapping
trapeze
trapezium
  trapeziums *or*
  trapezia
trapezius
  trapeziuses
trapezohedral
trapezohedron
  trapezohedrons *or*
  trapezohedra
trapezoid
trapped
trapper
trapping
trappings
Trappist
traps
trash
trashy
  trashier
  trashiest
trattoria
trauma
traumatic
traumatically
traumatise
  traumatises
  traumatised
  traumatising
traumatize
  traumatizes
  traumatized

traumatizing
travail
travel
  travels
  travelled
  travelling
traveller
travelogue
traverse
  traverses
  traversed
  traversing
travesty
  travesties
trawl
  trawls
  trawled
  trawling
trawler
tray (= for carrying
  things → trait)
treacherous
treachery
  treacheries
treacle
tread
  treads
  trod
  trodden *or*
  trod
  treading
treadle
treadmill
treadwheel
treason
treasure
  treasures
  treasured
  treasuring
treasurer

treasury
  treasuries
treat
  treats
  treated
  treating
treatise
treatment
treaty
  treaties
treble
  trebles
  trebled
  trebling
tree
  trees
trefoil
trek
  treks
  trekked
  trekking
trellis
tremble
  trembles
  trembled
  trembling
trembler
tremendous
tremolo
  tremolos
tremor
tremulous
trench
trenchant
trencher
trenches
trend
  trendily
  trendiness
trendsetter

trendy
  trendier
  trendiest
Treorchy
trepan
  trepans
  trepanned
  trepanning
trepanner
trepidation
trespass
  trespasses
  trespassed
  trespassing
tress
trestle
trews
triad
trial
triangle
triangular
triangulate
  triangulates
  triangulated
  triangulating
triangulation
Triassic
triathlon
tribalism
tribe
tribulation
tribunal
tribune
tributary
  tributaries
tribute
trice
tricentenary
  tricentenaries
tricentennial

trivialising

triceps
triceratops
trichologist
trichology
trick
  tricks
  tricked
  tricking
trickery
  trickeries
trickier
trickiest
trickily
trickiness
trickle
  trickles
  trickled
  trickling
tricksiness
tricksy
  tricksier
  tricksiest
tricky
  trickier
  trickiest
tricolour
tricot
tricycle
trident
tried
triel = trial
triennial
triennium
  trienniums or
  triennia
trier
tries
triffid
trifle
  trifles

trifled
trifling
trigger
trigonometric
trigonometry
trihedral
trihedron
  trihedrons or
  trihedra
trike
trilateral
trilby
  trilbies
trilingual
trilithic
trilithon
trill
  trills
  trilled
  trilling
trillion
trilogy
  trilogies
trim
  trimmer
  trimmest
  trims
  trimmed
  trimming
trimaran
trimester
trimonthly
trims
trinitrotoluene
trinity
  trinities
trinket
trio
  trios
trip

trips
tripped
tripping
tripartite
tripe
triplane
triple
  triples
  tripled
  tripling
triplet
triplicate
tripod
tripos
tripped
tripper
tripping
trips
triptane
triptych
tripwire
trireme
trisection
trisector
trite
triumph
  triumphs
  triumphed
  triumphing
triumphal
triumphalism
triumphant
triumvirate
trivet
trivia
trivial
trivialise
  trivialises
  trivialised
  trivialising

triviality
  trivialities
trivialize
  trivializes
  trivialized
  trivializing
triweekly
trochee
trod
trodden
✗ troff = trough
troglodyte
troika
Trojan
troll
trolley
trolleybus
trollop
trombone
trombonist
troop (= of soldiers
  etc → troupe)
  troops
  trooped
  trooping
trooper (= soldier
  → trouper)
troopship
✗ trooso = trousseau
trope
trophy
  trophies
tropic
tropical
tropism
tropistic
troposphere
trot
  trots
  trotted

trotting
troth
trots
trotter
troubadour
trouble
  troubles
  troubled
  troubling
troublemaker
troubleshooter
troublesome
trough
trounce
  trounces
  trounced
  trouncing
troupe (= of actors
  → troop)
trouper (= troupe
  member → trooper)
trouser
trousers
trousseau
trousseaux or
  trousseaus
trout
trout
trowel
truant
✗ truble = trouble
✗ trublesome =
  troublesome
truce
truck
  trucks
  trucked
  trucking
trucker
truckle

truckload
truculent
trudge
  trudges
  trudged
  trudging
true
truelove
truer
truest
truffle
trug
truism
truistic
truly
trump
  trumps
  trumped
  trumping
trumpery
  trumperies
trumpet
  trumpets
  trumpeted
  trumpeting
trumpeter
trumps
truncate
  truncates
  truncated
  truncating
truncheon
trundle
  trundles
  trundled
  trundling
trunk
  trunks
✗ trupe = troop or
  troupe

truper = trooper *or*
trouper
Truro
truso = trousseau
truss
  trusses
  trussed
  trussing
trussing
trust
  trusts
  trusted
  trusting
trustee
trustworthily
trustworthiness
trustworthy
trusty
  trustier
  trustiest
truth
truthful
try
  tries
  tried
  trying
trying
tryout
trypsin
tryptophan
tryst
tsar
tsarina
tsetse
T-shirt
T-square
tub
tuba
  tubas *or*
  tubae

tubal
tubbiness
tubby
  tubbier
  tubbiest
tube
tuber
tubercle
tubercular
tuberculin
tuberculosis
tuberculous
tuberose
tuberous
tubing
tubs
tubular
✗ tuch = touch
✗ tuching = touching
✗ tuchy = touchy
tuck
  tucks
  tucked
  tucking
tucker
Tuesday
✗ tuff = tough
✗ tuffen = toughen
tuffet
tuft
tufted
tug
  tugs
  tugged
  tugging
tugboat
tuition
tulip
tulle (= fabric →
  tool)

tum
tumble
  tumbles
  tumbled
  tumbling
tumbledown
tumbler
tumbleweed
tumbrel
tumbril
tumefacient
tumefaction
tumescence
tumescent
tummy
  tummies
tumour
tumult
tumultuous
tumulus
tun (= beer cask
  → ton; tonne)
tuna
  tuna *or*
  tunas
tundra
tune
  tunes
  tuned
  tuning
tuneful
tuneless
tuner
✗ tung = tongue
tungsten
tunic
Tunisia
tunnage
tunnel
  tunnels

tunnelled
tunnelling
tunny
tunnies *or*
tunny
tuns
tup
  tups
  tupped
  tupping
tuppence
tuppenny
turban
turbid
turbidity
turbine
turbocharger
turbofan
turbogenerator
turbojet
turboprop
turbosupercharger
turbot
turbulence
turbulent
turd
tureen
turf
  turfs *or*
  turves
  turfs
  turfed
  turfing
turgid
turkey
Turkey
Turkish
Turkmenistan
turmeric
turmoil

turn (= turn round
  → tern)
turns
turned
turning
turnabout
turnaround
turncoat
turner
turnip
turnkey
turnout
turnover
turnpike
turnround
turnstile
turntable
turpentine
turpitude
turps
turquoise
turret
turreted
turtle
turtledove
turtleneck
turves
tush
✗ tushay = touché
tushery
tusk
tusked
tusker
tussle
  tussles
  tussled
  tussling
tussock
tut
  tuts

tutted
tutting
tutee
tutelage
tutor
tutorial
tuts
tutted
tutti-frutti
tutting
tutu
✗ tuwards = towards
tuxedo
  tuxedos
TV
twaddle
twain
twang
  twangs
  twanged
  twanging
twat
tweak
  tweaks
  tweaked
  tweaking
twee
tweed
tweedy
  tweedier
  tweediest
tweet
  tweets
  tweeted
  tweeting
tweeter
tweezers
twelfth
✗ twelth = twelfth
twelve

twelvemonth
twentieth
twenty
  twenties
twerp
twice
Twickenham
twiddle
  twiddled
  twiddling
twig
  twigs
  twigged
  twigging
twilight
twilit
twill
win
  twins
  twinned
  twinning
twine
twinge
twinkle
  twinkles
  twinkled
  twinkling
twinset
twirl
  twirls
  twirled
  twirling
twirp
twist
  twists
  twisted
  twisting
twister
twit

twitch
  twitches
  twitched
  twitching
twitter
  twitters
  twittered
  twitting
twixt
two (= number
  → to; too)
✗ twoddle = twaddle
twofold
twopence
twopenny
twosome
Twyford
tycoon
tying
tyke
tymbal
tympan
tympani
tympanic
tympanist
tympanum
  tympanums or
  tympana
Tyne and Wear
type
  types
  typed
  typing
typecast
typeface
typescript
typesetter
typewriter
typhoid
typhoon

typhus
typical
typify
  typifies
  typified
  typifying
typist
typographer
typography
typology
tyrannical
tyrannise
  tyrannises
  tyrannised
  tyrannising
tyrannize
  tyrannizes
  tyrannized
  tyrannizing
tyrannosaur
tyranny
  tyrannies
tyrant
tyre (= on a wheel
  → tire)
Tyrone
tzar
tzarina
tzatziki

U

ubiquitous
U-boat
✗ucaliptus = eucalyptus
✗ucarist = Eucharist
udder
uf try euph
UFO
ufologist
ufology
Uganda
✗ugenic = eugenic
✗ugenics = eugenics
ugh
ugli
  uglis or
  uglies
uglily
ugliness
ugly
  uglier
  ugliest
uh-huh
uh-uh
ukelele
Ukraine
Ukrainian
ukulele
ulcer
ulceration
ulcerous
ulna

ulnae or
  ulnas
✗ulogy = eulogy
ulterior
ultimate
ultimatum
  ultimatums or
  ultimata
ultra
ultramarine
ultramodern
ultrared
ultrasonic
ultrasound
ultraviolet
ululate
ululates
ululated
ululating
um
umber
umbilical
umbilicus
  umbilici
umbilicus
umbrage
umbrella
umlaut
✗umlowt = umlaut
umpire
  umpires
  umpired
  umpiring
umpteen
unabated
unable
unaccompanied
unaccountable
unaccustomed
✗unaceptable =

unacceptable
unadvised
unadvisedly
unaffected
unalienable
unalloyed
unanimity
unanimous
unanswerable
unanswerably
unappetising
unapproachable
unapt
unarguable
unarguably
unarmed
unashamed
unashamedly
unasked
unassailable
unassuming
unattached
unattended
unauthorised
unavoidable
unaware
unawares
unbalanced
✗unbarable =
  unbearable
unbearable
unbearably
unbeatable
unbeaten
unbecoming
unbeknown
unbelievable
unbeliever
unbelieving
unbending

unbiased
unbiassed
unbidden
unborn
unbowed
unbridled
unbroken
unburden
  unburdens
  unburdened
  unburdening
unbutton
  unbuttons
  unbuttoned
  unbuttoning
uncalled-for
uncannily
uncanniness
uncanny
uncap
  uncaps
  uncapped
  uncapping
✗uncaracteristic =
  uncharacteristic
uncared-for
unceasing
unceremonious
uncertain
uncertainty
  uncertainities
uncharted
unchristian
uncircumcised
uncivilised
uncivilized
unclassified
uncle
unclean
unclear

uncoil
  uncoils
  uncoiled
  uncoiling
uncomfortable
uncomfortably
uncommercial
uncommitted
uncommon
uncommunicative
uncompromising
unconcerned
unconditional
unconditioned
unconnected
unconscionable
unconscionably
unconscious
✗unconshenable =
  unconscionable
✗unconshenably =
  unconscionably
✗unconshus =
  unconscious
unconstitutional
uncontrollable
unconventional
uncoordinated
uncork
  uncorks
  uncorked
  uncorking
uncouple
  uncouples
  uncoupled
  uncoupling
uncouth
uncover
  uncovers
  uncovered

uncovering
unction
unctuous
uncurl
  uncurls
  uncurled
  uncurling
undaunted
undecided
undemonstrative
undeniable
under
underachieve
  underachieves
  underachieved
  underachieving
underage
underarm
underbelly
undercarriage
undercharge
  undercharges
  undercharged
  undercharging
underclass
underclothes
underclothing
undercover
undercurrent
underdeveloped
underdog
underdone
underestimate
  underestimates
  underestimated
  underestimating
underfoot
undergarment
undergo
  undergoes

underwent
undergone
undergoing
undergraduate
underground
undergrowth
underhand
underline
　underlines
　underlined
　underlining
underling
underlying
undermine
　undermines
　undermined
　undermining
underneath
undernourish
　undernourishes
　undernourishing
underpants
underpass
underpin
　underpins
　underpinned
　underpinning
underprivileged
underrate
　underrates
　underrated
　underrating
✗ underrite =
　underwrite
undersecretary
　undersecretaries
undershirt
underside
undersigned
undersized

understand
understands
understood
understanding
understudy
　understudies
　understudied
　understudying
undertake
　undertakes
　undertook
　undertaken
　undertaking
undertaker
undertaking
undertone
undertow
underwater
underwear
underweight
underworld
underwrite
　underwrites
　underwrote
　underwritten
　underwriting
underwriter
undescended
undesirable
undetermined
undid
undies
undistinguished
undo
　undoes
　undid
　undone
　undoing
undoubted
undoubtedly

undress
　undresses
　undressed
　undressing
undue
undulant
undulate
　undulates
　undulated
　undulating
undulation
undulatory
unduly
undying
unearned
unearth
　unearths
　unearthed
　unearthing
　unearthliness
　unearthly
unease
uneasily
uneasiness
uneasy
uneconomic
uneconomical
✗ uneec = unique
unemployable
unemployed
unemployment
unequal
unequalled
unequally
unequivocal
unerring
✗ unerth = unearth
uneven
uneventful
unexceptionable

unexceptional
unexpected
unexperienced
unfailing
unfair
unfairly
unfaithful
unfamiliar
unfamiliarity
unfasten
  unfastens
  unfastened
  unfastening
unfathomable
unfathomably
unfavourable
unfavourably
unfazed
unfeeling
unfertilised
unfit
unflappable
unflinching
unfold
  unfolds
  unfolded
  unfolding
unforgettable
unfortunate
unfounded
unfriendliness
unfriendly
unfurl
  unfurls
  unfurled
  unfurling
ungainliness
ungainly
✗ ungarded =
  unguarded

✗ ungent = unguent
ungrateful
ungrudging
unguent
✗ unguvernable =
  ungovernable
unhappily
unhappiness
unhappy
unhealthily
unhealthiness
unhealthy
unheard-of
unhesitating
unhesitatingly
✗ unhigenic =
  unhygienic
✗ unholesome =
  unwholesome
unhoped-for
unhurried
unicorn
unicycle
unidirectional
✗ unien = onion
unification
uniform
uniformity
unify
  unifies
  unified
  unifying
unilateral
unimproved
uninspired
unintelligent
uninterested
union
unique
unisex

unison
unit
Unitarian
unitary
unite
  unites
  united
  uniting
United Kingdom
United States of
  America
unity
universal
universe
university
  universities
unjust
unkempt
unkind
unknowingly
unknown
unlace
  unlaces
  unlaced
  unlacing
unlawful
unleaded
unleash
  unleashes
  unleashed
  unleashing
unleavened
unless
unlicensed
unlike
unlikeable
unlikeliness
unlikely
unlimited
unlisted

unload
  unloads
  unloaded
  unloading
unlock
  unlocks
  unlocked
  unlocking
unlooked-for
unluckily
unluckiness
unlucky
unmade
unmanned
unmarked
unmarried
unmentionable
unmentionably
unmerciful
unmistakable
unmistakeable
unmitigated
unnamed
unnatural
unnecessarily
unnecessariness
unnecessary
unoccupied
unofficial
✗ unolterable =
  unalterable
✗ unoltered =
  unaltered
unorganised
unorganized
unorthodox
unpack
  unpacks
  unpacked
  unpacking

unpaid
unparalleled
unpasteurised
unpick
  unpicks
  unpicked
  unpicking
unpleasant
unplug
  unplugs
  unplugged
unpopular
unprecedented
unpredictable
unpremeditated
unprepared
unprincipled
unprintable
unproductive
unprofessional
unprofitable
unprofitably
unputdownable
unqualified
unquestionable
unquestionably
unquote
✗ unrap = unwrap
unravel
  unravels
  unravelled
  unravelling
unread
unreadable
unreal
unreasonable
unreasonably
unrecognisable
unrefined
unrelenting

unremitting
unrequited
unreserved
unreservedly
unrest
unrestrained
unripe
✗ unritten =
  unwritten
unrivalled
unroll
  unrolls
  unrolled
  unrolling
unruffled
unruliness
unruly
unsaid
unsaturated
unsavoury
unscathed
unscientific
unscratched
unscrupulous
unseasonable
unseasonably
unseemliness
unseemly
unseen
unselfish
unshakable
unshakably
unshakeable
unshakeably
✗ unshore = unsure
unsightliness
unsightly
unskilful
unskilled
unsociable

unsociably
unsophisticated
unsound
unsparing
unsparingly
unspeakable
unspeakably
unspecialised
unspoiled
unspoken
unstable
unsteadily
unsteadiness
unsteady
unstoppable
unstoppably
unstructured
unstuck
unstudied
unsubstantial
unsung
unsupportable
unsure
unsuspected
unsuspecting
unswerving
untangle
  untangles
  untangled
  untangling
untenable
unthinkable
unthinkably
unthinking
unthought-of
untidily
untidiness
untidy
untie
  unties

untied
untying
until
untimeliness
untimely
untitled
unto
untold
untouchable
untouched
untoward
untried
untrue
untruthful
untuck
  untucks
  untucked
  untucking
✗ unty = untie
✗ unuc = eunuch
unused
unusual
unvarnished
unveil
  unveils
  unveiled
  unveiling
unwaged
unwanted (= not
  wanted → un-
  wonted)
unwarily
unwariness
unwarranted
unwarily
unwariness
unwary
unwelcome
unwell
unwieldy

unwilling
unwind
  unwinds
  unwinded
  unwound
  unwinding
unwise
unwitting
unwonted (= un-
  usual → unwanted)
unworldliness
unworldly
unwrap
  unwraps
  unwrapped
  unwrapping
unwritten
unzip
  unzips
  unzipped
  unzipping
up
  ups
  upped
  upping
upbeat
upbraid
  upbraids
  upbraided
  upbraiding
upbringing
upcoming
update
  updates
  updated
  updating
updraught
upend
  upends
  upended

upending
upfront
upgrade
upgrades
upgraded
upgrading
uph try euph
upheaval
upheld
uphill
uphold
upholds
upheld
upholding
upholster
upholsters
upholstered
upholstering
upholsterer
upholstery
upkeep
uplifting
upmost
upon
upped
upper
uppercut
uppermost
upping
uppish
uppity
upright
uprising
upriver
uproar
uproarious
uproot
uproots
uprooted
uprooting

ups
upsadaisy
upscale
upset
upsets
upset
upsetting
upshot
upside-down
upsilon
upstage
upstages
upstaged
upstaging
upstairs
upstanding
upstart
upstream
upstretched
upsurge
upsy-daisy
uptake
uptight
upturn
upward
upwards
upwind
ur try eur
uranium
Uranus
urban
urbane
urchin
Urdu
urea
ureter
urethra
urethras or
urethrae

urethral
urge
urges
urged
urging
urgency
urgent
uric
urinal
urinary
urinate
urinates
urinated
urinating
urine
urn (= container
→ earn)
urogenital
urology
ursine
urticaria
Uruguay
us
USA
usable
usage
use
uses
used
using
useable
useful
useless
user
✗userer = usurer
usher
ushers
ushered
ushering
usherette

usual
usurer
usurious
usurp
  usurps
  usurped
  usurping
usurper
usury
  usuries
utensil
uterine
uterus
  uteri
✗ uthanasia =
  euthanasia
utilise
  utilises
  utilised
  utilising
utilitarian
utilitarianism
utility
  utilities
utilize
  utilizes
  utilized
  utilizing
utmost
Utopian
utter
  utters
  uttered
  uttering
utterance
utterly
uttermost
U-turn
uvula (noun)
  uvulas *or*

uvulae
uvular (adj.)
uxorious
Uzbekistan

V

vac
vacancy
  vacancies
vacant
vacate
  vacates
  vacated
  vacating
vacation
vaccinate
  vaccinates
  vaccinated
  vaccinating
vaccination
vaccine
vacillate
  vacillates
  vacillated
  vacillating
✗ vacsinate =
  vaccinate
✗ vacsine = vaccine
✗ vacume = vacuum
vacuous
vacuum
vagabond
vagary
  vagaries
✗ vage = vague
✗ vagely = vaguely
vagina
vaginal

vagrancy
vagrant
vain (= proud →
  vane)
vainglory
valance
✗ valay = valet
vale (= valley →
  veil)
valediction
valedictory
valency
  valencies
valentine
valet
valiant
valid
validate
validity
valley
valour
valuable
valuation
value
  values
  valued
  valuing
valuer
valve
vamoose
vamp
vampire
van
Vancouver
vandal
vandalise
  vandalises
  vandalised
  vandalising
vandalism

vandalize
  vandalizes
  vandalized
  vandalizing
vane (= weather
vane → vain; vein)
Van Gogh, Vincent
vanguard
vanilla
vanish
  vanishes
  vanished
  vanishing
vanity
  vanities
vanquish
  vanquishes
  vanquished
  vanquishing
vantage
✗ vaperize = vaporize
vapid
vapidity
vaporise
  vaporises
  vaporised
  vaporising
vaporize
  vaporizes
  vaporized
  vaporizing
vapour
variable
variance
variant
variation
varicoloured
varicose
varied
variegated

varies
varietal
variety
  varieties
various
varlet
varmint
varnish
  varnishes
  varnished
  varnishing
✗ vars = vase
vary
  varies
  varied
  varying
vascular
vase
vasectomy
  vasectomies
vassal
vast
vat
VAT
vaudeville
vault (= jump over
  → volt)
  vaults
  vaulted
  vaulting
vaunt
  vaunts
  vaunted
  vaunting
VCR
V-Day
✗ veacle = vehicle
veal
✗ veamence =
  vehemence

veament =
 vehement
vector
veer
 veers
 veered
 veering
veesavee = vis à vis ✗
veg
vegan
vegetable
vegetarian
vegetarianism
vegetate
 vegetates
 vegetated
 vegetating
vegetation
vegetative
veggie
vehement
vehicle
vehicular
veil (= draw a veil
 over → vale)
veiled
vein (= blood car-
 rier → vein; vane)
veld
veldt
vellum
velocipede
velocity
 velocities
velodrome
velour
velours
velvet
velveteen
venal

vend
vends
vended
vending
vendetta
vendor
veneer
venem = venom ✗
venerable
veneration
venereal
Venzuela
vengeance
vengeful
venial
venison
venom
venous
vent
vents
vented
venting
ventilate
ventilates
ventilated
ventilating
ventilation
ventilator
ventral
ventricle
ventriloquism
ventriloquist
venture
ventures
ventured
venturing
venturesome
venue
veracious
veracity

veranda
verandah
verb
verbal
verbalise
verbalises
verbalised
verbalising
verbalize
verbalizes
verbalized
verbalizing
verbatim
verbena
verbiage
verbose
verbosity
verdict
verdigris
verge
verges
verged
verging
verger
verification
verify
verifies
verified
verifying
verisimilitude
veritable
vermicelli
✗ vermichelli =
 vermicelli
vermilion
vermillion
vermin
verminous
vermouth
vernacular

vernal	veterinarian	viscountess
verruca	ve†erinary	victim
verrucae *or*	veto	victimised
verrucas	vetoes	victimized
versatile	vetoed	victor
versatility	vetoing	Victoria
verse	vex	Victorian
versed	vexes	victorious
version	vexed	victory
verso	vexing	victories
versus	vexation	victual
vertebra	vexatious	victualler
vertebrae	via	victuals
vertebrate	viable	video
vertex	viaduct	videos
vertices *or*	vial try viol	videoed
vertexes	vial (= small bottle	videoing
vertical	→ vile; viol)	videodisk
vertigo	viand	videotext
verve	vibes	vie
very	vibrant	vies
vesicle	vibrate	vied
vespers	vibrates	vying
Vespucci, Amerigo	vibrated	Vietnam
vessel	vibrating	view
vest	vibration	views
vestal	vibrato	viewed
vested	vibrator	viewing
vestibule	vicar	viewer
vestige	vicarage	✗ vigerus = vigorous
vestigial	vicarious	vigil
vestment	vice	vigilance
vestry	✗ vicer = vicar	vigilant
vestries	✗ vicerage = vicarage	vigilante
Vesuvius	vichyssoise	vignette
vet	vicinity	vigorous
vets	vicinities	vigour
vetted	vicious	Viking
vetting	✗ vicount = viscount	vile (= horrible
veteran	✗ vicountess =	→ vial; viol)

villa
village
villager
villain (= baddie)
villainous
villainy
villein (= serf)
villen = villain
villi
villige = village
villous (adj.)
villus (noun)
villi
vim
vinaigrette
vindicate
vindicates
vindicated
vindicating
vindication
vindictive
vindictively
vine
vinegar
vineyard
viniculture
viniette = vignette
vinigrette =
  vinaigrette
vino
vinos
vintage
vintner
vinyard = vineyard
vinyl
viol (= instrument
  → vial; vile)
viola
violate
violates

violated
violating
violence
violent
violet
violin
violinist
violoncello
violoncellos
VIP
viper
virago
viragoes *or*
  viragos
viral
✗ virelence = virulence
✗ virelent = virulent
Virgil
virgin
virginal
virginity
virile
virility
virtual
virtually
virtue
virtuoso
virtuous
virulence
virulent
virus
visa
visage
vis-à-vis
viscose
viscosity
viscount
viscountess
viscous
✗ visera = viscera

✗ viserel = visceral
✗ vishus = vicious
visibility
visible
vision
visionary
  visionaries
visit
  visits
  visited
  visiting
visitor
visor
vista
visual
visualise
  visualises
  visualised
  visualising
visualize
  visualizes
  visualized
  visualizing
vital
vitality
  vitalities
vitamin
viticulture
vitreous
vitriol
vitriolic
✗ vitrius = vitreous
✗ vittle = victual
✗ vittles = victuals
vituperation
vituperative
viva
vivacious
vivacity
  vivacities

vivarium
  vivariums *or*
  vivaria
vivid
viviparous
vivisection
vixen
viz
vizier
vizor
vocabulary
  vocabularies
vocal
vocalic
vocalise
  vocalises
  vocalised
  vocalising
vocalist
vocalize
  vocalizes
  vocalized
  vocalizing
vocation
vocational
vocative
vociferous
vodka
✗ voge = vogue
vogue
voice
  voices
  voiced
  voicing
void
voile
volatile
vol-au-vent
volcanic
volcano

volcanoes *or*
  volcanos
vole
✗ volenteer =
  volunteer
✗ volenterily =
  voluntarily
volition
volley
  volleys
  volleyed
  volleying
volleyball
✗ volovon =
  vol au vent
volt (= unit of
  potential → vault)
voltage
voltameter
voltammeter
volte-face
  volte-face
✗ voltfass = volte face
voltmeter
voluble
volume
volumeter
volumetric
volumetry
voluminous
voluntarily
voluntary
volunteer
  volunteers
  volunteered
  volunteering
voluptuous
vomit
  vomits
  vomited

vomiting
Vonnegut, Kurt
voodoo
  voodoos
voracious
voracity
vortex
  vortexes *or*
  vortices
vote
  votes
  voted
  voting
voter
votive
vouch
  vouches
  vouched
  vouching
voucher
vow
  vows
  vowed
  vowing
vowel
voyage
voyeur
voyeurism
✗ vue = view
vulgar
vulgarism
vulgarity
  vulgarities
vulnerability
vulnerable
vulpine
vulture
vulva
vying

W

wa try wha
wackily
wackiness
wacky
  wackier
  wackiest
wad
wadding
waddle
  waddles
  waddled
  waddling
wade (= in water
  → weighed)
  wades
  waded
  wading
wader
  waders
wafer
waffle
  waffles
  waffled
  waffling
waft
  wafts
  wafted
  wafting
wag
  wags
  wagged
  wagging

wage
waggle
  waggles
  waggled
  waggling
waggon
wagon
wagon-lit
  wagons-lits
wags
wagtail
waif
wail (= cry
  → whale)
  wails
  wailed
  wailing
wainscot
waist (= part of the
  body → waste)
waistband
waistcoat
waistline
wait (= wait for
  someone
  → weight)
  waits
  waited
  waiting
waiter
waitress
waive (= waive a
  fee etc → wave)
  waives
  waived
  waiving
waiver (= relin-
  quishment
  → waver)
wake

wakes
woke
woken
waking
wakeful
waken
  wakens
  wakened
  wakening
walk
  walks
  walked
  walking
walkabout
walkie-talkie
walkout
walkover
walkway
walky-talky
  walky-talkies
wall
wallaby
  wallabies
Wallasey
walled
wallet
wallflower
wallop
  wallops
  walloped
  walloping
wallow
  wallows
  wallowed
  wallowing
wallpaper
wally
  wallies
walnut
walrus

Walsall
waltz
  waltzes
  waltzed
  waltzing
wampum
wan
wand
wander
  wanders
  wandered
  wandering
wanderlust
wane
  wanes
  waned
  waning
wangle
  wangles
  wangled
  wangling
wank
  wanks
  wanked
  wanking
wanker
want
  wants
  wanted
  wanting
wanton
war
  wars
  warred (= fought
    → ward)
  warring
warble
  warbles
  warbled
  warbling

warbler
ward (= ward of
  court → warred)
warden
warder
wardrobe
✗ ware = wear
warehouse
wares (= goods →
  wears)
warfare
Warhol, Andy
warhorse
warier
wariest
warily
wariness
warlike
warlock
warlord
warm
warmonger
warmth
warn
  warns
  warned
  warning
warpath
warped
warplane
warrant
  warrants
  warranted
  warranting
warrantor
warranty
  warranties
warren
warring
warrior

wart
wary
  warier
  wariest
Warwick
Warwickshire
was
wash
  washes
  washed
  washing
washable
washbasin
washer
washout
washy
wasn't
wasp
waspish
wassail
wastage
waste (= rubbish
  → waist)
  wastes
  wasted
  wasting
wastebasket
wasteful
wasteland
wastepaper
waster
watch
  watches
  watched
  watching
watchable
watchdog
watchful
watchstrap
✗ wate = weight

wate = weight *or*
  wait
water
  waters
  watered
  watering
waterborne
watercolour
watercress
waterfall
waterfowl
wateriness
waterlogged
watermelon
waterproof
watertight
waterworks
watery
watt (= unit of
  power → what)
wattage
wattle
Waugh, Evelyn
wave (= wave your
  hand → waive)
  waves
  waved
  waving
waveband
wavelength
waver (= hesitate
  → waiver)
  wavers
  wavered
  wavering
wavily
waviness
wavy
  wavier
  waviest

✗ wawk = walk
wawl try wal
✗ wawm = warm
✗ wawt = wart
wax
  waxes
  waxed
  waxing
  waxiness
  waxwing
  waxwork
  waxy
  waxier
  waxiest
way (= road
  → weigh; whey)
  waylay
  waylays
  waylaid
  waylaying
  wayside
  wayward
WC
we try whe
we (= us → wee)
weak (= feeble
  → week)
weaken
  weakens
  weakened
  weakening
weakling
weak-willed
weal (= mark on the
  skin → we'll;
  wheel)
weald
wealth
  wealthily
  wealthiness

wealthy
  wealthier
  wealthiest
wean
  weans
  weaned
  weaning
weapon
weaponry
wear
  wears (= wears
    clothes
    → wares)
  wore
  worn
  wearing
wearable
wearily
weariness
wearisome
weary
  wearies
  wearied
  wearying
  wearier
  weariest
weasel
weather (= climate
  → whether
  weathers
  weathered
  weathering
weathercock
weave (cloth
  → we've)
  weaves
  wove
  woven
  weaving
weaver

web
webbed
webbing
wed
  weds
  wed *or*
  wedded
  wedding
we'd (= we would
  → weed)
wedge
  wedges
  wedged
  wedging
wedlock
Wednesday
wee (= tiny → we)
  wees (= urinates
    → wheeze)
  weed (= urinated
    → we'd; weed)
  weeing
weed (= plant
  → we'd; weed)
  weeds
  weeded
  weeding
weedily
weediness
weedkiller
weedy
  weedier
  weediest
week (= seven days
  → weak)
weekday
weekend
weekly
weeny
weeny-bopper

weep
  weeps
  wept
  weeping
weepiness
weepy
  weepier
  weepiest
weevil
weigh (= measure
  weight of → way;
  whey)
  weighs
  weighed
  weighing
weighbridge
weight (= heavy
  object → wait)
weightily
weightiness
weighting
weightlifting
weighty
  weightier
  weightiest
weir (= on a river
  → we're)
weird
weirdo
welcome
  welcomes
  welcomed
  welcoming
weld
  welds
  welded
  welding
welfare
well
we'll (= we will

→ weal; wheel)
wellbeing
wellies
wellingtons
wellspring
welly
  wellies
Welsh
welt
welterweight
wench
wend
  wends
  wended
  wending
went
wept
were (= they were
  out → whirr)
we're (= we are
  → weir)
weren't
werewolf
  werewolves
✗ wering = wearing
west
westerly
western
Westmorland
westward
westwards
wet
  wets
  wet *or*
  wetted
  wetting
  wetter
  wettest
we've (= we have
  → weave)

Weybridge
Weymouth
whack
  whacks
  whacked
  whacking
whale (= large
  mammal → wail)
whalebone
whaler
whaling
wham
wharf
  wharves or
  wharfs
what (= question
  → watt)
whatever
whatnot
whatsit
whatsoever
wheat
wheaten
wheatmeal
wheedle
  wheedles
  wheedled
  wheedling
wheel (= on a car
  → weal; we'll)
  wheels
  wheeled
  wheeling
wheelbarrow
wheelchair
wheeler-dealer
wheelie
wheeze (= pant →
  wees)
  wheezes

wheezed
wheezing
whelk
whelp
when
whenever
where
whereabouts
whereas
whereat
whereby
wherein
whereof
whereon
whereupon
wherever
wherewithal
whet
  whets
  whetted
  whetting
whew
whey (= curds and
  whey → way;
  weigh)
which (= which one
  → witch)
whichever
whicker
whiff
whiffy
while (= during
  → wile)
whilst
whim
whimper
  whimpers
  whimpered

whimpering
whimsical
whine (= moan →
  wine)
  whines
  whined (=
  moaned →
  wind)
  whining
whinge
  whinges
  whinged
  whinging
whinny
  whinnies
  whinnied
  whinnying
whip
  whips
  whipped
  whipping
whiplash
whippet
whir (= noise
  → were)
  whirs
  whirred
  whirring
whirl (= spin
  → whorl)
  whirls
  whirled
  whirling
whirligig
whirlpool
whirlwind
whirr (= noise
  → were)
  whirrs
  whirred (= made

a noise → word)
whirring
whisk
  whisks
  whisked
  whisking
whisker
whiskey (= Irish)
whisky (= Scotch)
whisper
  whisper
  whispered
  whispering
whist
whistle
  whistles
  whistled
  whistling
whistler
whit (= jot → wit)
white
whitebait
whiten
  whitens
  whitened
  whitening
whiteout
whitewash
whither (= where
  → wither)
whiting
Whitsun
whitter
whittle
  whittles
  whittled
  whittling
whiz
  whizzes

whizzed
whizzing
whizz
  whizzes
  whizzed
  whizzing
who
whoa
whoever
whole (= complete
  → hole)
wholefood
wholehearted
wholemeal
wholesale
wholesome
who'll
wholly (= comple-
  tely → holy)
whom
whomever
whomsoever
whoop (= shout
  → hoop)
whoops
whooped
whooping
whoopee
whoosh
whopping
whore (= prostitute
  → hoar)
whorl (= pattern
  → whirl)
whorled
who's (= who is)
whose (= of who)
why
wi try whi

wick
wicked
wicker
wickerwork
wicket
wicketkeeper
widdershins
wide
widen
  widens
  widened
  widening
widespread
widget
Widnes
widow
widower
width
widthwise
✗ wie = why
wield
  wields
  wielded
  wielding
  wieldy
✗ wier = weir
✗ wierd = weird
✗ wierdo = weirdo
wife
  wives
wig
wiggle
  wiggles
  wiggled
  wiggling
Wight, Isle of
wigwam
wild
wildcat
Wilde, Oscar

wildebeest
wilderness
wildfire
wildfowl
wildibeast =
  wildebeest
wildlife
vile (= trickery
  → while)
wilier
wiliest
wiliness
will
  wills
  willed
  willing
will-o'-the-wisp
willow
willowy
willpower
willy-nilly
wilt
  wilts
  wilted
  wilting
wily
  wilier
  wiliest
wimmen = women
wimp
wimple
win
  wins
  won (= won the
    game → one)
  winning
wince
  winces
  winced

wincing
winceyette
winch
winches
winched
winching
✗ winciyette =
  winceyette
wind (= wind a
  clock → whined)
winds
winded
wound
winding
windcheater
windfall
windier
windiest
windily
windiness
windlass
windmill
window
windowpane
windowsill
windpipe
windscreen
windshield
windsock
Windsor
windsurfing
windswept
windy
  windier
  windiest
wine (= drink
  → whine)
wineglass
wineglassful
winery

wineries
wing
winger
wingspan
wink
winks
winked
winking
winkle
winner
winning
Winnipeg
winnow
winnows
winnowed
winnowing
wins
winsome
winter
wintertime
wintrier
wintriest
wintry
wipe
  wipes
  wiped
  wiping
wipeout
wiper
wire
  wires
  wired
  wiring
wireless
wiring
✗ wirlpool = whirlpool
✗ wirlwind =
  whirlwind
wiry
wirier

wiriest
Wisconsin
wisdom
wise
wisecrack
wish
  wishes
  wished
  wishing
wishbone
wishful
wishy-washy
wisp
wispily
wispiness
wispy
  wispier
  wispiest
wisteria
wistful
wit (= repartee → whit)
witch (= magic → which)
witchcraft
with
withdraw
  withdraws
  withdrew
  withdrawn
  withdrawing
withdrawal
wither (= droop → whither)
withhold
  withholds
  withheld
  withholding
within
without

withstand
withstands
withstood
withstanding
witless
witness
  witnesses
  witnessed
  witnessing
witticism
wittily
wittiness
witty
  wittier
  wittiest
wives
wizard
wizardry
wizened
wo try wa
✗ woa = whoa
woad
wobble
  wobbles
  wobbled
  wobbling
wobbly
wod try wad
Wodehouse, P.G.
wodge
woe
woebegone
woeful
✗ woffle = waffle
✗ woft = waft
wog
woggle
wok (= Chinese)
woke
woken

wold
wolf
  wolves
wolfhound
✗ wollet = wallet
✗ wollop = wallop
✗ wollow = wallow
✗ wolly = wally
✗ woltz = waltz
woman
  women
womanish
womankind
womanly
womb
wombat
women
womenfolk
won (= won the game → one)
wonder
  wonders
  wondered
  wondering
wonderful
wonderment
wondrous
wonky
  wonkier
  wonkiest
wont (= as is my wont)
won't (= will not)
woo
  woos
  wooed
  wooing
wood (= forest → would)
woodcarving

wounded

woodcutter
wooded
wooden
woodier
woodiest
woodlark
woodlouse
  woodlice
woodpecker
woodshed
woodwind
woodwork
woodworm
woody
  woodier
  woodiest
wooed
woof
  woofs
  woofed
  woofing
woofer
wooing
wool
Woolf, Virginia
woollen
woolliness
woolly
  woollier
  woolliest
woolsack
✗ woom = womb
✗ woond = wound
✗ woop = whoop
✗ woopee = whoopee
woos
✗ woosh = whoosh
woozily
wooziness
woozy

woozier
wooziest
wop
✗ wopper = whopper
Worcester
wor try wa
word (= group of
  letters → whirred)
wordily
wordiness
wording
wordless
wordy
  wordier
  wordiest
wore
✗ worf = wharf
work
  works
  worked
  working
workable
workaholic
workbench
worker
workforce
workload
workmanship
workmate
workplace
workshop
workshy
worktop
world
worldly
worldwide
worm
  worms
  wormed
  worming

wormcast
wormery
  wormeries
wormwood
wormy
  wormier
  wormiest
worn
worrisome
worry
  worries
  worried
  worrying
worse
worsen
  worsens
  worsened
  worsening
worship
  worships
  worshipped
  worshipping
worshipful
worst
worsted
worth
worthily
worthiness
worthless
worthwhile
worthy
  worthier
  worthiest
✗ wot = what
would (= would you
  mind → wood)
wouldn't
wound
  wounds
  wounded

wounding
wove
woven
wow
wrack
wraith
wrangle
  wrangles
  wrangled
  wrangling
wrap
  wraps
  wrapped (=
    wrapped up
    → rapt)
  wrapping
wraparound
wrapover
wrapper
wrath
wrathful
wreak (= wreak
  havoc → reek)
  wreaks
  wreaked
  wreaking
wreath
wreathe
  wreathes
  wreathed
  wreathing
wreck
  wrecks
  wrecked
  wrecking
wren
wrench
wrestle
  wrestles
  wrestled

wrestling
  wrestling
wretch
wretched
Wrexham
wriggle
  wriggles
  wriggled
  wriggling
wring (= squeeze
  → ring)
  wrings
  wrung
  wringing
wringer
wrinkle
  wrinkles
  wrinkled
  wrinkling
wrist
wristband
wristwatch
writ
write (= with a pen
  → right; rite)
  writes
  wrote (= wrote a
    letter → rote)
  written
  writing
writer
writhe
  writhes
  writhed
  writhing
writing
written
wrong
  wrongs
  wronged

wronging
wrongdoer
wrongful
wrote
✗ wroth = wrath
wrought
wrung (= squeezed
  → rung)
wry (= a wry smile
  → rye)
✗ wulf = wolf
✗ wuman = woman
wun try one
✗ wun = won or one
✗ wunce = once
✗ wunder = wonder
✗ wunderful =
  wonderful
✗ wundrous =
  wondrous
✗ wuppee = whoopee
wur try wor
✗ wur = were or whirr
✗ wurl = whorl or
  whirl
wych-elm
wych-hazel
Wymondham
Wyoming
wyvern

xylophonist
xylose

X

Y

xabalioni =
  zabaglione
X-chromosome
xenia
xenon
xenophile
xenophobe
xenophobia
Xerox℠
  Xeroxes
  Xeroxed
  Xeroxing
Xhosa
  Xhosas *or*
  Xhosa
xi
  xis
Xmas
x-ray
  x-rays
  x-rayed
  x-raying
X-ray
  X-rays
  X-rayed
  X-raying
xylan
xylem
xylene
xylocarp
xylophone
xylophonic

yacht
  yachts
  yachted
  yachting
yachtsman
  yachtsmen
yackety-yak
yah
yahoo
  yahoos
yahooism
Yahweh
yak
  yaks
  yakked
  yakking
Yakut
yam
yammer
  yammers
  yammered
  yammering
yank
  yanks
  yanked
  yanking
Yankee
yap
  yaps
  yapped
  yapping
Yarborough

yard
yardage
yardarm
Yardie
yardstick
Yarmouth
yarmulke
yarn
yarrow
yashmac
yashmak
yaw (= to pitch →
  yore; your; you're)
  yaws
  yawed
  yawing
yawl
yawn
  yawns
  yawned
  yawning
Y-chromosome
ye
yea
yeah
year
yearbook
yearling
yearlong
yearn
  yearns
  yearned
  yearning
yeast
yeastily
yeastiness
yeasty
  yeastier
  yeastiest
Yeats, W.B.

yell
  yells
  yelled
  yelling
yellow
  yellows
  yellowed
  yellowing
yellowbird
yellowhammer
yellowtail
yelp
  yelps
  yelped
  yelping
Yemen
yen
yeoman
  yeomen
  yeomanry
Yeovil
yep
✗yern = yearn
yes
yeshiva
  yeshivahs or
  yeshivoth
yesterday
yesteryear
yet
yeti
yew (= tree → you)
Y-fronts
Yiddish
yield
  yields
  yielded
  yielding
yin
yippee

ylang-ylang
YMCA
yo
yob
yobbos
yobs
yodel
  yodels
  yodelled
  yodelling
yoga
yogh
yoghourt
yoghurt
yogi
yogic
yogurt
yoke (= on oxen
  → yolk)
yokes
yoked
yoking
yokel
yolk (= of an egg
  → yoke)
✗yoman = yeoman
yomp
  yomps
  yomped
  yomping
yon
yonder
yonks
yoo-hoo
yore (= days of →
  yaw; your; you're)
yorker
✗yorself = yourself
Yoruba
✗yot = yacht

Z

you (= me and you
→ yew)
you'd
you'll (= you will
→ yule)
young
youngster
your (= belonging
to you → yaw;
yore; you're)
you're (= you are
→ yaw; yore; your)
yours
yourself
  yourselves
youth
youthful
you've
yowl
  yowls
  yowled
  yowling
yo-yo
  yo-yos
  yo-yoed
  yo-yoing
ytterbia
ytterbite
ytterbium
yttria
yttrium
yuan
  yuan
yucca
yuck
yuckily
yuckiness
yucky
  yuckier
  yuckiest

Yugoslav
Yugoslavia
yuk
yukkily
yukkiness
yukky
  yukkier
  yukkiest
yule (= Christmas
→ you'll)
yummy
  yummier
  yummiest
yum-yum
X yung = young
X yungster = youngster
yup
yuppie
yuppy
  yuppies
yurt
Yvonne

zabaglione
Zaïre
Zambezi
Zambia
zanily
zaniness
zany
  zanier
  zaniest
Zanzibar
zap
  zaps
  zapped
  zapping
zapping
zappy
  zappier
  zappiest
X zar = czar or tsar or
  tzar
X zarina = czarina or
  tsarina or tzarina
zarzuela
zeal
zealot
zealotry
zealous
zebec
zebeck
zebra
zebu
zed

✗ zeenon = xenon
✗ zeerox = Xerox
zemstvo
   zemstvos
Zen
zenana
zenith
✗ zenofobia =
   xenophobia
✗ zenon = xenon
✗ zenophobia =
   xenophobia
zeolite
zeolitic
zephyr
zeppelin
zero
   zeros or
   zeroes
   zeroes
   zeroed
   zeroing
zest
zeta
zeugma
zidovudine
ziggurat
zigzag
zilch
✗ zilem = xylem
zillion
   zillions or
   zillion
✗ zilophone =
   xylophone
Zimbabwe
zimmer
zinc
zincate
zincite

Zinfandel
zing
   zings
   zinged
   zinging
zinnia
Zion
Zionism
zip
   zips
   zipped
   zipping
zipper
zippy
   zippier
   zippiest
zircalloy
zircon
zirconium
zit
zither
zloty
   zlotys or
   zloty
zodiac
zodiacal
Zoë
Zohar
zombie
   zombies
zonal
zonate
zonation
zone
   zones
   zoned
   zoning
zonked
zoo
zoological

zoologist
zoology
zoom
   zooms
   zoomed
   zooming
Zoroastrian
Zoroastrianism
zounds
zucchetto
   zucchettos
zucchini
   zucchini or
   zucchinis
Zulu
   Zulu or
   Zulus
zwieback
zwitterion
zygospore
zygote
zygotene
zygotic
zygotically
zymotic
zymotically